AN INTRODUCTION
TO PREHISTORIC
ARCHEOLOGY

AN INTRODUCTION TO PREHISTORIC ARCHEOLOGY

Frank Hole
Rice University

Robert F. Heizer
University of California, Berkeley

HOLT, RINEHART AND WINSTON

New York   Chicago   San Francisco   Toronto   London

June, 1966

23695–0115

Printed in the United States of America

PREFACE

Most students will never excavate an archeological site; indeed, they should not, but if as intelligent laymen they read reports of excavations or descriptions of life in prehistoric times, they need to be able to judge them in the light of current scientific procedure and belief. The purpose of this book is to introduce the study of man's past by showing how archeologists reconstruct human history from the artifacts that have survived. It attempts to show that the aims of archeologists are closely related to those of historians, but that archeologists must depend upon data, techniques, and services foreign to historians. To help the reader understand the complexity of prehistoric archeology, the work brings together in an introductory way relevant background material that is not available in any other single publication. Although the text was written with the beginning student in mind, it can be used in a variety of ways. In itself the book presents a balanced and systematic overview of the history, method, and theory of archeology. It is liberally supplied with both brief examples as illustrations and references to published works where the reader can find detailed information. As a reference work the book will also be valuable for the advanced student who wishes to inquire more fully into particular topics. The extensive bibliography at the end of the book lists all references cited in the text.

We accept full responsibility for the form and content of this presentation, but we should like to acknowledge the advice given on matters of style by Edward Norbeck, Rice University, and Hubert Mewhinney, Houston. Our thanks go also to Mrs. Edna Flood and Miss Linda Handjian of the Archeological Research Facility, University of California, Berkeley, and to Mrs. Deni Seinfeld and John Durham, Rice University, for help in preparing the manuscript.

Houston, Texas   F. HOLE
Berkeley, Calif.   R. F. HEIZER
January 1965

v

CONTENTS

Preface   *v*

PART 1   INTRODUCING THE STUDY OF PREHISTORY

Chapter 1   *What Is Prehistoric Archeology?*   3
Some Definitions   3
Archeology as a Study of Man's Past   5
Archeologists   10
Some Difficulties in Doing Archeology   10

Chapter 2   *Kinds of Archeology and Archeologists*   12
Dilettantes, Bargain Hunters,
        and Deep Sea Divers   14
Texts, Temples, and Tombs   24
Protohistory   26
Adam and Beyond   29
Salvage Archeology   31

Chapter 3   *Archeological Sites*   33
Kinds of Sites   33
How Is a Site Made?   38
How To Find Sites   46

Chapter 4   *Context*   49
Stratigraphy   49
Deriving Stratigraphy from Stratification   60
Time   64
Culture and Space   66

Chapter 5   *Preservation*   68
What Is Preserved?   68
What Is Willfully Destroyed?   77
What Is Recovered?   80
What Is Reported?   81

PART 2 ACQUIRING THE FACTS OF PREHISTORY

Chapter 6   *Survey*   85
             The Problem 85
             How To Find Sites 87
             Judging the Contents of Sites 90
             Designations for Sites 99

Chapter 7   *Excavation and Recording*   101
             The Object of Excavation 102
             Kinds of Excavations 103
             How To Dig 106
             Keeping Records 111
             Preservation of Artifacts 114
             The Staff 117

Chapter 8   *Classification and Description*   119
             Classification 119
             Description 124

Chapter 9   *Technical Analyses*   130
             Analysis of Pottery 130
             Analysis of Metal and Stone 132
             Analysis of Weaving 132
             Analysis of Soil 133
             Analysis of Animal and Plant Remains 134
             Chemical Analysis of Residues 138
             Analysis of Sites 139
             The Problem of Hoaxes and Fakes 140

PART 3 DATING THE EVENTS IN PREHISTORY

Chapter 10   *Dating by Physical-Chemical Methods*   145
             Radiocarbon Dating 145
             Other Radioactive Dating Methods 151
             Magnetic Dating 153
             Chemical Analysis 155
             Patination 157
             Hydration of Obsidian 158

Chapter 11   *Geochronology*   160
    Varve Analysis   160
    Beaches, Terraces, and Dunes   161
    Correlation of Pleistocene Features   163
    Rate of Sedimentation   165
    Location of Sites   165

Chapter 12   *Methods for Dating, Using Plant and*
           Animal Remains   167
    Palynology   167
    Paleontology   170
    Dendrochronology   172

Chapter 13   *Other Methods for Dating*   175
    Astronomical Dating   175
    Calendars   176
    Sequence Dating   177
    Cross Dating   180
    Rate of Accumulation   181
    Geographical Location   183

PART 4   DESCRIBING AND INTERPRETING PREHISTORY

Chapter 14   *Prehistoric Economy*   187
    What Is Economy?   187
    Diet   189
    Technology   197
    Trade   201
    Standards of Exchange   203
    Shelter   204
    Transportation and Travel   209

Chapter 15   *Determining the Use of Artifacts*   210
    Ethnographic Analogy   211
    Context   214
    Experiments   214
    Social Correlates   216
    Natural or Man Made?   217

Chapter 16   *Prehistoric Society*   220
              Demography   220
              Social Organization   225
              Identifying Prehistoric Cultures   229
              Religion   231
              Specialization   232

Chapter 17   *Writing Culture History*   234
              Site Reports   236
              Regional Histories   237
              Models of Prehistory   239

Bibliography   251

Index   293

PART 1

INTRODUCING THE STUDY OF PREHISTORY

1

WHAT IS PREHISTORIC ARCHEOLOGY?

SOME DEFINITIONS

Archeology means many things. We can agree that it is the science of ancient things—this is implied in the Greek roots of the word. We can also agree that archeology is concerned with man's past, but beyond these simple statements agreement ends. Instead of a well-defined science we find a host of related disciplines, each with its own subject matter and method of study. We shall not be concerned with all kinds of archeology; our emphasis will be on prehistoric archeology, and we shall say only enough of other types to give an impression of how they relate to one another.

As background for this discussion we will define a number of terms that might otherwise cause confusion. In the parts of the world where English is spoken it is usual to divide man's past into the *historic* and the *prehistoric*. If we define the historic past as that which has been recorded by writing, the prehistoric part is that which was not recorded by writing. The prehistorian, or archeologist, lacking the written records used by historians, must work with other artifacts that are usually recovered through excavation by archeologists.

3

The word "prehistoric" is so familiar and widely used that we might assume that the term has been in use for a very long time. This is not the case, however; the first modern use of the word dates from just over one hundred years ago, in 1851, when Daniel Wilson used it in the title of his *The Archaeology and Prehistoric Annals of Scotland*. Somewhat earlier, in 1833, Tournal proposed that the "Age of Man" could be divided into a "Prehistoric Period which extended from the time of man's appearance on the surface of the earth to the beginning of the most ancient traditions" and a "Historic Period which hardly dates beyond seven thousand years ago." Wilson wrote, in explanation, "Man may be assumed to be prehistoric wherever his chroniclings of himself are unde-signed, and his history is wholly recoverable by induction." The story of the rise of archeology as a separate study of man's ancient past can be read in works by Casson (1939), Ceram (1958), Daniel (1950, 1959, 1962), Hamy (1870), Heizer (1962a), Laming-Emperaire (1963), Shorr (1935), and T. Wilson (1899).

As a point of reference, history began about 3000 B.C. The earliest writing yet found is on clay tablets from the site of Warka in Mesopotamia (modern southern Iraq). It was not until several hundred years later, however, that writing was used widely for keeping records and for communication. By 2000 B.C. most of Southwest Asia was under the political influence of literate peoples. By contrast, England was prehistoric until the beginning of the Christian era, and the prehistory of the American Indian ended only with the coming of Europeans in the sixteenth century A.D.

For practical purposes the line dividing prehistory from history is hard to define. Even in Southwest Asia, where writing began, only the major political centers were really within the sphere of literacy until nearly the present day. Archeology is a major source of history in such places, even though the past several thousand years have been part of the historic era. If we stop to think about it, although written documents are the most important source of history, archeology can broaden our knowledge, even of the past in the United States. In recent years, for example, U.S. Federal or State governmental agencies, or historical societies, have investigated a great many sites occupied by non-Indians in the post-Columbian period (Harrington 1952, 1955). Such historic sites examined by archeologists include early settlements at Jamestown and Williamsburg, Virginia (Cotter 1958; Wertenbaker 1953), and the Spanish missions in New Mexico and California (Bennyhoff and Elsasser 1954; Toulouse 1949; Treganza 1956).

Today information is recorded in diaries, books, magazines, newspapers, and official records, but still a vast amount goes unrecorded and will vanish from man's record unless it is recovered by a future archeologist. A hundred years ago, when paper was more costly and printing processes less mechanized, much more went unrecorded, and information that can supplement our written history still lies in the ground, awaiting an archeologist's interest. Thus, archeology can contribute to knowledge of the whole of man's past; it need not stop where history begins.

To make the division of human history more precise, we can distinguish a period of protohistory. *Protohistory* is the study of peoples who were living after history began, but who themselves did not have writing. When the French coined the term *protohistoire* (Daniel 1955), however, they did not have the Australian aborigines or the Amazonian Indians in mind; they were concerned with peoples in western Europe, contemporary with, but not part of, the civilizations of the Mediterranean and Southwest Asia. Grahame Clark (1954) made a useful distinction in this regard when he described protohistory as "secondary prehistory," because it has to be studied with reference to the history of contemporary civilization. Archeology, which could be studied apart from civilization, was called "primary prehistory." By Clark's definition, this book is concerned with primary prehistory and the subject matter is world-wide.

Archeology records and interprets man's past. Prehistoric archeology deals with one segment of this past. One can also distinguish several other kinds of archeology by their subject matter, the way they developed historically, and the way they are studied.

ARCHEOLOGY AS A STUDY OF MAN'S PAST

"It is often, and I think rightly, held that archaeology should not be counted a separate field of study so much as a method of reconstructing the past from the surviving traces of former societies" (G. Clark 1954:7). Clark thinks of prehistory as an extension of history. A century and a half ago J. Hodgson (1822:xvi) had the same idea when he wrote:

> The vulgar antiquary, while he walks among the ruins of a city, is struck with wonder, and fixes his observation most upon their extent, their state of preservation. . . . He is an admirer of coins on account of their rarity, their age, the beauty of their rust, or from some accidental variety which marks them . . . He values his collection of manuscripts . . . merely because they are old. . . . But the judicious antiquary considers the various

objects of his contemplation with a learned eye; and imposes a value upon them in proportion to the quantity of light they throw upon the several departments of the history of the people to which they belong.

In the United States we usually think of prehistory as a subfield of anthropology, the most inclusive of the various studies of man. But no matter how it is defined, archeology deals with man in the past; its concern is with culture seen in the perspective of time. Prehistory, as a special example of archeology, deals with noncivilized peoples whose closest living counterparts are studied by ethnologists. A liaison with anthropology rather than history has thus been natural for prehistorians.

However, prehistorians are concerned with more than culture. Their special needs require close cooperation among a wide range of scientists who study the past. Geologists, paleontologists, palynologists, chemists, physicists, botanists, linguists, and astronomers have all contributed toward understanding man's prehistory.

History and Archeology

History is concerned with more than a sequence of dates that denote events in the past; it is an ordering of knowledge about man's past into understandable contexts. In other words, history is an interpretation. In this sense, there are no grounds for differentiating between the aims of history and prehistory (Childe 1953; Grimes 1954; Kroeber 1957). What we shall stress in this book are the ways in which prehistorians obtain and interpret their facts.

Histories are written to help us understand life in the past. This is different from a mere antiquarian concern with the past or from an esthetic concern for old art. For example, one who admires the obelisk of Luxor in the Place de la Concorde in Paris (see Fig. 1) or the bust of Nefertiti in the Berlin Museum is not ordinarily experiencing a historical appreciation, nor were the persons responsible for placing these treasures far from their Egyptian context acting as archeologists or historians. Similarly, collections of arrowheads found in local museums contribute nothing to history unless the objects are placed in a human context. When objects—arrowheads or obelisks—are frankly placed to be admired in their own right, as objects, they have lost their historical value. As Dorothy Garrod has written (1946:27), "Man's tools are the instruments of his response to the world in which he lives, but they are much more—they are the weapons of his conquest of that world . . . and the clue to its interpretation." In many museums, tools become works of art, and religious paraphernalia become treasures, all without

Fig. 1. The Obelisk of Luxor which once stood alongside the Nile now attracts tourists in the Place de la Concorde, Paris.

value except their intrinsic worth or beauty. Mere collection and admiration of objects are not historical activities for, though they may deal with archeological remains, they stop short of cultural interpretation.

Culture and Archeology

Any study of man, past or present, must be concerned with culture. Culture has long been the concern of anthropologists, and culture or various aspects of it has been defined many times, but the various uses of the word need not concern us here. For most archeologists, culture takes such tangible forms as tools, pottery, burials, house styles, ornaments, and art, as these things are repeatedly found together. Artifacts are part of a people's material culture, but an ax is not culture, nor is a burial or a house. It is only when certain kinds of axes, burials, and houses are found together in several sites that archeologists refer to the repeated associations of artifacts as evidence of a culture. All this implies is a kind of grouping an ethnologist would call a "tribe," or a "people," or a "society." We expect that people who occupy a common territory and share a common material culture will also share such things as language, ideas about right and wrong, preferences in art, religion, and other intangible traits. These elements of nonmaterial culture are not recovered by prehistoric archeologists, but every effort is made by archeologists to make inferences about the social or nonmaterial aspects of the dead cultures they examine. In this sense archeology is "paleo-anthropology."

Archeologists do not always deal with associations as large as whole cultures. The *artifact* is the smallest cultural unit of concern to archeologists. Artifacts are things of any kind that have been altered or constructed by man. Knives, houses, roads, art, language, and this book are examples of artifacts. A larger unit of culture is sometimes called the *industry*. An industry consists of all the artifacts of one kind found at a site. There may be a chipped-stone industry, a ceramic industry, a basket industry, and a bone-tool industry. All the industries taken together at one site constitute an *assemblage*. If several similar assemblages are found at several sites, an archeologist will describe them as a culture. Childe (1948:51) says:

> An archaeological culture is an assemblage of artifacts that recurs repeatedly associated together in dwellings of the same kind and with burials of the same rite. The arbitrary peculiarities of all cultural traits are assumed to be concrete expressions of the common social traditions that bind together a culture. Artifacts hang together in assemblages, not only because they were used in the same age, but also because they were used by

the same people, made or executed in accordance with techniques, rites or styles prescribed by a social tradition, handed on by precept and example and modifiable in the same way.

Cultures exist only in a context of time and space. Simply stated, context is association—a thing in its environment. The one thing that keeps a Parisian or a tourist from enjoying a historical appreciation of the obelisk of Luxor is that it has been removed from the context that would have given it correct historical meaning and placed instead in the middle of the heavy Paris traffic. In Luxor the obelisk was among the ruins of which it was a part. Enlightened probing of these ruins has revealed the cultural context into which the obelisk fitted. In addition, at Luxor there are the sun and the sand and the Nile; these comprise the geographical context. Inserted into the contexts of culture and geography, the obelisk has far different meaning and evokes far different appreciation than it does in Paris surrounded by fountains, palaces, motorcars, and tourists. As Childe (1956:5) put it, with a different example (the Elgin marbles) in mind, "Indeed we tear down the frieze from a temple in a sunny clime and set it at eye-level in a room in murky London to appreciate its beauty!" (see Chap. 4).

Natural Science and Archeology

Despite its necessary preoccupation with culture, archeology relies greatly upon the natural sciences for much of its basic information. Peoples living in the prehistoric past were intimately involved with their natural environment. In fact the main features of the economic and social life of many peoples can be directly related to the environment in which they lived. The study of the relation of man or any other organism to its environment is called *ecology*. Unlike prehistoric man, we are tied to a man-made environment and many features of our lives are related to it. To help understand how people lived in the past, therefore, archeologists are as interested in environment as in artifacts.

Most information about prehistoric environment comes from geologists, who study the earth's landscape and how it developed; and from botanists and zoologists, who are interested in the history of plants and animals. Archeologists are responsible for integrating these varied data and describing an ecology for prehistoric man (see Chaps. 14 and 16). Helm (1962) has written a survey of the ecological approach in anthropology, with many citations. Two outstanding examples of the application of ecological method in archeology are by J. G. D. Clark (1952) and Wendorf (1961).

There has been an equal value in the contributions of scientists who have worked out methods for dating the past (see Chaps. 10–13). Still other specialists have applied their technical skills to the analysis and interpretation of artifacts (see Chap. 9). Prehistorians work with limited data, and, to realize their potential, apply the most modern techniques to their recovery and interpretation.

ARCHEOLOGISTS

Archeologists are persons who use data taken from archeological contexts as a guide to recreating and interpreting the past. Most archeologists excavate. By our modern standards, we identify as archeologists only those who are professionally employed as such. As a practical matter, it is rare for a nonprofessional to have the full range of requisite skills and understanding to carry through a substantial piece of excavation, analysis, and reporting. On the other hand, there are many amateurs who do archeology and their work has sometimes been of great importance. For the most part amateurs contribute by discovering sites, helping in digging them, and making preliminary analyses of the excavated material.

The academic training of a professional archeologist is protracted. In the United States he must obtain the Ph.D. degree. Persons who wish to become archeologists should begin by getting a broad college background in the humanities and in the social and natural sciences (Kenyon 1961; Rowe 1954; Sturtevant 1958). In addition, they must develop at least a reading knowledge of the modern languages they will need in their research. After college a student must plan on at least four years of graduate school, which will lead to a specialization in one of the branches of archeology. Following receipt of the Ph.D. degree, many archeologists teach in a university and excavate during the summers or on sabbatical leaves. Others work as curators in museums or in state and national parks, or they may be ·employed by state and national governments to do salvage archeology in areas that will be destroyed by the construction of roads and dams.

SOME DIFFICULTIES IN DOING ARCHEOLOGY

Archeologists often work under trying conditions. The climate may be extremely uncomfortable (cf. Judd 1930:1–2; Lloyd 1963:71), as in the Mexican or Amazonian tropical lowlands, the African deserts, or the high Andean altiplano where intense heat or cold or high humidity can cause real discomfort and misery. W. B. Emery, who excavated in Nubia between 1921 and 1931, records that by ten o'clock in the morning the temperature was 120 degrees Fahrenheit, and at one o'clock at night had lowered to slightly over 100 degrees.

Official permits to excavate in foreign countries are usually secured from a governmental agency. Negotiations over excavation permits can be very drawn out and can consume much valuable time. Creel (1937:17, 156) tells us that in China there was such feeling against opening graves that 60 percent of an archeologist's time and energy went into protracted negotiations to secure a clearance to excavate, and 40 percent into actual work. Rassam (1897:55–56) records the kinds of problems encountered in securing a concession to excavate in Greece and Turkey where international politics, in his day, favored one country or another. Generally speaking, even today, an American archeologist wishing to excavate in most countries can expect the negotiations over an agreement to cover several months. Braidwood (1960:123), referring to antiquities protection laws of some foreign countries that forbid export of any objects, says, "These laws serve only to prevent the completion of a good job by serious professional archeologists." But as we shall see below, many of these laws were written as a reaction against the looting of national treasures by irresponsible collectors.

Beyond these problems, there may be actual physical danger in field work. Dust from digging dry caves has caused some deaths among archeologists, as have falling rocks from the ceilings of caves and collapsing walls in deep trenches. Hazards of disease in regions where sanitary conditions are very poor and medical facilities are unobtainable have brought an abrupt end to many archeological expeditions and death to some archeologists. While these may be extreme examples, field excavation in foreign lands is rarely easy and often hazardous, and almost all archeologists can tell truthful stories of real adventure and hardship.

Local politics may require the excavator to walk a tightrope in an effort to keep his dig from being closed down, and crews of local workmen may get erroneous ideas about what is being done, leading to strained relations between crew and the director of the excavation (T. Clark 1903; Coon 1957:167; A. H. Layard 1849:2:86–87).

Archeologists rarely write biographies and their experiences in the field are usually recounted, if at all, in the most offhand and matter of fact way, somewhere in their technical reports. The reader who wishes to learn about the adventures of some archeologists, who at times use their wives or children as spokesmen, may consult the works of L. Braidwood (1953), Breasted (1948), Crawford (1955), J. Evans (1943), A. H. Layard (1903), E. Lothrop (1948), Petrie (1931), and Woolley (1953).

KINDS OF
ARCHEOLOGY AND
ARCHEOLOGISTS

There are many kinds of archeology and archeologists. Archeologists, unlike doctors or lawyers, are not licensed to practice their profession and can, without penalty of the law, be impersonated. Indeed, any person, subject only to his conscience, can call himself an archeologist. When advertisements describe persons as archeologists, or when news stories tell of archeological discoveries, the average reader finds it hard to judge who is really an archeologist and whether the matter warrants his serious consideration. Some of the aspects of archeology are described here so that the student may begin to evaluate the claims he reads.

"Who is an archeologist?" Is the farmer who plows up arrow points and puts them in old cigar boxes an archeologist? Or the student of ancient languages? Or the high school boy who excavates the local Indian mound on Sundays and then writes a report on his activities? Or the Bedouin in Jordan who searches caves for Dead Sea scrolls in the hope that he may become rich? Or the college instructor in a department of anthropology who takes his students on summer digs? Or the author of popular books dealing with archeology? Or the skin diver who brings up amphorae from sunken ships?

This is not an exhaustive list of the kinds of persons who might be called archeologists, but it illustrates a point. And it should raise the question again, "Which of these persons is an archeologist?" The answer is very simple. None of these persons is necessarily an archeologist; all may be archeologists, and all are doing one or more of the jobs done by archeologists.

To answer the question more precisely and to begin the discussion of the modern study of prehistoric archeology, it will help to take a brief look into the history of the subject to see how it began and how it developed.

As an academic discipline, archeology has a history of only a little more than one hundred years, but a few persons were practicing a form of archeology by the end of the fourteenth century. Early archeology, spurred on by an interest in ancient Greece and Rome, was mainly directed toward recovering coins and objects of art. The emphasis was on collecting and cataloguing, usually for personal rather than for public pleasure.

It was out of this tradition of interest in the past that the concept of the romance of archeology was born. In fact, some of the finest tales of adventure and exploration stem from the romantic lure that discovering and collecting held. The words of early travelers who happily faced privation, disease, and sometimes death as they sought their treasures across the globe quicken the pulse even today. This is true despite the fact that, as M. Wheeler (1956:241) remarked, ". . . romance is merely adventure remembered in tranquillity, devoid of the ills and anxieties, fleas, fevers, thirst, and toothache, which are liable to be the more insistent experience."

Without doubt, the most persistent motive throughout the history of archeology has been to collect antiquities. In some cases excavation was needed; in others, not. In some cases collection was an end in itself; in others it was a step toward a broader end. Whatever curious turns it has taken, collection has traditionally been in the center of archeology. But the emphasis has shifted. Today private collecting is done mostly by amateurs and persons of means, and is actively shunned by professionals.

Although collecting is a central activity of archeology, it does not fully describe the subject. When artifacts, whether they be cuneiform texts, Greek statues, flint tools, or bits of pottery, are collected, archeologists must describe, classify, and record the information recovered. When this is done, the data are interpreted. The differences among the various kinds of archeology are largely in the geographical areas and particular times studied, and in the way the data are interpreted. The following sections will be concerned with describing four broad subjects of archeology and telling something of their development historically.

DILETTANTES, BARGAIN HUNTERS, AND DEEP SEA DIVERS

The history of "treasure hunting" is highlighted by cultivated gentlemen of the arts, brash performers for fame and prestige, highwaymen with official backing, cowboys, and submarine adventurers. At their best, these men stirred the imaginations of a complacent self-centered world; at their worst, they wrought irreparable damage to the record of man's past.

The history of treasure hunting must be viewed against the slow development of archeology, the emergence of a conscience about how it should be done, and the appearance of an educated public and appreciative governments who acted to protect their ancient remains from destruction. We shall want to judge the men involved, but we must remember that our criticisms of their work depend on knowledge not available a hundred or more years ago. Were we to judge work done in 1800 by the standards of today, we would generally find it damnable.

The earliest record we have of archeology was actually discovered by much later-day archeologists. The first archeologist who appears in history is Nabonidus, last of the kings of Babylon (555–538 B.C.) and father of Belshazzar. Nabonidus became intensely interested in the past of Babylonian culture and conducted excavations of ancient buildings, saved what he found, and established a museum in which his discoveries were displayed.

Tombs in which were buried persons of importance together with articles of value such as jewelry and precious metals have, since earliest times, been the targets for robbers (Parrott 1939). As Emery (1961:129) neatly observes, the Egyptians believed "you could take it with you," and as a result of this belief they buried a wealth of materials with their dead. Belzoni and others of his ilk were doing nothing new. The robbing of royal tombs in ancient times is well-known as modern excavators often find that they are searching several thousand years too late. For example, in 1120 B.C. there was an official investigation and list of tomb robberies made in Egypt (Peet 1943; J. A. Wilson 1956:282–285), and there is a historical account from China of the opening of an ancient tomb in

A.D. 281 (Creel 1937:25). Examples where archeologists have found evidence of previous looting occur in the Shang tombs at Anyang in China (Creel 1937:216); in the ship tomb of the Viking queen at Oseberg (reprinted in Heizer 1959b:52); in the log tomb of the Scythian chieftain at Pizirik, Siberia (reprinted in Heizer 1959b: 84–92); and in the royal tombs of Ur (reprinted in Heizer 1959b:2–10). Another early record of grave plundering is mentioned by Strabo. When Julius Caesar established a Roman colony for veterans of his campaigns on the site of ancient Corinth, former cemeteries were discovered and looted for bronze vessels that were sold to Roman collectors who prized items of Greek manufacture. The Spanish conquistadors in Mexico, Panama, and Peru soon learned that they could "mine" ancient cemeteries for gold objects and proceeded to do so as soon as the native peoples were conquered. Fernandez de Oviedo, a Spanish chronicler, wrote a detailed report on the opening of a tomb in Darien in 1522, and if we are willing to call this archeology, his is one of the earliest archeological reports from the New World.

In the fifteenth century, 2000 years after Nabonidus, the large scale collecting of art treasures began in Italy and flourished, especially in Rome, under the example of such popes as Sixtus IV (1471–1484) and his immediate successors. To supplement the technique of merely removing standing monuments, Alexander VI, who was pope between 1492 and 1503, began excavating to help his collecting. During the fifteenth century it became fashionable for influential men of affairs as well as of the church to furnish their homes with the abundant ancient statuary. These men of the Italian Renaissance were known as *dilettanti*, to describe their delight in the fine arts.

The collector's spirit did not remain confined to Italy. With the spread of the Renaissance, collectors from all over Europe began to accumulate objects that would later become the nuclei of many of the world's famous museums. It was during this time that the city of Herculaneum, buried under a thick deposit of volcanic material thrown out of Vesuvius in A.D. 79—at which time Pompeii was also buried—was "mined" for Roman sculptures, which were sold to rich collectors.

When Thomas Howard, the Earl of Arundel, visited Italy in the early seventeenth century, he began his extensive collection of art from Greece, Italy, and Southwest Asia. His example of travel and collection was not lost on other young Englishmen of means who, for the next 200 years, were to follow Howard to the Mediterranean. The extent of Arundel's zeal can be seen today in the Ashmolean Museum, which retains the nucleus of his once much larger collection of marbles. Howard's collection, not appreciated by his descendants, was partly destroyed and then dispersed.

By the beginning of the nineteenth century, the scene of large scale collecting had begun to shift to the site of the most ancient civilizations. It was on the desert valleys of the Nile, Tigris, and Euphrates that the great feats of treasure hunting were performed. Until the end of the eighteenth century, the Western world knew little of the riches that awaited discovery in Southwest Asia. A few mud bricks with undecipherable inscriptions on them, a handful of cylinder seals, and tales of some imposing cities in ruins were all that had reached Europe since the Crusades. The establishment of a British consulate in Bagdad in 1802 marked the opening of Southwest Asia for the Western world and its treasure hunters.

The occupant of the British Residency in Bagdad for most of its first twenty-five years was Claudius Rich, a precocious student of languages and an astute politician. Rich's wide interests were shown in his careful surveying of prominent archeological sites and especially in his collecting. After his untimely death in 1821, some seven thousand pounds of antiquities, including ancient coins, Syriac manuscripts, and about one thousand pounds of clay tablets, cylinders, and bricks with cuneiform inscriptions gathered by him were deposited at the British Museum.

A contemporary, Henry Creswick Rawlinson, was a British (Indian) Army officer, horseman, adventurer, and student of ancient inscriptions. With remarkable energy and devotion, Rawlinson visited virtually every ancient monument of consequence in what is now modern Iran. His interest was mainly to collect samples of the ancient writing that had not yet been deciphered. As evidence of his travels one frequently finds Rawlinson's name carved into cliffs that were once reserved for the inscriptions of kings. But Rawlinson's fame lies not in his arduous journeys nor in his artistry with a chisel, but in his recording and translating of the long lost inscriptions that describe Persia's former opulence. By 1837, working in his spare time, he had accomplished the translations that were to gain him the title "Father of Cuneiform" (Cleator 1962: 90–96).

In Egypt, collecting of antiquities was begun during the fifteenth century by Italian humanists who were interested in the religious texts that the Romans had reported being on the obelisks (Giehlow 1915). A by-product of these activities was the pillaging of sites and tombs (Dannenfeldt 1959). This interest in the ancient Egyptian language received its biggest boost with the discovery of the Rosetta stone in 1799. It was discovered by one of Napoleon's field officers, André Joseph Boussard, who was directing excavations for fortifications at Fort Rachid (later Fort Julien) about seven kilometers from Rosetta (near Alexandria) in the Nile delta. The Greek inscription was soon translated by archeological experts attached to the French forces, and from this it was learned that the stone referred to a general synod of Egyptian priests at Memphis in honor of Ptolemy V. The importance of the stone was realized, and it was entrusted to General Jacques Francois de Menou who kept the stone, for safekeeping, in his house. The British army in 1801 forced the surrender of General Menou, and included in the articles of capitulation was the provision that all Egyptian antiquities collected by the French should be delivered over. General Menou, in an attempt to save the Rosetta Stone, claimed the stone as his personal property, but the English commander, Lord Hutchinson, through his envoy, Turner, ignored this nicety and seized the stone, which was taken off to England in 1802 where it was deposited (along with the Elgin Marbles secured by no more legal means) in the British Museum.

Rubbings of the trilingual inscription on the Rosetta Stone were made by the French before it passed from their hands, and these provided French scholars with what they needed. While the British worked hard at finding the key to the Rosetta inscriptions, so also did the French, and the answer was finally provided by Champollion in 1822. Champollion had predecessors, among whom may be mentioned Silvestre de Sacy, J. D. Akerblad, H. P. Ameilhon, James Bailey, and Arthur Young, and their work have been described by D. C. Allen (1960) and Doblhofer (1959, Chap. 2).

The earliest archeology had been done by men whose primary business lay along quite different lines, but by the middle of the nineteenth century archeology received an impetus that it had not hitherto enjoyed. Both the French and British, sensing the great treasure that awaited the enterprising, supported men whose sole job was to recover antiquities.

One of the first of these men was Austen Henry Layard, who, under British auspices, undertook to dig the site of Nimrud, Mesopotamia, one of the ancient Assyrian capitals. As Layard approached the task his expectations mounted and he recorded a dream he had as follows: "Visions of palaces underground, of gigantic monsters, of sculptured figures, and endless inscriptions, floated before me. After forming plan after plan for removing the earth, and extricating these treasures, I fancied myself wandering in a maze of chambers from which I could find no outlet" (Lloyd 1955:126). When two palaces were discovered in the first day of excavation, the news spread rapidly, and soon the French entered the scene. With the lure of gold for the taking, agents of the two countries frantically dashed around staking out claims on sites about whose contents they knew nothing.

In spite of the promise of treasure for the British Museum, Layard, in contrast to his French counterpart, Paul Emile Botta, was never able to finance properly a really serious excavation. He was reduced to an expedient more the rule than the exception in those days. It can be stated simply: "to obtain the largest possible number of well-preserved objects of art at the least possible outlay of time and money" (Lloyd 1955:133). Though he sorely regretted it, as he dug through Nimrud Layard saw many of the treasures disintegrate before his eyes. Frescoes, sculpture, and metal work frequently crumbled to bits when exposed to air and handling. Layard, in common with his competitors, had no knowledge of how to preserve the priceless objects and no time in which to experiment.

In the ensuing years French and British archeologists even vied with each other at the same site. In 1853 a British subject, Hormuzd Rassam, enviously saw the French diggers approach a particularly likely looking spot on the site of Nineveh. Rassam took his workmen and had them excavate at night, stopping at dawn before the French came on the scene. By this simple subterfuge Rassam's men discovered a picture gallery and library in the palace of Ashur-bani-pal, an Assyrian king who lived between 669–633 B.C. Lacking time and funds, the men hacked their way through the palace, preserving little that was not intact and thereby losing much. Rassam (1897:395–396) wrote:

> Early the next day I . . . examined the localities where collections of unbaked clay tablets had been discovered, and was glad to find that important relics had crowned our labors. I found, to my great vexation, that a large number of the records had crumbled to pieces as soon as they were removed, as they were found in damp soil impregnated with nitre. Had I had an Assyrian copyist with me, we might have preserved, at all events, the history of the documents, though part of the originals would have been lost.

Rassam later learned that mud tablets could be baked and thus preserved, and wrote: "Our excavations at Aboo-Habba were carried out without much interruption for eighteen months altogether, during which time we must have discovered between sixty and seventy thousand inscribed tablets, a large number of which fell to pieces before we could have them baked." (On preserving clay cuneiform tablets by baking, see Delougaz 1933; Parkinson 1951.)

As an example of the manner in which digging was done more than a century ago in Mesopotamia, we quote Loftus' (1859:52–53) account of his efforts to collect glazed coffins from the site of Warka (Uruk) in southern Mesopotamia:

> The object of my second visit to Warkah was to collect a series of such antiquities as it afforded, and more especially to obtain one of the glazed coffins which might be sent to the British Museum. As the colour of those near the surface is affected by exposure, I tried to procure a good specimen from below; but, the deeper I dug, the more saturated with moisture and brittle they became, so that, the moment an attempt was made to move one, it fell to pieces. Finding it impossible to succeed at any depth, I came to the conclusion that the only chance for me was to try at the surface. As the Arabs were much more adept at digging with their spears and hands than with the spades which I had brought with me, I permitted them to follow their own mode of searching. Their cupidity is attracted by the treasures contained within the coffins, to procure which many hundreds are broken and searched every year. Their method of proceeding is simple enough: they pierce the loose soil with their spears, until they chance to strike against some solid substance; by the vibration produced, the Arab knows at once whether he has hit upon a coffin or the vault containing one. The spear is then thrown aside, and, after the fashion of a mole, the wild fellow digs a hole with his hands. If an obstacle presents itself, the spear is again had recourse to, and in this manner perseverance secures the object of search. When the coffin is rifled, a hole is broken through the bottom to ascertain if there be one below. In riding or walking over the mounds considerable care is requisite on account of the innumerable holes made by the Arabs, who of course never take the trouble to fill them up again.
>
> During every day of my stay several coffins were uncovered, and numerous expedients adopted to remove one unbroken; but not-withstanding every precaution, they broke with their own weight. Pieces of carpet and Arab abbas were tied tightly round them, the earth inside was either partially or wholly removed, and poles were placed below to give support; all however to no purpose.

But as if these feats of looting and mass destruction were not enough, a crowning blow to Assyriology occurred in 1855 with the destruction by Arab vandals of some three hundred cases of antiquities collected by Place from the Palace of Sardanapalus. Disappointed in the cargo, the Arabs capsized the rafts carrying it as they were about to enter the Persian Gulf below Bagdad and there they await recovery at some future date by an enterprising archeologist who can locate and raise them from the mud.

Lloyd (1963:35) described the great despoiled Near Eastern site of

Khafaje that "when we first visited it, looked like a battlefield. The main mound . . . was completely honeycombed with holes large enough to be shell craters, surrounded by mountains of discarded earth." Lloyd also records that since 1930 in the Lurish province of western Iran between 400 and 500 burial grounds, each containing about 200 graves "have been excavated commercially [for bronze objects] without any assistance from archeologists."

No tale of treasure hunting should fail to mention one of the most extraordinary persons ever to be called an archeologist. Giovanni Battista Belzoni was perhaps the most outrageous and audacious looter of them all (Clair 1957). Working in the early 1800s, partly under the auspices of the British Consul in Cairo, Belzoni capped his richly varied life as circus strong man and hydraulic engineer by dedicating himself to robbing tombs. Belzoni, whom Mayes (1961:296) somewhat inappropriately described as "the man who laid the foundations of an English Egyptology," was a giant of a man whose deeds assumed gigantic proportions.

Belzoni's career in Egypt began in Thebes. His first efforts are described as follows: "Every step I took I crushed a mummy in some part or other. When my weight bore on the body of an Egyptian it crushed like a band-box. I sank altogether among the broken mummies with a crash of bones, rags and wooden cases. . . . I could not avoid being covered with bones, legs, arms and heads rolling from above" (Daniel 1950: 155–156). Moving from tombs to outdoor projects, Belzoni excavated Abu Simbel, he opened the second pyramid, he recovered the eight ton head of Rameses II from Thebes, and he would probably have succeeded in the prodigious engineering feat of sending the Philae obelisk out of the country had he not been intercepted by a better armed band of brigands who claimed it for themselves. But Belzoni (1820, 1:239–240, 294) was not altogether a crude wrecker and collector if we may judge him by his time-consuming efforts to make wax castings of the interior of two elaborate Egyptian tombs with the aim of bringing these back to Europe and making exact reproductions for showing to the public. Belzoni was not the seed from which British Egyptology sprang but the autumn brilliance of a leaf that happily was soon to wither and fall. Howard Carter, famous for his excavation of the tomb of Tutankhamen in 1923, had this to say about Belzoni's day: "Those were the great days of excavating. Anything to which a fancy was taken, from a scarab to an obelisk, was just appropriated, and if there was difference with a brother excavator, one laid for him with a gun" (as quoted in Daniel 1950:156).

By the end of the nineteenth century, archeologists had come to recognize the part that texts would play in unraveling the history of the area, and they began to dig primarily to recover the ancient writings. Some of these were inscribed on stone and clay, but others (especially from Egypt) were papyrus rolls containing Egyptian texts as well as Greek and Roman literary writings (Woolley 1958:48–51). With this change in emphasis, archeology took a historical bent and became more leisurely and scholarly than it had been in the days when the museums were empty and so were many of the excavators' heads.

A fascination with the extreme age of cave-dwelling man, whose remains dated from the latter part of the Pleistocene or ice age, developed just over a century ago in western Europe. By the end of the nineteenth century many sites, the scenes of occupation lasting thousands of years, had been systematically "quarried." Gangs of workmen were hired to obtain the few carvings of bone and ivory, figurines of clay and stone, and superbly made tools of flint and bone that had been produced so many thousands of years before. The lure was not so much the intrinsic value of the artifacts as it was the great age that they implied. In recent years, in an attempt to salvage what remains, many of the dumpheaps outside the caves left by unscientific diggers of the nineteenth century have been systematically re-excavated in order to recover the tools that were overlooked or discarded by the earlier diggers. In this way some idea of the total assemblage that occurred in the cave or shelter can be determined, though the material is lacking in associational context. Men such as Otto Hauser, a Swiss dealer in antiquities, became wealthy collecting and selling material to the museums that would bid the highest. All over the continent and England as well, gentlemen spent their holidays excavating in the local sites. But these looting operations gradually died out as the historical importance of the antiquities was recognized.

A happy exception to the prevailing role was the famous and successful research team of Henry Christy, an English banker, and Edward Lartet, a French magistrate who abandoned the law for paleontology. Between 1863 and 1865, when Christy died from an illness contracted in digging a cave in Belgium, the two men excavated in the famous French paleolithic sites of La Madeleine (from which the Magdalenian culture was named), Le Moustier (type site of the Mousterian culture), Les Eyzies, Laugerie Haute, and others. Their cooperative work was intelligently done, and among their important accomplishments were the first recognition of paleolithic engraved art, recognition and definition of the Upper Paleolithic as distinct from the Lower Paleolithic, and the first classification of paleolithic cultures based upon associated fauna (Daniel 1950:100; Breuil 1941).

In the United States, when the West had been wrested from the Indians and opened to cattle grazing, cowboys became pioneers in archeological discovery. At the successful conclusion of the Mexican War, engineers of the U.S. Army were dispatched to the newly acquired territories of the southwestern United States, and their reports contained descriptions of prehistoric sites that were soon to encourage American archeologists to investigate them. In the late 1800s members of the Wetherill family, early settlers in Colorado, discovered at Mesa Verde some of the most impressive and best preserved prehistoric remains in the western hemisphere. In 1888 Richard Wetherill and Charley Mason, looking for a stray herd, came upon one of the largest cliff dwellings ever built—"Cliff Palace." After their discovery the Wetherill brothers explored the Mesa Verde canyons in detail, and archeologists soon followed suit. A Swedish archeologist, Baron Gustav Nordenskiöld, wrote the first comprehensive account of the ruins in 1893, and, in retrospect, this seems to have been an open invitation for looters to try their luck also.

Meso-America and Peru, centers of the New World civilizations, have been the scene of even greater looting. There is scarcely an art shop or decorator's atelier in the United States that does not feature some pieces of pre-Columbian art, usually finely modeled pottery, stone sculptures, or jade carvings. These antiquities are smuggled out of the countries of their origin; conveniently, the rural natives dig them up in their free time, thus sparing a modern collector the burden of becoming a latter-day Belzoni.

One more aspect of treasure hunting should be considered. As practiced under water to recover objects long since sunk, it has been called with some derision "archaeological salvage" (de Borhegyi 1961:44). Particularly in the Mediterranean, where traders have been moving goods by ship for thousands of years, there are numerous wrecks lying in relatively shallow waters that are easily accessible to divers. Soon after the invention of the aqualung in the 1940s, a growing group of sportsmen-adventurers discovered that treasure awaited their search. It was exceedingly simple. For example:

> As soon as word got out that an archaeological discovery (a sunken ship) had been made at Anthéor, amateur divers rushed from all parts of

the French Riviera and with thoughtless enthusiasm carried off hundreds of souvenirs of their visit. One day in 1949 an American yacht anchored over the wrecks, and the owner arranged a special show for his guests. He put the davits of his ship at the disposal of the divers swimming there so that they could bring up heavy articles from the sea bottom (de Borhegyi 1961:10).

Not all underwater archeology is disreputable and, in fact, there are exciting possibilities for future research as archeologists develop adequate techniques of recovery and recording (see Bass 1963; Dumas 1962; Frost 1963; Goggin 1960; Ryan and Bass 1962; Silverberg 1963; Throckmorton and Bullitt 1963).

Long ago the potential of underwater archeology was recognized. Sir Charles Lyell (1872, 2, Chap. 46) cites a considerable number of known instances of submarine archeological materials, and his list of the numbers of British vessels wrecked between 1793 and 1829 provides a hint of the possibilities for archeology that exist on the ocean bottom. Lyell concludes by saying that "it is probable that a greater number of monuments of the skill and industry of man will, in the course of ages, be collected together in the bed of the ocean than will exist at any one time on the surface of the continents." For an early account of traditions, some of them probably based on fact, of settlements below the present surface of lakes or the ocean, see the Lord Bishop of St. David's account (1859).

During the exceedingly dry winter of 1853–1854 when lake levels fell far below normal, the pilings of Neolithic and Bronze Age houses were found on the exposed margins of certain Swiss lakes. In order to retrieve additional similar remains, archeologists sometimes resorted to draining lakes (Brisse and Routrou 1876; Geoffrey 1876). As we now know, an enormous amount of unique material was lost before adequate techniques for preserving water-logged wood were developed.

For persons living in the fifteenth or even during much of the nineteenth century, looting was a wholly respectable practice (T. Wright 1844). But as soon as it was shown that serious archeological study could pay dividends in knowledge ultimately far greater than the price an object alone might bring, educated persons engaged in looting have found themselves working against the main stream of public conscience. When measured against the life history of archeology, looting is the activity of thoughtless children; adults are expected to be better informed and to set a creditable example. Evidence of man's past is destructible, and once destroyed, it can never be restored.

TEXTS, TEMPLES, AND TOMBS

The title of this section recalls the previous one, for most of the treasure hunters were dealing with temples, texts, and tombs. But the important thing is the purpose toward which the work is directed. Here we will deal with studies of the ancient civilizations and their immediate antecedents. Such work is usually done by persons trained in the humanities.

Classical archeology received its greatest impetus from Heinrich Schliemann, though he did not originate scientific classical studies. In fact, some would deny that his methods should be dignified by the term archeology. Schliemann's impatience with getting to the bottom of sites left him with little taste for working out precise stratigraphic associations. In his later years his associate, Dorpfeld, brought some order to his digs, but his early work amounted to little more than the recovery of objects. By contrast, Schliemann's predecessor, Giuseppe Fiorelli, who excavated Pompeii in 1860, attempted to restore a picture of the whole Roman city. Fiorelli said that the discovery of art objects was of only secondary importance; yet it was Schliemann, not Fiorelli, whose work was followed by the world and whose example was emulated by later workers. While Schliemann's excavation methods left much to be desired, they were nevertheless far better than the work of his predecessors in the eastern Mediterranean area.

Childhood reading about the sacking of Troy during the Homeric period so impressed Schliemann that after he made his fortune as a merchant he began to study ancient history. He wanted to corroborate Homer by finding Troy. In his several seasons of excavation between 1869 and 1889 he was successful in finding a convincing Troy (Hissarlik) and other great sites. In Mycenaean shaft tombs he found treasure that was described then as being "one of the most important discoveries of past human civilization that has ever been made" (Daniel 1950:138). He also found remains of an even earlier, previously unknown, prehistoric Greek life and so opened a whole new world for classical scholarship. But Schliemann's influence was most effectual in that he opened the eyes of the world to the possibilities of excavation directed toward solving problems rather than solely to the recovery of objects of art.

The recent history of classical archeology has been one of continuing discovery and interpretation. The Egyptian hieroglyphs had been deciphered by Schliemann's time, and Greek writing could be read, but other ancient scripts have not been deciphered to this day. A pre-Greek civilization, Minoan, was responsible for two forms of writing, the more recent of which, Linear B, was shown only in 1952 to be a form of ancient Greek (Chadwick 1961). The earlier form, Linear A, is still to be deciphered adequately. Early cuneiform inscriptions from Mesopotamia, writing on Hittite documents from Anatolia, and the written Mohenjo-daro script of the Indus Valley civilization still cannot be read.

Classical archeologists are often students of ancient languages. In this respect their work is to supplement written history by combining archeology with philology. Note, for example, the map of Homeric Greece and the outlying Mediterranean regions that it has been possible to draw based upon geographical details contained in the Iliad (Page 1959). Archeologists who deal with the Mesopotamian and Egyptian civilizations, however, are often trained in art or architecture rather than languages. Their job is as much to discover facts of prehistory as to add to knowledge of written history. The persons who transcribe the ancient texts are called epigraphists; they may never participate in the actual excavation of a site.

Writing is not the only concern of classical scholars. Art fascinates many students and some study coins (for some unusual and highly interesting publications that deal with cultural rather than financial or numismatic aspects of coins, see the recent work of Zeuner (1963) on domestication of animals; M. Grant (1958) on Roman history as illustrated on coins; and D. Allen's (1958) excursion into life in the late pre-Roman times in Britain as illustrated by devices on Belgic coins); others prefer architecture; and, of course, there is the old mainstay of most archeology, pottery, which serves as a means of determining chronology as well as cultural connections between different societies (Colton 1953; Ford 1962; Shepard 1956).

In spite of the diversity of topics and approaches, when ancient civilizations are studied, the emphasis usually rests on the material qualities of civilization—art in its various forms, monumental architecture, and literature. These subjects are studied in the divisions of the humanities at the larger universities. Within this broad area, however, research is divided among departments of oriental languages (including those of Southwest Asia), the classics, art and architecture, and, sometimes, ancient history.

Schliemann's work set the tone of what is still being done. The significant changes since his time have been in the development of more precise techniques for acquiring information. As knowledge has accumulated, it has been possible to plan excavation more intelligently. As better techniques for excavating, recovering, and preserving antiquities have been developed, archeologists have been able to learn more. Classical archeologists have defined their aims and devoted their time to recapturing history in ever more sophisticated ways.

PROTOHISTORY

Christian Jurgensen Thomsen, curator of the National Museum in Copenhagen in 1836, devised a method for sorting and displaying the antiquities in his charge. His method was to keep separately the objects of stone, bronze, and iron. This was the birth of the Three-Age system (Heizer 1962a:10–26; 1962b) that has plagued more constructive archeological thought to the present day. On the difficulties of applying the Three-Age system to European archeology see Childe (1944a, 1944b) and Daniel (1943). Nevertheless, it soon became apparent through the excavations carried out by Thomsen's associates, among them J. J. A. Worsaae (Rowe 1962a), that in Denmark there was an actual stratigraphic succession of flint, bronze, and iron. With this clue it was natural for archeologists to conclude that man had gone through these three stages almost everywhere.

The principle of superposition or stratification (sometimes called Steno's Law) was first devised by Nicolaus Steno (1638–1686), a Danish medical doctor attached to the court of Ferdinand II, Grand Duke of Tuscany. Steno's *Prodromus* was published in 1669 (for translation of a part of this work see Heizer 1962a:4–10). When the principle of stratigraphic succession was applied, archeology could be used to extend local history by recording evidence of past cultures in their proper chronological order. Building on this foundation, enterprising archeologists in Europe turned their attention to uncovering their national past and in the process gathered information that showed the spread of civilization across the Western world.

Without writing which can be deciphered, archeology becomes what Albright (1957:49) calls "anepigraphic" (the science of unwritten documents), or what C. Hawkes (1954) calls "text-free." This kind of archeology discovers lost or forgotten civilizations such as the Minoan of Crete, the Hittite of Asia Minor, and the Harappan of India—it literally *creates* these. The Scythians of South Russia who had no writing[1]

---

[1]The recently discovered Sakiz treasure in Iran is ascribable to the Scythians. A metal plate in the board bears a hieroglyphic inscription that is not in any otherwise known scripts and may be a Scythian form of writing (Ghirshman 1961:109).

were, however, pretty well described by Herodotus, and by combining Greek documents and archeology, we know a great deal about them. Unlike their colleagues who were working with Greek and Roman materials, archeologists in western Europe could not readily name the peoples whose past they were excavating. True enough, the British had historical knowledge of the Celts and the Angles and Saxons, but before them, nothing. And in most of Europe there was no knowledge at all of whom the early inhabitants had been. Modern national names would not describe the peoples who, thousands of years earlier, had not been grouped into those transitory political allegiances. With nothing to fall back on, archeologists named prehistoric people after some of their most characteristic artifacts. Thus we have the curious spectacle of the "Beaker-folk" whose movements have been traced to the Rhineland, Holland, and finally, by about 1800 B.C., to the British Isles. Another group, perhaps having its origin in the steppes of central Asia, was named the "Battle-axe Culture." Somewhere in Europe the Beaker-folk and the Battle-axe people met and both seem to have entered Britain at about the same time. It is anybody's guess what these people called themselves or what their language was.

In most areas it was when the people took to farming rather than hunting that they came under the influence of the Mediterranean and Southwest Asian civilizations, and these centers continued to influence the outlying areas for much of their history. Accordingly it has been natural for scholars concerned with peripheral areas to study their material in terms of the influential civilizations. How else could they compare one area with another, or interpret fragmentary data that were only complete in the centers of diffusion? Thomsen in 1836 already saw clearly that the later prehistory of northern Europe would have to be understood as derivative from the Mediterranean area of civilization. Dawkins (1880:447) also saw the possibility of dating the later prehistoric cultures of Europe by referring these to the dated remains of the Mediterranean area when he wrote: "It is a question equally interesting to the historian and to the archaeologist, to ascertain the extent to which the light of their culture [that is, of Egypt, Assyria, Etruria, Greece, and Phoenecia] penetrated the darkness of central, western and northern Europe, and to see whether it be possible . . . to bring the Historic period in the Mediterranean region into relation with the Prehistoric period north of the Alps." This was not done until G. Montelius in the last decade of the nineteenth century effectively tied the two chronologies together (Bibby 1956:176–182).

Archeology in the biblical lands has made clear a great many brief or cryptic references in the Bible to sites, people, customs, and historical events, so that archeology in this case actually has been able to add a great deal of specific detail to the historical documentation (D. W. Thomas 1961). In the Migration Period (or Dark Ages), after the decline of Rome in the third century A.D., Northwest Europe lost direct contact with the literate Mediterranean world, and for a period of about half a millennium lapsed back into what was essentially a "nonhistorical" phase, which we know mainly from archeological rather than documentary evidence. The study of protohistory has therefore been closely allied to the humanistic traditions that produced the classical scholars. This is in contrast to prehistoric archeology, which is concerned with peoples who lived before or beyond the influence of civilization.

Piggott (1959, Chap. 5) has provided us with an excellent discussion of the degrees to which societies can be called historic. Peoples lacking writing (or whose writing cannot be deciphered) but who lived in the penumbra of literate civilizations may be known to us by name, and something of their history may have been recorded by their neighbors. The Scythians of South Russia, described by Herodotus and Strabo, the occupants of the Land of Punt (Somaliland) with whom the Egyptians traded and whose customs they recorded (W. S. Smith 1958:136–138), and the Celts of Europe, known from writings of Caesar, Tacitus, and others, belong to the category of nonliterate barbarians living beyond the borders of the civilized world where writing and reading were practiced. But the fact that they are named and described and the knowledge that certain events of ancient history involved them brings them into focus as "real" and identifiable people rather than belonging to that shadowy, nameless kind of group (so familiar to the prehistorian) whose very existence is a fact discovered by archeologists. This kind of knowledge about preliterate societies is not limited to the peoples living on the fringes of the Greek and Egyptian and Roman worlds, but indeed is equally true of all of the primitive cultures of the Old and New Worlds that are known to us from the writings and museum collections compiled by travelers, explorers, and ethnologists. Christopher Columbus and Hernando Cortes wrote, or caused to have written, records of societies whose traces now are solely archeological, and in so doing they were instrumental in permitting these extinct groups, in the last instant of their life, to enter into the historical arena and, as a result, avoid the fate of so many human groups of prehistory, which was to live and die anonymously.

In the New World the great native empires of the Aztecs and Incas, which were brought to a sudden and bloody end by the Spanish conquest in the early sixteenth century, managed to incorporate some of their history in Spanish accounts. These "histories" take the form of traditional genealogies of important families and main events in the lives of certain individuals, including the ruling dynasties. Thus, for the Peruvian rulers there are lists of emperors that are very useful in identifying and dating archeological sites of the late Inca period (Rowe 1944:56–59; 1945a, 1945b). The Homeric epic was a memorized tale that happened to get recorded in writing while it was still remembered in detail, and it has been argued (Albright 1957:73; Daniel 1950:15; Griffiths 1956; Lang 1908; Myres, 1908:127–128; Page 1959: Chap. 6) that the *Iliad* describes an actual historical situation referring to the end of the Bronze Age. Piggott (1959:104) uses the term "conditional literacy" to characterize the surviving written records of societies such as that of the Myceneans in Linear B script (Chadwick 1961) and which are almost exclusively bookkeeping accounts recording the amount of production or inventories of goods. While these official business records, made by clerks who were a specialist minority in the society, can tell us a great deal about the economic and political structure of the Myceneans (Chadwick 1959), they do not contain literary or historical accounts. The famous Peruvian knotted string mnemonic records called quipus (Locke 1912) were probably similar in function, and Rowe (1944:57) believes that these were never used for keeping dates. The surviving books (codices) of the Maya and Aztec peoples, while known to represent only the barest fraction of such records existing at the time of the Spanish conquest, are of the greatest importance in our understanding of the later history and calendars of these societies. Thus a variety of situations are involved when we refer to a society as historical (cf. Albright 1957:64–76).

ADAM AND BEYOND

Unlike other kinds of archeology, prehistory is not primarily aligned with humanistic or even historic academic disciplines. Prehistory has always been closely allied with anthropology, which developed at about the same time, and with geology which supplied the evidence of great age for antiquities. Two facets of prehistory center on evolutionary studies. The first is the cultural evolution of man; the second is his biological evolution. Neither study has a history going back much before the time of Darwin, when the concept of evolution was first clearly shown to the world. Quite by chance the year 1859 marked both the publication of Charles Darwin's great book *On the Origin of Species,* which presented the theory of evolution by natural selection, and the birth of Paleolithic archeology. In that year several British geologists (John Evans, Prestwich, Flower, and Falconer) visited Amiens, France, where they verified the claims made by Jacques Boucher Crêvecoeur de Perthes that rude flaked stone implements occurred at great depths from the present surface in the Pleistocene (then called "antediluvian") gravels of the Somme River. Such ancient and crude tools fitted well with the idea implied (but not stated) by Darwin of the progress of man from lower forms. No primitive fossil human bones were known in 1859 except for the first of the Neanderthal skulls, discovered in 1856, about which a controversy was raging over whether it was the skull of a primitive form of man or that of a pathological idiot (see Heizer 1962a, Chaps. 2, 3; Oakley 1964).

The early prehistorians recognized that the remains they were digging up had their closest counterparts among living primitives rather than among civilized peoples. It was natural for them to turn to anthropologists, and especially ethnologists, who were gathering information on primitive peoples, rather than to historians and humanists, for their inspiration and interpretation. The development of man's technology from simple to complex over the long span of his existence was readily attributed to cultural evolution. As a result many prehistorians have been more concerned with discovering and interpreting the universal trends of culture evolution than with working out the details of short-range local sequences of cultures. The earliest attempts at describing cultural evolution were based largely on analogy with living primitives, who were thought to exhibit various "stages" of cultural evolution. Though this has been a persistent notion, detailed work on particular sequences has demonstrated that human history has been remarkably varied and cannot be described by any single system of stages of development (South 1955; Steward 1955; L. A. White 1947).

Few prehistorians are competent to understand the details of biological evolution; therefore they work closely with physical anthropologists when skeletons are found or when they must make interpretations based on man's biological capacities. Because man's early history of development is more closely tied to biology than to culture as we know it today, archeological interpretations of fossil man as frequently draw on theories of biology as they do on anthropology. The extent to which cultural and biological evolution have gone along side-by-side, and the way in which culture has helped to shape man's body, are neatly discussed by Washburn (1959, 1960) and Washburn and Howell (1960).

American archeology is a somewhat different case. Because the earliest men to reach America were modern physically, there is no major current interest in the biological evolution of the American Indian. Neither is there much concern with the Indian's cultural evolution, although his culture underwent striking changes in the 15,000–20,000 years that he has occupied the continent. Rather, the main effort in American archeology has been to work out regional sequences of occupation (Jennings and Norbeck 1964). Archeologists have recently begun to consider the pancontinental development of culture, especially as it relates to the development of civilizations and their influence thereafter. The publications by Willey (1955, 1960) and Willey and Phillips (1958) illustrate the wider consideration of New World cultural development.

Prehistory can thus be contrasted with treasure hunting, art history, philology, history and even protohistory in its inspiration and method. This contrast holds in spite of the fact that the ends of these studies—to understand man's past—are essentially the same. This is the reason why we have entitled this book *The Study of Prehistoric Archeology* rather than simply *The Study of Archeology*. The aims, methods, and results described in the remainder of this book pertain to prehistoric archeology.

SALVAGE ARCHEOLOGY

In the past few decades there has been an increasing awareness that something ought to be done to rescue archeological sites from the onslaughts of modern construction. In the United States, where dams and highways are being built, responsible agencies frequently appropriate money to salvage the sites that will be covered with water or otherwise obliterated. The most dramatic appeal to salvage has been in Egypt where the Aswan dam will bury many monuments of Egyptian history. In response to the appeal, several foreign governments have sponsored archeological teams to excavate and record affected sites (Brew 1961).

Salvage archeology is a special case. It is done only if there is appreciation of the value in preserving information about the human past. In this sense, it is not new. As early as 1627 Charles I of England officially declared that "the study of antiquities . . . is very serviceable to the general good of the State and Commonwealth." And positive action was being taken to preserve sites a hundred years ago in Britain when a Roman amphitheater was successfully saved from destruction because it stood in a railroad right-of-way (Jessup 1961:200–201). Salvage archeology is usually based on the premise that some work is better than no work. As a result certain methods are often used that would not be considered proper on more leisurely excavations. In many areas salvage archeology has been the only *systematic* investigation made and has contributed knowledge of enormous value. In this respect its methods should be emulated, but in two ways salvage archeology runs counter to practices that will be advocated here. First, salvage archeologists must be indiscriminate and take the sites as they come. That is, it is not possible to be very selective when the atmosphere is one of a rescue operation. Salvage archeologists are altruistic in that they put aside their scholarly interests in problems of their own devising for the general good of future archeology. Second, salvage archeologists must operate under the pressure of time and thus may be forced to ignore many of the refined techniques of modern archeology. The resultant loss in information is rationalized by saying that, after all, something was saved.

On the other hand, we owe a great deal to salvage archeologists who, working under pressure, have developed techniques for survey and excavation that make even the normal paced digs easier (Wendorf 1962; Dittert and Wendorf 1963). But perhaps their most important contribution has been to demonstrate the value of really intensive studies of whole areas, a practice, regrettably, followed by too few archeologists; many who have the time often get themselves tied too closely to individual sites and thus lose valuable perspective on distribution and variation.

3

ARCHEOLOGICAL SITES

KINDS OF SITES

Archeology is concerned with sites. A *site* is any place, large or small, where artifacts are found. The variety of prehistoric sites is limited only by the number and kind of places where prehistoric men lived and left their equipment, or where their artifacts have come to rest. A site may be as large as a city or as small as the spot where an arrowhead lies.

In spite of the great variety of individual sites, there are broader groupings into which all sites can be fitted for easier understanding. Sites are sometimes classified by the artifacts found there (for example, Paleolithic, Bronze Age, or Desert Culture), by location (for example, lake-side, valley-bottom, or cave), by the activity represented (for example, kill-site, camp site, quarry site, living site), by permanence of habitation (for example, permanent, seasonal, infrequently, or single occupation), or by archeological context (for example, stratified, non-stratified, surface find). None of these classifications can account for all the possible kinds of sites. The following descriptions are grouped by activities.

Habitation Sites

Habitation sites are the most important. In a sense all archeological sites imply habitation, though it may have been relatively short, but for convenience here, a habitation site is one around which a group of people centered their daily activities. Some habitation sites were occupied the year round. These frequently have the remains of houses, but they may be caves or rock shelters or even open areas in which no trace of a permanent shelter remains. Seasonally occupied sites generally have fewer traces of architecture. We know from ethnography that prehistoric men may have sought shelter in various sorts of constructions ranging from temporary brush windbreaks, lean-tos, and tipis to semisubterranean houses made of logs and earth that could be lived in year after year, mud brick or rough masonry houses, and so on. In areas where shelters were not needed, habitation sites may show nothing more than the remains of fire and a scatter of refuse and artifacts. The most ancient structure, an arc-shaped pile of stones, which perhaps served as a windbreak, has recently been discovered in Olduvai Gorge, Kenya, by L. S. B. Leakey. By the potassium-argon dating method this shelter, if it is correctly identified as such, is nearly two million years old (Leakey and Lawick 1963:147).

Sites that are ordinarily close to settlements are agricultural fields and terraces, irrigation canals, roads, bridges, and aqueducts.

Identification of sites built for *defense* is rare for prehistoric times though from the location of some we must infer that their builders had defense in mind. Such examples as the cliff dwellings in Mesa Verde, Colorado, are striking; and the remains of Inca fortresses in the central Andes attest to recurrent warfare between local groups. Palisaded villages of later prehistoric times in the eastern United States such as Aztalan, Wisconsin, also attest to the social practice of serious warfare and the need for living in defensible villages.

Trading Centers

Trading centers have been reported from a few places though they are hard to recognize with certainty. Trading on a scale large enough to necessitate trade centers must have been unusual for prehistoric peoples. Sites centrally situated between the Maya and Aztec areas have been identified as ports of trade though of course they were habitation sites as well (Chapman 1957). In Turkey archeologists have found a site on nonarable land that was favorably placed for the salt and obsidian trade (Mellaart 1958). Cleared pathways across open ground, or roads such as the Roman roads of Britain, Maya causeways (Morley 1946:339–341), and Inca highways (von Hagen 1952, 1955) are features related to trade. Photographs of trails in desert southern California are shown in Schroeder (1952) and Johnston and Johnston (1957).

Kill Sites

It is common in the United States to find *kill sites*. These are places where one or more animals were killed by hunters, some of whom may have had no permanent dwellings. At kill sites archeologists find the bones of the animals, projectile points used for killing them, and the tools for butchering. Frequently there is associated a fireplace in which the animal was cooked. Outside the Americas it is less common to find kill sites, though certain remains from the African Acheulian, situated at the edges of rivers and lakes, must have been combination kill and habitation sites (J. D. Clark 1960). The amount of bone and stone tools suggests seasonal, or perhaps permanent year-round, camps. In Africa these are called "living floors."

Quarry Sites

Quarry sites are common throughout the world. At the Alibates ranch in Texas, prehistoric men quarried for a widely used multicolored flint. Flint mines, dug into the chalk deposits at such places as Grimes Graves, are well-known sites in England. Mining for metal ores throughout Europe and in Mesoamerica has also left sites. In grim testimony of the dangers of some prehistoric activities, archeologists have uncovered bones, and in some cases, the bodies of miners who were crushed by falling rock. Quarry sites may be workshop areas where ores were smelted, flint was chipped, or soapstone was worked into bowls (Bryan 1950; Ball 1941; Heizer and Treganza 1944). Analysis of stone from quarry sites may help answer the question of where a particular stone originated, and a study of the distribution of finished artifacts made from the stone may tell the archeologist a great deal about ancient trade relations. An interesting example is the petrological analysis of British stone axes of the Neolithic and Bronze Ages (Keiller et al. 1941).

Ceremonial Sites

Ceremonial sites are also common. The imposing megalithic construction at Stonehenge is rivaled by the much older caves in France and Spain where remarkable paintings, carvings, and reliefs are found. Chogga Zambil in southwest Iran, an Elamite ziggurat of the thirteenth century B.C., is one of the largest known religious structures ever built, and the enormous ceremonial precincts in Meso-America evoke admiration the world around. Ceremonial centers need not be attached to habitation area, but if they are monumental in size, they cannot have been far from a supply of labor. Ordinarily, however, there are no dwellings other than those of religious functionaries within the area of a ceremonial site. For example, La Venta, a large Meso-American ceremonial center, was erected some distance away from the area where the population lived (Drucker et al. 1959 and Heizer 1960a). J. Eric Thompson (1950:6), in discussing Maya ceremonial centers, has proposed that there existed among these people two classes—one the general "lay" or peasant population that lived their own life in villages, farmed, and provided labor to build the ritual centers; and a "hierarchial" group of educated priests who administered the religion for the benefit of the masses. The contrasting type of life and location of living areas of the two elements of the same population would, therefore, leave quite different archeological traces.

Burial Sites

Burial sites have attracted looters since early historic times, and many archeologists concentrate their efforts on cemeteries. These range from isolated burials in shallow holes to elaborate masonry constructions, earth mounds, and megalithic monuments. Their variety is illustrated by the earth mounds used by the Hopewell Indians of Ohio, the platform burials used in the northern woodlands, simple cremations in the Cochise site of Cienega in Arizona, the Neanderthal burials at La Ferrassie, France, the royal tombs of Ur, and, most remarkable of all, the pyramids of Egypt, which were simultaneously imposing funerary monuments and housings for royal tombs. It was long thought that the pyramids of the New World served only as elevated platforms on which to build religious temples, but the discovery in 1950 by Ruz, the Mexican archeologist, changed this opinion. At the Classic Maya site of Palenque in the state of Chiapas, Mexico the pyramid and Temple of the Inscriptions were built over a great burial chamber (Ruz 1952). M. Coe (1956) has argued that the main purpose of Meso-American pyramids may have been to house tombs of high priests and kings.

Burials may also be found in the garbage dumps of large villages; they may be under the floors of houses; or they may occur singly away from habitation sites. At times certain cemeteries, or sections of a cemetery, may have been reserved for persons of one sex or age or social rank. Usually, however, cemeteries contain a sample of the whole population that died in the period of the cemetery's use. As examples of special cemeteries we note those for children in Pennsylvania (Farabee 1919); separate cemeteries for men in the Desert Fayum (Caton-Thompson and Gardner 1934); and the Roman cemetery at Ziegelfeld in Upper

Austria where special areas were reserved for children, for victims of epidemics, and for persons belonging to "an elevated social group, very like the clergy" (Kloiber 1957).

Surface Scatters

Surface scatters are sites that ordinarily cannot be classified by activity. These sites have a geological or geographical context but no archeological associations. The numerous finds of flint tools in river gravels around the world can sometimes be classified as surface scatters. In most cases such tools were secondarily deposited by water that moved them from the spot where they were dropped by prehistoric man. In these sites flint tools are found alone, without associated fireplaces, houses, or bones. In fact, the first ancient tools of man to be identified as such were found in river gravels by Jacques Boucher de Crêvecoeur de Perthes, a customs official of Abbeville, France, who exhibited his finds in 1838. His work began the systematic search for objects of the European paleolithic period. In the United States knowledge of the distribution of early big game hunters is based largely on surface finds. Isolated projectile points and other artifacts are found by farmers plowing in their fields or by persons who accidentally come upon them while walking. Flints are sometimes found on the surface in situations that suggest activities. For example, in West Iran, in hilly country on the edges of large valleys, one frequently finds flints on the tops of hills, as if hunters had waited and watched for their quarry there.

Petroglyphs and Pictographs

Petroglyphs and pictographs are painted pictures of animals, men, mythical beings, or geometric and curvilinear designs whose meaning cannot be interpreted with any reliability. They are usually found on exposed, flat, rock surfaces, either in the open air or on the protected walls of caves and shelters. Painted or pecked designs are spread over most of the world, and vary from the great painted caves of France and Spain, such as Lascaux and Altamira (Breuil 1952), and the marvelous painted art of South Africa (Lowe 1956), to rude designs pecked on boulders in the western United States (Steward 1929; Heizer and Baumhoff 1962) and some quite remarkable painted caves in Texas and California (Gebhard 1960; Jackson 1938; C. Grant 1964). We are all familiar with the propensity of tourists to carve, scratch, or paint their names on monuments, public walls, and the like. The practice was apparently just as common in antiquity, and the inscriptions of Spanish and American explorers on the walls of Morro Rock, New Mexico, actually constitute a valuable historical record (Hodge 1937). When the inscriptions scrawled on Egyptian monuments by Bonaparte's soldiers had been studied they provided information not otherwise known. The ancient Egyptian habit of inscribing signatures on monuments has often proved valuable to archeologists who can sometimes date sections of sites, determine for what length of time the walls were standing in good condition, or identify architects by name (Winlock 1942:47, 103). In the same way an intimate insight into the life of the common people at Pompeii is afforded by a careful study of the *graffiti* on the walls of that city (Tanzer 1939).

Large "intaglio" figures of animals, humans, or geometric forms constitute a special kind of pictographic site, as do the giant desert figures along the lower Colorado River (Harner 1953; Setzler 1952), the "medicine wheels" and effigy figures in the Great Plains (Wedel 1961:228–233, 266–270), the immense figures on the coastal desert of Peru (Reiche 1949; Kosok and Reiche 1949), and the giant, turf-cut figure in Wessex illustrated by Stone (1958, Plate 72).

HOW IS A SITE MADE?

Perhaps the two questions most frequently asked of archeologists are, "How is a site made?" and "How do you know where to look for sites?" Sites result from human activity. We see this easily in pyramids and mounds that were built as memorials to the dead, but it may be harder to understand how other sites accumulated. We might question the 50 feet of debris through which an archeologist digs in a cave, or the enormous habitation sites that sometimes reach a height of 100 feet and a circumference of a mile. At first it may be hard to understand how persons, living a normal life, could eventually pile up so much dirt. We must recognize two things. First, in prehistoric times standards of cleanliness were not very high and, second, the most spectacular accumulations are the remains of houses built on top of one another.

Mongait (1960:23) mentions mounds (*tells*) in Turkestan that were occupied between the tenth and seventh centuries B.C. where the depth of refuse is as much as 34 meters (about 114 feet). Woolley at Ur in Mesopotamia dug over 90 feet to reach the base of the great mound, and Lloyd (1963:94) reports that the Sultantepe mound in Anatolia rises to a height of over 150 feet. In the absence of easily gotten stone in most of this area, people built their houses of mud, placed roof beams on top of the walls, and then covered them with a thick layer of mud and

Fig. 2.   Detail of a typical Near-Eastern mud-walled house showing position of roof beams.

branches (see Fig. 2). In about a generation, after normal wear and through erosion by rain, such houses became unsafe for further occupation. Thrifty villagers would build a new house nearby and take the roof beams from the old one. Without its roof, the walls of a house rapidly disintegrate in the wind and rain, and eventually leave a featureless mound where the old house stood (see Fig. 3). After leveling, new houses are often built on these mounds. The second house might be two or more feet higher than the original house. In Southwest Asia, where people like to live close together, they often build on top of an old house rather than on flat land. In many cases a wall surrounding the town or perhaps planted fields prevent sidewise expansion. In time—some sites have had almost continuous occupation for 5000 years—the mound builds up. Lloyd (1963, Fig. 1) shows in a series of diagrams how mounds grow.

Two interesting instances of the process of disintegration of abandoned Indian dwellings in southern Arizona and northern Mexico are given in detail by Halseth (1933) and Woodward (1933). Through such observable instances of the decay and disintegration of posts, roofs, and floors archeologists may secure valuable hints which will enable them to reconstruct the original appearance of the houses they excavate (Pyddoke 1961, Chap. 11).

The mound is such a conspicuous feature of the landscape in Southwest Asia and so conspicuously absent by comparison in the rest of the world that one must ask why. Childe (1962:56) says that there "are no tells in the woodland zone of Eurasia, north of the Po valley and the Hungarian plain." There are at least two reasons for this. First, the building material in Europe was usually wood; and second, the sites in Eurasia generally have not been occupied for so long as those in Southwest Asia. In Europe, outside of caves, an occupation of 1000 years duration is almost unknown. Where wood is used in building, it disintegrates and does not leave a mound. Where stone is used, it is frequently reused for new buildings, so there may not be the constant addition of new material. Under these conditions only small mounds accumulate. In modern cities, when old buildings are razed, they are rarely leveled to their original surface. In the course of repaving, street levels are raised. And so, even in the United States, mounds are growing. J. C. Wylie (1959:9) calculates that in our own civilization "every thousand people . . . discard nearly a ton of rubbish every day of their lives." Some of this remains in the living area and thus adds to the rising surface of our cities.

This discussion has so far excluded the conscious building of mounds

Fig. 3.   Houses of mud bricks in the process of disintegration.

by the deliberate heaping up of dirt or stone. The practice of building mounds on which to place houses, public buildings and temples was common in the eastern United States as well as in Meso-America (see Figs. 4 and 5). Indians in the Great Lakes region of the United States often made mounds for purposes of burial, some of them being in the form of animals, birds, and serpents.

The accumulation of debris in caves can be explained as the joint result of man and nature (Schmid 1963). A family moving into a cave might bring in some branches or grass to cover the damp, hard floor where they wanted to sit and sleep. They might even bring in some rocks to sit on. They would bring in wood and branches to build fires. The hunters would kill animals and bring their bodies into the cave. When they had finished their meals they would throw the bones to one side. On muddy days they would track in dirt. They would never sweep out the cave. As natural erosion of the cave or rock shelter took place, bits of rock and dirt would flake off the ceiling. Sometimes a major rock-fall would bury the whole floor. Dust carried by wind might add appreciable quantities of fine soil over long periods of time, and water carrying sediments might also add to the filling process. If occupation along with natural events continued for thousands of years the cave might finally be filled to its top.

The archeology of central California provides us with some examples of the composition of prehistoric refuse deposits. Beginning about fifty years ago, E. W. Gifford screened samples of fifteen shell mounds and determined the relative proportions of fish and mammal bone, marine shell, charcoal, ash, stone, and fine soil. He determined (1916:15) that the average mound contained the following percentages: fish remains, 0.031; other vertebrate remains, 0.055; shell, 52.07; charcoal, 0.22; ash, 12.27; stone, 7.5; residue (soil, earth), 27.84. These deposits are made up of the day-by-day leavings of people living on the spot. Since Gifford's initial work, additional investigation along these lines has been carried out in California (Heizer 1960b:94 ff.).

For a variety of reasons some locations are more attractive than others, and these spots may be continuously occupied or frequently re-occupied. A common cause of the successive use of the same spot may lie in its presumed religious sanctity. Often a shrine or church existed there, and later peoples, perhaps of a different religion, took advantage of the same site to build their religious structure. Immediately following the Spanish conquest of Mexico in the first quarter of the sixteenth century, the major Aztec shrines were razed, and important Catholic churches

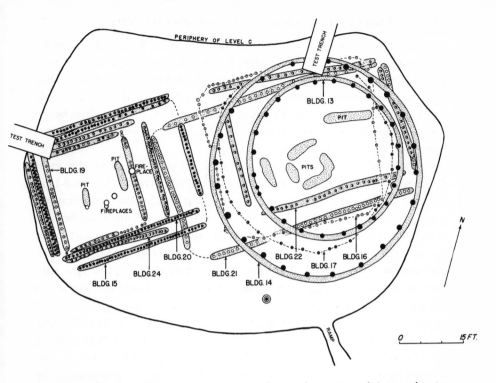

Fig. 4. Plan view of summit of mound in the southeast United States showing the remains of superimposed buildings. The whole village, of which this mound is a part, was surrounded by a defensive stockade. (T. M. N. Lewis and M. Kneberg, *Hiwassee Island*. By permission of the University of Tennessee Press.)

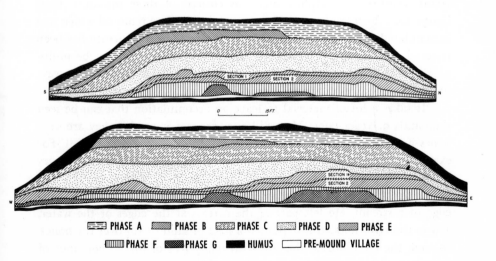

Fig. 5. Section through mound at Hiwassee Island showing the successive stages of construction. (T. M. N. Lewis and M. Kneberg, *Hiwassee Island*. By permission of the University of Tennessee Press.)

were built on their sites (see Ricard 1933;196–199; Montgomery, Smith and Brew 1949:265–272). In Europe, nearly without exception, the great cathedrals stand on the sites of pre-Christian shrines or temples. In Denmark it is commonly noted that flattopped tumuli occur within churchyards. This association of prehistoric sites and Christian churches is explained by the early belief that the heathen precepts were thus rendered harmless (Andersen 1951b:133).

The modern Marsh Arabs have their island villages in the great drowned area of the lower Tigris and Euphrates rivers. The same land has not always been covered with water, but in the last few centuries when the ancient system of dikes fell into disrepair the land became inundated. In ancient times the land was dotted with towns and cities, and it is the tops of these *tells* or mounds, rising above the marsh waters, that are now occupied by the Arab villages (Salim 1962:7, 95). Any still-existing structure dating from classical antiquity is likely to have had a history of multiple successive uses since the time it was first built and served its original purpose. Take for example the Roman amphitheatre at Nimes in Provence, France. It was built just before the beginning of the Christian era and measures 131 meters long by 100 meters wide and seated 21,000 spectators. In the fifth century A.D. it was transformed by the Visigoths into a fortress by filling the arches, adding towers and excavating an encircling moat. Then in the Middle Ages the poor took possession of the arena and in it built houses which accomodated 2000 occupants (see Fig. 6). The little city also had its own chapel. In the nineteenth century the amphitheater was cleared of these squatters, their houses torn down and removed, and 20 feet of refuse removed which had accumulated over the original floor. Today this great structure has been restored and is used as a bullfight arena. Examples need not be multiplied; those given above are cited merely to illustrate some of the ways in which successive occupation may come about.

It takes a lot of material to leave an accumulation that can be seen thousands of years later. Most kill sites are not mounds—they are only bones and stones lying in or under a natural accumulation of soil. For examples of bison and mammoth kill sites in North America see Haury et al. (1953, 1959) and Wormington (1949:25, 29–30, 43–47, 92, 95). The following situation is typical. Assume that a hunter killed a bison at the edge of a stream. He left part of the carcass at the edges of the water, and as the river flooded it deposited a load of sand or silt over the bones. In time the river buried the site with many feet of dirt. Thousands of years later the action of the river changed from aggrading to degrading,

Fig. 6. Roman arena reoccupied by a medieval town, Arles, France. (Cie des Arts Photomécaniques, Paris.)

and the site was exposed again, this time in the vertical bank of the new stream.

In summary, depth of deposit in sites is often directly related to the cleanliness of the people living in them and to the material they used to build with. Sites that are lying far beneath the present surface are the result of geologic action and their position has no direct bearing on the personal habits of their occupants.

HOW TO FIND SITES

There are special ways to find sites, but most sites have been discovered by sheer luck. As a general rule, wherever the surface of the earth is disturbed, evidences of the earlier presence of man may be uncovered. Fortuitous discovery of sites will always be important. Two extreme instances of such lucky discoveries resulted from violent events. Adaura cave near Palermo, Sicily, was opened by the demolition of artillery ammunition during World War II (Blanc 1953), and a tidal wave uncovered the hitherto unknown archeological deposits on the northeast coast of Nuka Hiva, Marquesas Islands.

On the other hand, one can, quite deliberately, find sites if he knows just what to look for. There are two approaches: a person can begin with an area and ask, "What is there?"; or he can begin with a kind of site in mind and ask, "Where can I find one?"

To answer the first question, a person must familiarize himself with the landscape. He will soon learn what is natural in any area. He will learn how the hills look, how the grass grows, where there are trees, and what the sources of water are. He will begin to notice when things look out of place. An unnatural contour to a hill, an unusual kind of vegetation growing in a particular spot, or soil differing in color from that of the surrounding area are all clues to sites. In short, the observer must train himself to look for the unusual. Direct inspection of suspicious or "unnatural" features of the landscape should tell whether or not a site is present. British archeologists have perfected several methods of detecting such sites from indications on the surface. Roman roads and camps, buried walls, camp sites, and so on, can all be found by a trained observer (Crawford 1953). For other examples of site survey see Heizer (1959a, Chap. 7). If the unnatural contour is strewn with flint or pottery, it indicates an archeological site. If the grass grows more luxuriantly in the outline of a rectangle, it may mark the borders of an ancient ditch or house.

Inspection of the landscape is sometimes facilitated by aerial photography, which often shows up features better than ground level viewing will. Photographs can also be taken with special films and filters to show features not visible to the human eye. But, in essence, aerial photography is based on the premise that sites will appear as something unusual on the landscape. Publications dealing with the use of aerial photography in the detecting of archeological sites are by Miller (1957) and Solecki (1957).

Some archeologists get in the habit of watching wherever building involves the moving of a lot of dirt. But we need not always wait for construction crews to expose sites. Rivers may do the same thing. Perhaps the most spectacular such site is Olduvai Gorge in Tanganyika, where many hundred thousand years of human occupation along the edge of a lake can be seen in the sides of the eroded gorge. As one goes from the top to the bottom of the gorge each successive layer is older than the preceding one. Similar finds, though less impressive, are often made in the United States. Persons who scan the cut banks of streams sometimes find flints, bones, and layers of charcoal weathering out.

Caves should also be examined. Men usually lived toward the front of caves. In fact, they sometimes leveled a terrace in front to give themselves room to work in the daylight. If the archeological deposit has been covered by rockfall or soil after the abandonment of occupation, artifacts will at times be found just below the cave where they are eroding out of the steep or rocky slope. The caves where men lived were often situated on hillsides or cliffs where they could survey the surrounding countryside. Cave-dwellers were not much interested in deep and dark underground caverns such as Mammoth Cave in Kentucky, except for special ceremonial purposes.

Instead of random searching, many archeologists decide what they want to find and then go out to find it. A discovery comparable to Schliemann's finding Troy was made by a Dutch doctor, Eugene Dubois, who went to Java in 1890 to find a fossil man, and did—*Pithecanthropus erectus* (Lasker 1961:91 f). Ordinarily, deliberate discovery of particular kinds of sites depends on careful evaluation of available information.

The present-day landscape is usually a clue to where sites are situated. For prehistoric people, one of the most important limitations on the location of sites was availability of water. Sites are usually—but by no means always—close to a river, lake, or spring. Beyond this limitation, however, hunters liked to camp near concentrations of game or in places where they could see game migrating. Farming groups often preferred to plant on certain types of soil. Before population pressure grew too great and before special farming tools were developed, most agricultural sites were probably situated in places whose locations can be predicted with a little foresight and study. In addition to knowing the landscape and its potentials and limitations, therefore, it is necessary to know something of the requirements and capabilities of prehistoric man.

Guesses as to where sites should be are generally based on knowledge of where sites of particular kinds have been found before. That is, if all sites of a particular kind are always found at the edges of lakes, a person looking for more of the same would be well advised to look along lakes. By the same token, a person interested in finding where the domestication of wheat began should look where wild wheat grows.

However, our knowledge of the present does not always lead us directly to knowledge of the past. The world's present climatic pattern is only a few thousand years old. What is now pleasant country may have been under ice a few thousand years ago. Or land that is now grassless rock and sand dunes may have been well watered not too long ago. Archeologists, therefore, must know not only in what kind of environment sites would be found, but they must know what kind of environment existed when the sites would have been occupied. For information about prehistoric environments archeologists depend on geologists, paleobotanists, and paleozoologists, who study plants and animals and the countryside in which they lived. See the publications of North (1937), Pewe (1954), and Judson (1961) for discussions of the relationship of geology and archeology.

CONTEXT

Three elements comprise archeological context: space, time, and culture. If any of these elements cannot be specified, the basic framework for describing and interpreting culture history is incomplete. All sites have geographical context (that is, context in space). The sites or the artifacts in them can often be dated. The culture represented in the sites is defined in terms of the kinds of artifacts found, their date, and the location of the sites. A single arrowhead found on the surface ordinarily cannot be dated, nor can it be associated directly with other artifacts even though its cultural relations (for example, Folsom point type) may be known. It therefore has, properly speaking, no archeological context. By contrast, all objects found and recorded as occurring in one level of a cave can be related to one another and to other finds in the levels above and below. Such an association of artifacts may also be referable to similar associations at other caves. It is easier to interpret the significance of an assemblage when there are other similar assemblages from several sites. The context in which any artifact is found determines the extent to which one can make interpretations about it.

STRATIGRAPHY

Stratigraphy has to do both with space and with time. Use of stratigraphy is fundamental to archeological research and interpretation. It helps us assess the association of objects and their relative ages. The

49

principle of stratigraphy can be stated very simply: if there are layers, those laid down first will be found on the bottom. This idea is so simple that most authors give only passing reference to it; yet interpretation of stratigraphy is one of the most difficult jobs for the excavator (see Fig. 7). All serious students should read Wheeler's (1956) and Pyddoke's (1961) discussions of the subject. As Wheeler puts it, "The first rule about stratification is that there is no invariable rule" (Wheeler 1956:62).

Stratigraphic layers in a site may consist of many things. In a cave or rock shelter, debris from daily living may accumulate as it is packed down under foot. If the cave should be abandoned for some time, chips and flakes falling from the roof and walls as a result of natural weathering will cover with a sterile layer the debris left by people, or wind or water may wash in a layer of soil that contains no artifacts. The result is a series of superimposed natural and cultural layers that can be seen as the cave is excavated. Occupational debris, likely to be rich in organic matter and to contain charcoal, is usually dark in color whereas the sterile accumulation deposited by non-human agency is generally lighter colored (see Fig. 8).

One must remember that even occupation sites may not have been lived in continuously, and that in such cases the stratigraphic record will have gaps or temporal discontinuities. The archeologist may or may not be aware that these lacunae occur from a visual inspection of stratigraphic profiles, and his chief hint of a discontinuity may come from his analysis of the artifacts. Phillips, Ford, and Griffin (1941:233) were able to identify gaps in their ceramic sequence in a stratigraphic pit, and a particularly interesting example is provided at the site of Jericho (Kenyon 1960:198; Zeuner 1954) where an occupational hiatus between the Neolithic and Bronze Age settlements was marked by an immature soil. The time required for development of this immature soil was estimated by Zeuner at 300 ± 100 years on the basis of soil development at Jericho since its abandonment in the Byzantine period, while Kenyon on other grounds calculates this time lapse at about 180 years (1580–1400 B.C.).

Archeologists working at several sites in Palestine before World War I failed to recognize chronological gaps with the result that the chronology was not only incomplete, but also was compressed (Albright 1957:55–56). Such failures to recognize hiatuses in a sequence are of course usually more common in the early stages of investigation of an area.

In open sites, if there have been permanent buildings, the layers are usually made of house floors. As they are successively rebuilt, there is usually a discernible gap between the floors. The floors thus serve to

Fig. 7. One of the earliest instances of the recognition of stratigraphy in American archeology. The painting, done in 1850, shows a Mississippian mound being excavated under the supervision of Dr. Montroville Dickeson. (Courtesy of the City Art Museum, St. Louis.)

Fig. 8. Excavation of Kunji cave, Iran, showing the clear-cut layering of the deposits. The dark bands were caused by the decomposition of organic material whereas the lighter strata are composed largely of disintegrated stone from the roof of the cave. The age of these layers extends back to 40,000 years.

(see Fig. 10). These sites are often referred to as "unstratified," the term in this case meaning that they do not evidence natural stratification. If analysis of artifacts that have been collected with information on their place of occurrence shows that there is a difference between types of objects found at different depths, the archeologist may then speak of cultural phases or levels. There may be an early cultural phase at the bottom of the site, which is different from a late cultural phase found in the upper deposits. One may even go so far as to speak of the site as being *culturally* stratified, although this use of the term is not common.

When an archeologist deals with an unstratified deposit in which he can distinguish no differences in texture or color, what must he do? Does he treat the entire deposit as a single unit of deposition and simply record his finds as occurring within this homogeneous matrix? If he did this, he would be following too literally the recommendation of Wheeler (1956, Chap. 4) to dig by natural levels. The method widely used by archeologists in excavating such sites is to establish arbitrary levels and to treat each level, which may be as thin or as thick as he deems desirable, as though it were a natural stratigraphic level. It is a method of establishing some kind of stratigraphic control, even though it be an arbitrary one, in the absence of visible layers. One of the authors (Hole) has seen rock shelters in Iran with as much as 15 feet of archeological deposit, representing thousands of years of occupation, which have no natural stratigraphy. Any cultural succession in such sites is demonstrable only by analysis of the artifacts, which have been segregated by arbitrary levels.

Wheeler (1956:70) refers to the method of arbitrary or metrical stratigraphy as an "old outworn system," and he is absolutely correct in saying this if that system is employed in archeological deposits that are composed of distinguishable natural levels or layers (see also Newell and Krieger 1949:65 and Willey and McGimsey 1954). He is not so correct, and, in fact, may be wholly wrong, in referring to the system as outworn if he is referring to unstratified deposits. Collections made and recorded by arbitrary levels often, when analyzed, show differences in type or frequency of types from level to level. These differences, which result from differences in cultural practices, are as "real" as anything that can be determined by following natural layers. A justification of the method of digging by arbitrary levels has been written by Heizer (1959a:40–41), Phillips, Ford, and Griffin (1951:240–241), and R. H. Thompson (1955).

The best method of excavation is to remove separate layers after

Fig. 10. Deposit at Gar Arjeneh, Iran, showing the lack of visible stratification that is common to rock shelters of this sort. The bulk of the deposit is composed of disintegrated rock fallen from the overhang. Tools and bones are interspersed throughout. The deposit is partly contemporary with that in Kunji cave (see Fig. 8).

they are exposed over a wide area. R. J. Braidwood (1960:97–108), Lloyd (1963:94–96), and Kenyon (1961:68–114) have written clear descriptions of how an excavation of this sort is done. The natural stratification can often be determined by means of a test pit. Archeologists use the findings from test pits to guide them in recognizing the layers they will expect to encounter when they clear an extensive area. A variation of this is to use balks or stratigraphic control walls between pits or areas. Wheeler discusses this technique and illustrates it with two photographs of sites in India (Wheeler 1956, Chap. 5, Plates 4, 5). A good deal of archeology is small scale work, however, and if an archeologist is limited with regard to funds, size of work crew, or time, he may only be able to excavate a series of test pits or a trench. Lloyd (1963:64) describes the method of one archeologist who covered sites with test pits. While these pits were dug with great care, and all finds were meticulously recorded, Lloyd concludes that "this process could have been prolonged indefinitely without any prospect whatever of coming to understand the anatomy of the mound." The choice of the two alternatives (area exposure or test pitting) is clearly stated by Kathleen Kenyon, a leading British archeologist, who says (1957:41–43):

> There was a phase in Palestinian archaeology in which expeditions set out with the aim of excavating a site completely, and of removing each occupation level over the whole site from the uppermost to the lowest. This was a reaction against earlier methods in which pits or trenches were sunk which never gave an adequate idea of any of the phases discovered. The aim of this total clearance was to gain a complete picture of each successive period. There is something to be said for this idea. But it has two serious disadvantages. Scientifically, it has the disadvantage that nothing is left for posterity. I have already stressed the fact that archaeological methods are always improving, and should continue to do so. Therefore, material should be left for future excavators to test the results of their predecessors on all sites of major importance, though the complete excavation of smaller sites is desirable in theory. The second serious disadvantage is that though a number of long-term plans have been made to carry out the complete excavation of a large site, no single one has ever been carried through. Changes of circumstances, in the resources available to the expedition, or due to political events, have always suspended operations, with the result that much time has been spent on preliminaries and in dealing with less important superficial areas, and the really interesting levels have hardly been reached.
>
> We have now come back to the idea of more limited excavation. But the limited excavation must be to a set plan. We must decide what problems we hope to solve and how that solution can best be attained. I have already referred to the problems which were uppermost in our mind in deciding

upon Jericho as a site for excavation. They concern in fact the beginning and end of ancient Jericho, the question whether the end of the Bronze Age occupation could be ascribed to the period of Joshua, and the examination of the extremely early occupation revealed by Professor Garstang. In between lay many long centuries in which Jericho was a very important town, on which our excavations would undoubtedly throw light, but our initial operations were planned to throw light on these two main problems.

As Kenyon points out, important sites must be restudied as techniques improve and this can be done most effectively if an undisturbed block of the original deposits that show stratigraphy remain. Museum collections from archeological sites may be restudied whenever the occasion requires, but new insights can be secured from re-excavation that inspection of already collected material divorced from its context can never supply.

There are several examples of sites that have been excavated by the two methods—arbitrary levels and natural layers. The reader will find it worthwhile to compare the occurrence of pottery types collected by digging arbitrary levels in Tularosa and Cordova caves, New Mexico (Martin, Rinaldo, Bluhm and Cutler 1952, Fig. 26, Table 2) with the profile of stratigraphic layers (op. cit., Fig. 25), and note that there is a general correlation of the two, but also that collecting of potsherds by natural layers would have produced a much sharper ceramic sequence. At the site of Pachacamac on the central coast of Peru, Strong and Corbett (1943) excavated two large "cuts" (that is, trenches) in the refuse deposits and collected materials by what they call "stratigraphic blocks," each of which was one meter long, one meter wide, and one-half meter thick. When the excavation was finished, the actual stratigraphy exposed on the vertical wall of the trench was recorded (op. cit., Fig. 5). After analysis of the pottery recovered from the trench, the proportions of each ceramic style were indicated on a grid diagram of the stratigraphic blocks (op. cit., Fig. 20). By comparing the two figures, one can see that there is a very rough correlation of ceramic styles, as they occur in stratigraphic blocks, with the actual stratigraphic layers. The case is instructive in showing that greater accuracy in recovering context would have been effected by collecting pottery by actual stratigraphic layers.[1] Willey (1939) reports on an investigation of a village site in Georgia where he began

[1] Strong in 1932 excavated the Signal Butte site in Nebraska by proper methods. He writes: "The deposit was taken down layer by layer, according to (grid) squares, and each layer was carefully cleared off prior to excavation to prevent mixture of artifacts." We do not know why Strong did not employ this same technique at Pachacamac, but it was not because he was ignorant of the proper method.

collecting potsherds by arbitrary three-inch levels. The percentages of Swift Creek to Lamar pottery in successive levels suggested that Swift Creek was earlier.

> These figures, however, were not conclusive. Obviously pits, roots, and other intrusive features had disturbed the natural midden deposits to such an extent that artificial three-inch levels would not give a true time-depositional picture. . . . To correct this, a technique was employed whereby each sherd was plotted in relation to the soil strata and to other sherds. This was done in the usual manner, isolating a block for stratigraphic purposes by cutting a narrow trench on the four sides of a ten foot square. Beginning on one face, the soil profiles were recorded and then a one-foot strip the length of the block was peeled down from the top.

Willey's report illustrates the necessity of assessing results as an excavation progresses so that methods can be changed to suit the circumstances. After changing his techniques, Willey was able to affirm definitely that Swift Creek preceded Lamar.

In most instances where natural stratigraphy exists, it is wrong to dig a large area by arbitrary units because no horizon in any site is absolutely level throughout its extent. Contemporary houses may often be built on different absolute levels so that excavation by arbitrary depth units will cut through strata of different ages and mix them. The inappropriate use of a system of absolute levels has been effectively depicted by Wheeler (1956, Fig. 11). In Wheeler's drawing, pits have been dug into lower levels. Later filling of the pits introduced more recent material at the same level as older artifacts.

A method which has been used to great advantage is the technique of isolating a block. By this method a square trench is excavated so as to leave standing a block of deposit on whose four sides the natural layers can be clearly seen. The block is then peeled down layer by layer. For examples of the use of this technique see Bird (1943:253, 257, Fig. 24), Schmidt (1928), Troels-Smith (1960: Plates 1–3), and Webb and de Jarnette (1942:95 ff., Fig. 27, Plate 162). One advantage of this method is that samples of artifacts from an area of constant dimensions can be secured. This makes it easier to compute the proportions of artifacts and leads to interpretations that would otherwise not be possible (cf. Heizer 1960:101–102).

As a check on results it is sometimes useful to be able to refer back to the stratigraphy after the excavations have been concluded. To facilitate this, soil scientists have developed methods of securing a vertical sample of stratification by attaching a heavy cloth or board to the sides of the excavation, fixing the soil to this backing with an adhesive, and then removing the backing with a thin layer of soil attached. This vertical panel can then be removed to the museum and used to check texture, color, and other features of the original profile at leisure. For details see Dumond (1963), Fryxell and Daugherty (1963:18), Smith, McCreery, and Moodie (1952), and Smith and Moodie (1947).

DERIVING STRATIGRAPHY FROM STRATIFICATION

A practical problem for all field archeologists is to decide what the observed stratification indicates. Does it accurately reflect the sequence of cultures? Are two or more cultural horizons mixed, or are the strata reversed?

A striking example of reversed stratigraphy was found in the American Southwest where, at the large site of Chetro Ketl in Chaco Canyon, New Mexico, the people excavated their well-stratified garbage dump in order to build a large semisubterranean ceremonial chamber. The excavated garbage dump was thus overturned and resulted in the formation of a new dump that had the most recent material on the bottom and the oldest on the top (Hawley 1934, 1937). N. M. Judd (1959:176–177) cites a similar case of partly reversed ceramic stratigraphy at Pueblo Bonito, New Mexico. Judd, who knew in general what to expect in the way of ceramic stratigraphy from the work of earlier investigators, accidentally selected the prehistoric dump as a spot to make a stratigraphic pit. Recognizing that pottery types were not appearing in their correct sequence, he sought for, and found, the cause of the reversal in the kiva pit which had been excavated nearby. It is fortunate that N. C. Nelson, who carried out the first systematic stratigraphic examinations in refuse heaps in the American Southwest (Nelson 1916; Woodbury 1960) did not happen to select an overturned refuse dump to demonstrate the method!

Although reversed stratigraphy is rare in archeological deposits, archeologists can expect it to occur in a variety of circumstances. Winlock (1942:75 ff.) describes an apparent instance of Eleventh Dynasty Egyptian materials overlying deposits of the older Eighteenth Dynasty. The "reversal" of order resulted from a misinterpretation of the sequence of the construction of two buildings. The sinking of floating peat islands which were occupied by prehistoric hunters in Denmark (J. D. Clark 1960:147) has apparently led to the deposition of cultural materials out of their proper order. E. W. Gifford (1951:223) writes of Fijian peoples who disrupt archeological deposits while digging deep earth ovens. Discussions of the various processes by which mixing and disruption, including reversal of normal stratigraphy, can occur are found in Colton (1946:297 ff.), Dietz (1955), Holmes (1893:238–239), Pyddoke (1961:85), Rowe (1961), and Tolstoy (1958:8–9).

The present authors may appear to be laboring the point of stratigraphy, but it is nevertheless extremely important to recognize that normal deposition of layers is subject to a wide variety of disturbance. For this reason, the examples cited above are well worth reading and bearing in mind. We should like to impress upon the reader that archeological deposits must be carefully studied and that assumptions that relative age of materials can be determined from their relative depth of occurrence may be misleading. Depth per se tells nothing about age (see Fig. 11).

In the absence of floors or rockfalls, differences that show stratigraphy may be subtle. In villages where houses were built of dirt taken from around the site, it is often hard to distinguish layering. In these instances only freshly exposed and slightly damp layers may be visible, except to the well-trained observer. In the glare of the noonday sun subtle changes in stratigraphy are often lost because of the intense reflections or because the dirt dries out. A special photographic technique employing infrared sensitive film is often successful in providing pictures that show contrast between layers that are not visible to the naked eye (Beuttner-Janusch 1954). Deetz and Dethlefsen (1963) have outlined a method of detecting nonvisible stratigraphic differences in an apparently homogeneous or unstratified midden profile by making pH determinations at fixed points.

Considering the difficulties in analyzing stratigraphy, archeologists must use the greatest caution in drawing conclusions. Almost all interpretations of time, space, and culture contexts depend on stratigraphy. The refinements of laboratory techniques for analysis are wasted if archeologists cannot specify the stratigraphic position of their artifacts. Pyddoke (1961:17) writes:

> The vertical side of any excavator's trench displays a section through superimposed strata, and almost every archaeologist today will record the thickness and extent of these layers and carefully note the exact position of his 'finds,' but an excavation report is not complete unless the writer sets out to explain the manner in which the layers were deposited. To understand his site properly the stratigrapher must always ask himself how his finds reached the position in which he discovered them; his little sequence of strata can no longer be regarded just as a heaven-sent means of separating cultural levels, nor can deposits be regarded as meaningless and 'barren' simply because no recognizable artefacts or organic remains are discovered in them. They are all equally important parts of the continuing record.

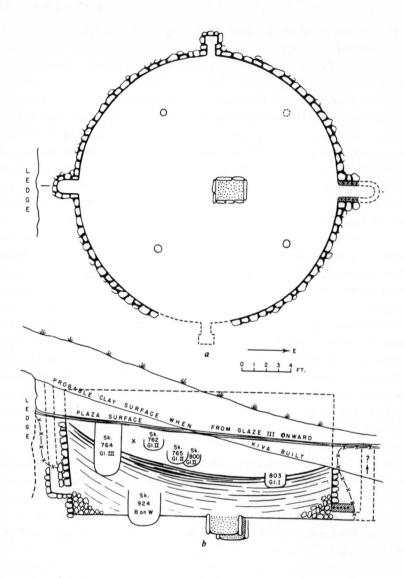

Fig. 11. Abandonment of kiva (underground ceremonial chamber) during black-on-white phase is shown by skeleton 924 whose burial pit is cut into the floor of the kiva. Subsequent filling of the kiva and the placing of burials into the fill continued during the Glaze I, II, and III phases. Note, however, that the depth of the burials below the surface is no true indication of their age. Skeleton 764 of the Glaze III phase is the same depth below the surface as skeleton 803 which belongs to the Glaze I phase. (A. V. Kidder, "Pecos, New Mexico: Archaeological Notes." *Papers of the Robert S. Peabody Foundation for Archaeology*, Vol. 5. By permission of The R. S. Peabody Foundation and The Trustees of Phillips Academy.)

A further point should be stressed. Once the stratification has been determined it is still necessary to verify the association of the objects in each horizon. We generally assume, usually correctly, that objects found associated together at one level in a particular layer in an archeological site were made and used at the same time. By "the same time" is meant, of course, approximately the same time as, for example, in a period of ten years, or as long as a person's lifetime. If this were not true, association of objects would mean little to the archeologist.

The rule of associated objects being contemporaneous may be upset, however, by the preservation of heirlooms or curiosities that people acquire and that finally come to rest in association with much younger objects. In certain societies valued goods are handed down from generation to generation. The Yurok tribe in northwest California passed valuable obsidian blades from father to son, and it is conceivable that examples of these seen by ethnologists around 1900 may have been a century old. Foster (1960b) conducted an "age census" of pots used in the households of the Mexican Indian town of Tzintzuntzan and found only one vessel whose age was as much as forty to fifty years. Foster's observations bear out the assumption made by archeologists that pottery vessels have a relatively short life. Examples of the use of antiques are in the occurrence of prehistoric projectile points in historic period Seneca graves in New York (Ritchie 1954:67–68) and ceramic vessels of Nazca type in Middle Ica period graves on the Peruvian coast (Kroeber and Strong 1924:116). The re-use of stelae and sculptured monuments of earlier manufacture by the Maya builders of Piedras Negras is mentioned by W. R. Coe (1959:155). A similar instance of the modern use of ancient pieces is seen in the collecting of Babylonian cuneiform cylinders as good-luck charms by Persian pilgrims who were visiting Moslem shrines (Rich 1819:58).

Two instances of the deliberate copying of ancient artifacts serve to illustrate another possible source of confusion for archeologists. In the Late Period in the seventh century B.C. in Egypt there was deliberate imitation of Old and Middle Kingdom relief carving and literature dating from one to two thousand years earlier (W. S. Smith 1958:240–241; Aldred 1961:155). The modern Eskimos of Point Barrow were observed by Ford (1959:220) to copy a prehistoric boot pattern that was shown to them by an archeologist, and we have here another instance of a revived form. An archeologist might assume that the ancient quarries were still being worked in the fourteenth century A.D. when he found a Cairo mosque built of the same limestone that covered the great pyramid—an assumption that would be wrong because it is known that Sultan Hasan, in A.D. 1356, stripped off large amounts of the outer limestone casing of the pyramid of Cheops to build the mosque. R. B. Dixon (1903:136–137) noted that the Maidu Indians of northern California used stone bowl mortars to grind acorns in, but that these mortars were always archeological pieces which they found on ancient sites. A final example is that provided by Gadow (1908:17), who observed Mexican Indians making clay figurines in prehistoric molds and selling them to tourists.

It is generally assumed that the objects found in graves represent pieces which were made and used during the lifetime of the person buried. Ordinarily this assumption is true. But a special situation is presented by family tombs or collective sepulchers which may have been used as a depository for corpses for a period of several generations. In this instance, even though the offerings placed with the bodies may pertain to a long period, it will be difficult to isolate the styles of artifacts typical of any particular part of the period because they will be mixed indiscriminately. The use of grave lots (material contained in a single grave) as a means of developing a sequence of types has been discussed by Rowe (1962), who takes up the special problem of collective tombs. For dating of artifacts in tombs see also Childe (1946:3–13), Daniel (1958:48–50), Kenyon (1960:188–190), Petrie (1899), and Stone (1958:34).

TIME

When an archeologist asks, "How old is it?" his question is more than a matter of idle curiosity. For many analyses one must know the sequence in time of what has been found. After an archeologist identifies and describes his artifacts, he usually compares them with artifacts from sites dated relatively older or younger than the one in question. The study of culture change and of evolution, for example, depends on knowing which find is the earlier. The question of age is vitally important in evaluating the cultural significance of two things. For example, the similarity of two objects of the same age at different sites may imply trade, whereas the similarity of two objects of widely different ages may suggest a long cultural tradition. Knowing the relative ages may also help establish association. In the case of the famous Piltdown hoax, part of the proof of the deception depended upon the fact that the skull and jaw, which were claimed to have been found associated, were not of the same age (Weiner 1955). An archeologist may find an ambiguous specimen and want to know to which of two cultures it belongs. If he can date one or the other he may be able to solve his problem. These and many more practical applications of dating constantly face the archeologist; therefore, he must know the relative ages of sites and artifacts before he can make intelligent judgments of their cultural significance.

At the outset it should be noted that two kinds of time—relative and absolute—are important in archeology. In fact this is only a convenient distinction: all dating is relative. Absolute dates are those that are keyed to our modern calendar. Our calendar is based on recurring astronomical events, but it is arranged relative to the date of Christ. The ancient Maya, for example, had a different system that was just as absolute as ours (J. E. S. Thompson 1950).

A relative date tells us simply that one thing is older than another. Archeological material is dated in relation to other archeological material. Thus, the Piltdown jaw was dated as relatively younger than the skull. Absolute dates automatically give relative ages; thus, by reading the birth dates of George Washington and Abraham Lincoln, we can tell immediately that relative to Washington, Lincoln was younger.

There are differing degrees of accuracy in all dating, whether we call it absolute or relative. With modern techniques we are able to give dates that are expressed in terms of the Christian calendar, but which are only absolute within a mathematically expressed margin of error. In some cases because of the possible error, these dates would be less useful to archeologists than sound relative dates. For example, when two closely similar sites are found, it is useful to know which is earlier. If the absolute date of each site (for example, 5200 ± 200 and 5100 ± 200) has a margin of error of 200 years more or less, the archeologist can never be really sure which is earlier since the true date in these cases will fall between 5000 and 5400 years in one case, and 4900 and 5300 years in the other, the overlap being between 5000 and 5300 years. By contrast, if the archeologist can find some way to date one site relative to the other rather than relative to the Christian calendar, he can tell which is the older.

Besides the methods for dating one must also consider what is to be dated. The best method is to date the article—a site or an artifact in the site—itself. Another method is to date the immediate context in which the artifact or site lies. Thus it may be possible to date the beach deposit in which a site is found, or the hearth in which an artifact is found. If so, we then infer that the artifact is the same age as its context. The third, and least accurate, method is to date similar occurrences. Thus, if the beach in which a site is found cannot be dated, a similar one elsewhere may be dated; or sometimes the geological stratum in which a site is found can be dated some miles from the site; or, in some instances where geological formations have been traced around the world, it may be possible to get a date from another continent that will give an estimate for the age of a site. In short, although absolute and relative ages can be given for many archeological occurrences, the dependability of these age determinations may vary considerably. An interesting example of geological cross-dating comes from Java where tektites (also called billitonites)—small, chemically distinct drops of glass of cosmic origin—fell during the Middle Pleistocene. Conveniently for archeologists they have been found in the upper Trinil beds in Java where *Pithecanthropus* fossil human remains were found, and also in the Philippines in association with the teeth of stegodons and elephants (von Koenigswald 1956:104–105). The age of the tektites of Java has subsequently been determined because some of them underlie the basalts, which by the potassium-argon method can be shown to be 500,000 years old (Gentner and Lippolt 1963:82). *Pithecanthropus* and the stegodons and elephants, therefore, are older than a half-million years.

CULTURE AND SPACE

The remaining aspects of archeological context, culture, and space can be considered together. Without culture, space is simply geography, and without space there is no culture in the usually accepted sense of the word.

When assemblages from contemporary sites are compared, some are more alike than others. Groupings of sites with similar assemblages become cultures. That is, cultures are made up of similar archeological assemblages, which are found within a restricted geographical area. There are some exceptions. Recent mass migrations and exportation of ways of life negate the generalization. However, it is to be doubted that in prehistoric times one could find a parallel to transplanted modern English culture in such widely spaced places as Hong Kong, Nairobi, and Sydney.

In the absence of history, an archeologist must give an arbitrary name to the cultures. He may name them after the region in which they are found (for example, Desert Culture), after the site in which the assemblage was first identified (Badarian after the Egyptian site of Badari), or after a characteristic artifact industry in the assemblage (Beaker Culture after the kind of pottery). As one goes back in time he finds he can distinguish fewer and fewer separate cultures. This is because the diffusion of technological innovations over wide areas (but not over whole continents) kept pace with invention. As we approach the present, invention proceeds more and more rapidly, and cultures, as we know them through their artifacts, become more and more restricted geographically. The increasing differentiation is partly an outcome of the invention of specialized equipment to deal with local situations.

Many of the cultural differences that we observe now in Europe between people living in various countries might not be obvious archeologically. Evidence of such things as dress, language, and art—in the absence of graphic arts—would not ordinarily be preserved. Even though people over most of Europe used similar tools during the early stages of the last glaciation and are therefore hard to differentiate archeologically, we have no reason to assume that they spoke the same language, told the same legends around their campfires, believed in the same gods, or painted their faces in the same way. As archeologists we can only distinguish cultures when we can distinguish differences. Many peoples in the past left us very little with which to distinguish differences. Specific ways for identifying cultures from artifacts and the ways to interpret archeological date in cultural terms are given in Part 4 of this book.

The boundary lines we draw between cultures are arbitrary. People living along the Rhine share elements of French and German culture; in many ways they are not typical of other groups of French or Germans living further west or east. For every culture there is a center in which it finds its clearest expression. Groups on the geographical edges may grade indistinguishably from one culture to another. There are few clear cut lines. All archeologists could read with profit Kroeber's (1963:4–6; 1936) and Driver's (1962) discussions of the problem of defining culture areas, how to draw boundaries between culture areas, and how to define the climax group within a culture area.

In summary, context, with its aspects of time, space, and culture, is central in archeological studies. The use of stratigraphy to establish associations and relative ages of artifacts allows interpretations to be made about culture. For archeology culture consists of repeated associations of artifacts as they occur in time and space.

5

PRESERVATION

WHAT IS PRESERVED?

Archeology depends upon preservation. Whatever an archeologist's skills, his restoration of prehistory depends directly on the amount of material preserved. Preservation is predictable, yet whimsical. In a given environment we can predict what kinds of things may remain after a certain time, yet frequently, by accident, only a small part of the potentially preserved material will remain and, also frequently, from the viewpoint of archeology, the wrong things will be preserved (Childe 1956: 10–13; R. J. Braidwood 1946:108–112).

Man's world is animal, vegetable, and mineral. Of the three, the minerals are most likely to be preserved under any conditions, but even metal may oxidize and fired clay may disintegrate. With the exception of stone and gold, very few inorganic artifacts last under adverse conditions.

Today's large buildings, being framed with steel, would soon disintegrate if left untended. Our automobiles will be reduced to window glass and spark plug insulators. Our tools will rust, our books and papers will rot, and our landscapes will be littered with imperishable "throw away" bottles rather than beer cans. Without historical records, an archeologist in fifty or a hundred thousand years would have to use a great deal of imagination to recapture a reasonably accurate picture of what life is like today. The reader interested in how modern cultures or sites might be reconstructed by future archeologists can consult Nathan (1960), Slosson (1928), and Lancaster (1949). Wylie (1959:106–107) in his excellent book on the disposal of modern wastes, writes:

> Times change and the character of refuse changes with changing habits in home and industry; the stream of refuse flowing from any community provides material from which a comprehensive record of the life and interests of the people could be written. Local and national newspapers still clean and legible would furnish relevant facts, while these along with periodicals and magazines would reveal reading habits and interests. The quantity of tins would indicate a decline in home cooking and to the more discerning investigator they would give a clue to the economic strain that is forcing an increasing number of housewives to go out to work. The quantity of coal ash and cinders would surely indicate the inefficiency of the open fire and the certainty of a polluted atmosphere. Bottles and, still more revealing, their metal caps, would establish drinking tastes while scraps of food, decaying vegetable wastes would reveal what the people eat. Discarded clothing, household furnishings, and odd surprising things would supply all the evidence required to complete the story.

But under some conditions our cities would survive virtually intact. The best environments for preservation of organic remains are the very wet, the very dry, and the very cold. If oxygen can be excluded, very wet environments may even preserve metal. The worst environments are those that are alternately wet and dry, hot and cold. Cornwall (1958: 68–71) has written an excellent discussion of the chemical nature of soils and their special preservative effects.

Preservation thus depends upon environment. There is a complicated and little understood chemistry that determines how the environment will affect particular artifacts. From the standpoint of preservation, the tropics have the worst environments. Their heavy rains, acid soils, warm climate, vegetation, insects, and erosion combine to destroy almost everything built or dropped by man. Because of this, some of man's brightest history has been destroyed in southeast Asia. Even with any conceivable techniques, the archeologist will never learn very much of prehistory from that area. Destruction does not take long. Archeologists clear jungle from Mayan temples only to watch them disappear back into the forest after a few years. W. H. Holmes (1897:102) actually records that the site of Chichen Itza in Yucatan was cleared for a hacienda in the last century, but in fifty years the jungle growth had completely covered it again. As vegetation takes hold, its prying roots slowly tear the structures apart. Heavy rains have long since washed most of the plaster facades from the buildings and paintings are rarely preserved.

Occasionally some fluke of preservation will indicate a fact of pre-history that would normally have been lost. Surprisingly, for example, some Maya paintings have been preserved just because of the humidity. In some temples water has deposited a thin film of lime that excludes air and dirt from the paintings. The same thing happened in southern France with some of the 10,000- to 20,000-year-old cave paintings. But nature is fickle on this score, for if too much lime is deposited paintings are obscured or obliterated. In Mayan Guatemala a few wooden lintels remain, but little other organic material has been preserved. Archeological knowledge of the Maya comes largely from their buildings, stone, tools, a few metal artifacts, tombs, and most of all, from interpretation of the codices—the books written in an unintelligible script.

The tropics are wet, but the ground in which artifacts lie is usually very acid. The best remains, preserved by moisture, have come from northern Europe, Scandinavia, and the Arctic, where bogs have sealed artifacts in a wet and airless tomb or low temperatures have prevented decay. Whole bodies have been found in bogs. The Tollund man, buried with the noose that strangled him still around his neck, is a famous example (Glob 1954). His preservation was so perfect that the species of plants he ate for his last meal could be identified in the contents of his stomach. Schlabow *et al.* (1958) describes in detail two bodies found in a bog at Windeby in Schleswig-Holstein, Germany: one a female who still wore a blindfold (see Fig. 12); the second a male who met death by strangulation with a hazel root rope. The circumstances suggest that the persons were put to death for transgression of laws, probably those deal-ing with adultery, and were buried in graves dug into the swamp. They date from the early post-Christian iron age in the second or third cen-tury A.D. In addition to the archeological recovery, the article referred to contains detailed information on the anatomical, histological, and roent-genographic examination of the bodies. Of special interest is the discus-sion of the well-preserved brains and references to a surprisingly large number of other prehistoric brains. Such peatbog bodies have been known for a long time (Barrington 1783; Bibby 1956, Chap. 27; Broholm and Hald 1940; Lyell 1876:2:508 ff.; Thorvildsen (1952). De Laet (1957: 26) describes in detail the hermetically sealed oak coffins found under layers of stones and earth, which contain marvelously preserved organic materials dating from the Bronze Age. In Switzerland and neighboring countries the remains of villages situated on lakeside marshes found beneath the water surface have remained water-logged and well-preserved for several thousand years. The evidence recovered from the mucky

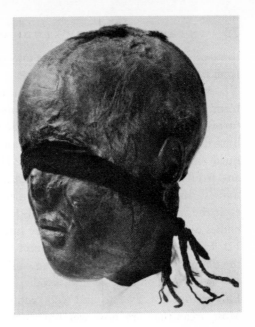

Fig. 12 (*right*). Head of Windeby Bog-body No. 1 with blindfold. (K. Schlabow, *et al.*, "Zwei Moorleichen-funde aus dem Domlands-moor," *Praehistorische Zeitschrift*, Vol. 36.)

Fig. 13 (*below*). Tattooing on the body of a man from the Pazyryk burial mound, in the Altai Mountains of Russia. (A. Mongait, *Archaeology in the U.S.S.R.*, Foreign Languages Publishing House, Moscow.)

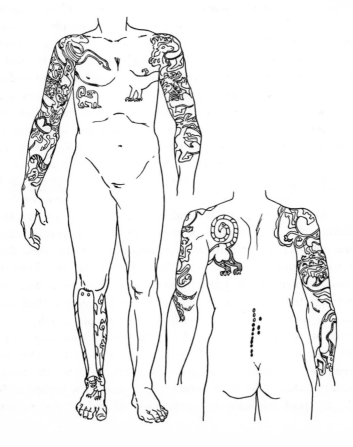

slime of one such well-preserved site may give more information than that from hundreds of poorly preserved ones.

A remarkable example of how man unwittingly helped nature comes from Russia, where tombs of warrior horsemen yield the complete burial furnishings. Two thousand years ago Scythian inhabitants of the Altai buried their leaders in tombs more than 12 feet deep. The tombs were lined with logs and covered with rocks. Moisture rapidly filled the shafts and froze during the first winter to such a degree that it never completely thawed during the summer. The deep freeze thus created has preserved even the most fragile silk, felt, wood, leather, metal, and, of course, the bodies of men and animals that were interred with them (Mongait 1959: 171 ff.; Rice 1957). The preservation of human bodies was so perfect that the designs of complicated tattooing could be readily copied (see Fig. 13).

It is commonplace to find wooden structures dating from our era in Europe, but it is rare to find wood more than a few thousand years old. Most areas that are now wet have been so for only a relatively short time; bogs in Europe are usually a direct outcome of Pleistocene conditions. Occasionally wood is preserved from sites occupied during the Ice Age. Dawkins (1880:269–271) gives us the details of a remarkable find of a complete wooden house of the Neolithic period in Ireland. This famous discovery, made in 1833, is called the Drumkelin house after the name of the bog in Donegal County where it was found. From Europe there are a few examples of wooden spears that may be more than 100,000 years old (Movius 1950). A possible wooden club and large pieces of a tree along with pollen, seeds, and nuts have been recovered by J. Desmond Clark from Kalambo Falls in Northern Rhodesia in an environment that has remained wet for 50,000 or more years. We do not know how many such localities there are, and must depend upon accidents of discovery just as much as we depend upon accidents of preservation. A particularly interesting example of preservation is the several footprints of Lower and Upper Paleolithic men impressed in the mud floor of certain Italian and French caves (Vallois 1928; Blanc and Pales 1960). These foot imprints are of great interest to physical anthropologists because they are the only evidence of the flesh proportions of these ancient humans who are otherwise known only from their bony remains.

There are other conditions where the preservation may be nearly total. In Poland a woolly rhinoceros of the type hunted by man during the Pleistocene was found impregnated with oil and salt. The beast had been washed into a pool by a flooding river and then buried with silt. By luck, this pool was saturated with crude oil and salt from a natural oil seep. In Siberia whole mammoths have been found in the places where they were frozen many thousands of years ago. Contrary to earlier popular opinion, the animals were not trapped by an overnight change of climate. The mammoths evidently fell into crevices in the snow and were buried eventually by silt in a natural icebox. We have yet to find the body of a man preserved under either of these extraordinary conditions.

Almost perfect preservation also occurs in exceptionally dry environments. Even without mummification, Egyptian bodies would have been well-preserved by the dry atmosphere of much of Egypt. Naturally preserved bodies have also been found in the American Southwest in caves, and in graves along the coast of Peru. In all these places the most fragile textiles, basketry, and wood and leather objects may be preserved. Possibly the most spectacular example of mass destruction and preservation with it occurred in A.D. 79 when Vesuvius erupted, burying Pompeii and Herculaneum in a flood of mud and ash. Although bodies were not preserved, their casts were (Mairui, Bianchi, and Battaglia 1961). Inorganic objects remained in a perfect state, and the carbonized remains of complete loaves of bread, so perfectly preserved that they still bear the name of the baker stamped upon them, have been recovered (Tanzer 1939:23). Carbonized papyrus scrolls discovered in 1753 at Herculaneum are described by Lyell (1877:1:651–652), the methods devised by Piaggi to unroll them are described by H. G. Bennett (1806), and the apparatus is shown by Ceram (1958:29).

A unique situation came to light at the site of Jericho where Zeuner (1955b; see also Kenyon 1960) was able to determine the reasons for the preservation in Bronze Age tombs of cloth and wooden furniture. The tombs had been cut into limestone, the burials and offerings deposited, and the tombs walled up. Carbon monoxide and methane gases seeping into the closed tombs through cracks in the rock replaced the normal air that would have permitted bacteria to live. As a result, organic materials that would normally have decayed within a few years after being deposited were preserved. Most archeologists work with poorly preserved sites. Even in very dry areas, such as Southwest Asia and the American Southwest, very little is preserved unless it has been isolated from the small amount of moisture that does occur. To witness the torrential rains and flash floods that seasonally soak such areas makes one appreciate how accidental preservation is. Even in areas of extreme cold, if there is any thawing at all, rot will occur, and if wet areas should dry, new oxygen, and with it destruction, will enter.

Most open sites are subject to alternate wetting and drying, and organic materials disintegrate or are destroyed by bacteria in a fairly short time. If one counts the number of objects recovered from a dry cave in the western United States, he cannot fail to be impressed with the large amount of perishable items made of horn, leather, or vegetal materials that would rapidly disappear in an open site.

Table 1 presents the count of items recovered from six sites where dry conditions have preserved organic materials that would normally have disappeared. The two sites from Chile are from the very dry north coast where conditions of preservation are similar to those prevailing along the narrow Peruvian coast. The two sites in New Mexico are from protected caves in a dry region where conditions of preservation are

	Playa Miller, Chile	Punta Pichalo, Chile	Cordova Cave, New Mexico	Tularosa Cave, New Mexico	Humboldt Cave, Nevada	Lovelock Cave, Nevada
Imperishable						
Stone	494	6389	1577	1546	87	95
Metal	17	1				
Pottery	24,871	1414	751	5470		
Shell	1	222	2	4	2	7
Bone	29	228	23	55	272	530
Antler			8	1		
Perishable						
Wood	55	945	394	762	113	310
Rush, cane, twine basketry	323	1552	628	3473	2982	7535
Skin, wool, feather	750	442	40	594	49	320
Vegetal food	299	48	2000	28,000		
Hoof, horn				3	15	20

TABLE 1

Occurrence in six dry open or cave sites of perishable and imperishable objects. Two Chilean open sites from Bird (1943:191–216, 253–278); two New Mexico cave sites from Martin et al. (1952); two Nevada cave sites from Loud and Harrington (1929); Heizer and Krieger (1956). Unworked stones of various kinds reported as found are included; unmodified food animal bone is counted; human burials (2 at Playa Miller, 42 at Punta Pichalo, 2 at Tularosa Cave, 32 at Lovelock Cave) are each counted as one bone. (We are indebted to Mr. Ronald Weber for preparing this and the following table.)

| | Imperishable | | Perishable | |
Sites	No. items	Percent	No. items	Percent
Playa Miller	25,412	95	1427	5
Punta Pichalo	8253	73	2987	27
Cordova cave	2361	43	3062	57
Tularosa cave	7296	19	33,832	81
Humboldt cave	361	10	3159	90
Lovelock cave	632	7	8285	93

TABLE 2

Summary of Table 1 showing total numbers of imperishable and perishable items from six sites. In many open sites perishable items are totally absent. The two largest figures (at Playa Miller and Tularosa Cave) are ascribable respectively to the great abundance of potsherds and maize cobs.

optimal, and the same situation holds for the two Nevada cave sites. The average annual rainfall in these areas ranges from less than one inch to not over eight inches. Table 2 summarizes the counts in Table 1 and presents the proportional amounts in percent of total number of items of perishable and imperishable pieces. It is easy to see how deficient our knowledge of material culture items would be for an open site in Nevada, for example, where not more than ten percent of the items that find their way into the trash layers are of durable materials.

In the dry deposits of Lovelock Cave, Nevada, cordage was perfectly preserved, and details on the size and mesh of nets could be determined. One hundred forty-two pieces of braid gave evidence that the prehistoric occupants of the cave knew how to braid, 3, 5, 6, 7, 16, and 18 strands; and 404 knots proved to belong to 8 types (mesh or sheet-bend, overhand, reef, granny, slip, clove hitch, "necktie" or timber-hitch, and wrap knots). Details of the methods of stringing shell beads were also evidenced (see Fig. 14). This listing of some of the details observable about cordage illustrates clearly the degree of complexity in one single aspect of prehistoric technology that is ordinarily totally absent in open sites.

If a technique or type of artifact does not make its appearance after a considerable amount of archeological investigation has been carried out in an area, it may be permissible to suggest that the prehistoric peoples did not know or possess that technique or tool. If the technique or implement is of the kind that would not leave, even under relatively favorable conditions, any palpable trace, the archeologist would then

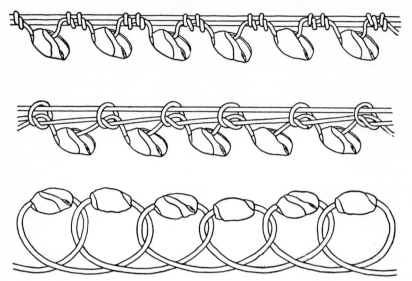

Fig. 14. Beads recovered from Lovelock Cave, Nevada, showing details of their stringing. The dry environment of the cave preserved organic material that would ordinarily be absent from archeological sites. (L. L. Loud and M. R. Harrington, "Lovelock Cave," *University of California Publications in American Archaeology and Ethnology*, Vol. 25, No. 1.)

admit that there was no way of telling whether it may or may not have once occurred in the area he is interested in. By way of example, slings made of cordage were widely known ethnographically in the New World, but they had not appeared archeologically up to 1960 in North America, even in collections secured from dry cave deposits. Arguing from this negative evidence, one author proposed that the sling was introduced to the Indians of North America in historic times. While this seemed unlikely, there was no way (except possibly through linguistic analysis, which was never done) to verify or disprove the recent spread of this weapon. Now, however, at least three prehistoric North American slings (all from dry caves in western Nevada) are known, and the theory of historic introduction is shown by archeological facts to be incorrect. Inferring that culture traits are absent simply because they are not proved to be archeologically present must be done with judgment and only after consideration of all relevant evidence.

A discussion of the preservation of artifacts should not omit consideration of sites. Ideally, for archeologists, the occupants of a site would decide on the spur of the moment to abandon their homes and forthwith walk off, taking nothing with them and leaving everything where it lay. The site would then become rapidly buried and when excavated after many years, an archeologist would discover everything just as it was left on the day of abandonment. As we have pointed out above, this ideal is a fantasy because objects disintegrate. We have not mentioned, however, the effects of man and nature on the sites themselves.

Without trying to give an exhaustive list of the ways in which nature manages to disturb and disarrange archeological sites and strata, we may mention the natural soil-building process that tends to bury objects lying on the surface of the earth (Grinnell 1924; Wood 1963:293–294; Woolley 1960:24–30); the burial of settlements by drifting sand in Africa, Europe (Lyell 1876:2:514–516), and Asia (Stein 1907; Woolley 1958:122–129); burial under volcanic ash as at Pompeii (Lyell 1876:1: Chaps. 23, 24) and certain Pueblo sites in Arizona (Colton 1932); covering by molten lava that hardens to solid basalt as at the pre-Classic site of Cuicuilco on the outskirts of Mexico City (Cummings 1933) and at certain locations in Europe (Laming 1952). Settlements on the edge of the sea may become destroyed as the ocean wears away the shore (Lyell 1876:1:515, Chap. 20); the shoreline may subside allowing encroaching water to engulf a settlement (Henry Ellis 1847); floods may bury occupation sites under thick deposits of mud (Lyell 1876:1:351); and a recent instance is provided by the 1962 avalanche in Peru that caused the death of 3500 persons (McDowell and Fletcher 1962). A well known case of the destruction of a site is that of the Palace of Minos in Crete. An earthquake, perhaps, combined with conquest, was followed by fire. The year, 1400 B.C., has been determined, and even the month (March) as evidenced by smoke stains that could only have been caused by the *Notios,* the strong southwest wind, which achieves maximum force in that month (A. Evans 1921–1935:4:942–946). A kind of reenactment of accumulation and advance of ice sheets, which covered traces of man's presence during the Pleistocene is to be seen in the recent ice advances that gradually overwhelmed settlements in Southeast Alaska (de Laguna 1958) and in the Mont Blanc range in southern France (Matthes 1956:154; Dyson 1962:178–184).

WHAT IS WILLFULLY DESTROYED?

Man himself destroys many sites and artifacts. The robbing of ancient tombs has already been mentioned. During the Paleolithic, when the numbers of men were not great and the economy was based upon hunting and collecting, there may not have been any very profound changes imposed by man on the earth's surface. But when he became a farmer and acquired a tool kit that allowed him to quarry stone, dig ditches and pits, and domesticate animals, which in some areas turned wooded country into deserts by overgrazing, man began to make profound changes in the earth's face (W. L. Thomas 1956; Heizer 1955).

Claudius Rich (1818:40) wrote: "A ruined city . . . is a quarry above ground." The unfortunate truth of this pithy statement can be documented by hundreds of instances of the pillaging of ancient buildings for construction materials. Some sites where stone was employed have been leveled and others so greatly damaged that they are like the Abbey of St. Martin in Tours, of which Henry James in *A Little Tour in France* says, "What we see today may be called the ruin of a ruin." The Greek Temple of the Giants at Agrigentum, Sicily, was destroyed in the eighteenth century to provide material for a breakwater (Daux 1948:121), and about 1800, great sculptures of Nineveh were broken up to furnish materials to repair a bridge (A. H. Layard 1853:122). The great pre-Inca site of Tiahuanaco in the Bolivian altiplano near Lake Titicaca contained immense quantities of beautifully sculptured stone blocks. The nearby village by the same name consists of houses with sculptured doorways taken from the ancient site, and the large church, built in the seventeenth century by Pedro de Castillo, is constructed entirely of stones carried from the nearby ruins (Posnansky 1945:2:52). When the railroad was built between La Paz and Guaqui, Bolivia, on the shore of Lake Titicaca, the site of Tiahuanaco provided a convenient source of stone for building bridges, and Posnansky (*ibid.*, 166) records the fact that "an immense statue around which there was entwined a snake from the chest to the feet, was divided and set in cement in bridges." Many of the immense stones at the Tiahuanaco site proved to be too heavy to transport (some weigh 100 tons) and, it being beyond the imagination of the local people after the Spanish conquest to understand that such large stones had been brought from distant sources, the belief grew that these colossal stones were made of concrete and must contain gold. Accordingly, many of the great blocks were split open with steel chisels in order to find the gold. A few failures did not seem to be sufficient evidence that the story was untrue for everywhere on the site one can see scores of these sundered blocks. The lure of gold was so great, the Tiahuanaco site so impressive, and the imagination of ignorant people so active, that a Spanish miner in the seventeenth century went to the great effort of digging a hole over 20 feet deep, 120 feet wide, and 250 feet long in the top of the Akapana, a great, flattopped mound of earth. Local recollection of this activity having been lost, the pit (which contains water) is now believed by the townspeople to be the ancient reservoir that served the prehistoric occupants of the city.

Winlock (1942:11) found clear evidence of the nearly total destruction of an immense mortuary temple in ancient times at Deir-el-Bahri, Egypt. In southern Utah, J. W. Powell (1961:107–108), in referring to a three-story pueblo ruin at the mouth of the Kanab River where it enters the Colorado River, wrote, "The structure was one of the best found in this land of ruins. The Mormon people settling here have used the stones of the old pueblo in building their homes, and now no vestiges of the ancient structure remain."

Wars have caused immense destruction to ancient sites. One of the best known instances is the Parthenon in Athens, which, while being used in 1687 by the Turks as a powder magazine, received a direct hit by a Venetian shell, blowing out the interior.

When religious iconoclasm inspires the destruction of the sacred monuments of other religions it leads to destruction of archeological evidence. Moorehead (1961:109) describes the defacement of Egyptian monuments by Coptic priests, and Duignan (1958) records that by 1531, roughly ten years after the conquest of Mexico by Hernando Cortes, the Franciscan priests had torn down 500 Aztec temples and broken up 20,000 stone idols. Inca religious sites in Peru suffered a similar fate, and a book by Father Joseph de Arriaga, in 1621, records the destruction of large numbers of various types of native temples and shrines: 477 Chapkas, 603 main Huacas, 3410 Konopas, 617 Halkis, 45 Mamazuras, 180 Huankas, and so on. By contrast, religious sanctity of a spot may serve to protect a site. Rawlinson (1850:419) wrote that an ancient site opposite Mosul had not been excavated because "the spot, indeed, is so much revered by the Mohammedans, as the supposed sepulcher of the prophet Jonas, that it is very doubtful if Europeans will be ever permitted to examine it." On the other hand, Layard at Nineveh found that his Arab workmen were continually trying to batter out the eyes of sculptured animals and persons because they were the idols of unbelievers. A probable ancient instance of religious iconoclasm is to be seen in the mutilation of twenty-four of the total of forty-five sculptured monuments from the Olmec site of La Venta in the state of Tabasco, Mexico (Heizer 1961:55). Stephens (1842:2:187) tells the story of the President of Guatemala, who, about 1810, received a present of a small gold image from the archeological site of Santa Cruz del Quiche. Intrigued with the possibility of getting gold, he ordered a "commission" to explore the site for hidden treasure, and in the process the palace was destroyed. The Indians were roused "by the destruction of their ancient capital, rose, and threatened to kill the workmen unless they left the country."

One continuing cause of the loss of archeological information lies in the increasing number of collectors of ancient art objects. Such collecting goes back to Classical times (Wace 1949), but today, among wealthy persons who can afford it, very high prices are paid for prehistoric stone sculptures, metalwork, and ceramic vessels. The availability of a market encourages surreptitious and illegal digging, often by needy local people who usually realize very little for their labors. The looting of sites is a regular business, both in the New World—in Mexico, Guatemala, and Peru—and in Egypt and the Middle East. While the objects found may be preserved, in the course of changing hands through dealers and collectors, their context may be forgotten. Then identification of their source and age can only be determined by referring to similar pieces in archeological reports or museum collections. While most countries have very strict laws governing the excavation and prohibiting the unauthorized export of archeological materials, these regulations usually are observed only by reputable archeologists. On the other hand, antiquities dealers encourage unauthorized digging and manage quite successfully, through the simple expedient of bribes, to remove vast quantities of material to their galleries in New York, San Francisco, Los Angeles, London, Paris, Rome, and other capitals of the art conscious world.

WHAT IS RECOVERED?

Much is preserved that is not recovered from ordinary excavations. Belzoni, or even Schliemann and Layard, recovered only a small part of the available information. When Sir Leonard Woolley went to Mesopotamia in 1922 to excavate at the great site of Ur, he found the Royal cemetery within a few weeks, but kept it secret until four years later. It took Woolley all that time to train his men and himself so that he was confident of doing a good job. His excavation stands as a *tour de force* of technical skill. In one instance he was able to restore a completely disintegrated harp by filling with plaster the open cavity in the ground where it had laid. But for all his skill, he still discarded much that might have been saved. Creel (1937:41–42) has shown by astute reasoning based upon indirect evidence that bamboo books existed in Shang Dynasty times in China in the third millennium B.C. No actual traces of such books have ever been found, but there is no question that they once existed.

For all the palaces and tombs that have been excavated in the centers of early civilization, there has been very little attempt to discover how people lived. In many cases we do not even know what people ate. What is worse, we know very little about the effect of civilization on the lives of the common people. Our information comes from texts and sometimes pictures (Tanzer 1939; Gentili and Edwards 1957), but only rarely from the excavation of houses. Preoccupation with one kind of information— art, architecture, epigraphy—implies a corresponding blindness about other kinds of information.

Often there are things present that an archeologist does not think significant at the time of the excavation. For example, he may map a site, but later be unable to tell which houses were occupied at what time. The positions of tools within houses or their distribution among houses may tell what kinds of activities were going on and where. Workmen under the direction of an unimaginative archeologist will not recover this kind of information. Men trained to pick up bronzes and potsherds will blithely hack through bones or charcoal.

An archeologist must take care to recover what is preserved, and he must preserve what is recovered. Countless objects have been destroyed within a few hours of their excavation because they dried out or fell apart. Metal will often turn to dust; in fact it may appear only as a rusty stain in the ground. Basketry, textiles, and wood may dry out and disintegrate. Almost all excavated objects are damp when first taken out of the ground. A few minutes in the hot sun may destroy them. Objects taken from bogs are subject to shrinking and cracking that can be countered by proper use of preservatives. Bones that threaten to fall apart can be reinforced with plaster, papier mâché, glue, or plastic compounds. There is no lack of techniques for preservation, but the excavator must know enough to use them.

WHAT IS REPORTED?

If there is a big difference between what is preserved and what is recovered, there is a bigger difference between what is recovered and what is reported. Archeologists are notoriously slow in reporting the results of their excavations. Many reports are never written, and many that are written are never published. It is safe to say that there is much more excavated archeological material unpublished than published, and for practical purposes this information is lost. Because the sites were destroyed in the process of excavation, if there is never a publication, the information is lost forever.

An excavator may publish only part of his material. He may do the pottery or temples, or may report on only the very finest objects from among a large group. In this regard it is common to see a group of artifacts labeled "typical" or "characteristic" of the site in question. It would often be more accurate to say that they were the finest, the most elaborate, or the most exotic. Mud bricks are typical; gold pins are not. Another archeologist might dig for years and never find one of the so-called "typical" objects. Such reporting can be a misleading weighting of the evidence.

Archeologists may also fill in blanks without explicitly saying so. They may guess that such an such happened and report it as fact, or they may leave out material that does not fit their preconceptions. More will be said about excavation technique and report writing in another chapter; this short discussion should point up that what we understand about prehistory is based on many variables. Part of the archeological context is the human filter through which information about preserved antiquities must pass before they are eventually described in print.

PART 2

ACQUIRING THE FACTS OF PREHISTORY

SURVEY

Except when they have been discovered previously, the archeologist's first problem in the field is to find sites. He usually begins with a survey. But before he takes to the field, he should decide exactly what he wants to accomplish. The kind of survey he will do, as well as where he will do it, depends on the kind of information he wants to obtain.

THE PROBLEM

Modern archeologists are concerned about general problems of history. They want to learn about and preserve knowledge of man's past. Because excavation is destruction, conscientious archeologists weigh the probable value of their efforts against the loss resulting from them. We can no longer justify excavation to recover art or texts alone when the excavation destroys much other information. Most archeologists today, whatever their personal interests, take care to recover information that is of interest to other archeologists as well.

There are other factors that determine what archeologists do. There is a trend today toward seeing prehistory in the perspective of world history and planning excavations that will contribute toward filling in unknown periods or areas. This may sometimes mean leaving sites which contain treasure in favor of those which will help put the richer sites in their proper historical place.

Regional Studies

Universities, museums, or amateur archeological societies sometimes set out to discover just what the archeological resources of their state or area are. Their aim is to intensively survey and plot all sites within certain geographical limits. There is no urgency to such survey, and it is not necessarily keyed to future excavation. The follow-up to such studies usually depends on the personal interests of individual archeologists. Aside from satisfying curiosity, regional studies are the firmest ground work for future excavation. In fact, serious archeology is predicated on such surveys. Sometimes areas to be surveyed are selected for a definite reason. A small valley may be chosen because the archeologist thinks a full story of its prehistory will contribute toward understanding the general history of an area more than scattered work might do. There are some excellent examples of just such work, and their benefits have been proved; unfortunately they are rare. For some notable examples see MacNeish (1958, 1964) and Willey (1953).

Culture History

Most people are interested in the histories of their regions. In the Americas there is less concern with this perhaps than in Europe because the American past is Indian history. However, in Europe and other parts of the world, prehistoric people are usually considered part of a people's national identity. Sites are thus sought specifically to contribute toward understanding the national past. An outstanding, though none too exemplary, instance of this occurred when the Nazis conducted excavations to help prove the superiority of the Nordic race (G. Clark 1957: 259–261). The history of the peoples who make up present-day Europe has been traced in detail and is being pushed farther back in time as new data from prehistory are uncovered (Childe 1958).

Special Problems

Archeologists may be interested in problems that require finding special kinds of sites. For example, since World War II there has been extensive effort in Southwest Asia to discover how, when, and where domestication of animals and plants took place (R. Braidwood and Howe 1960; Reed 1961). Similar work is being done in Meso-America (Mac-Neish 1964). In both instances it was necessary for archeologists to define the area in which it seemed most probable that domestication first occurred. They then had to go to the areas and find sites that could be excavated. Other archeologists have attempted, like Schliemann, to find sites for which historical records existed. In all such instances it is first necessary to eliminate those areas in which one need not look.

Student Training

Many sites are dug to train students in the proper techniques of excavation. In Great Britain, Roman sites are used; in the United States, Indian sites. Usually the sites are chosen so that students will receive training in certain techniques rather than for the light they may shed upon archeological problems.

HOW TO FIND SITES

Whatever the reason for finding sites may be, there is the practical problem of how to find them. The methods used in a survey depend on the kind of sites desired, the terrain in which they lie, and the ingenuity of the archeologist. Laming-Emperaire (1963:80) estimates that 25 percent of known archeological sites are discovered by chance or accident, over 70 percent by systematic search, and not more than 2 to 3 percent by all of the various methods that are called "scientific," among which are included aerial photography, electrical prospection, and so on.

Most sites are found when someone walks over them. Archeologists usually grid an area and systematically work back and forth across it, examining the the ground. The best method is to walk, but in some regions most of the sites can be found by criss-crossing the area by horse or jeep, stopping only to examine suspicious features. Braidwood and Howe (1960:20) believe a survey on foot produces the best results and in Iraqi Kurdistan employed local men, who as boys had herded sheep and goats and knew of sites, to make surface collections.

Along with collecting artifacts a surveyor will map the position of sites and make notes about them. This information is best recorded on standardized forms. The design of the forms will vary depending on the kind of base maps available for the area, the amount of work done previously, and the expected total of sites. Two forms used are shown in Figs. 15 and 16. Other examples are shown in the handbooks on field archeology.

Occasionally there are no artifacts on the surface of sites to give a clue that men once lived there. These spots can sometimes be recognized as sites through the use of special techniques. For example, they can sometimes be detected through vegetation. In semiarid lands vegetation will grow best where water collects. Old canals that have silted in to the level of the surrounding land may retain subsurface moisture better and

ARCHEOLOGICAL SITE SURVEY RECORD

1. Site................................ 2. Map... 3. County...................................

4. Twp.......................... Range..................... ; .... ¼ of.............. ¼ of Sec.............................

5. Location ....

....

.... 6. On contour elevation ....

7. Previous designations for site...

8. Owner.................................. 9. Address ....

10. Previous owners, dates...

11. Present tenant ....

12. Attitude toward excavation ....

13. Description of site..

....

14. Area .... 15. Depth................... 16. Height....................................

17. Vegetation... 18. Nearest water.............................

19. Soil of site.. 20. Surrounding soil type..................

21. Previous excavation ....

22. Cultivation .... 23. Erosion......................................

24. Buildings, roads, etc. ....

25. Possibility of destruction..

26. House pits...

27. Other features..

28. Burials...

29. Artifacts...

....

....

30. Remarks...

31. Published references ....

32. UCMA Accession No. .... 33. Sketch map ....

34. Date .... 35. Recorded by........................... 36. Photos........................

Fig. 15.   Archeological Site Survey Form.

SITE SURVEY

Date.......................... 19.........   Number...

Location: map............................. grid.................................. detail.....................................

....

Estimated time range:...

Size: .... Facing: ....

Type: mound........., open scatter........., shelter........., cave........., other.........................

Situation: cliff face............., hill............., spur........., terrace........., valley bottom............., dune...................

Water: spring............., wet wadi............., dry wadi............., lake............., swamp............., other..........................

Condition: occupied........., plowed.........cropped........., fallow........., potted........, eroded........., other.............

Excavation potential:.. Access road:........................

Landowner:... Photo ....

Artifacts: yield-L........., M........., H......... . Chpd stone..................., grd stone................., sherds...................

Remarks:... Over: ....

Fig. 16. Archeological Site Survey Form. The details included on a form depend on the area, maps available, previous work, and the intent of the survey.

allow a more luxuriant growth of grass. Buried buildings may alter the soil chemistry or drainage so that certain kinds of plants will grow where they will not grow in the unaltered landscape. Some instances of the association of particular species of plants with archeological site soils are given in Heizer (1959b:207–213) and Woolley (1960:31–34). Zeiner (1946) has written a most interesting report on the botany of the Angel Mounds site in Indiana. At the Angel Mounds, by observing the pH of the soil and counting the frequency of different species of plants, it was determined that the precise course of the palisade wall that enclosed the village could be plotted without excavation. The slight difference in number of species of plants growing on the surface above buried walls or ditches often shows up clearly on aerial photographs. An archeologist must not only have an eye for the unusual, but he must also be in the right spot at the right time; in many places the differences in vegetation are visible for only a few days or weeks.

Aerial survey is one of the most useful means for finding sites, especially so where there is a minimum of vegetation and where large areas are to be surveyed (Bradford 1957). Photos taken at the proper altitude and time of day show things that are invisible on the ground. It is often possible to map many of the buildings and streets of a town or city directly from the photos. When used in conjunction with surface inspection, aerial photos give information that could otherwise only be learned by excavation (Reeves 1936).

One of the most successful uses of aerial photos to plot the distribution of sites was made in southern Iraq and Iran where the dry plains are suited to the technique. In several seasons of work Oriental Institute archeologists have mapped hundreds of sites covering 7000 years of history (Jacobsen and Adams 1958; Adams 1962). The intent was to discover the relation of irrigation canals to sites and distribution of population. Aerial photos not only speeded the work tremendously, but they also revealed many features that would probably not have been seen on the ground. Willey (1953) utilized aerial photographs most effectively in plotting the location, main features, and extent of archeological sites in the Viru Valley, Peru, as a preliminary to the actual field work. Not only was time saved, but more accurate and complete maps were secured. This particular method is best suited to large, open areas without heavy vegetal cover.

The use of aerial photos is a specialized job. It requires knowledge of what will appear on photos and what kinds of traces sites will leave. Sites frequently show up as nothing more than dark spots in otherwise gray fields or gray spots in otherwise dark fields. In most instances, it is necessary to walk over the areas noted on the photos to verify them as sites.

In some areas photos will reveal very ancient sites. In other areas the usefulness of the method decreases sharply with the age of the sites. In Europe, plowing and other intensive land use have gone far toward obliterating surface traces of ancient sites. By contrast, in Southwest Asia, where erosion and cultivation have not affected the land surface so greatly, sites will show unless they have been buried. There, on the alluvial plain, the accumulation of silt has probably covered most of the very early sites and accidental discovery will continue to be the principal means of finding settlement areas.

JUDGING THE CONTENTS OF SITES

Structural Features

On-the-ground survey and aerial photography are used to find sites. Once a site is located, there are ways to determine what features are in it. One way is to use magnetometry, usually called "magnetic surveying." The proton magnetometer is a sensitive instrument that measures the intensity of the earth's gravitational field directly below the instrument (Aitken 1961, 1963; Johnston 1964; Linington 1961, 1963). When readings are taken at intervals across a site, the presence of underground archeological features is recorded as variations in the strength of the magnetic field. A plot of the readings will show a profile of "peaks and valleys" that can be interpreted as archeological features (see Fig. 17). The interpretation usually requires some test excavation because one cannot tell a priori whether a ditch or a wall will have the higher value and thus appear as a peak on the profile (Black and Johnston 1962).

Magnetometry depends upon the fact that protons act as miniature bar magnets and gyroscopes. In the presence of a magnetic field the protons align themselves with the magnetic field in the same manner as a magnet, but they are slowed in this act by the gyroscopic action. While they incline toward the desired alignment, they gyrate at a rate that is directly proportional to the magnetic intensity. The magnetic intensity thus shows in the gyration rate.

A disadvantage to using magnetometry is that pieces of metal, whether they be in the ground, on the operator's clothing, underground wires, overhead power lines, automobiles, buildings, pipelines, and other metal artifacts, will affect the instrument. On the other hand, instruments for detecting metals below the surface can take advantage of this situation to locate objects (Olsen 1963). See Andersen (1951a) for an account of a successful search with a mine detector for a deeply buried metal hoard.

In archeological sites differences in humic content from one place to another are responsible for differences in the intensity of the magnetic field. Thus when pits are filled with organic material, they register a greater intensity than the ground into which they were dug. The shape of the underground features also determines their magnetic intensity. Magnetometry has great potential for special applications, but wider testing under varying field conditions will be necessary before the tool becomes a standard item of archeological equipment.

Another method for finding features within known sites is to measure the electrical resistance of the earth. This method is called resistivity surveying and is dependent upon water content of the soil; thus it lends itself well to archeological sites where there are several kinds of structures (Linington 1961; Aitken 1961). For example, stone walls have a higher electrical resistance than the surrounding soil or clay. The equipment needed is more cumbersome and generally more time consuming than that for magnetometry.

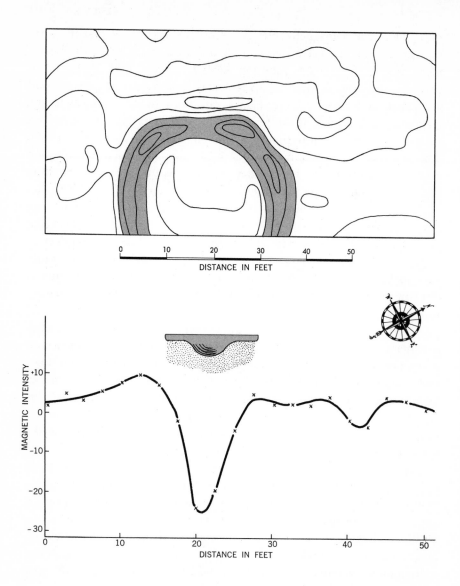

Fig. 17. Magnetometer survey of a ring ditch at Stanton Harcourt, Oxon. A magnetic contour diagram is given with a sample magnetic profile and sketch ditch section. The ditch was cut down into natural gravel and was filled with mixed gravel (dashed) and then uniform loamy earth (solid black). (R. E. Linington, "The Application of Geophysics to Archaeology," *American Scientist*, Vol. 51 (1963) p. 60.)

The technique involves placing electrodes in the ground at regular intervals and sending an electric current through one of them. The amount of resistance in the ground between two electrodes is measured as the ratio of voltage across the electrodes to the current flowing through them. The system requires the use of at least four electrodes, a generator, and a measuring device. When operated by two persons this method is as efficient as magnetometry.

There have been relatively few applications of resistivity surveying although in theory it should be useful in many circumstances. The major problems are that rain soaked ground and a high water table will seriously affect the readings. Natural geological phenomena may also cause trouble. For example, pockets of clay or soil in surrounding rock may be indistinguishable from archeological features. Rocky soil also causes trouble because the interference caused by rocks may obscure archeological features.

Other methods have been used for discovering what is below the surface of a site. The probe is a simple device made of a rod of spring steel with a ball bearing welded to its tip. An experienced operator can quickly tell differences in compactness of soil and can even find bone, stone, and metal. When the operator pushes the probe into the ground he can sometimes tell the kind of objects he strikes by their feel and sound. The probe is especially useful for finding pits and stone walls. An auger may also serve to test the depth of a refuse deposit or to determine the position of subsurface features (Ford and Webb 1956:21). Another method is to thump the ground with a large wooden mallet and listen to the sound. If sites are lying over compact soil or bedrock, a practiced thumper can tell by the sound where the walls and pits are.

Cameras have been used to examine the insides of Etruscan tombs. When a tomb is found, a hole is drilled in its top and a camera with a flash gun is lowered to take pictures of the interior (Lerici 1959). When the contents have been thus revealed one can decide whether or not to excavate.

In some instances it is also possible to map the visible features on a site and attain a good idea of the sort of site it is. This is especially useful where walls are visible as courses of stones flush with the surface, but where it is hard to perceive the plan from ground level (see Figs. 18 and 19). Or, if a site is obscured by heavy vegetation, it is possible to plot buildings that to all practical purposes are invisible. To do this requires two persons, one with a compass and one with a drawing board. One person with a compass stands on the corner of a building and sights

Fig. 18. Surface indications of a house in the Deh Luran valley, Iran. The upper part of the walls, made of clay, have completely eroded away leaving only the stone foundations. See Fig. 19 for a plan drawing of the house.

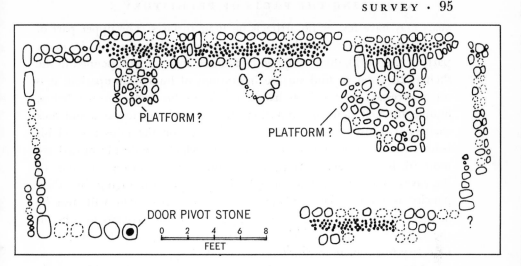

Fig. 19. Plan of a house mapped from the surface of a site in the Deh Luran valley, Iran. The figure in Fig. 18 is examining what would be the upper left-hand corner of this drawing.

both the drawing board and the second person, who is also at a corner. The second person may not be able to see the drawing board. In this manner, by shooting from a known position to an unknown position, a whole town can be mapped expeditiously (Detweiler 1948; Debenham 1947).

Age and Culture

Another object of survey is to pick up artifacts that will identify the contents of sites. If an area is archeologically unknown, it is necessary to pick up a representative sample of the material on the surface. This material can later be compared with other collections. One assumes that the surface sample is representative of the contents of the site. That is, it is assumed that there should be present sherds or other artifacts that represent each of the cultures in a site. This assumption is not always true, but it is used as a general guide. It is also assumed that the finds made on the surface of sites having similar contents will be similar. Comparison should thus reveal how many sites of each culture are present.

The kinds of artifacts found on the surface varies with the age of the site, soil chemistry, climatic conditions, vegetation, and previous survey. Caves that have been abandoned for hundreds or thousands of years may have few or no artifacts on their surfaces. The upper part of the fill may be sterile rock, dirt, and, as is so often the case in many parts of the world, dung dropped by animals that are kept penned in the shelter. In order to find surface indications of human occupation, it is often necessary to crawl on hands and knees for some minutes before finding the first signs of habitation. As one walks up to caves and rock shelters it is usually best to begin the search on the talus a good bit below the cave opening. Flints and sherds which are deeply buried are more likely to be exposed on eroded talus slopes than on the floors of the caves. The surface finds may be few and unencouraging, but their paucity is no necessary indication that the cave's yield will also be meager. When caves have been cleaned out, *all* the artifacts may be on the talus. Sometimes previous occupants swept out all the dirt. It is necessary to excavate to find out.

The surface signs on open sites may also be misleading. Mounds or middens may be covered with pottery and flint, or they may be barren. In Southwest Asia it is usually hard to find artifacts on mounds that are covered with close-cropped turf. Centuries of trampling by sheep and goats have usually beaten the surface into a hard layer and broken all sherds into small pieces. But it is not always easier to find sherds in newly plowed mounds. In fact we have surveyed mounds of which one half was recently plowed and the other fallow. There was no consistency as to which half contained the more material. We have also seen mounds that by the shape, size, and position must have resulted from human habitation, but on which no artifacts could be found.

Conditions for collecting also depend on whether a site has been looted or eroded. If graves have been looted, pottery is frequently thrown out onto the surface. Sites situated alongside streams may be cut by the water and have fresh sections exposed from which good examples of pottery can be taken.

The degree to which precise information about the age and cultural contents of sites can be learned from surface materials has been hotly debated. In an effort to make surveys more dependable, special sampling techniques have been worked out. For a number of reasons these techniques have not been generally used. Most workers prefer to look for "type artifacts" rather than attempt random sampling. A third method is to dig small test pits to try to obtain more artifacts than occur on the surface and to find out their stratigraphic relationships.

The most common technique is to pick up everything. The process varies with the manpower available, but the following is typical. Each person takes a bag and picks up all the pottery and stone from a portion of the whole site. The aim is to cover the whole site and pick up as much as possible. After the collections are made they are dumped in a central spot, and the most diagnostic pieces (type artifacts) are selected. If the archeologist has any knowledge of the area beforehand, he will be able to recognize certain types of pottery and stone tools. His selection will emphasize those items that he recognizes. Thus, painted sherds will ordinarily be more valuable in identifying the culture and date of a site than unpainted ones. The principle behind the use of the type artifact is that certain well-defined types occur within sharply defined limits of time. Although painted designs on pots are likely to change rapidly through time, unpainted utility pottery may seldom change. If an archeologist knows the area well, he will be able to tell with fair accuracy just how long a site was occupied and what its relations to other sites in other areas is. The total collection from the surface is thus broken into smaller dated units (parts of assemblages), which are defined by the diagnostic type artifacts.

The other survey technique consists of trying to obtain a "random sample" of the sherds on the surface. The reason is that deliberate selection of type artifacts can lead to undue emphasis on certain types and neglect of others, possibly leading to misinterpretation. Furthermore, when there are no easily datable type artifacts, changes through time may be seen best in the relative frequencies of different types. For example, during the early occupation of a site, type A may have been most abundant with type B in the minority, later type B might become dominant, with some A remaining and some C beginning. Still later all type A might be gone, type C would be dominant, and types B and D minor elements. The differences between the phases are seen in the differences in frequencies of types. On the surface of a stratified site it would be very difficult to separate assemblages, but where sites were occupied for only a short time it may be possible to determine the frequency of the various types for one moment in time. It is not possible to do so by deliberately selecting only the best examples.

The usual method for sampling is to grid the site and pick up only that pottery within certain grid squares. No pottery in these grids is left out. When the material has been lumped the percentages of the various types can be calculated. It is assumed that pottery of all types was distributed at random across the site and that it occurs on the surface in the same proportion as in the ground. No such technique has yet been used on very large sites that had a long occupation. The problems of collecting a good sample, by whatever method, from Near Eastern tells which are at times a mile or so in circumference, 50 to 100 feet high, and which were occupied for 5000 years, are tremendous.

Percentages are usually calculated from raw numbers of sherds. Sometimes relative percentages are based on weights of various sherd types, and some archeologists count only rim sherds or pieces from different pots where two or more sherds can be fitted together. The problem with these various statistical sampling techniques is that some sherds weigh more than others because the pots from which they came were thicker. Others break more easily. A calculation of weight or raw number is thus useful only in special circumstances (Baumhoff and Heizer 1959).

There has developed a general agreement among American archeologists that a surface sherd collection of at least one hundred fragments will contain representatives of the pottery types present at the site. The seriation graphs, which presume to show variable popularity of pottery types through time (see, for example, Ford 1962), are accurate only to the extent that the samples upon which they are based reliably reflect the actual contents of the site. Students concerned with the problem of making adequate surface collections should read the papers of Alcock (1951), Ragir (1964), Spaulding (1960), and Vescelius (1955).

No serious archeologist would contend that the surface of a site is always a microcosm of its contents. The only way to tell whether or not it is, is to sample the surface and then dig the site. A few archeologists, among them Spier (1917), Tolstoy (1958), and Ford (1949, 1951) have examined in particular—by comparing surface potsherd collections with collections made from test pits dug in the same sites—the assumption that the surface materials do represent a sample of the pottery contained in the deposit. From our own experience we believe that the presence of artifacts on the surface is dependent upon so many variables, both natural and cultural, that it is unwise to use surface indications as more than a rough guide to a site's contents. Even preliminary test examination of a refuse deposit may not yield a sample that is representative. For instances where an original excavation was followed by a second exploration with rather different sampling results see Greengo (1954) on shell species represented in the 1948 and 1952 excavations of the Monagrillo shellmound in Panama; Kroeber (1925:932, Table 17) on artifact class frequencies from the 1902 and 1906 excavations of the Emeryville shellmound on the San Francisco Bay; and Phillips, Ford, and Griffin (1951:233) on problems in recovering a normal sequence of pottery types in refuse deposits in the Mississippi Valley. It should be assumed that buried materials will move both up and down because of later disturbance by people digging pits (for disposal of garbage, corpses, for storage, and so on), and by burrowing animals.

A technique to supplement surface survey is to test dig a site. This means to dig a small hole that plumbs the depth of the site. Its purpose is to find out the stratigraphic relations of artifacts and whether the site is worth extensive excavation. This is a particularly valuable technique to use in caves where surface material may be sparse. Furthermore, in caves one usually cannot tell just how deep the deposit is from looking at the cave walls and the floor of the infilling. One should not plan a season's dig at an untested cave; it might only contain a few inches or a few feet of debris.

Techniques for surveying are of variable dependability and their use depends on the archeologist's needs. No survey can substitute for excavation; there is too much guesswork and too many gaps in surface survey. This is especially true with magnetic or resistivity surveying because one has a hard time translating the readings into specific archeological features. These systems are of no value in deciding questions of age, nor are they of value when more than one level is present. Magnetic or resistivity surveying cannot sort out superposition. This kind of information comes best from artifacts, and artifacts with context are secured by proper excavation.

DESIGNATIONS FOR SITES

Every site that is of sufficient importance to be mentioned in publication or recorded for a file of archeological data must have a designation. Usually sites are given the local name or the name of some geographical feature nearby.

In some areas archeologists have worked out a uniform site designation system for large areas such as counties, states, or countries in order to achieve some uniformity. In the United States the most widely employed system is that developed by the Smithsonian Institution in connection with the River Basin Survey program of archeological salvage. In this system a hyphenated, three-unit symbol is employed, the first being a number representing the state (for example, California is number 6); the second is a three-letter abbreviation representing the county within the state (for example, in California, SJo signifies San Joaquin County); and the third, a number representing the order of assignment of numbers to sites within each county, usually in the order of their being entered into the permanent master file of sites. Thus the fifty-third site recorded in San Joaquin County, California, would be rendered 6–SJo–53. Other systems are described in Cole and Deuel (1937:22–24), Gladwin and Gladwin (1928b), and Shaeffer (1960). For Canada, a grid system of site designations has been proposed by Bordon (1952), and a system of geographical coordinates has been proposed for site reference in Switzerland (Staub 1951). Uniform site designation systems are probably necessary to record large numbers of sites, but at present and for some time to come important sites will be more familiarly known by the names that have been selected for them by the archeologist who excavates and reports on his findings.

7

EXCAVATION AND RECORDING

The knowledge that a particular site exists is not in itself sufficient reason to excavate it. No site should be dug unless new information can be learned from it. The clever use of modern techniques for excavation and analysis is wasted if it is not directed toward and designed for the solution of a particular problem. The suitability of approaches and the scope of the dig should develop naturally out of an archeologist's intention. As R. J. C. Atkinson says in *Stonehenge* in a review of the development of archeological thought about this impressive site, "It is now no longer considered sufficient, or even justifiable, to excavate a site in a repetitive manner, merely waiting, like Mr. Micawber, for something to turn up. On the contrary, every excavation and every part of one must be planned to answer a limited number of quite definite questions." W. H. Sears (1961), in an attempt to draw inferences about the social and religious systems of prehistoric North American Indians, found that the older literature is grossly deficient in relevant information. His study points up the fact that archeologists should excavate to answer problems rather than simply to observe and collect what comes to light, or to dig for information on chronology to the practical exclusion of other information. Before an archeologist can estimate a site's potential worth, he must have a thorough knowledge of the area and past excavations in it.

101

He can then tell just how each site relates to what is known and what is not known.

Sometimes many sites in an area are worth digging and the problem of selecting one becomes difficult. Some archeologists compare archeology to a military campaign because of the many factors that must be balanced before the best approach can be selected. Starting with a problem and some sites that will help solve the problem, the archeologist has to consider the size and difficulty to dig, the time available for excavation, sources of equipment, cost, and the number and quality of workmen and supervisors available. When these factors have been considered, one or more sites will be selected as suitable for digging. The presence of a good access road or permission to dig from a landowner may tip the balance in favor of a particular site. Often the choice is not so clear cut, but it is unusual to have very many equally good sites. It is especially important to pick a job that can be carried through to completion. Many sites cannot be excavated in a single season, but must be revisited repeatedly, as in the instance of Pecos Pueblo, New Mexico (Kidder 1958), which was excavated in ten field seasons between 1915 and 1929, or Pueblo Bonito, New Mexico (Judd 1954), which was worked annually in each field season from 1921 through 1927. Perhaps the longest continuously excavated site in the world is Susa, in Iranian Khuzistan, where field parties have been in residence since the 1880s.

The elements of a military campaign are evident in the actual excavation: there is the training of labor; the orderly assignment of the men and supervisors; the ordering of supplies; and the recording of data. Above all, the job should be done with precision and economy. As M. Wheeler (1956:80) noted, it is axiomatic "that an untidy excavation is a bad one."

THE OBJECT OF EXCAVATION

Sites are not dug only to find out what they contain. If this were true, quarrying would be a sufficient technique. M. Wheeler (1956:150) describes the excavation at a Roman town that "was dug like potatoes," and many similar examples could be quoted. Preferably, archeologists try to do two things in an excavation regardless of the size of the site, its type, or how large an excavation is planned. They want to discover the cultural sequence in the site, and to expose whole cultural levels separately. They do this to find out how the people lived during each cultural period. Their procedure is to find the vertical relations of one cultural level to another, and the horizontal relations of objects within each cultural level. These jobs depend on careful stratigraphic control. The purpose of the dig and the resources available to carry it out determine how large an area will be dug and the techniques that will be used. There is no general rule that will apply to all situations.

KINDS OF EXCAVATIONS

Test Pits

Many excavations begin with test pits and in fact many end with test pits. Test pits (or soundings, *sondages*) are used to find out quickly and cheaply what sort of things are in a site. They may be used to determine the depths of occupation in various places, the sequence of levels, and the location of particular features. They may be used to obtain a larger sample of material than from surface survey alone. In short, test pits are tools, not ends in themselves. Test pits cannot be expected to provide a sample of the site's contents sufficiently large or representative to enable archeologists to say with any confidence how typical or unique the materials that they secure from it are. There is no rule about what percentage of a site must be dug, or how many burials must be uncovered, or how many potsherds or flint tools must be collected before archeologists can say that they have a representative sample. How much of a site is excavated will rest on the availability of time, funds, labor, weather, and the archeologist's judgment about whether he has a large enough sample.

A test pit may be a trench cutting across a site, or it may be one or more rectangular pits. Rectangular pits may be dug into the site wherever an archeologist thinks they will give him useful information. They are used to establish the depth of deposit in various places and to find out what the stratigraphy is. Test pits must be large enough to enable the workers to reach the undisturbed subsoil. Even ground water should not prevent the pit from being excavated to the bottom of the cultural deposits. M. Wheeler (1956:73) notes that at Arikamedu, in India, pits were successfully dug to base 11 feet below sea level, and at Mohenjo-daro, with the use of pumps, a depth of 10 feet below the water table was reached. Long trenches are often used to find buried buildings or walls, though they may also be used to correlate stratigraphies in various parts of a large mound. A variation, the step-trench, is often used on large sites. A step-trench runs from the top of a mound to its base (Lloyd 1963, Plate 2). At the base it will cut into sterile soil to establish the depth of deposit. As the trench cuts in toward the center of the mound, steps are left so that the bottom of the trench does not reach sterile ground. The trench is designed to find both early and later materials. The oldest should be on the bottom, but once it is found there is no point in digging it repeatedly by trenching from the summit to the base. In fact, on a large site it would be impossible to dig a narrow trench from top to bottom. The step-trench is a compromise.

Test pits are dug to prevent expensive and time-consuming excavation in the wrong place and to solve specific problems of stratigraphy. There is no way to generalize about how many pits should be put into a site. Some sites will not need any pits, others may need several. Archeologists show their ability to guess in the placement of test pits. American archeologists often dig 5 by 5 foot pits, but much larger units are required in the large, deep sites of the Near East and India. Wheeler (1956:83) suggests making the sides of the squares equal in length to the anticipated depth of the site.

Excavation of Large Areas

Any large scale dig will expose wide areas so that a good bit of each cultural level may be seen. When a village is being dug, archeologists usually try to expose several houses and special work areas if they are present (see Fig. 20). The object is to learn about the range of activities going on when the site was occupied. The exposure of large areas frequently grows out of the expansion of test pits. Frequently, and generally where the site is large, more than one large area will be dug.

As with test pits, there is no rule that will tell how large an area to dig. An interesting but not too successful attempt to combine the advantages of test pits and excavations of large areas was Braidwood's at Jarmo in Northeast Iraq (Braidwood and Howe 1960, Fig. 6). The excavators gridded the whole site and dug a checkerboard of squares. They hoped to correlate the levels in one square with those in another by interpolating through the unexcavated squares. Unfortunately, because of the undulating stratigraphy so common in a large mound, they were unable to accomplish their intent so that in this instance the experiment was a failure (Lloyd 1963:76–77). Braidwood and Howe (1960:39) say, "The underlying strata of archeological sites may pitch and toss in ways which their present surface contours seldom suggest; the conventional lecture-hall analogy of archeologists that the layers in a mound are like the layers of a cake is a vast over simplification."

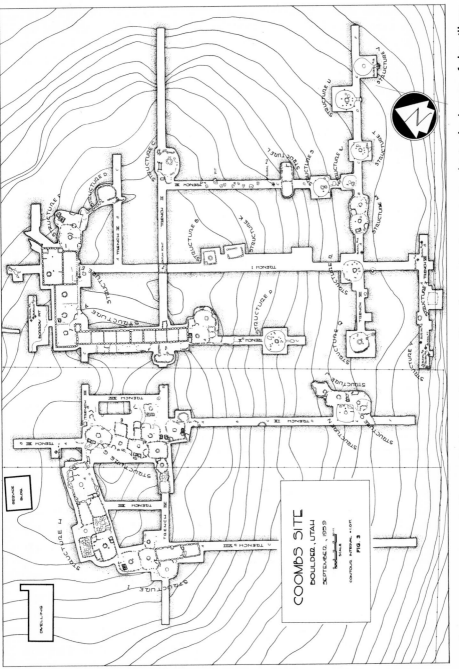

Fig. 20. Plan of the Coombs Site, Utah, showing the excavation of an extensive area to obtain the layout of the village. (R. H. Lister, J. R. Ambler, and F. C. Lister, "The Coombs Site," Part II. *University of Utah, Anthropological Papers*, No. 41.)

In the excavation of large areas the entire expanse must never be completely cleared and exposed, but standing exposures (pillars, walls, or baulks) must be left for back-checking on stratigraphy. It is not advisable to completely excavate any site if there is a chance to leave part of it untouched for future workers. New techniques that will surely be developed in the future can then be applied to important sites with the prospect of gaining new kinds of information (see Fig. 21).

HOW TO DIG

"There is no method proper to the excavation of a British site which is not applicable—nay, must be applied—to a site in Africa or Asia (M. Wheeler 1956:36). Lloyd 1963:30) disagrees with Wheeler's statement on the grounds that British and Near East sites may be so different that quite different methods of excavation must be employed. Lloyd also disparages "American expeditions with their multiple card-indexes and photographic kite-balloons, often seeming to be involved in trying to apply a kind of methodism under obstinately unsuitable circumstances." Another archeologist (G. Clark 1954:7) suggests that all archeologists, whether working with the Paleolithic or with Greek art, should have training in prehistoric archeology because it requires greater discipline to recover a maximum amount of data. In spite of these bits of advice, there are no rules for digging a particular site, except that care must be used to apply the best techniques for digging and recording. The way a site is dug depends upon the archeologist's capabilities and upon the site itself. As G. Clark (1957:108) says, the archeologist must have powers of observation, pertinacity, and adaptability.

If care, combined with observation, pertinacity, and adaptability, is a necessary requirement, then how is one to dig? This depends upon the situation. Bulldozers are often used to clear sterile overburden from deeply buried sites or from sites that must be dug quickly because of impending construction (Wedel 1951). On the other hand, some European paleolithic sites are dug from top to bottom with no tool larger than a screwdriver bent in the shape of a hook.

The tools used vary with a person's preference. In the United States, long-handled shovels and trowels are the most popular. In Great Britain, many use a cultivating fork instead of a shovel. In Southwest Asia, the pick is a universal instrument. None of these is necessarily better for loosening dirt than the others. Aside from the basic earthmoving tools, there is an assortment of ice picks, dental tools, hooks, brushes, knives,

Fig. 21. General view (*top*) and close-up (*bottom*) of the excavations at Tiahuanaco, Bolivia, showing the technique of excavating large areas and leaving regularly spaced balks to preserve evidence of stratigraphy. (Centro de Investigaciones Arqueologicas en Tiwanaku.)

spatulas, bellows, coal scoops, and scrapers to choose from. Again, the use of any of these depends on the excavator's preference and the job to be done. Digging in other lands and using local laborers may pose some problems. For example, one of the present authors found that in southeastern Mexico many of the pick and shovel men hired to do the digging on a large site did not know how to use either the pick or the shovel, and they had to be instructed in their use. In many instances the local laborers will have some method of moving earth that they are familiar with and would prefer to use rather than push a wheelbarrow. Thus, Arab diggers in Mesopotamian sites prefer to carry out earth in baskets, and while this may seem inefficient, if they are allowed to indulge their preference more work may get done than by forcing them to adopt another means.

Basically, there are two ways to expose a site (see Fig. 22). One is to strip an area horizontally. To do this the surface is scraped with a shovel and the area is peeled down by thin layers. The advantages of this method is that it enables the worker to see features in their extent. Differences in soil color, which indicate archeological features such as post holes, appear in their proper position. To offset such advantages, it is hard to recognize and keep track of subtle stratigraphic changes when you come down on top of them.

The second method is to dig into an area against a vertical face. That is, the workers begin by cutting a trench into a level and then proceed across the area by cutting away at the vertical edge. They always see the area being excavated in section. In this way it is easier to follow changes in stratigraphy. When loose, ashy levels are being followed across an area, this is an ideal method and it is the only way possible to dig in very hard ground. When the soil is too compact it cannot be easily scraped off with a shovel or trowel. Complete reliance on following a vertical face may mean that features that are most easily seen from the top will be missed. There are two ways to get around these problems.

When one is stripping an area horizontally, it is possible to dig what Wheeler calls "control-pits." These are small pits dug within the larger area. The object is to see ahead of time what is below, a form of "peeking," as it were, so that stratigraphy is anticipated and will not be missed in stripping a level. The other method makes up for the problems of excavating against a vertical face. The edge against which the workers are picking or shoveling will usually be six to nine inches in height if they are working through an area that may contain houses, fireplaces,

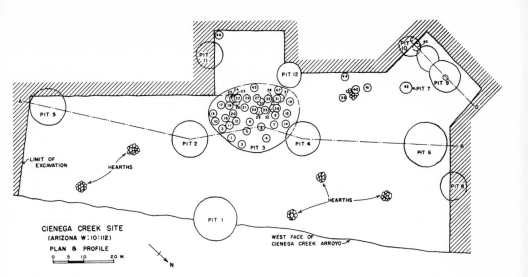

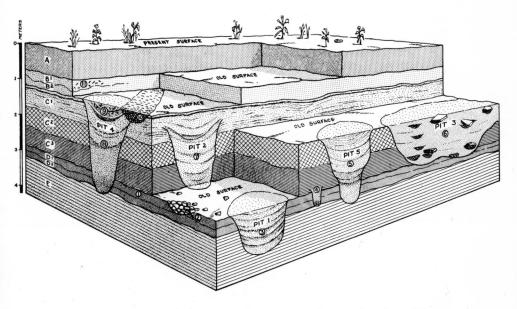

Fig. 22. Plan (*top*) and block (*bottom*) diagram of the Cienega Site, Arizona, showing the deposits both horizontally and vertically. The block diagram summarizes the sequence of cultural features in relation to the geological stratigraphy. Excavators must establish controls on the digging that will allow them to reconstruct the deposits in this manner. (E. W. Haury "An Alluvial Site on the San Carlos Indian Reservation, Arizona," *American Antiquity,* Vol. 23.)

or other features. When each level is finished, the surface should be scraped with trowels or shovels and then brushed to remove loose dirt. This brings out the details of soil color changes and it is often possible to see features which might otherwise be missed from the narrow perspective of a vertical face. The control pit is usually used even with the vertical face; again, so that stratigraphy can be foreseen.

"How deep should each level be?" The answer depends on what a level is. In a site where there are well-defined buildings, each rebuilding can be considered a level. The number of buildings that can be referred to such "time-based" levels will depend on the site. A cultural level is one that contains a contemporaneous assemblage. A cultural level might include several phases of rebuilding, but an archeologist cannot usually state this in the field. It is better at first to consider stratigraphic levels separately and to combine them later if appropriate. The standard method of recording stratigraphy of a section is described by Atkinson (1946:154, 166–170), Heizer (1958:75–77), Kenyon (1961:123–135), and Wheeler (1956:68–79).

The advisability of excavating by arbitrary levels has been debated, but there is no other method to use in the absence of stratigraphy. The size of the levels depends upon the tools used and the archeologist's experience in guessing what may be significant. Arbitrary levels are usually the depth of a small pick or shovel, 6 to 9 inches. Where there is a lot of fill in rooms or buildings, and where stratigraphic levels may be several feet or even yards apart, digging usually proceeds by such levels as the workers can easily manage. The digging levels in this case would not be the same as the recognized stratigraphic levels; that is, they would be thinner.

The method for dealing with particular kinds of features are well-described in the handbooks on excavation, but can be learned only by experience and practice. It is sufficient to say that there are special techniques for excavating bogs; shellmounds; sites having brick, mud, or wood walls; for clearing burials and tombs; and even sunken ships lying on the sea bottom.

Under certain circumstances, tunnels have been driven into large archeological sites in order to learn something about superposition of structures. Layard's tunneling operations of a hundred years ago at Nineveh could not be justified today as good technique, for he dug tunnels in order to make as many discoveries of sculptures as possible in a limited time. At the great pyramid of Teotihuacan in the Valley of Mexico a tunnel was driven into the center of the structure at ground level in order to determine whether the pyramid had all been built at one time or consisted of a series of superimposed structures, each later one encasing the earlier surfaces and increasing the size (Millon and Drewitt 1961). A similar tunnel driven into the great earth pyramid of Cholula in the Valley of Puebla, Mexico, yielded rich results, showing that no fewer than five superimposed structures were present (Marquina 1951, Plate 36). Few excavators will ever be required to explore sites by tunnels, but it is of interest to know, if this is the only method available for sounding a huge, solid structure, that, properly done, useful results can be obtained. An alternative method of exploring Meso-American earth pyramids that often contain tombs is outlined by Kidder, Jennings, and Shook (1946:27–28, 90–92).

KEEPING RECORDS

Because excavation destroys primary evidence, it is essential to keep good records. There is no point at all in excavating carefully if accurate records are not made and preserved.

Mapping and Plotting

All excavated sites should be mapped, but the kind of mapping that must be done before and during excavation varies with the site. A basic plan of the site will show its relation to roads, streams, towns, and so on. A more detailed plan should show the contours of the site and the areas excavated. On very large sites it may be necessary to use surveying equipment, but on smaller sites plotting with a compass, tape, and hand level is ordinarily sufficient. Some archeologists insist upon taking measurements as though they were going to build a bridge; such accuracy is not warranted in most instances. The use of a transit on simple sites is usually a waste of time, though it may be necessary to use this instrument to keep track of the complicated stratigraphy on a large mound.

Plans of sites are usually approximations because without total excavation it is difficult to tell the limits of a site. However, the recording of objects within the excavation must be done with precision. Permanent features, such as walls, floors, hearths, concentration of stones, graves, and so on, are ordinarily plotted in three dimensions. To facilitate recording, most archeologists set datum stakes along the edges of the excavations. Measurements can be taken laterally from the stakes. Thus walls of houses can be measured relative to the sides of the excavation and their depth below a datum point on the surface of the site. If walls must be removed to get at something lower, a three dimensional record enables an archeologist to restore their location later, either in a model or on a drawing. Special artifacts may also be recorded in this way, though it is more usual for such things as flint tools and potsherds to be removed and a record made of the level and grid square in which they occurred. Thus the archeologist will record the fact that a certain group of sherds came from a particular level and square; but will not know precisely where each item lay with reference to the others unless he records these facts during excavation.

The decision as to whether all finds should be recorded with equal accuracy depends on the judgment of the archeologist about what is important. As a practical matter, objects that occur in great quantity or are so small that they cannot be seen easily during excavation but are caught when the dirt is screened, will be recorded only by level. When very small objects are anticipated, all dirt is screened after it is removed from the excavation. Such a practice precludes recording the precise location. If the archeologist recognizes an unusual cluster of flints, sherds, or rocks, he may decide to have them left in place until he can judge whether their position is of special significance. It is always wise to err on the safe side, though it is hard for an archeologist to justify too slow an operation when he is pressed for time or money.

A neat excavation is essential to accurate recording. If possible the sides of the dig should be kept straight. The only exception to this is where the sides will not hold if they are vertical. In some loose soils—shellmounds and sand—edges may not hold. If the side of the dig will hold vertically for only several feet, it is possible to step it in and begin another vertical cut. In no instance where it can be avoided should the sides slope toward the bottom. Keeping the sides vertical makes it easier to keep accurate records. It is very difficult to plot the true positions of artifacts and features against a sloping side. The comparability of levels is also reduced if the area at the bottom is much smaller than the top.

It is of little use here to give specific descriptions of methods for numbering levels or bagging artifacts except to note that it is customary to number levels from the top down. Level 1 will therefore be the first dug, and some larger number will indicate the last and oldest level reached. In other words, the numbering reverses the order in which the levels accumulated and follows the order in which they are excavated.

As an excavation progresses, the records of stratigraphy in the form of diagrammatic profiles of sections accumulate. Archeologists should take care to correlate their drawings of stratigraphic sections in the field.

Otherwise they may return home and find that they have failed to make a record of how the levels in one section relate to those in another. Few archeologists succeed in making notations of all relevant points while engaged in the excavation, but these errors of omission should be kept at a minimum. It is better to have more notes than necessary than too few. To accomplish this it is often useful to record data on forms prepared for the purpose.

Photography is a necessary part of recording. Used in conjunction with drawn sections, it helps show the stratigraphic relations of various features and levels. Alongside the plans of the levels, photographs add a measure of reality that drawings can never achieve. It is regular practice to photograph all sections and features. Often drawings can be made directly from the photos, but in any case they serve as useful checks on the drawings. No matter how hard an archeologist tries to observe and record everything of significance in his profiles, he often fails to recognize, until he returns home, the importance of some aspect of the exposure. On many occasions clear photographs of the exposures in question will answer his questions. Both black-and-white and color photographs should be taken as features not apparent on one photograph may show up on the other. Many stratigraphic exposures show clearly distinguishable color differences between the layers when they are first excavated, but after a time dust collects on the exposed face and the once apparent color differences fade. Exposures should be brushed or scraped—working from the top down—to clean them of loose dust and scalings. A hand bellows or air pump and a sharp trowel may serve equally well for this purpose. If done with care, features exposed in the vertical wall, such as postmolds, pit outlines, or boundary lines between levels, can be lightly incised with the tip of a trowel to make certain that they will appear in the photograph. Care must be taken not to unduly accentuate such lines or to emphasize doubtful points lest this amount to falsification of evidence. Original color distinctions in the profile may often be reconstituted by spraying a fine mist on the face with a pressure sprayer of the type that home gardners use to spray pesticides on garden plants (Bruce-Mitford 1956:236).

Any dig at certain times will get to look "messy," and a fair amount of housekeeping is required to keep tools, bags, boxes, and other items picked up. A messy dig may lead to inadvertent loss of specimens or tools that get set aside and covered. When photographs are taken of an excavation, it is good practice to remove paper bags, boxes, tools, and dirt piles in addition to cleaning the vertical faces and straightening out bulges or unsquared corners. Useful guides to archeological photography are by Cookson (1954) and Frantz (1950).

It would be possible to map an excavation entirely by photographs. A tripod of sufficient height to include the total area of an excavation unit could be placed over the unit when needed. All photos would thus be of standard scale and from the same perspective. A series of such photographs taken over the entire site could be made into a mosaic in the same manner as aerial photos. Use of this sort of system might result in recording some features that might otherwise be overlooked, but it is also true that photos may miss important features. The photo technique is valuable when portions of a site are excavated at different times. Some features that are visible only when seen over the total area may not show up on a map but will be evident in a photo mosaic. One technique of photographic recording has been outlined by Merrill (1941a, 1941b).

Photographs taken of the whole site from a distance will show the relationship of the site to local features of terrain. Usually at least one such photograph appears in every full archeological report. Such pictures may be taken from a high elevation in the vicinity, or from a low-flying airplane or helicopter.

Examples of poor photography and poor photographic reproduction in publications are as common as poorly done sketches and plans. Mapping and photography are necessary to good recording, but unless the operator has sufficient skill to use the equipment, its use is no guarantee that the records will be good. The capabilities of the archeologist and his staff are seen in the attention they pay to the technical aspects of excavation and recording. Poorly illustrated reports are all too often a good indication that the excavations were poorly recorded and that the reports are second rate.

PRESERVATION OF ARTIFACTS

Excavation and preservation of artifacts go hand in hand. It sometimes happens, as at Ur, that objects must be "fabricated" in the ground before they can be excavated. It was only after Woolley had poured plaster into holes in the ground and then excavated the resulting casts that he could be sure what had lain in the ground. Sometimes archeologists uncover bones in a very bad condition and they must often take great pains to solidify them. Once bones or artifacts are protected they can be taken to a laboratory for final excavation and restoration. In such instances excavation merely means getting the things out of the ground safely. Full exposure, cleaning, and repair take place under the better controlled and more leisurely conditions of a laboratory. The archeologist should be aware of the fact that cleaning of objects is both subjective and destructive (Biek 1963b). He may clean a piece to the point where it has been altered, and if he removes the oxidation or patina from a stone or metal object, he may be removing something that will provide valuable information. Over-cleaning and restoration should not be done casually, and it is better not to do anything than to do too much. The magnitude of the problem of preservation should not be underestimated. In each area where work has been done, archeologists have developed special techniques for preserving artifacts. The techniques are developed best in Europe and Great Britain, where perishable and especially fragile materials are more likely to be preserved than elsewhere. It is beyond the scope of the present work to attempt to describe the varied methods for preservation of materials in the field or their repair and restoration in the laboratory. The reader is referred to Rowe's (1953) excellent summary, and the handbooks of Leechman (1931) and Plenderleith (1956) for methods and materials used. An extremely useful source of information is the volume of abstracts of publications (Gettens and Usilton 1955) dealing with technical methods employed in treating organic and inorganic objects of artistic or archeological nature.

Waterlogged artifacts may be preserved by one of several methods. Furniture from the Oseberg Viking ship in Norway was preserved by one of these. This ship-tomb was filled with remarkable grave furniture, including elaborately carved sleighs, one of which was fragmented into 1068 pieces of wood, each of which had to be treated separately. The procedure was to boil them in an alum solution, dry, and then soak with linseed oil. In this way the pieces kept their original shape and size and could be fitted back together (Heizer 1959a:29–52). Another method recently described is to treat old, waterlogged wood with a solution of polyethylene glycol that reduces shrinkage and hardens the material (Seborg and Inverarity 1962). At the Mesolithic site of Star Carr in England, the excavator devised a large vacuum tank in which animal bones were impregnated with preservative solution (J. G. D. Clark 1954, Plate 2i).

Those artifacts that come out of the excavation in good shape can be sent immediately to a museum. Unfortunately much loss occurs in storage. Items that were dry may rot; others may disintegrate in shipment if they are not properly packed for transport or are roughly jostled; and some specimens are affected by heat, insects, or dirt.

Even though an archeologist's immediate responsibility is to remove artifacts from the ground safely, he must not overlook their future well being. Instances of improper preservation in the field, resulting in later destruction, are legion. For example, bones may be coated with various substances that at first appear to preserve them; later, when they are unpacked in the laboratory, they may have disintegrated. Varnish applied over damp bone is notorious in this respect. Other preparations may harden bone but be unremovable in the laboratory except with destruction of the bone.

Preservation is not limited to techniques for keeping things from rotting, shrinking, and disintegrating. It also means recovering a maximum amount of data. It means examining sherds or lumps of clay for possible impressions or "casts" of plant seeds. How much insight into what particular cereals were being cultivated, and the relative importance of different species in the diet, can be gained from identifying and counting casts or impressions of seeds in clay, may be learned in an article by Helbaek (1953; see also J. G. D. Clark 1960:193–194). Preservation means saving charcoal for dating, and plant and animal remains for identification. It means plotting associations. In short, preservation means throwing away nothing that might provide a lead to cultural interpretations. An archeologist may be primarily interested in architecture or flints, but if he ignores making records of the rocks on which people sat or with which they boiled water, he is missing—and therefore not preserving—relevant archeological data. The same is true of keeping records. Records keep track of association. Artifacts and features that turn up in the laboratory without records of their locus and associations have, for practical purposes, been lost. At times an excavation produces more material than can be saved. Preliminary analysis in the field is often sufficient to enable an archeologist to discard a weighty collection of flint scrap, potsherds, grinding tools, or whatnot, whose characteristics have been sufficiently recorded and which are impractical to save. Such excess materials are best abandoned at the site where they were excavated, but it is essential that these modern caches or hordes of prehistoric materials be abandoned in such a way that some future archeologist will not mistake them for anything but what they are.

One way of doing this is to mix in with the redeposited materials several modern coins, or a few glass bottles, and thus mark the deposit as a secondary one. A statement that such leavings have been buried should be entered in the notes as well as in the publication. Judd (1959: 212–213) has provided a detailed description of wall repairs made at

Pueblo del Arroyo in New Mexico in the seasons of 1923–1926 and this will prove a valuable record to future students of Pueblo masonry in allowing them to distinguish between reconstructed and original masonry sections.

THE STAFF

The composition of the supervisory and technical staff of an excavation cannot be taken for granted. Most digs consist of an archeologist and his assistant, along with varying numbers of workmen. Technical help, advice, and analysis are usually obtained catch as catch can. This is not an ideal situation, but on some digs such a staff will suffice. At the opposite extreme, Wheeler's staff for large digs consisted of "a director, a deputy director, a supervisor for each area under excavation, a trained foreman, a small-find recorder, a pottery-assistant, a photographer, a surveyor, a chemist, a draftsman, and, according to need, an epigraphist or numismatist" (M. Wheeler 1956:153). American archeologists are only just beginning to write of their experiences in the operation of excavations. Two recent statements, both having to do with salvage archeology, are by Wendorf (1962) and Jennings (1963).

Wheeler was concerned with historical sites. For prehistoric sites he would have had to add a zoologist, a paleobotanist, a palynologist, a geologist, a mineralogist, a pedologist, and possibly others as well, though he could leave the epigraphists and numismatists at home. There is not less need for specialists at prehistoric sites—indeed there may be need for a greater variety. This is because the prehistorian must rely upon the natural scientists for basic information much more than the historian. On a practical basis, one person may well control two or more specialties so that a mere listing does not indicate the number of persons involved. As examples of archeological projects on which a number of specialists in different fields cooperated, and whose reporting includes contributions from the several specialists, we cite the Boylston Street Fishweir in Boston (F. Johnson 1942), an Early Man site in Wyoming (Moss 1951b), and Braidwood and Howe's (1960) survey and excavation in Iraqi Kurdistan.

It is the rare prehistorian who can take such a staff to the field with him. Most analyses are made by technicians in their home laboratories, though it is common for them to visit sites being excavated. In fact, it is important that these persons have a chance to do some work at archeological sites. Only in this way will they be able to appreciate the conditions under which samples are obtained. At the site they can also make valuable suggestions about taking samples and preserving specimens. Furthermore, as a guide to what is happening in the site, an archeologist needs a running analysis of the plants and animals encountered. It is often as revealing as a running analysis of pottery or coins.

Excavations are chronically understaffed. For most sites the problem is lack of supervision and analysis rather than labor. In Wheeler's organization, like a military chain of command, each man is assigned responsibility for a certain segment of the operation and supervision of a certain number of workers. However, no matter how the staff is organized, care must be taken to ensure that someone is present at all times in all areas under excavation. In this way proper records can be kept. Routine excavation is often dull work and requires little supervision, but when the unexpected occurs prompt and efficient supervision is necessary. An incalculable number of artifacts have been destroyed by careless workmen, or stolen by dishonest ones, under loose supervision.

Like every archeological operation, the selection of a staff must be planned with due regard to the unique circumstances of each dig. No factor is as important to the outcome of an excavation as the cooperative efforts performed day after day by the group of individuals who, collectively, comprise the staff.

CLASSIFICATION AND DESCRIPTION

Excavation is only one of an archeologist's many jobs. Ultimately, the data recovered in excavation should be written into the history of a region. However, before he can write any kind of history an archeologist must put his information into a cultural and chronological context (Rouse 1953, 1955).

An archeologist works with three kinds of data: artifactual; non-artifactual (for example, bones and charcoal); and the geographical or chronological positions of the sites. After he has analyzed and interpreted these data an archeologist can write a history, but the first step is analysis. Classification—which for the most part means naming artifacts—and a description of all data are basic to archeological analysis.

CLASSIFICATION

In order to bring system to a chaotic assemblage of data, one must put all items into convenient categories. With animal bones this means putting the sheep in one pile, the cattle in another. This is one kind of classification. Classifications are also used to help describe tools, houses, and even sites. Archeological classifications are intended to simplify making comparisons among artifacts from several sites so that chronological and cultural relationships can be established (Rouse 1960; Krieger 1960). A *type* is the most frequently used unit of comparison with artifacts.

Classification is a tool that can be made to work for many purposes. Theoretically, there is an almost infinite number of typologies for any body of material. Different typologies can help in understanding chronology, the relation of one part of a site to another, or the relations between sites or areas. Unfortunately, as J. G. D. Clark (1952:1) says, "The overwhelming proportion of archeological evidence has been gathered rather by accident than by design and studied more as an exercise in classification than as a source of history." It is quite possible to get lost among the trees of typology and never see the forest of which they are a part. There has been considerable controversy over typology among American archeologists, much less among Europeans. Most of the discussion has centered upon what the type is or should be.

There are several issues involved in deciding what a type is. First, how much difference should there be between types? The process of classification in archeology is similar to the definition of a species in biology or paleontology. With some conspicuous exceptions, members of different biological species cannot be interbred. In paleontology, of course, this crucial test cannot be applied; skeletons do not interbreed under any circumstances. Even with the criterion of interbreeding, some workers lump a great many variants into single species, others maximize the differences and distinguish many species. The same distinctions can be made with artifacts. There is no way to establish rules for the amount of difference that separates types of artifacts because, as with the animals, the makers of the tools are dead and cannot indicate what types they recognized.

Functional Types[1]

Archeologists find it easy to classify a bow or arrow if they are lucky enough to find them preserved. They are able to recognize and name their use because they know that similar tools are used by living peoples. However, if they should find several variations of bows and arrows at one site, they will have a hard time trying to decide whether they should

---

[1]The headings Functional Types, Convenient Types, and Cultural Types, are not in general use. We do not necessarily advocate the adoption of these terms and we use them here only for convenience and clarity.

take notice of the differences. They will wonder whether variously shaped arrowheads were used for different kinds of game, resulted from accidents in manufacture, or from preferences of their makers. In short, once archeologists get beyond very gross classification of material of known use, they run into difficulty. Classification of stone or bone tools is even more difficult. One can call a piece of chipped flint a "knife" and still be in doubt about whether it was really a knife, a javelin tip, a scraper, or something else. It is common for some archeologists to name artifacts after their presumed use even though there is no way to check the guess. This practice has resulted in a great deal of misunderstanding by uncritical readers. Furthermore, giving an artifact a name describing its function often leads to inaccurate comparison. For example, when a person reads the term "knife" in several reports he is likely to assume that the same implement is being described in each instance. A check of accompanying illustrations may reveal that very different objects are being described by the same term.

The greatest pressure for giving functional names to artifacts comes from people who know the material the least. More and more, professional archeologists are shying away from such commitments *in their basic reports*. Interpretations about use should properly come after an artifact has been described in such terms that it can be readily comprehended and compared. After the basic descriptions have been made, the analyst should try to discover what functional types are represented. Only when the use of an artifact is unmistakable is it appropriate to name functional types. The distinction between basic description and interpretation of function should always be clearly made.

Convenient Types

An opposite approach to naming functional types is to define types as being those variations of artifacts that can be used to make comparisons. Sir Flinders Petrie (1901), for example, was less concerned over what the ancient Egyptians were thinking about when they made different styles of jar handles than over the fact that he could set up a chronology based upon their changes. Similarly, when American archeologists describe projectile points, they go to great lengths to discern differences that may help define geographical and chronological versions of cultures. An aborigine who was given a handful of different "types" might, unlike an archeologist, see no noteworthy differences among them. For archeologists, however, the aborigine's opinion is irrelevant because typing helps the archeologist. As Jennings (1957:98) remarks, "I view . . .

types not as synonomous with cultural truth but as an invention of the analyst for his own convenience."

A distinction has been made by some American archeologists between "designed" and "discovered" types. A designed type is said to be empirically derived, and to serve the purpose of helping to distinguish—by means of forms or shape—different segments of the cultural continuum. Designed types are arbitrary and are imposed by the classifier upon the objects without consideration of the purpose the object may have served its maker (MacWhite 1956:12). Discovered types are assumed to reflect the models that the makers had in mind. Discovered types are, therefore, "real" and reflect forms that were culturally significant to their makers. A similar idea was expressed some years ago by Burkitt (1933:59) when he wrote:

> The classification of gravers [burins] is a matter of some controversy. They can be classified according to type, or they can be classified according to the method of their manufacture. Neither of these systems is perfect, and, indeed, the student must always remember that he is not making rules for prehistoric man, but deducing laws from facts. He is in the position of a grammarian, not of the inventor of a language.

Daniel (1960:87) observes that there was a large amount of "hybridization of ideas and plans" of Breton Passage Graves, and says that "too exact a classification of the wide variety of Breton monuments can only be, at worst, an academic exercise, and at best, a learned arrangement of observer-determined categories."

Convenient ("designed") types are probably the most commonly used in archeology. Whenever a report lists types without giving any basis for them the reader is justified in assuming that the archeologist finds it convenient to so group his material; he probably has no other rationale behind his classification. This sort of typology has definite limits and is gradually being replaced by other methods. The use of purely arbitrary types results in different archeologists choosing various types to describe the same assemblage. Because of this, more than for any other single reason, it is hard to make comparisons of archeological data. Most archeologists assume that they are doing a good job and that other archeologists understand what they are doing. Unfortunately, this is not always the case. A person who wants to sum up the results of many excavations must himself handle the material or at least be sufficiently familiar with the excavators and their techniques to make judgments about what they report. Too often synthesizers overlook the extremely variable quality of reporting; this in addition to the very variable quality of excavation.

Cultural Types

Persons make things (artifacts) the way they think things ought to be made. Some archeologists try to discover the ideal that the makers were trying to copy. "The term *type* is intended to represent the perfect example, exhibiting all the characteristics which differentiate it from other types" (Byers and Johnson 1940:33). Ideal types ("discovered types") are assumed to be those that the makers of the artifacts would recognize. In practice, however, the ideal is rarely achieved. When flint breaks oddly or a pot fires faultily or a metal casting is imperfect, these artifacts vary somewhat from the ideal. Making due allowance for such aberrations, archeologists try to find the ideal to which a series of artifacts conforms. These types are commonly established by visual inspection of the ranges of variation in an artifact industry. Except as a preliminary assessment of a small assemblage, ideal types cannot be described on the basis of one example. In the basic description, ideal types are not functional types.

Another way to discover cultural types is to use statistical analysis to discriminate clusters of attributes that occur in significant frequencies (see, for example, Driver 1961; Kroeber 1940b; Witherspoon 1961). The method depends on the fact that people do things by habit and preference; that is, they have an ideal in mind when making artifacts. Most artifacts are the result of several separate stages of manufacture. Very likely there are alternate ways to accomplish each stage and the way chosen may have no significant bearing on the use to which the artifact is put. The particular way a piece is made can, to a large degree, show the peculiar notions the maker had about how the job ought to be done. Some methods of manufacture are characteristic of individuals or groups of people. If archeologists can distinguish these differences in method of manufacture and end result, they have an easy way of distinguishing between cultural groups *even though to all intents and purposes the finished artifacts are functionally identical.*

To discover types statistically one must first describe artifacts by their attributes. Attributes are recognizable features such as size, shape, color, material, and decoration. A single pot may have many attributes. In one industry there may be several shapes and sizes of pots, two or three different kinds of tempering material, and a dozen or more kinds of decoration. Analysis attempts to discover which combinations of attributes are found in association in such frequency that they are probably not accidental. Archeologists look for "a consistent assemblage of attributes whose combined properties give a characteristic pattern. . . . Classification into types is a process of discovery of combinations of attributes favored by the makers of the artifacts, not an arbitrary procedure of the classifier" (Spaulding 1953:305). According to Spaulding (1953:306; see also Ford 1954), types discovered by cluster analysis "cannot fail to have historical meaning."

Many archeologists have shied away from using statistical techniques, partly because of the sampling problems in any excavation and partly because the limitations and opportunities of statistical techniques are poorly understood by them. Statistical treatment is invaluable in the simultaneous handling of many variables. It will yield data, but as Spaulding (1953:393) has pointed out, the archeologist still must interpret them.

In practice, most archeologists use several approaches to typology because no one method is useful all the time. But the most useful tool in all cases is the archeologist's brain.

Archeological data are destroyed by nonhuman agencies as they lie in the ground; they are destroyed by man during excavation and handling; and to one degree or another they are altered again as they pass the filter of archeological analysis. To help overcome analytical looseness, a concern with methodology has developed in American archeology and, to a lesser degree, in European archeology.

DESCRIPTION

Description of artifacts goes hand in hand with classification. It should be brief, readily understood, and comparable with other descriptions.

Verbal Descriptions

All descriptions begin with words. Purely verbal descriptions, however, are easily misunderstood even by speakers of one language. Translations to other languages are even more difficult because descriptive terms frequently have no direct counterparts in other languages. Verbal descriptions are best when they define the attributes of artifacts.

Pictorial Descriptions

The most common, and in some ways the best, kind of description is a drawing or photograph of the artifact. However, the ideal sought is seldom attained. To draw artifacts requires the hand of a skilled draftsman, just as photographs require the skilled use of a camera. Reports are filled with poor examples of each technique, and one looks far to find good examples of either. Archeologists are ordinarily not capable of doing the work themselves.

Drawings can show details that will not appear on photographs, but they are highly susceptible to personal interpretation. Artists usually emphasize those features that seem most important to them. Their interpretation may be entirely correct, but the reader has no way to judge for himself. Sometimes an archeologist has the drawings emphasize or, in some notorious instances, create those features that he desires.

It is difficult to make good photographs of artifacts. Success or failure depends upon the kinds of light, perspective, focal length of lenses, background, and developing and printing techniques used. In the hands of a skilled operator the camera can be made to do what the archeologist wishes and, like a drawing, a photograph can misrepresent.

If the shape of an artifact is important, it is common to represent it by an outline. This is a stylized description. Stylized drawings are ordinarily taken to be ideal types. They may not duplicate the outline of any single specimen. These drawings are easy to make and easy to understand. But many artifacts cannot be understood by their shape alone. For these one must use a more representational technique. The usual practice is to draw particular artifacts as faithfully as possible (see Fig. 23).

The use of outline drawings is relatively new and is usually coupled with some sort of statistical treatment (Bohmers 1956; Kleindienst 1961). In this technique, types and their variants are outlined and keyed to columns in summary tables (see Fig. 24). The reader can look in the table to find that x number of type A, variant n, were present in level 7. If the classifications are accurate, this is a better method than drawing all the artifacts from level 7 or even all those of type A.

Whether photographs or drawings are used, there must be a good set of representations of the artifact types. Without them no report is very intelligible. This does not necessarily mean that drawings must accompany each report, but descriptions must refer to readily available sources.

Statistical Descriptions

Statistical descriptions may be simple tabulations of data or descriptions of the combinations of attributes of artifacts. All basic reports should contain a numerical listing of artifacts and most will also have a calculation of the frequencies in which various artifacts occur. The use of statistical techniques often permits more exact description than words or illustrations alone, and may help to discriminate between

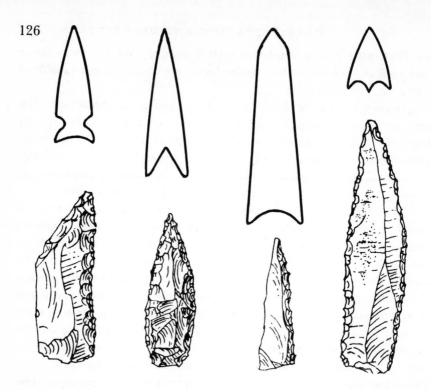

Fig. 23. Outline and detail drawing of artifacts. The style to be used in illustrating artifacts depends on their important features. Outline drawings are sufficient where the gross shape of a tool is important but techniques of chipping can only be depicted by a careful drawing of the details.

associations of attributes or artifacts that are not readily observable by any other method. Moberg (1961) has discussed the great variety of quantitative methods presently available for archeological description and analysis.

Mention has been made of the use of statistics in discovering artifact types, a process that follows logically after basic description. However, statistics are also used for basic description. For example, it may be useful to describe the sizes of certain artifacts. Statistics can describe the range, the mean, and the standard deviation in size. These three statistics may be sufficient to describe an artifact type or they may help to discriminate between variations of a type found at different sites. That is, even though the same type may have been used at different places, two different sizes of the type may have been made.

Statistics can also help tell whether the observed variations seem to be random. This is especially useful because it will help avoid the error of emphasizing attributes that are the result of accident rather than design.

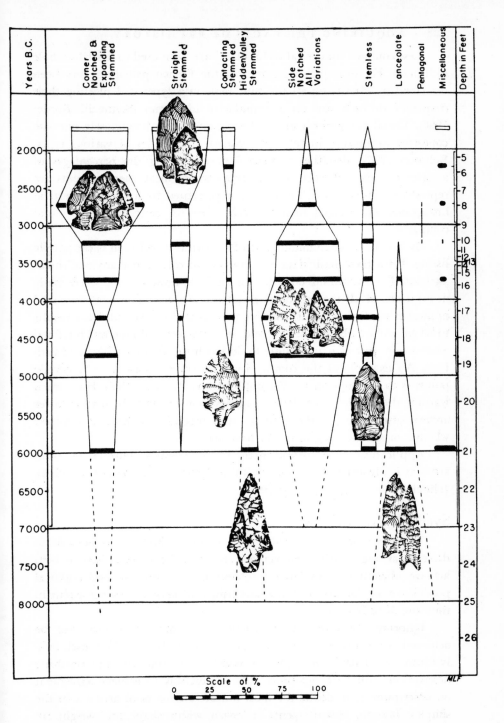

Fig. 24. Chart illustrating technique of graphically representing changes in frequency of projectile points of various types in relation to time. (M. L. Fowler, "Summary Report of Modoc Rock Shelter," *Illinois State Museum, Report of Investigations,* No. 8.)

Less complex numerical techniques have been used to describe whole industries. For example, a segment of the French paleolithic has been described by classifying all the flint tools into types and plotting their frequency in each site on a cumulative histogram (Sonneville-Bordes 1960). Visual comparison of the histograms shows how closely one site conforms to another in terms of relative frequencies of various types. Bohmers (1963) describes a method of comparing the percentages of a series of clearly defined artifact types whose mean measurements are represented graphically. These data, represented by a series of vertical histograms, are ranged next to each other for convenience of visual comparison.

By far the most common kind of statistical description is the simple listing. With these basic data it is possible to carry out many additional analyses. For maximum potential in analysis, however, one needs basic descriptions of all the attributes of all the artifacts. The labor involved in measuring, listing, and tabulating these is prohibitive unless the results to be gained are obvious beforehand. It is possible to do too much refined observation, just as it is possible to do too little, about attributes of artifacts. An example of the complexity of attributes present in projectile points is to be found in the list published by Binford (1963). How much warrant there is for such detailed observation can only be decided after archeologists have put the typology into practice and have determined whether or not meaningful results have been achieved.

Application of statistical methods to determine chronology from artifacts is illustrated by Brainerd (1951), Dempsey and Baumhoff (1963), Jelinek (1962a), and Robinson (1951).

Symbolic Descriptions

There has been considerable concern over whether it is possible to describe artifacts entirely objectively. Statistics have been used to help achieve objectivity. The main problem is not over the philosophical possibilities of description but that various workers are not consistent in their use of basic terms.

Ignoring the question of whether true objectivity can ever be achieved, some workers conclude that, to the extent to which each analyst can understand and apply a standard terminology, the resulting descriptions will be comparable. The easiest way to achieve agreement on description is to define the most minute attributes of artifacts in the simplest fashion. Measurements of length, width, shape, and weight are examples of attributes that can be easily defined. It is also possible to define design elements, and combinations of elements, by using a symbolic notation. When description has been reduced to a formal language of symbols, it is easily handled mechanically and readily compared to other similar descriptions (*cf.* Whiteford 1947; Binford 1963).

The most ambitious attempts to make such descriptions have been at the Center of Documentary Analysis for Archaeology in Paris (Gardin 1958). Their initial work includes the classification and recording of such diverse data as epic tales, bronze axes, and linear elements of design. As attributes in each of these areas were observed, they were given symbols and their occurrence was recorded on punched cards. The basic data thus stored can then be recalled by inserting sorting needles into stacks of the cards and withdrawing those on which certain attributes or clusters of attributes occurred. Although the French did not do so, business machines could easily be used for the mechanical sorting.

The advantage of recording each artifact mechanically is that unlimited numbers of attributes can be accommodated, and the data are readily available for statistical analysis. If one is interested in learning the association of axes with convex bits, holes for hafting, and trapezoidal sections, one can quickly do so by inserting needles in a stack of edgepunched cards. By this method it is possible to change the constitution of types without a basic reanalysis of the artifacts. Each worker can select whatever clusters he wishes and no change will have been necessary in the basic description.

Archeological reports are filled with descriptions of variable quality that add up to an enormous bulk. The use of a coding system coupled with mechanical handling of data would eliminate long verbal and graphic descriptions and greatly facilitate the comparison of material. Today large libraries are required to store the basic data; with punched cards it would be possible to store the same data in a relatively few cubic feet and at much less expense (Hymes 1963).

The advantages of mechanical recording and statistical analysis are obvious. As archeologists become more aware of their possibilities they will be used more frequently. It takes a great deal of time to create the descriptive systems on which basic recording must be based and for each analyst to learn the system. For the present these are the two most important obstacles that prevent universal adoption of such techniques.

In spite of archeologists' traditional preoccupation with classification, there have never been devised any universally accepted systems. Until these are developed, archeology will continue to be plagued by descriptions that are not comparable with one another. It is worth the effort to develop and learn better methods of handling basic data.

9

TECHNICAL ANALYSES

Most of the interpretations archeologists make about culture are based upon artifacts. These interpretations sometimes depend on technical analyses that must be made by metallurgists, chemists, physicists, geologists, biologists, and zoologists. Usually, technical analyses are made to discover methods of manufacture and to identify the mineral or chemical composition of artifacts. These data can be used as evidence of trade between areas and to indicate the technical processes and skills of the artisans. Other kinds of analyses can be applied to sites and to noncultural materials. Analyses of the physical condition of sites may tell how they were formed, how long they were occupied, and, perhaps, what they contained if visual traces are gone. Analyses of plants and animals give information on prehistoric diet, climate, land use, and chronology.

ANALYSIS OF POTTERY

Classification of ceramics depends upon knowledge of their attributes. Such attributes as shape, texture, and design are readily identified visually by an archeologist, but there are other qualities whose presence may be equally valuable for identification. Among these are the way pots were made, firing conditions, kind of paste or glaze used, and other surface finishing. These kinds of data may help to distinguish between wares at one site, or to determine the place where the pottery was made. Other qualities, such as hardness, porosity, luster, strength, color, and mineral content can also be readily determined, but often such details are of little use to archeologists. No technical analysis is worth the time and trouble unless it helps to solve an archeological problem.

The main tools used by a ceramist are binocular and petrographic microscopes. With these he can identify most of the culturally important attributes of sherds. For preliminary analysis, a binocular microscope is necessary in the identification of paste and tempering material. Often nothing more is needed. If more detailed analysis is required, the petrographic microscope will reveal the mineral composition of the tempering material used in the pottery. These analyses can help establish whether pots were manufactured locally. With sufficient information from other areas it may also be possible to find the place of origin of pots that were made elsewhere. As a case in point, Shepard (1963:21–22; see also Judd 1954:235) noted the abundance of a painted pottery with sanidine basalt temper of nonlocal origin at Pueblo Bonito, New Mexico, and proposes that this pottery may have been manufactured at a source some fifty miles distant. While large-scale import from such a distance is possible, the alternative possibility that foreign potters came to Pueblo Bonito carrying temper material (rather than bulky and breakable pots) and made their distinctive pottery on the spot might be considered. A good example of petrographic analysis of potsherds is the report of Williams (1956) on the tempering materials in the pottery of several sites in central Mexico.

Other techniques depend on the use of chemical reagents to test the presence or absence of certain chemicals in sherds. These tests can often be made by archeologists, but if quantitative determinations are desired it is usually necessary to turn to a chemist or a ceramist. Spectographic analysis and differential thermal analysis are two other techniques for identifying the chemical composition of sherds.

The best single source available on the technical study of pottery is Shepard's (1956) handbook. Also useful are the manuals setting forth standards of pottery description by March (1934) and Colton (1953); and several general papers on the cultural implications of pottery technology studies by Matson (1951, 1960). Matson's papers are particularly useful because they contain numerous bibliographic references. A widely used standard for recording the color of pottery is the loose-leaf *Munsell Soil Color Charts* (Munsell Color Co., Baltimore, Maryland), which contain color chips that permit close matching of hue.

ANALYSIS OF METAL AND STONE

Analysis of metal artifacts can yield valuable information about techniques of manufacture and chemical composition (Coghlan 1960a, 1960b; Caley 1949). Similar analyses can be made on the composition of the stone in artifacts. Such knowledge can lead to information about where the artifact was made and where the stone or metal or ore was obtained (Bastian 1961; Pittioni 1960). Techniques similar to those used for ceramic analysis are employed.

It is equally interesting to learn how metal artifacts were made. Details of manufacture that cannot be determined by simple visual inspection may be discovered by photomicrographic examination of portions of artifacts (Drier 1961). Such discoveries go a long way toward enlarging our knowledge of the technical skills of prehistoric peoples. In some instances it is possible to identify the work done by individual smiths or factories because of peculiarities of manufacture that are not easily seen with the naked eye. The spectographic analysis of faience beads found in tombs of the Wessex culture, England, by Stone and Thomas (1956) proved that these beads were of Egyptian origin and dated from about 1400 B.C., thereby providing the English archeologists with an important fixed date in British prehistory.

A highly technical method of petrographic analysis called "fabric analysis," employed by L. Weiss (1954) can prove that two fragments of marble once were part of the same sculptured stele, and some important matchings of what were necessarily considered fragments of separate stelae have been made by application of this technique.

ANALYSIS OF WEAVING

Analysis of textiles can provide a wide range of information. To begin with, it is possible to identify the material used. Study of the fibers may lead to conclusions about whether plants or animals were domesticated. Identification of the fibers may show that they are not native to the area. Analysis of the dyes tells a great deal about the technical skill of prehistoric man and may also give some clues about trade if the pigments are identified as originating in an area other than that in which the textiles were found. Study of the kind of weaving and type of loom used gives data on technical skill and, in many instances, on cultural relationships. Where actual basketry that was once present has not survived, impressions or casts of basketry may be recorded on soft clay that was later fired, and by a study of these imprints a great deal about the basketry techniques may be learned (Holmes 1881; Miner 1936; Munger and Adams 1941; and Rachlin 1955).

Basketry and matting are studied in similar ways. A classification of basketry techniques by Balfet (1952) is recommended.

ANALYSIS OF SOIL

Analyses of soil can help date sites, indicate how deposits were formed, and tell something of the environment at the time of formation. The persons who study soil are called pedologists, but similar work may also be done by geologists and geographers.

It is often evident how a site accumulated and was buried. If not, the information may be obtained through detailed analysis of the sediments. In most instances one can discover whether sites resulted from natural or man-made deposition; the pedologist can distinguish between water-laid, wind-laid, and man-laid deposits. This is important because it helps to show whether the artifacts are *in situ* and provides information about the environment at the time of deposition.

Through analysis of buried soil horizons one can tell something of the climatic conditions that produced them. In some instances (for example, on the Mediterranean coast) one can correlate some of the buried soils in caves with those in dunes to arrive at a rough relative chronology (Howell 1959, Wright 1962). However identification of these soils is a job for a specialist who must be familiar with the chemistry of soil formation. Two soils having the same appearance may result from different causes. Facile nontechnical comparisons based upon visual observation by an archeologist are generally undependable. Rates of soil weathering and development of soil profiles offer a promising lead for archeological dating. The reader may consult Atkinson (1957) and Cornwall (1958:200–203) for more extended discussion.

The sediments in caves can also be interpreted to give information on climate. Angularity and size of particles and color of sediments are some of the features looked for. There is still disagreement on exactly what conditions produced certain effects, but rough guide lines have been laid down and they seem to correlate with information on climate derived from other sources. For an extended discussion of this question as it relates to a specific series of sites, see Movius (1960).

Pedologists, through chemical analysis of the soil, may also be able to tell whether an observed feature in the earth is natural or man-made.

For example, there may be a question whether a hole once held a post or resulted from a burrowing animal, or perhaps just from the digging by the inhabitants of a site. Analysis of the humic content of the pit compared with soil nearby may tell whether a wooden post rotted there. In acid soils bone is usually destroyed by chemical action. Solecki (1953: 382–383) was able to show in the Natrium site, West Virginia, from a very high phosphate concentration in what were believed to be grave pits—but in which no visible signs of bone were apparent—that the pits had at one time contained burials. Bone will ordinarily not be preserved in soil more acid than that having a pH (hydrogen ion value) of 6.3 or less. A pH value of 7.0 is neutral; values above 7.0 indicate basic or alkaline soils; those below 7.0 are acid.

Pedological methods applied to archeological soils are discussed and illustrated in publications by S. F. Cook (1963); S. F. Cook and Heizer (1962); Cornwall (1953, 1960, 1963); Deetz and Dethlefsen (1963); Dietz (1957); Heizer (1953:17–18); Lotspeich (1961); and Parsons (1962).

Just as with other technical analyses, those of soils can produce far more information than the archeologist can use. Such analyses are only useful when the problems they can help solve are well-defined.

ANALYSIS OF ANIMAL AND PLANT REMAINS

Aside from artifacts, the largest source of information about prehistoric life and times comes from studying the bones of animals that people ate and the plants they ate or lived with. Identification of faunal and floral vestiges are made by zoologists and botanists.

Most analyses of bones are simple identifications of the species present (Cornwall 1956; Olsen 1961a, 1961b). Many site reports include such a listing but fail to describe the implications of the presence of these species for prehistoric man. For a review of a sample of the archeological-zoological literature on this subject, see Heizer (1960b). If we know the species present, we can determine the meat diet of prehistoric man, and, by computing the frequencies of animals, we can get an idea of the relative importance of each species. For a method of calculating the minimum individuals, see T. E. White (1953b). For examples of the use of the technique in Iran, see Hole and Flannery (1962:126–127); North America, Lehmer (1954:170); W. T. Stein (1963:216–219); and Switzerland, Kuhn (1938: 256); Wettstein (1924). By knowing the number of animals that were brought to the area where people had their houses and cooked their meals, it is possible to estimate the amount of meat available. T. E. White (1953a) does this by estimating the dressed weight of game animals.

We should mention at this point that conclusions regarding total number of individual animals may be incorrect due to disappearance, through chemical action or mechanical breaking, of certain of the bones. The example of the Solutrean 4 layer in the site of Badegoule in southern France (Bouchud 1954) is given here. The layer produced 2577 adult reindeer teeth that theoretically should have shown the following proportions:

> 1032 incisors   (normal incisor-premolar ratio of 3/2)
> 744 premolars ⎱
> 744 molars   ⎰ (normal premolar-molar ratio of 1/1)
> ―――
> 2580

The teeth recovered show the following actual distribution:

> 144 incisors   (actual incisor-premolar ration of 1/7)
> 989 premolars ⎱
> 1444 molars   ⎰ (actual premolar-molar ratio of 17/25)
> ―――
> 2577

The newborn reindeer has four incisors and three premolars in each half of the jaw. The 186 teeth of newborn animals found should, therefore, have had the following proportions:

> 104 incisors   (normal incisor-premolar ratio 4/3)
> 78 premolars
> ―――
> 182

The teeth actually found are divided as follows:

> 12 incisors   (actual incisor-premolar ratio 1/15)
> 174 premolars
> ―――
> 186

Apparently in these instances there has been differential disappearance of certain teeth, which has skewed the normally expected proportions. Since the teeth of reindeer did not, so far as known, serve as material from which artifacts were made, the imbalance of expected numbers of kinds of teeth cannot be attributed to cultural practices by the persons who killed the reindeer for food.

Another caution about interpreting the number of animals is that the presence of twenty-five mice, one horse, and a deer does not mean that the people were primarily mouse eaters. In the first place, twenty-five mice give less meat than even a baby deer. In the second place, small rodents probably inhabited most archeological sites and often died natural deaths in the deposits. Others were probably killed as pests. It is not reasonable to assume that they were ever a very important part of the diet of prehistoric man although such allegations have been made. Similarly, the listing of infrequent birds, snakes, and miscellaneous scavenger carnivores in the site gives little clue to the diet of man since their presence in the archeological deposits may not have been due to human agency. Jewell (1958) shows that concentrations of the bones of water voles in Wiltshire barrows does not indicate a wetter situation in the Bronze Age at the site, but that the bones were introduced into the site by roosting birds who disgorged pellets containing the bones of animals caught elsewhere. Matteson (1959) has shown clearly that terrestrial snails may live and die on refuse middens and leave their shells to be discovered by an archeologist who may assume incorrectly that they provided part of the diet of the human occupants.

On the other hand, Watson (1955) has sounded a cautionary note in calling attention to the situation in New Guinea where meat resources are rare and considerable reliance is placed on small feral mammals, worms, and insects that would not leave any bones. The example points up once more the incompleteness of the archeological record.

Special feasts may leave evidence whose nature would be difficult to interpret from archeological evidence. For example, in the Mt. Hagen district of New Guinea great feasts are held at intervals of several years. At these times numbers of pigs are killed, roasted, and eaten. There is a record of 1100 animals being killed at one such feast (Riesenfeld 1950: 425; Salisbury 1962). Since pigs are eaten only on such festive occasions, the great accumulation of discarded bones that one supposes results from such a feasting orgy would refer to one single event of this sort. Since only certain villages hold such feasts, there would eventually be a great concentration of pig bones in these sites and not in others.

If the data secured from bones are properly weighted, a great deal of information can be derived about diet. We have mentioned how, by calculating the sizes of various species, one can tell approximately how much meat could have been consumed. By noting which parts of the body are represented one can tell whether the hunters brought whole or partial carcasses back to camp. This must be taken into account in any calculation of the amount of meat available. One can also tell, by examining the bone, how animals were butchered. In some instances meat was separated at the joints; in others, long bones were simply hacked

TECHNICAL ANALYSES · 137

through. Variations in techniques of butchering can give information about cultural associations. Interpretations of the cultural significance of fragmentary animal bones in refuse deposits must be made with caution since the archeologist does not know what cultural practices (Grahame Clark calls these "social choices") may have been involved in hunting, butchering, bringing back the kill to the site, or in disposing of the bones after the animal was eaten. This subject is discussed by Heizer (1960b). Kehoe and Kehoe (1960) present a detailed analysis of bones recovered from a bison kill site in Montana and demonstrate that they can distinguish different cultural groups and whether such a kill site was the result of activity of hunters sent out from villages or that of nomadic hunters. Actually, archeologists often reach a conclusion that seems to be supported by the data they have recovered from the excavation, but that conclusion may not be nearly so correct as the archeologist implies. In illustration, note the paper by Davis (1959) in which he critically examines the evidence for certain conclusions made by Southwestern archeologists on changes of diet in successive prehistoric cultures.

The kinds of animals and plants present in a site may give information about climate. The large animals are not always as sensitive indicators of climate as small ones may be (Heizer 1960b:121–123). For inferences about climate, plants and snails seem to be the most sensitive of all indicators. The reader may wish to follow up the matter of the importance of snails and molluscs as ecological indicators by consulting the papers of Allen and Cheatum (1961), Burchell (1961), Lambert (1960), and Matteson (1960). The bones of microfauna (such as mice), while of little value in determining diet, must be saved for the climatic clues they can give. Plants and animals are often found within narrow ecological zones (Sears 1953). When these zones are known, it is possible to infer that flora and fauna found in sites came from similar zones. Inferences can be made from pollen, impressions of plants in clay, and from preserved plants. It is more difficult to make inferences from small mammals because they are often burrowers and may have entered a site long after its abandonment. Their presence, while an indication of climatic conditions, may be related to a climate quite different from that which prevailed while the site was occupied by man.

Both flora and fauna can give information that a site was occupied at a certain time of year. When caches of ripe seeds are found, one infers that the site was occupied during or soon after the harvest season. If animals of a certain age are found, it may indicate seasonal slaughter. When migratory birds are found, one can tell the seasons when they would have been present. It is easier to tell when a site was occupied than to say that it was not occupied at a particular time. For a more extended discussion of what kinds of evidence indicate whether a site was seasonally or permanently occupied, see Heizer (1960b). J. G. D. Clark (1954:94–95) presents evidence of seasonal occupation at Star Carr, England, and MacNeish (1964) does the same for the Tehuacan valley in Mexico.

Valuable clues to diet may also be derived from analysis of human feces. These are often preserved in dry sites and may contain the bones of small mammals along with seed and vegetal matter that can be identified. This is a field of investigation that has been badly neglected. Citations to analysis of feces from archeological sites are given in Heizer (1960b:108–109). E. O. Callen of McGill University, Canada, has perfected a technique of soaking coprolites preserved in dry archeological sites for seventy-two hours in a 0.5 percent aqueous solution of trisodium phosphate. The softened mass is then sedimented and a detailed microscopic examination made of all of the solid matter that remains. Surprisingly rich results have been obtained by Callen and Cameron (1960) from an examination by this method of coprolites from the ancient dry site on the Peruvian coast named Huaca Prieta, and by Callen (1963) from cave sites in the state of Puebla, Mexico.

CHEMICAL ANALYSIS OF RESIDUES

At times qualitative chemical analysis may lead to the identification of some residue that an archeologist recovers. By way of example we cite the chemical analysis of cheese residues in Egyptian tubular jars of the First and Second Dynasties (Emery 1961:212), the determination that mercury poisoning was probably responsible for a prehistoric death (Aitken 1961:169; Hall 1963:185), chemical analyses of Egyptian beer and yeast residues (Lucas 1934:5–13; Winlock 1942:193), determination by microscopic examination of residues that wheat beer and mead had been contained in two north German drinking horns found in a peat bog (Grüss 1932), analyses of wine residues in Egyptian pots (Lucas 1934: 20), chemical analyses of "bog butter" (adipocere) preserved in wooden casks of Scottish bogs (Macadam 1882, 1889), and verification of the supposition that fat was used as fuel in lamps of the Ertobölle culture of Denmark through chemical analysis of scrapings from the basins of lamps (Mathiassen 1935). A similar demonstration that certain vessels from Irish sites were lamps was made by Moss (1910). An effort to determine by chemical analysis of "cakes" or "dottels" whether supposedly prehistoric "Puebloan tobacco pipes" were pipes for smoking tobacco was inconclusive (Dixon and Stetson 1922).

ANALYSIS OF SITES

Sites themselves, irrespective of the artifacts within them, may be analyzed. The discovery of buried sites has been facilitated by chemical analyses of the soil. Organic remains, especially bone, decompose and leave a high phosphate concentration in the soil. Where analyses of soil have been taken at short intervals over a wide area, sites may be found. High percentages of phosphate within a site may also indicate the former presence of bones (Solecki 1953). Finally, sites may be examined for the clues they give to age and past climate.

In North America geologists are often consulted by archeologists who have discovered evidence of Paleo-Indian implements in alluvial deposits. As examples, the reader may wish to consult Antevs' studies of the geology of the Naco and Lehner sites in southern Arizona where flint implements were found associated with bones of mammoths (Antevs 1953b, 1959); the geological study of the San Jon site in eastern New Mexico by Judson (1953); the geomorphological study of the Lime Creek area in Nebraska (Schultz, Lueninghoener, and Frankforter 1948); and the geological studies by Moss (1951a, 1951b) and Holmes (1951) of early man sites in the Eden Valley, Wyoming. These studies, which lead to conclusions about the age of sites and the prehistoric climate, are paralleled by similar work in Europe (Bordes 1954 and Müller-Beck 1957:5–23).

In a similar vein, it may one day be possible, by use of chemical analyses, to determine the kinds of activities that were carried out in particular spots within a site. Research has not yet progressed to the point where this can be done, but in a large site, with sufficiently refined qualitative chemical techniques, it might be possible to identify areas where grain was ground, acorns were leached, pottery was made, animals were butchered, and so on. Biek (1963b) in a recent book has provided the best review yet made of techniques that would be applicable to this kind of investigation.

Because sites are often too large to warrant complete excavation, sampling techniques have been attempted to allow selective excavation. Some attempts along this line have been made in California shell and earth mounds (for citations to methods and results see summary in

Heizer 1960b:94–99), but in principle the practice may be applicable to a wider variety of sites. A postulate basic to such sampling is that any given area within a site is likely to be very much like any other given area. If it is known a priori that some activities were carried out only in certain places, a random selection of areas to dig would produce undependable results.

Technical analyses are ancillary aids to archeology (Brothwell and Higgs 1963). In themselves they only provide data which archeologists can interpret. Before archeologists begin to dig they should have a clear idea of the kinds of information that they may be able to recover and also a clear idea of how the material can be analyzed. When analyses have been made, archeologists must take the data and, through interpretation, translate them into culturally meaningful information.

THE PROBLEM OF HOAXES AND FAKES

Most archeologists will not be bothered with the "planting" in their site of specimens that do not belong there. Occasionally, however, a malicious individual or a person who does not understand the serious nature of archeological investigation will play a practical joke and bury, for later "discovery" in apparently undisturbed ground, a specimen that he found elsewhere. Most archeologists will simply not stand for this kind of horseplay, and, if discovered, the practical joker will be packed off summarily. The most notorious instance of faking and planting of objects—in this case human bones—in a deposit is that of the Piltdown Man. The story of this hoax has been hold by Weiner (1955) who, with admirable courtesy, restrains himself from drawing the logical conclusion and naming the perpetrator. The demonstration by analytical chemical methods that the bones were forgeries was made by K. P. Oakley of the British Museum. An earlier instance in which a human lower jaw was said to have been discovered in Pleistocene gravels involved the father of Paleolithic archeology, Boucher de Perthes. Having offered a reward for new finds to the quarry workers in the Moulin-Quignon pit, the temptation was too much for one worker who in 1863 presented the jaw to Boucher de Perthes, claimed and received his reward. The jaw was finally shown to be more recent than it was alleged to be by application of flourine test (Oakley 1964:111–116).

Many forgeries make their appearance in museum collections (Wakeling 1912) where they may be taken as genuine until someone becomes suspicious of their authenticity and examines them from a new viewpoint (Plenderleith 1952; Cooney 1963). It was actually for this reason that the Piltdown hoax was exposed because it became increasingly difficult to see how the anomalies of the bones could be adjusted to what was otherwise known of human evolution. A more recent instance is the discovery that the remarkable Etruscan terracotta warrior statues in the Metropolitan Museum of Art in New York are forgeries (Von Bothmer and Noble 1961).

An increasing amount of faking is being done, mostly for financial gain. The forgers often work hand in hand with dealers who sell to private collectors and museums. Archeologists are often asked to give their opinion on whether a piece is genuine or a fake. If an archeologist is willing to provide such an opinion, he must base it upon his knowledge of what he has seen of undoubtedly genuine pieces that the specimen in question resembles. Often the proof that a piece is genuine must await complicated, time-consuming, and often expensive chemical and physical testing. For some of these tests see the references cited by Gettens and Usilton (1955). For a detailed account of the testing and authentication of Egyptian dynastic materials from Amarna see, Stross (1960). The archeologist should not forget that in ancient times there were also copiers and forgers (Partington 1947).

PART 3

DATING
THE EVENTS
IN PREHISTORY·

10

DATING BY PHYSICAL-CHEMICAL METHODS

A variety of techniques, ranging from calculating the rate of weathering on stone to measuring the disintegration of carbon isotopes, are included under physical-chemical methods for dating. Most of these techniques give relative dates although some give absolute dates. Since the present chapter cannot hope to cover the subject of archeological dating with any adequacy, we refer the reader to several general books and articles that contain fuller treatments of the subject: Aiken (1961); Bowen (1958); Brothwell and Higgs (1963:21–89); Griffin (1955); Heizer (1953); Libby (1955, 1961); Oakley (1953); Smiley (1955); Tilton and Hart (1963); Willis (1963); and Zeuner (1958, 1959).

RADIOCARBON DATING

For archeologists, one of the most important discoveries of the twentieth century was made just after World War II. In 1949 a method for determining the absolute age of certain ancient and previously undatable organic materials was announced (Arnold and Libby 1949; Broecker and Kulp 1956; Catch 1961, Chap. 7; and Kamen 1963). The method was devised to measure the amount of radioactive carbon remaining in ancient dead material. With this measurement it was possible to tell how long ago the plant or animal died. Thus archeologists could learn the approximate year in which a tree was cut for a house beam, how long ago a man represented by a mummy had died, or when the fire had been put out in a fireplace. The immediate enthusiasm of archeologists went far beyond the limits of the method as it was first developed. Most archeologists had had "guess dates" for their materials and they were aware that a system of absolute dating would probably invalidate some of their guesses. Unfortunately, some of the new dates were so far off the expected, and many so internally inconsistent, that some archeologists simply chose to ignore them. After this pendulum swing of enthusiasm, more sober judgments prevailed and the "bugs" in the system were largely worked out. The radiocarbon method for dating has proved itself useful when used with caution. In view of its importance, carbon-14 (C^{14}) dating will be described in some detail.

In essence, radiocarbon dating is based on the following argument. Neutrons produced by cosmic radiation enter the earth's atmosphere and react with the nitrogen isotope N^{14}. The reaction produces a heavy isotope of carbon, C^{14}, which is radioactive and has a half-life of about 5730 years.[1] Libby's (1955:2) equation describing the reaction is:

$$N^{14} + n = C^{14} + H^1$$

Chemically, C^{14} seems to behave exactly as ordinary nonradioactive carbon, C^{12}. Thus the C^{14} atoms readily mix with the oxygen in the earth's atmosphere along with C^{12} and eventually enter into all living things as part of the normal life process. As long as matter is living and hence in exchange with the atmosphere, it continues to receive C^{14} and C^{12} atoms in a constant proportion. After death the organism is no longer in exchange with the atmosphere and no longer receives atoms of carbon.

After the death of an organism the C^{14} begins to disintegrate at the rate of one half every 5730 years, so that by measuring the amount of radiocarbon remaining, one can establish the time when the plant or

[1] The original Libby value for the half-life of C^{14} was 5568 ± 30 years. Research currently being carried on at several laboratories will result in final agreement on determination for this constant. For the present, the Fifth Radiocarbon Dating Conference, Cambridge, 1962, has accepted 5570 ± 30 years (the original value) as the half-life of radiocarbon, and made the decision to use A.D. 1950 as the standard for computing dates B.P. The best value now obtainable for the half-life is, however, 5730 ± 40 years. To convert published dates to the new half-life, multiply them by 1.03 (*Radiocarbon*, 5, 1963, "Editorial Statement").

animal died. Half-life is measured by counting the number of beta radiations emitted per minute per gram of material. Modern C^{14} emits about 15 cpm/g whereas C^{14} 5700 years old should emit about 7.5 cpm/g. In the disintegration the C^{14} returns to N^{14}, emitting a beta particle in the process. Thus:

$$C^{14} = B- \; + N^{14}+$$

There were several assumptions about the process that had to be verified before it could be used with confidence. For example, it was necessary to verify that the rate of cosmic radiation through long periods of time had remained constant; that the concentration of C^{14} in the reservoir of exchangeable carbon on the earth and in the atmosphere had not changed; and that C^{14} is distributed evenly throughout the atmosphere and living matter. Verification of these assumptions involved such things as possible errors in the calculation of a half-life, instances of irregular distribution of C^{14} among living things, the effect of atom bomb explosions on the production of C^{14}, and the effect on the ratio of C^{14} to C^{12} of burning fossil fuels such as coal and oil. The suggested errors in measurement through such sources are relatively minor for dates beyond the range of history (Craig 1954; Libby 1963; Wickman 1952).

From the beginning it also had to be assumed that it was possible to obtain dependable samples of carbon from archeological contexts. Early results indicated that it was possible. One of the first samples run was a piece of wood from an Egyptian boat that had been dated by archeologists at 3750 years before the present. The date was based upon texts and other archeological evidence. The average age of three runs of the radiocarbon sample was 3621 ± 180 (C-81). After a series of similar results had been obtained there seemed little reason to question the essential validity of the assumption that archeological materials could be dated with fair precision. Research since Libby's original announcement has gone far in an effort to achieve better laboratory techniques in the preparation and counting of samples.

In the inevitable rush of enthusiasm archeologists began to submit samples to Libby and others for dating. After large numbers of dates had been released, it became apparent that the system was creating as many new problems as it was solving. The dates could not always be justified on archeological grounds. As the evidence was examined, several likely sources of error were pointed out (Anderson and Levi 1952); none of them, however, involved the fundamental assumptions about the nature of C^{14} (Libby 1963).

It has been thought that anomalous radiocarbon ages of shells of fresh-water molluscs are due to the incorporation of inactive carbon deriving from humus carried in solution in the water. Broecker (1964) disputes this but agrees that there are problems in dating shells. Keith and Anderson (1963) show that shells of river molluscs may yield age errors of up to several thousand years. Tauber (1958) has discussed some of the difficulties archeologists encounter in determining the significance of radiocarbon dates. A single radiocarbon date for an archeological level should be accepted with reserve and efforts made to verify such single dates with additional check runs or by other methods for dating. Wood charcoal and pottery associated together may not be of the same age, and a radiocarbon date of the charcoal could be misleading if applied to the ceramics. An instance of this occurred at the site of Cuicuilco in the Valley of Mexico where charcoal from preceramic earth fill gave an age of 6715 ± 90 years but was associated with pottery known on other grounds to date from 2700 to 2300 years old.

It is possible for a sample to become contaminated after it is removed from the ground. The first archeologists to submit samples often put them in paper boxes or padded them with cotton for shipping. This practice frequently resulted in mixing older with more recent carbon. Other archeologists treated samples with an organic preservative to keep them from falling apart, thus introducing young radiocarbon into the old sample. Again, modern carbon, or at least carbon of a different age, was introduced into the sample. It was also found that modern rootlets had frequently penetrated the charcoal as it lay in the ground. In some instances it was found that older carbon had been present. For example, where tar was used to coat wood, it had introduced older carbon into the sample. Another source of error lay in the fact that humic acids from the surface soil sometimes percolate into underlying archeological horizons. Here again, modern carbon can be introduced into an old sample. By the time archeologists began to recognize the many possible sources for contamination, physicists and chemists had begun to improve upon the original techniques for preparing the samples and counting them. All the recently developed methods for counting samples use similar techniques for their initial preparation. Washing samples in acid and alkali solutions and subsequently burning them has added considerably to the dependability of the determinations. This is an important fact that must be considered when one uses dates run between 1950 and 1955.

Libby's original apparatus was primitive compared to that now in use. He used what is called the "screen-wall" technique in which he reduced the organic material to carbon and then smeared it on the inner surface of a specially built Geiger counter. By contrast, modern methods change the carbon to a gas—carbon dioxide (CO_2), acetylene (C_2H_2), or methane (CH_4)—and count it in a proportional counter (for photos of apparatus see Briggs and Weaver 1958). There has been a considerable gain in accuracy over the older technique because the sample is not handled after it has been made ready for conversion to a gas. This has eliminated the danger of radioactive contamination from the atmosphere, a disruptive factor introduced by atomic bomb tests. Further, with the gas proportional counters, a much smaller sample will suffice.

Two other methods are now being used by laboratories making radiocarbon determinations. One involves using CO_2 in a Geiger-Muller counter rather than solid carbon as Libby first tried. The other uses the liquid scintillation spectrometer. Neither of these methods has yet proved better for routine work than use of the gas proportional counter.

Another important refinement is that of isotopic enrichment. With the original methods the effective range of radiocarbon dating was about 30,000 years. With the more modern systems 50,000 years is the practical limit, but for samples of great importance an elaborate, expensive, and time-consuming process of isotopic enrichment can be carried out that will enable the scientist to ascertain the dates of material as old as 70,000 years (Haring, deVries and deVries 1958). On a practical basis, however, with isotopic enrichment the problems of contamination become much greater the older the sample is. A practical example will make this clear.

> The addition of 1 percent of modern carbon to a sample that is 5570 years old increases the specific radioactivity by 2 percent, so that the measured age of the sample is too small by 160 years, an error of 3 percent. For a sample that is 23,000 years old, the addition of 1 percent of modern carbon increases the specific radioactivity by 16 percent, corresponding to 1,300 years, an error of 5 percent. But for a sample that is 67,000 years old, the addition of 1 percent of modern carbon makes the radioactivity 40 times what it should be. The indicated age would be 37,000 years; this bears no relation to the true age and depends only on the degree of contamination (Aitken 1961:97).

Quite apart from matters of possible contamination, no sample is worth dating unless it is archeologically dependable. Archeologists must make sure that their samples are from undisturbed deposits. They should be prepared to tell the laboratory technicians how the sample was collected, the kind of deposit in which it was found, the kind of pretreatment he has given it—washing or sorting out of foreign material by hand—whether there were roots or humus-rich soil horizons near the sample, and anything else that might bear on its dependability. Here the responsibility rests squarely upon the shoulders of archeologists, who must take care to submit only samples of high quality.

It is necessary before leaving the subject of radiocarbon dating to mention two more topics. The first is the statistical expression of the dates and what it means (Spaulding 1958). All dates are expressed in terms of a plus or minus factor. Thus the date for the Egyptian boat mentioned above was given as 3621 ± 180 years before the present. The plus or minus 180 is the range of one standard deviation; it indicates that 68 percent of the time the true age of the sample will lie between 3441–3801 years before present. If we double the plus or minus factors, there will be a 95 percent probability—19 chances out of 20—that the true age lies within these limits (that is, 3261–3981 years before present). But "there are *no* limits within which the true age lies with absolute certainty" (Aitken 1961:98).

The second matter is the use of B.P. (before present) as opposed to B.C. (before Christ) or A.D. (anno Domini) when stating the age of a sample. For archeologists, the use of B.P. dates makes little sense. The machines count years before the present, but archeologists need not. When dates are written B.P., persons reading them must continually update them. As the years pass, converting dates to our calendar becomes more difficult if one does not know the year in which the laboratory determination of age was performed. The same event may on occasion be stated to have occurred at different times if various individuals employ a different *P* date in reckoning the B.C. or A.D. date. The compromise adopted in 1962 by the Fifth Radiocarbon Dating Conference to use A.D. 1950 as the standard for computing dates B.P. is not entirely satisfying although it is much preferable to using a constantly changing date. The main problem that will arise from using A.D. 1950 is that dates published prior to the agreement will have to be adjusted. A second problem is that archeologists as well as nonprofessionals have difficulty adjusting their thinking about the past when they must use several time scales. The mistakes made when one must shift between A.D. and B.C. are annoying at best.

Jelinek (1962) has provided a very useful list of radiocarbon dates of archeological materials. In an annual volume entitled *Radiocarbon*, published by the American Journal of Science, appear lists of dates determined by the fifty-six (in 1963) active radiocarbon laboratories.

OTHER RADIOACTIVE DATING METHODS

Several methods of dating are based on the radioactive decay of minerals. Many of these cannot be applied to archeological materials because they are most effective on extremely old material or because they are based on material which is ordinarily not found in archeological sites. One method which may become valuable for dating very old archeological deposits is based upon the decay of potassium-40.

Potassium-Argon Dating

Measurement of the ratio of potassium-40 (K^{40}) to the gas argon-40 (A^{40}) in many minerals extends the range of absolute dating far beyond the limits of radiocarbon. This method depends upon the fact that radioactive K^{40} decays at a known rate to form A^{40}. By measuring the ratio of K^{40} to A^{40} in a mass spectrometer, one can calculate the age of the rocks (Carr and Kulp 1957; Gentner and Lippolt 1963; Curtis 1961; for a bibliography of geochronology see Anonymous 1962). K-A dating depends upon these assumptions: that there was no argon trapped in the sample at the time of its formation; that no argon was added or lost during the lifetime of the sample; and that measuring techniques are accurate. Of the three assumptions, the second is known to be incorrect in many instances; certain rocks leak argon at a greater rate than others. For example, mica retains 80–100 percent of its argon whereas feldspars retain 40–85 percent. Accurate dating of some of these minerals must await clearer definition of the factors that cause the leaking.

The value of the K-A dating is that rocks associated with a site may be dated. Thus far the major application of the method on archeological materials has been at Olduvai Gorge in Tanganyika, where L. S. B. Leakey has found some of the oldest known fossil hominid bones. At Olduvai the beds containing the fossils are composed of volcanic tuffs (consolidated volcanic ash) alternating with clays. It appears from the freshness of the tools and bones that vulcanism occurred repeatedly while the site was being occupied, and that the material was covered by tuff soon after it was laid down. The tuffs thus make excellent dating material. The K-A dates from the lowest levels at Olduvai average 1,750,000 years. This figure is much larger than would have been expected by many workers, and it has been questioned on stratigraphic and technical grounds (Howell 1962a).

Most archeological sites cannot be dated by K-A. It would do no good to date rocks brought into a site by man because they might well be millions of years older than the site. The major application of this method to archeology would seem to be at those sites where there has been volcanic activity that has caused the deposition of potassium-rich materials either shortly before or shortly after occupation by man.

Thermoluminescence

In 1960 Kennedy and Knopff (1960:147–148) announced a potentially interesting method for dating archeological materials. This method was based on the fact that objects such as pottery that have been heated in the past could be dated by measurement of their thermoluminescent glow (Aitken 1961:86–87; Hall 1963; Tite and Waine 1962). Although the principle of thermoluminescence was well known, it was necessary to verify the practicality of routinely dating archeological materials.

Subsequent research has shown that thermoluminescence dating techniques will only work on material that has not been altered since its initial date of firing. Unfortunately most ceramics have undergone some chemical alteration that affects the thermoluminescent glow and cannot be distinguished from the glow produced by radiation damage since the pot was fired (George Kennedy, personal communication, June 10, 1964). This problem limits the possible applications of the method so severely that, at least for the foreseeable future, it will not become an important tool for archeological dating.

While an exact method of dating may yet be developed by thermoluminescence, this time has not yet arrived (Hall 1963). One good use of the method would be for the detection of modern ceramic fakes since it should be very easy to determine whether a pot was anciently or recently made, even though it is impossible to give its exact age.

Natural Low-Level Radioactivity (Beta Activity)

Buried archeological materials will vary in low level radioactivity in the form of beta and alpha activity measured with a proportional flow counter. Correlations between radioactivity of the soil matrix environment and the material (bone or teeth are excellent subjects) can be determined. The method has been described by Jelinek and Fitting (1963), and applications of the method to the Texas Midland site bones (Oakley and Rixon 1958); Piltdown bones (Bowie and Davidson 1955); Arlington Springs bones, Santa Rosa Island, California (Oakley 1963a); bones from the Llano Estacado region of Texas (Oakley 1961); and the Lagow Sandpit, Texas (Oakley and Howells 1961), have been made.

The method shows great promise as a means of making distinctions in relative age of two finds, of detecting intrusion of recent bones in older deposits, and checking archeological materials for their fit with postulated climatic history.

MAGNETIC DATING

Magnetic dating can also give absolute dates. Variations in the angle of declination between magnetic north and true north and in the angle of dip of a magnetic needle have been recorded for 400 years in London and for shorter periods in other cities (see Fig. 25). These measurements have shown that the magnetic field of the earth, as expressed in terms of angles of declination and dip, has changed although not in easily predictable ways. Other studies have shown that a record of past angles of declination and dip is trapped in baked clay. In unfired clay the magnetic fields of the magnetite and hematite grains occur at random. When clay is fired the grains are aligned with the magnetic field of the earth surrounding them. On cooling, the alignment of grains is "frozen" and can be recorded so long as the clay is preserved intact. This permanent alignment of grains is called *thermo-remanent magnetism.* Where records of past angles of declination and dip have been kept, it is possible to compare the values obtained from a piece of clay with the plotted values of historic records and arrive at the date of the archeological specimen.

In practice the method is severely restricted by inadequate records. In addition, for any given time the angles of dip and declination vary considerably from place to place. Reference to Fig. 25 will show how the values for the same years in Boston, London, Rome, and Paris differ. Thus one must not only have good records of change, but also have them for areas near archeological sites. One thousand miles is a *maximum* distance for extrapolation of data, but there are ways of getting around this limitation.

The problem for the archeologist is to obtain samples of baked clay that can be dated by radiocarbon or some other means. When a number of such samples from one area have been recorded, one can plot a curve that shows the variation in angles of dip and declination through time. When a series of clay samples of known dates has been measured, one can measure samples that have no independent dates. By comparing these with the scale one can calculate their age.

This method may become valuable for archeology although it has

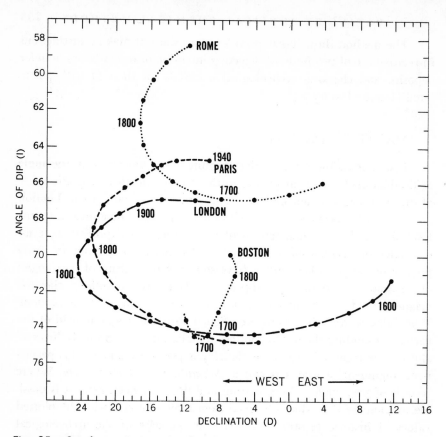

Fig. 25. Secular variation—London, Paris, Rome, and Boston. The time scale is indicated by dots at 20-year intervals. Prior to 1900 the curves shown are those obtained by Bauer (1899) using recorded observations of declination and dip to determine an empirical formula. Bauer's extrapolations into periods when only declination was measured have been omitted. Subsequent to 1900 the data have been taken from Vestine *et al.*, (1947). (M. J. Aitken, *Physics and Archaeology.* Courtesy of John Wiley & Sons, Inc.)

been tried in detail only in Great Britain (Aitken 1960, 1961; Cook and Belshe 1959; Cook 1963) and Japan (Watanabe 1959). The Research Laboratory for Archaeology and the History of Art at Oxford University is doing the most active investigation of magnetic dating at this time, and the results of these inquiries are published in the annual volumes of *Archaeometry.* Magnetic dating is useful, partly because it can give absolute dates, and partly because baked clay is present in so many archeological sites. Fireplaces and pottery kilns are the most common and, as we shall see, perhaps the best subjects for measuring, but bricks and pottery can also be used.

There are many difficulties in magnetic dating. Some of these result from the problems of measurement and some from the nature of thermo-remnant magnetism. For example, the best material for dating is that which has remained where it was fired. Fireplaces are the best. Bricks have ordinarily been removed from the place where they were fired. It was thus difficult to align them in their original positions so that the deviation of the angles of declination and dip can be calculated. By the same token, pottery rarely can be used to establish declination unless it has remained in the kiln where it was fired. In fact, pottery is often a poor medium for measuring because it was frequently traded over great distances. On certain types of pots, however—those which are glazed or have considerable plastic decoration—it is possible to measure the angle of dip because they were probably fired standing on their bases and hence on a fairly level surface. Nevertheless, their angles of declination cannot be measured because there is no way of knowing what their alignment with respect to geographical north was when they were fired. In one instance it was possible to take a large series of pots made over a long period of time in a city in China and measure the variation in angle of dip. Scientists thus arrived at a simplified approximation of a dating standard (Aitken 1961:152).

The measurements themselves are usually made in a laboratory with special equipment. Only two determinations are made in the field. One is a calculation of geographic north; the other, a determination of magnetic north. Both of these readings are recorded on the sample before it is sent to the laboratory for measurement of thermo-remnant magnetism. Measurements in the laboratory are done with several kinds of sensitive magnets. Under certain circumstances there may be some alteration of the thermo-remnant magnetism. Laboratory methods have been worked out to allow for these and to determine whether the sample is suitable for measuring.

CHEMICAL ANALYSIS

The most important of the chemical techniques are the analyses of the fluorine, uranium, and nitrogen contents of bones. Quantitative differences in the amount of fluorine, nitrogen, and uranium may permit archeologists to reach a decision on the relative age of buried bones, and in many instances where there is an apparent association of the bones of extinct animals with those of man, to determine whether the human and animal bones are of the same or different ages. The reader is referred to publications by Cook and Ezra-Cohn (1959), Cook and

Heizer (1953), Heizer and Cook (1952), Oakley (1963b), and Oakley and Weiner (1955) that illustrate kinds of problems that can be solved by chemical analysis of bone. The first two analyses depend upon the fact that buried bones and teeth gradually absorb fluorine and uranium from the ground water. The absorption of these minerals occurs through the alteration of hydroxyapatite, the phosphate of which bones and teeth are mainly composed. The amount of fluorine can be determined by chemical analysis or through the x-ray crystallographic method (Baud 1960; Cook 1960; Oakley 1951). McConnell (1962) has questioned the reliability of the fluorine method as a means of determining the age of bones. The amount of absorbed uranium can be determined from the radioactivity of the material (Oakley 1955b). Whereas the fluorine and uranium content increases with age, nitrogen by contrast decreases in amount with prolonged burial owing to the disappearance of collagen in the bone. Nitrogen determination and some results obtained can be further studied in the publications of Oakley (1963b) and Cook and Heizer (1952, 1959).

Laboratory methods for extracting collagen (gelatin) from ancient bones have been devised (Sinex and Faris 1959), and this collagen is suitable for dating by the radiocarbon method (Berger, Horney, and Libby 1964). Oakley was able to extract a small amount of collagen from the Piltdown bones and H. deVries of the Groningen Radiocarbon Laboratory determined from this organic extract that the mandible was 500 ± 100 years old and the Piltdown skull 620 ± 100 years old (Oakley 1959). Fifty years ago Lyne (1916) examined the Piltdown mandible by x-ray. This examination should have shown that the characteristic roots of ape teeth were present, but radiographic techniques at this time were not sufficiently perfected to make this feature clearly apparent on the plates. A re-examination by x-ray in recent years would surely have shown the nature of the teeth clearly, but such tests were not made.

Analyses of organic material help to determine the relative ages of bone specimens from one place. Because of the complicated and poorly understood chemistry involved in the absorption of chemicals into bone or the disappearance of organic matter, it is not possible to compare specimens from different places with accuracy. In addition, bones, teeth, and antlers may take up fluorine at variable rates. It is known that temperature and humidity affect the chemical action, and environments differ greatly in their chemical make-up. In spite of the many limitations, chemical analyses may be very useful in helping to establish stratigraphy or association of one bone with another. There is as yet no method for deriving an absolute chronology from chemical analyses.

Schoute-Vanneck (1960) describes a method of relative dating of coastal shell middens. Shells of mussel (*Mytilus*) are dissolved in acetic acid and the ratio of conchylin (a substance similar to chiton) to calcium carbonate (lime) is determined. There is proved for South African coastal sites a progressive loss of conchylin over time. The method is now useful for relative dating, but if in the future the rates of decrease of conchylin can be determined, an absolute or chronometric dating method could be devised.

Progressive chemical changes occurring in animal skin (or leather) are claimed to follow a rate so that the age of ancient skin can be determined. Burton, Poole, and Read (1959) describe a technique where collagen fibers extracted from ancient skin are mounted for microscopic viewing. When these fibers are heated, the fibers begin to shrink, and the older the specimen the lower the shrinkage temperature. Fragments of the Dead Sea Scrolls written on parchment were found to produce "collagen fiber shrinkage temperature dates" that were in agreement with paleographic and radiocarbon age determinations. In theory almost any ancient preserved material will differ in its chemistry from modern material. In some cases the process of change can be invested with a rate or tempo, and thus provide a means of calculating the age of older materials.

Mention may be made here of attempts to determine the blood groups of ancient populations from their bones. Thieme and Otten (1957), in a review of earlier work, have concluded that the results achieved are undependable; on the other hand, M. Smith (1960) and Glemser (1963) feel that presently known techniques of paleoserology will yield useful and dependable results.

PATINATION

It has long been observed that the surface of rocks exposed to the atmosphere undergoes chemical alteration. The altered surfaces are said to be *patinated*. Many writers have suggested the possibility of using the amount of patina on stones as an index to their age. A recent evaluation of this method (Goodwin 1960) lists so many variables involved in patina formation that one must agree that absolute dates cannot be determined. Nevertheless, for certain problems observation of the amount of color of patina on a stone may be of use. In sites where there is a long sequence, the flints in the bottom levels may have more patina than those found in the upper levels. This is especially common in river gravels and terraces of rivers or lakes. When one has a large series of tools from several levels, it is sometimes possible to see clear-cut differences in the relative amounts of patina. With this knowledge it is then possible to assign dependable relative ages to artifacts from the same area. Successful use of differential patination on flint tools has been realized by Kelly and Hurst (1956), Hurst and Kelly (1961), Higgs (1959:212), and Sonneville-Bordes (1953). Additional cases are listed by Goodwin (1960). The famous Belzoni, referred to in the first chapter, noted three distinct types of patination on the sculptures on the granite cliffs at Aswan in Egypt, and suggested that by dating the sculptures of one style or age, the age of the other two degrees of patination could be calculated (Belzoni 1820: 1:360–361).

The variations between areas and even on the same tools greatly limit the use of patina for age determination. When used, it must always be with a firm basis in stratigraphy; it is no substitute for excavation (Schmalz 1960).

Glass that has been buried in soil or submerged under water will undergo surface alteration and form microscopically thin bands or layers, which can be counted. Some studies suggest that these bands are annual, and their total number is a register of the number of years the glass has been buried or immersed. Ages of nearly 1600 years have thus far been determined for archeological specimens (Brill 1961).

HYDRATION OF OBSIDIAN

Preliminary work with the rate of weathering of obsidian shows much more promise as a dating method. Obsidian is a natural volcanic glass with a high aluminum content, and does not weather rapidly. But "a freshly exposed surface of obsidian will take up water from the atmosphere to form a hydrated surface level" (Friedman and Smith 1960: 476; Friedman, Smith, and Clark 1963). The dating system follows from the fact that the hydration layer builds up at a constant rate. By measuring the thickness of the layer, it is possible to estimate the date when hydration began. Because of the complicated nature of hydration and its great variation under different conditions of temperature, and by reason of the chemical composition of obsidian, universal standards for dating by this method seem to be unattainable. However, series of "hydration dates" from sites in the tropics and temperate zones have yielded results that are comparable to those obtained by other methods (D. L. Clark 1961; Friedman and Smith 1960). Within strict geographical limits the system may have real merit, but it is not a universal substitute for other sorts of dating.

A measurement of the amount of hydration on obsidian can be used much as the patina on flint and the relative amounts of fluorine and nitrogen are used (Evans and Meggers 1960). Within one site it is possible to tell the relative age of samples, but obsidian-hydration dating has practical problems such as the fact that when it has been burned, as may be the case in archeological sites, it cannot be used to determine dates.

11

GEOCHRONOLOGY

Besides directly dating archeological materials by associated charcoal, one can often date them indirectly through geology. When archeological materials are found in a geological context, they can sometimes be dated indirectly by techniques of geochronology (Howell 1959; Smiley 1955b; Zeuner 1958).

VARVE ANALYSIS

This, the oldest technique for geochronology, was described in 1878 by the Swedish Baron Gerard De Geer, who did most of the pioneering work, although somewhat earlier Heer (1863:453–455) had recognized that varves are annually deposited layers of silt. Varve analysis depends upon the fact that certain clayey deposits are laminated. These laminations, or varves as they are called in Swedish, are annual layers of sediment deposited in lake basins by the runoff from melting glacial ice. Through a process similar to that used in tree-ring analysis, it is possible to measure the relative thickness of the varves and obtain a series to which one can compare new sections as they are discovered (De Geer 1912; Heizer 1953:9–12).

Varves are composed of coarse sediments at the bottom and fine sediments at the top; the finer sediments settle during the winter while the lake is frozen over. Varves may range in thickness from less than one-half inch to more than 15 inches, though these maximum and minimum values are seldom reached.

The use of varve analysis is restricted by several factors. First because varves accumulate only near ice, there are no varves in most of the world. Second, in many places where ice was present during the Pleistocene, it has receded and no longer supplies basins with sediments. Therefore, outside of Scandinavia it is difficult to find a continuous sequence of varves reaching the present. Varves linked with the present do not extend very far into the past. The longest sequence known goes back only 17,000 years. This is because places that now have lakes were covered during the height of the Pleistocene glaciation and were not receiving sediments. A final reservation is that varves are not only annual; depending on the amount of melting, layers may be deposited more or less frequently than annually (Flint 1952:293–297).

In spite of the limitations, analyses of varves have been made in the Baltic area, North America, South America, and Africa. Attempts at exact correlations of these several sequences have not been generally accepted.

Varve analysis can be used indirectly for archeological dating. Sites are not often found in glacial lakes, but sediments in glacial lakes may be correlated with other geologic features such as beaches left by varying water levels. When the sea levels, and hence their beaches, can be dated by reference to varves, it is then possible to date archeological material found in the beaches. The method lacks precision, however, because it is possible for archeological materials to have been incorporated into beach deposits long after the beaches were formed. In North America Ernst Antevs has made several attempts to relate Pleistocene geological formations in the American Southwest to events that produced varves in the northern parts of North America (Antevs 1948, 1952, 1953; Smiley 1955a, 1955b). The dates derived by the varve chronology are rather older than those for the same events as determined by the radiocarbon dating method (Flint and Deevey 1951; Antevs 1954, 1957, 1962).

BEACHES, TERRACES, AND DUNES

When archeological sites are found in association with datable geological phenomena, the archeological materials can be dated indirectly. During the Pleistocene, fluctuations in sea level left records useful for archeological interpretation (Zeuner 1959, Chap. 9). Much of the sea water was periodically locked on land in the form of ice and in interglacial times this water was returned to the seas. The alternate raising and lowering of the sea, called eustasy, resulted in changes in the sea level of at least 300 feet (Russell 1957; Fairbridge 1958). Our records of lower sea levels in the past would have been wiped out by the present sea level were it not for an accompanying movement, in some areas, of the land masses, called isostasy. Under the weight of the ice, land masses were depressed, and when the ice retreated the land sprang up again. In some places this isostatic action raised the land so high above sea level that traces of old, once much lower, shore lines are visible; without isostasy they would now be submerged. Outside of glaciated areas, tectonic action—movement of land masses whether or not they were covered by ice—has exposed Pleistocene shore lines. Some beaches that would have been submerged are now readily seen, but the opposite is also true— some land areas are now submerged that might not have been were it not for tectonic action (Howell 1962b).

Traces of old sea levels can frequently be dated relative to one another. Extensive work on such correlations has been carried out in the Baltic and Mediterranean, to the great advantage of prehistoric archeology (Zeuner 1958, Chap. 5).

Along the eastern Mediterranean coast it has been possible to relate certain kinds of sand dunes, or weathering horizons within them, to Pleistocene chronology (Howell 1959, 1962b). Sometimes archeological sites can be related not only to beaches but to dunes as well. Even better, in the Baltic, shore lines can sometimes be correlated with varve sequences so that absolute dating can be given to the beaches.

Lakes often form beaches, and where these are controlled by the climate they can be related to a Pleistocene chronology. Such is the case in western Utah, where Jennings (1957) found that Danger Cave could not have been occupied before a lowering of the Pleistocene "Lake Wendover." Thus he had a date before which the site could not have been occupied. In some instances the sinking or rising of shorelines provide a means of dating archeological sites when there is some idea of the rate at which the change in elevation is taking place. Examples are cited by Heizer (1953:11).

Terraces, former flood plains formed along streams as a result of the changing regime of the river, can be used in the same way as shore lines. During periods of aggradation a river will deposit silt and gravel and build up its bed while at other times the river will degrade or cut into its bed. During periods of relative stability a stream may cut a valley sidewise by flooding or meandering. Alternatively, it may build a flood plain by depositing silt and gravel in the river valley. Either process results in a relatively level valley floor over which the stream spreads during floods. Later degradation leaves remnants of the flood plain suspended well above the river. The lowering of the bed of a river ordinarily takes a long time, and in the natural course of events the flood plain should wear down at about the same rate as the stream bed. However, sometimes bits of the flood plain are preserved at the margins of the valleys where meanderings of the river have failed to remove them. After a time a series of flood plains at different elevations can be distinguished (Flint 1957:Fig. 12–4). Under certain conditions the heights of these remnants can be used as a means of correlating one terrace with another. This is the same method used on shore lines, but it is much more difficult to make correlations between rivers; in practice it is even difficult to identify parts of the same terrace on different stretches of the same river (Johnston 1944). If the aggradation or degradation of a river can be directly related to an ocean or lake, it may be possible to date one by the other.

Just as archeological material may be found in association with shore lines, so it is often found associated with terraces. A very detailed correlation of archeology with terraces was made along the Nile where a four-year study was undertaken in the late 1920s and 1930s by K. S. Sandford, a geologist, and W. J. Arkell, an archeologist. Their work (1929–1939) has long been a standard reference, but their results are questionable because they sometimes used archeological materials to date terraces, and at other times terraces to date artifacts.

CORRELATION OF PLEISTOCENE FEATURES

The greatest amount of Pleistocene geology has been done in Europe and along the Mediterranean coasts where some of the best evidence of the Pleistocene climatic succession is preserved. A considerable amount of prehistoric archeology has been done in the same areas so that European and Russian scholars have been the leaders in correlating Pleistocene events with prehistoric man. By contrast, in North America there had been relatively little habitation that can be related to the glacial stages of the Pleistocene. Man probably entered this hemisphere toward the end of the last glacial.

Moraines of various sorts and outwash features from the melting ice are well-known glacial features. Ordinarily, however, because of their nearness to glacial ice, they are not directly associated with human habitation. Areas suitable for man lay beyond the immediate margins of the ice. In much of Eurasia this was loess land, in some places several hundred feet deep. Loess "is a sediment commonly nonstratified and commonly unconsolidated, composed dominantly of silt-size particles, ordinarily with accessory clay and sand, and deposited primarily by the wind" (Flint 1957:181). The loess that covers large portions of southwest Russia, east Europe, and the middle western United States is thought to have been derived from moraines and other glacial debris.

The development of soil horizons in loess is exceptionally important in helping to establish the late Pleistocene chronology of Europe. In theory loess is deposited during glacial periods, whereas soils are developed in the loess during the warmer phases when plants grow better. When these soils are buried, as they were during the alternations of the Pleistocene climate, a layered sequence is built up. Because some soil horizons are deeper than others, a characteristic sequence of thinner and thicker soils can thus be compared, from one locality to another. Sometimes loesses include fauna that helps to identify them. For example, the snail, *Helicigona banatica,* (among others) is found in a soil in central Europe (Movius 1960:359). For a detailed discussion of the correlation of European Pleistocene soils see Wright (1961:961–966).

Loess regions were grasslands, especially suitable for grazing animals such as bison and mammoths. Hunters of these animals left their camp sites in the loess, and these sites can sometimes be associated with particular loess horizons. A striking example of this is in southern Moravia, where Dolni Vestonica and Pavlov, both sites of mammoth hunters, are associated with the "Paudorf" soil formation (Zeuner 1955a). This soil, now a marker in the Pleistocene chronology of the area, is estimated to have lasted about 4000 years, from about 27,000 to 23,000 B.C. The estimate is based on radiocarbon dates made on charcoal from the sites as well as on humus from the soil (Movius 1963:132).

By slowly compiling knowledge of local sequences, geologists have begun to establish reliable chronologies for the latter part of the Pleistocene, but for most of the Pleistocene—now thought to be about two million years long—the dating is much less precise (Flint 1957:289–301). There are two reasons for this: either datable remains are not present; or enough work has not yet been done. Such gross distinctions as the four Alpine glacials—Günz, Mindel, Riss, and Würm—are of little help to archeologists. In southern areas four "pluvials," presumably contemporary with the Alpine glacials, were identified. Thus in Africa, south of the Sahara, there are the Kageran, Kamasian, Kanjeran, and Gamblian pluvials. These would have been convenient segments to correlate from continent to continent if the events had been strictly contemporaneous; however, they were not. In fact, in Africa, on second look, there is little evidence for widespread pluvial phases (Flint 1959). To add to the difficulty, each Alpine glacial is now subdivided and there are more than four. In short, except for the very end of the Pleistocene, when radio-carbon dates and varve analysis are useful in making correlations, chronology based on geologic features is imprecise. This fact is overlooked in many publicatons on the subject.

RATE OF SEDIMENTATION

Geologists have made inferences about the length of time required to deposit a certain amount of sediment, or of the time required for leaching of glacial deposits (Kay 1931; Dreimanis 1957). Archeologists often estimate the duration of a site by its depth of deposit, but any estimate is a sheer guess. It is really not possible to say that a deposit in a cave has accumulated at the rate of 15 inches per 1000 years, or that a shell midden accumulated at the rate of 2 feet per 100 years. When such guesses have been checked with radiocarbon or other dating methods, they have usually been proven wrong (Heizer 1953:24–25; 1959b, Chap. 9). On the other hand, if the depth of deposit and the length of time it took to accumulate are both known, then one can say that, on the average, one foot of depth was added per century, or whatever. Even with such statistics, however, it is not possible to extrapolate these data from one site to another. There are too many variables to control. Geological deposition is as complex as deposition in an archeological site, and its short term characteristics are not so easily measured. The lifetime of a human observer is very short compared to the time it takes nature to do most of its work.

LOCATION OF SITES

In the desert portions of western North America water was scarce, and one usually finds evidences of man's presence in the vicinity of springs or creeks. The presence of chipped flint tools on the shorelines of lake basins in the southern California desert has led to the supposition that the stone tools date from the time when the lake held water, and that if one can date the time the water was there, the cultural materials can thus be dated. This seems reasonable, but there are at least two other possibilities that should be considered before the simple equation that age of the lake waters equals age of the implements can be accepted. First is the known fact that some of these lake basins occasionally fill even today as a result of very heavy rains. In 1938, for example, the basin of normally dry Lake Mohave received enough water in a period of thirteen days to form a lake 16 miles long, 2.5 miles wide, and 10 feet deep. In prehistoric times, say as recently as 150 years ago, such a lake would certainly have attracted the Indians of the vicinity to its shores, where they would have camped and left traces of their temporary occupation, however brief, until the lake dried by evaporation. Thus, implements found on the surface around the lake margins might be 15,000 years old and date from the Pleistocene when the country was better watered and the lake permanent, or they might be 150 years old. Mere association of this sort between implements and a geological feature may or may not be related in a single way and may refer to only a single event.

A second caution in accepting surface finds of stone implements as contemporaneous with Pleistocene age of lakes is illustrated by a statement of J. H. Steward (1937:105) who writes:

> In the southern end of Eureka Valley, near the northern end of Death Valley, California, there is a site bordering a playa and extending several miles. Thousands of flint flakes with relatively few artifacts mark it as predominantly a workshop, though the source of the flints is several miles distant in the mountains. The nearest water is a spring 3 to 5 miles away. There is no apparent reason why anyone should choose a place lacking water, having virtually no vegetation, and, in fact, devoid of anything of apparent use to man or beast, for a workshop or other purpose. Nevertheless, the presence here of large spherical stone mortars of the type used by Death Valley Shoshoni and at least one arrow point of the Shoshonean type is presumptive evidence that the Shoshoni visited the site, though it does not, of course, prove that they used it as a workshop. Although Mr. and Mrs. Campbell (1935, p. 26) have never found a camp site more than 3 miles from a water hole in southern Califoria, the writer has repeatedly received accounts from Shoshoni and Paiute informants of camps maintained by entire families and groups of families for days at a time 10 and even 20 miles from water when seeds, salt, flints, edible insects, or other important supplies made it worth while to do so. Water is used sparingly and when the [basketry] ollas in which it is transported are empty one or two persons make the long trip to replenish them. Remoteness from present water, then, is not, per se, the slightest proof that a site dates from the pluvial period.

Although there is a variety of methods for dating archeological materials by means of geology, none of the methods is simple. In all cases it is better to have several independent methods for dating particular events. Used alone, any method that depends on far-reaching correlations of geologic stratigraphy is likely to be undependable because of weak links in the chain of observations. Archeologists should use, but be aware of the many imprecisions of geochronologic dating.

12

METHODS FOR DATING, USING PLANT AND ANIMAL REMAINS

Botany and zoology are included under this heading, but we must affix "paleo" to the words because we are concerned with long dead remains of living things. Paleontology and paleobotany have become extremely useful avenues for determining ancient climates and the dates of deposits in which archeological materials occur.

PALYNOLOGY

Pollen analysis (palynology) was first developed in 1916 by the Swedish scientist Lennar von Post, who was interested in forest trees. Twenty years later the technique was extended to all plants that scatter pollen. It has subsequently been developed into a highly refined method for identifying end-Pleistocene and post-Pleistocene climatic changes and chronology (Martin and Gray 1962; Dimbleby 1963).

Accurate analysis depends upon plants distributing their pollen widely and the grains being sufficiently well-preserved to be identified. Pollen analysis is tedious. It is based on the identification of pollen from modern plants. When these have been identified, it is possible to take a standard number of grains from samples in a vertical stratigraphic section and count the number from each species of plant. By plotting the relative frequencies of various species through time, one can make a pollen diagram describing the changing vegetation for the area involved (see Fig. 26).

Deevey (1944:138–140) lists four conditions that must be fulfilled in order to apply the technique of pollen analysis to problems of prehistory in any area. These are: (1) there must have been, within the period encompassed by human occupation of the area, vegetational changes resulting from area-wide causes; (2) pollen grains must be properly preserved in the deposits; (3) the investigation must first establish a "standard pollen sequence" through study of natural deposits such as lakes and swamps; (4) the investigator must possess a knowledge of the regional plant ecology in order to properly interpret the pollen sequence in terms of vegetational and climatic changes in the past.

If pollen analysis is relatively simple in theory, it is exasperating in practice because under many conditions pollen is not preserved. The best conditions are in bogs where pollen has remained damp since it was deposited. It is simple to cut sections from peat bogs and plot the pollen diagrams. In Scandinavia, after several hundred such diagrams had been constructed, certain characteristic "zones" in the late glacial and post-glacial sequence stood out. These zones are easily identifiable between sites and can be used to indicate climate and chronology. Radiocarbon dating of the peat, combined with pollen analysis, gives the best chronology in the world for the period (Flint 1957:285–288).

Prehistoric sites found in bogs can thus be dated. However, even though a site is not in a bog, if pollen has been preserved in the cracks of implements (Clark 1957:47) or on the land surface covered by the site, it is possible to match the pollen frequencies from the site with those from a nearby bog. This may date the site.

Intensive studies of pollen are being made in the United States and Canada (for example, Heusser 1960; Schoenwetter 1962), Mexico (for example, Sears 1952), Southwest Asia (Van Zeist and Wright 1963), and South Africa (Van Zinderen Bakker 1960), but many of the results have not yet been directly applicable to the dating of prehistoric man. Except in England, Scandinavia, and the western United States, well-dated pollen sequences have not been found associated with archeological remains. The problems of beginning pollen studies in an area are enormous. First, one must study the modern flora, and then find good sequences of ancient pollen. The latter is very difficult in arid and semiarid parts of the world.

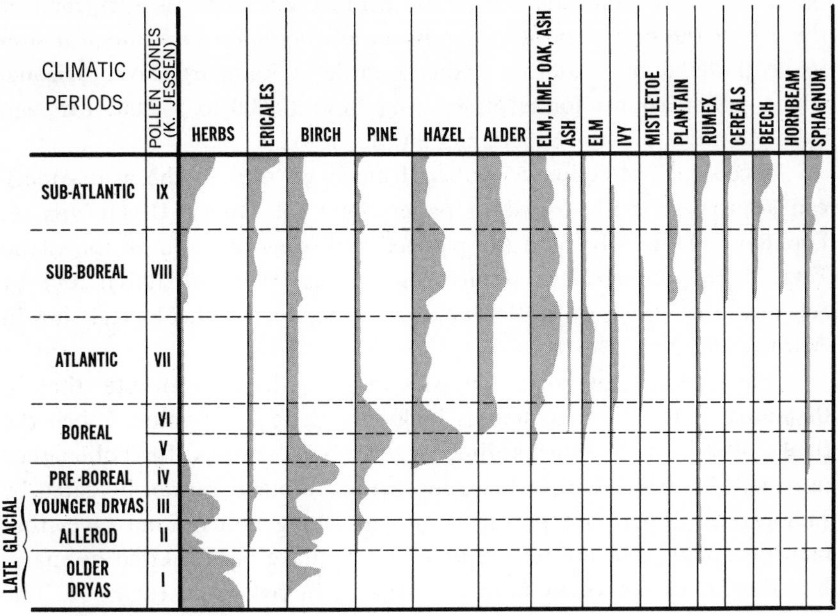

Fig. 26. Diagram showing development of vegetation in Jutland since the retreating ice-sheet uncovered the land. The diagram depicts the relative frequencies of pollen from each of the plant species listed. (G. Clark, *Archaeology and Society*, Cambridge: Harvard University Press, and London: Methuen and Company, Ltd.)

While acid peat or bog deposits are ideal sources of ancient pollen, dry silts, sands, and clays may contain enough pollen to provide a sequence. Dimbleby (1963:144) notes that acid soils with a pH of less than 5.5 may preserve pollen in large amounts. Oxidation and mineralization frequently destroy pollen, but grains are usually preserved in clays. Methods of extracting this pollen are always difficult (and at times impossible) to devise. In the past ten years pollen analysis has been applied to dry environments and to dry caves from which it had been assumed all pollens had disappeared (R. Anderson 1955; Kurtz and Anderson 1955; Sears and Roosma 1961).

Deevey (1951:178) says that "most American pollen stratigraphers have not looked hard enough [for pollen]." The five gram sample of breccia from Locality 1 at Choukoutien, site of the discovery of Peking Man, has yielded 132 pollen grains and 9 spores identifiable as deriving from 16 plants. The floristic assemblage, taken together with the faunal analysis, is considered by Kurtén and Vasari (1960) to indicate a cold (glacial) climate and the second or Mindel glaciation is identified as the age of the cave deposits. This is one of the oldest archeological sites to be pollen-dated. Another good example is Rampart Cave, Arizona, where pollen counts for levels ranging from 10,000 to 35,000 years ago were obtained (Martin, Sabels, and Shutler 1961).

Successful extraction of pollen from open sites in the arid American Southwest is illustrated in papers by F. E. Green, U. Hafsten, F. Foreman, and K. Clisby in the paleoecological monograph on the Llano Estacado region of New Mexico and Texas (Wendorf 1961); and by Schoenwetter (1962) on pollen analysis of eighteen archeological sites in Arizona and New Mexico.

The problem of pollen analysis in generally unfavorable (that is, dry) areas is to obtain sequences long enough to be of value. When the banks of streams or other sediments have been sampled for pollen they must still be dated. Unlike bogs, inorganic sediments cannot be dated by radiocarbon. There are problems also in taking pollen from caves that man occupied. The pollen frequencies may have been skewed by man's bringing in plants, or by animals bringing in pollen on their fur. The danger of mixing levels in an archeological site is also important, and in a cave with fallen rock pollen might enter through the interstices and be found many feet below its correct level.

However, pollen analysis can be very useful for both relative and absolute dating. Where only broad outlines of the climatic-floral history of a region have been worked out, it is often possible to identify pollen from an interglacial or glacial period without specifying the date. Where the chronology has been worked out in greater detail, one can place pollen profiles in terms of hundreds of years to give a rough absolute chronology.

Referring back to the discussion of changes in sea level and differences in shore elevation due to rising or subsidence, we may note here that pollen studies in salt marshes on the coast of the eastern United States have helped date these changes (Sears 1963; Deevey 1948).

PALEONTOLOGY

The study of bones in archeological sites may also give a rough basis for chronology. A change in climate will bring different animals as well as different plants into a region. Further, certain species of animals have become extinct since men appeared. Taking these two factors into account, one may use paleontology to establish relative dates. Thus one can assume a temperate climate if such species as *Elephas antiquus* (a forest elephant) are present, whereas *E. primigenius* (a steppe elephant) indicates a steppe or tundra environment of almost glacial conditions. For some periods during the Pleistocene even such gross estimates of dating as these can prove valuable. For the later stages of the Pleistocene it is often possible to get much finer distinctions. In France, for example, an alternation of the forest and steppe varieties of reindeer suggests the alternation of warm and cold stages during the final glaciation (Movius 1961:564).

In North America there was a sequence of extinction of mammals whose remains are found associated with those of early man. The mammoth, horse, camel, and several species of bison (Forbis 1956) all became extinct after the arrival of man in the New World. Although the exact dates for the extinction of these forms are not yet known, within a margin of error of perhaps 1000 years it is possible to say that man associated with mammoth remains lived before 6000 B.C. (Jelinek 1957: Hester 1960). The problem is that no species of mammal became extinct all at once. Instead, there is good reason to believe that small groups lingered on in isolated refuges long after the main body was extinct. Dating by means of faunal association is thus inexact and may at times be very misleading.

Smaller species of animals may give better evidence. Rodents and birds are often more sensitive indicators of climate than the larger mammals. Some molluscs and forms of snails are exceptionally sensitive to changes in climate (Lais 1936). Their presence or absence in archeological sites may therefore record the changes of climate in an area. When these changes can be related to varves, pollen, or soils, it is frequently possible to date them and the human remains found in association (Sparks 1963). In northern Ireland it has been possible to show changes in coastal environment since the time of human occupation through changes in tidal-zone molluscs found in archeological sites (Jope 1960).

It is hazardous to infer past climate from bones found in an archeological site. One must always recognize the fact that the bones were usually brought there by hunters and that they are not a random sample of the species around the site. This is a very important point to remember because many animals can live in a wide range of climate, and species that are more sensitive may not have been brought to the site. Furthermore, in places where men could choose among many species of game—anything from jackrabbits to mammoths—they may have hunted only one species. Thus a hunter living at the base of a mountain might habitually secure his food from the slopes of a mountain rather than from a valley or plain. If the hunter had a choice of food from a forest or plain, the choice of the former would lead the archeologist to believe he is dealing with a forest environment. In reality, both forest and tundra might have been within easy hunting range, yet they imply very different climates. These problems, with examples and citations to the literature, are discussed in more detail in Heizer (1960b).

One must also remember that inferences about the climatic tolerance of a species assumes that the tolerance has not changed over the millenia. This is not necessarily a safe assumption. Also, many species have a much greater range of tolerance than of preference. That is, some animals prefer one kind of environment but, under certain conditions, may be able to live in a different environment with little visible effect. The preferences and tolerances of various species are not in fact very well-known, and judgments about environment at the time archeological sites were occupied must be made with great caution.

If climate can be deduced from paleontology, it should be obvious that the climatic phase to which it refers may be fitted into a dated sequence.

DENDROCHRONOLOGY

Tree-ring dating, or dendrochronology, is severely restricted in application both in space and time. It has had its greatest use and development in North America, but as far as prehistoric man is concerned, it allows dating of only the archeology of the last 2000 years.

The method of tree-ring dating now in use was conceived about 1913 by Dr. A. E. Douglass, who was trying to determine whether tree rings held a record of past climate that could be related to sunspot cycles. Knowledge that some trees grew a ring each year and that by counting the rings one could determine the age of the tree had been known since the time of Leonardo da Vinci (Studhalter 1955). In the United States Reverend Manasseh Cutler in 1788 counted rings of trees growing on archeological sites at Marietta, Ohio, and concluded that the site was about 1000 years old. A similar attempt by M. Fiske, in 1820, yielded an age of 500 to 600 years for a Tennessee site; Squier and Davis, in their great volume on mounds of the Mississippi Valley, published in 1848, determined the minimum age of certain mounds by counting tree rings; Lapham (1855:75) calculated the minimum age of the aboriginal Wisconsin copper mining dumps at 395 years by counting tree rings; and other early examples of efforts to use this method are given by Fowke (1902:117–123). The actual inventor of tree-ring dating of archeological remains was Charles Babbage, who published a paper on the subject in 1838 (reprinted in Heizer 1962:48–51).

The method depends on the fact that trees growing in temperate zones have clearly defined annual rings of growth. After a winter period of dormancy, new growth cells are formed in the spring and continue to be added, though at reduced size, during the summer. If a person examines a cross section of a tree trunk, he can see these annual increments preserved as a series of concentric rings. To tell how old the tree is, it is only necessary to count the number of rings. For descriptions of principles and techniques see Bannister (1963), Giddings (1962), Glock (1937, 1955), and McGinnies (1963).

To get a chronology suitable for dating archeological materials, it is necessary to match series of rings from trees of various ages. The present chronology, which extends into the first century B.C., was developed by means of cross-dating. Because the size of tree rings depends upon the weather from year to year, one can match similar series of rings from the one tree to another. The relative sizes of rings for a given time will be similar and recognizable in properly selected samples. The system of cross-dating is illustrated in Fig. 27.

In principle the method is simple, but there are some practical problems. These are listed by Bannister and Smiley (1955:179) as follows:

> The establishment, in any given area, of a satisfactory tree-ring chronology, permitting the dating of prehistoric materials, is possible only when the following four conditions are met:
> 1. There must be trees that produce clearly defined annual rings as a result of a definite growing season.
> 2. Tree growth must be principally dependent upon one controlling factor.
> 3. There must have been an indigenous prehistoric population that made extensive use of wood.
> 4. The wood must be well enough preserved so that it still retains its cellular structure.

Conifers are the best trees for dating. In the American Southwest, where the system has been used most extensively, the Ponderosa pine (*Pinus ponderosa*) and a few other trees can be used. The longer sequences have come from the giant sequoia in California (*Sequoia gigantea*) and recently the bristlecone pine (*Pinus aristata*) found in the White Mountains of eastern California has been found to grow for over 4000 years (Schulman 1958). Unfortunately, wood from these trees does not occur in archeological sites and they are thus of no value for dating. A second difficulty is that the most dependable sequences come from trees growing in relatively arid climates where tree ring growth is dependent upon soil moisture. Much of the temperate world is not suitable because it has too much rain in the summer.

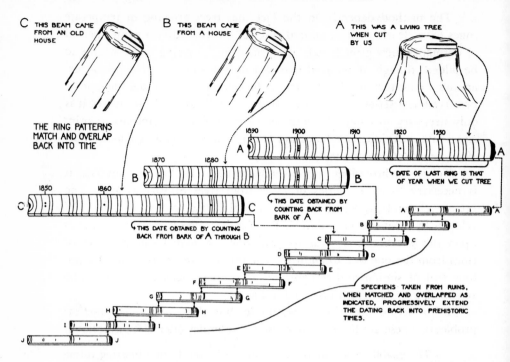

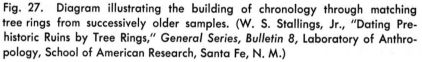

Fig. 27. Diagram illustrating the building of chronology through matching tree rings from successively older samples. (W. S. Stallings, Jr., "Dating Prehistoric Ruins by Tree Rings," *General Series, Bulletin 8,* Laboratory of Anthropology, School of American Research, Santa Fe, N. M.)

One must also find trees that have not tapped a permanent source of underground water. Trees from hillsides are better than those from river bottoms. The effect of permanent water may sometimes be just the opposite of the expected. In Europe it was found that trees living on the flood plains of rivers put on a very small ring during a wet year. By contrast, trees on the slopes put on large rings. The reason was that the trees on the flood plains were suffering from drowned roots.

When logs for dating are taken from archeological sites, other cautions must be observed. Any terminal date on a log, that is, its last ring, represents the time when the log was cut. It does not necessarily date the time the log was used. In areas where wood was relatively scarce and where it was necessary to cut it with primitive implements, logs were used repeatedly (Judd 1959:56; O'Bryan 1949). Bannister (1962) discusses four possible sources of error often involved in relating a tree ring date to its associated archeological material being dated.

13

OTHER METHODS
FOR DATING

ASTRONOMICAL DATING

For more than a hundred years there has been investigation of solar radiation and its effect on the earth's climate. Some of the early workers were interested in finding out what had caused the Pleistocene ice advances (Zeuner 1958:134–142). In an attempt to relate variations in solar radiation to climatic changes, the astronomical theory was devised. Without going into details, one may say that the theory is based upon the fact that the orbit of the earth undergoes perturbations so that the obliquity of the ecliptic, the eccentricity of the orbit, and the precession of the equinoxes have changed owing to the mutual attraction of the planets. This means that at intervals in the past the orientation of the earth relative to the sun has shifted. Parts of the earth then received more or less solar radiation. Accordingly, those areas receiving the greatest amount of radiation were the warmest.

Today the theory is not used to explain the cause of the ice advances, but only the fluctuations during the Pleistocene once the series of glaciations had started. The formulae on which the theory rests were devised by a number of mathematicians, of whom the most prominent is M. Milankovitch. Support for his theory from which dates can be derived for the various stages of the Pleistocene, comes mainly from Zeuner in his two major works, *Dating the Past* (1958) and *The Pleistocene Period* (1959, Chap. X). He believes there is a close correspondence between the dates arrived at with Milankovitch's calculations and elapsed time based on rates of sedimentation and with other time-reckoning methods used in geology (cf. Zeuner 1960). Many authors do not agree with Zeuner's dating of the Pleistocene. Even if one assumes that the theory is correct, the calculations themselves can be criticized for failure to take fully into account known sources of error (Flint 1957:300–301, 506–509).

CALENDARS

Strictly speaking, unless they are calendars, artifacts themselves do not give dates. Prehistoric people did not usually have exact calendars, although the Maya, who had an excellent calendric system, are prehistoric in the sense that they wrote no history that can be read. In the case of the Maya, it has not been possible to read very many of the glyphs they used for writing. Most of them that have been read so far pertain to the calendar, but a large number of glyphs are presumed to be literary in nature, rather than numerical or calendrical. The Maya are therefore literate, but for us they will remain (until their records can be deciphered), prehistoric. R. E. Smith (1955:3–4, 105–108) reminds us that even Maya stone stelae that bear inscribed dates, and from which one can tell when the city was occupied, can be used to date ceramic sequences only very rarely since stelae and pottery are not often directly associated.

Unfortunately, an exact correlation of the Maya calendar with our own (Christian) calendar is lacking. By the time of the Spanish conquest in the first half of the sixteenth century the Maya had stopped erecting dated stelae at regular intervals. There was, therefore, no direct link between 1520, the time of the Spanish arrival, and the last dated stelae, sometime before A.D. 1000.

Various workers have claimed to have the key to the Maya calendar. Even though its cyclic nature is known, authors disagree on its precise relation to our calendar. Two correlations differing by 260 years predominated and vied for approval over the years. When radiocarbon dating was first applied to the solution of the problem, the "Spinden correlation" appeared to be correct. Subsequent reanalysis with refined radiocarbon techniques and a more careful selection of material to be dated indicates that the Goodman-Thompson-Martinez correlation, which makes Maya dates 260 years younger than the Spinden correlation, is probably correct (Satterthwaite and Ralph 1960:165–184).

When stone stelae that bear dates in the Maya calendar system are found associated with structures, it is generally assumed that the stele was carved and set up on the date inscribed on the stone. As stelae were often erected at the time pyramids and temples were built and are clearly associated with these, one can usually date (that is, within 260 years, depending on which correlation is used) the structure itself and materials contained in it that were placed there at the time of its building. How-ever, this is not invariably the case; A. Smith (1929) and Ricketson (1937: 154–156) point out that dated stelae do not always date the building they are associated with, as older stelae were sometimes moved and re-erected without changing the date glyphs. The recarving of Maya stelae may also impose a problem of associational dating since the inscribed dates may refer to an earlier event not associated with the structure where the stele came to rest last (Baker 1962).

A similar problem has been encountered in connection with the ancient reusing of beams in Southwestern sites. While such beams may be dated by dendrochronology, the date may not refer to the age of the building or the room (O'Bryan 1949; Bannister 1962). The point is that even where absolute dating of particular pieces can be determined, these are not always precisely contemporaneous with associated features. A glance at the coins in your pocket or purse will show that there is a range of dates represented. If the coins in your pocket were found archeo-logically in a group you would date the hoard with reference to the latest or most recent minting date. The hoard cannot have been deposited earlier than the most recent coin, but can have been deposited later.

SEQUENCE DATING

Noncalendrical artifacts do not tell dates but if artifacts change in predictable ways through time, it may be possible to date them relative to one another. If one can build up either a generalized temporal se-quence of artifact types or associations of artifacts—as are implied in the very elementary "stone, bronze, and iron age" system, or a more special-ized one such as "Mousterian, Aurignacian, Solutrean, Magdalenian, Mesolithic"—he can take isolated examples and fit them into the stand-ard schemes. In this way archeologists can tell that a bronze knife must have been made later than a certain date; they cannot, with equal pre-cision, say that a particular flint tool was not contemporary, as flints were often used along with bronze. If an archeologist is familiar with sequences of paleolithic tool assemblages, he can look at a group of tools and tell whether it is representative of the Aurignacian or some other subdivision. By comparative typology he can thus date it within broad limits because the Aurignacian in general has been dated by radiocarbon. Even without absolute dates an archeologist could readily say that the material was earlier than the Magdalenian and other remains that are consistently found stratigraphically above the Aurignacian tools.

Sequences of artifacts are thus a key to relative chronologies, and at their best these tools may be referable to particular dated segments of prehistory. The system of relative dating depends on change that is nonreversible and continuous.

Pottery has traditionally been the most important artifact for purposes of dating. It is durable, being made of fired clay, and therefore accumulates in quantity rather than decaying and disappearing after it is broken and discarded. It is a medium of artistic and esthetic expression as the moist clay can be manipulated into different forms and can be decorated by surface impressions (stamping, molding, incising, and so on) or painting. Like any aspect of culture, the manufacture and functions of pottery are subject to patterning. That is, a group will not make every pot differently (nor, of course, every one exactly alike), but will usually settle upon a limited variety of shapes and decorative styles so that this becomes definable and recognizable as a ceramic pattern of the culture. Like all other parts of a culture, pottery changes over time, and by detecting these trends of change, an archeologist can trace associated cultural changes and make short-term time distinctions through careful study of the ceramic remains (Albright 1939; J. Gifford 1960; W. and H. S. Gladwin 1928b; Peake 1940:123; and Quimby 1960).

The recognition of the importance of potsherds as a guide to chronology in archeology could not come until reasonably exact excavation methods had been developed. Albright (1957:49 ff.) tells us that Furtwängler, who was primarily an art historian, was the first to see and use the significance of painted pottery for chronological purposes in classical studies, and that Petrie, in his report on the excavation of Tell el-Hesi (Lachish) in 1890, was the first archeologist to appreciate the importance of unpainted pottery for purposes of determining chronology (Petrie 1891:14–15, 40–41). Petrie wrote, "and once settle the pottery of a country, and the key is in our hands for all future explorations. A single glance at a mound of ruins, even without dismounting, will show as much to any one who knows the styles of the pottery, as weeks of work may reveal to the beginner" (Petrie 1891:40).

Sir Flinders Petrie, an Egyptologist whose work in Egypt began in

1881, developed the technique known as sequence dating (Albright 1957: 51–52). Predynastic Egypt was almost unknown and the graves that Petrie excavated at the site of Diospolis Parva could not be dated. The pottery from the graves was varied, but certain types were habitually found together. Petrie reasoned that different assemblages of pottery were of different ages. With this in mind, he analyzed such features as handles on pots and worked out a sequence showing their change into mere decorations. Such changes on pots were then correlated with changes in other artifacts from the graves, and he finally ended with a series of numbered pottery stages that he labeled "Sequence Dates" (Petrie 1901: 4–8; reprinted in Heizer 1959b:376–383). His series ran from s.d. 30 to s.d. 80, but Petrie had no way to tell what this range meant in terms of years. He began with s.d. 30 because he assumed (correctly) that he had not found the earliest Egyptian pottery. As a guess, Petrie suggested that s.d. 30 should be about 9000 b.c. We now know that s.d. 30 should be about 3500 b.c. (Emery 1961:28).

In the New World local styles of pottery had been identified and named in the Southwest by J. W. Fewkes, H. W. Holmes, F. H. Cushing, and other pioneer workers, but no clear idea of how to exploit pottery to extract time ordering was clearly worked out in North America until A. L. Kroeber in 1915, at Zuni Pueblo, collected surface potsherds from local sites and devised the method of surface seriation (Kroeber 1916; reprinted in Heizer 1960:383–393).

The method of sequence dating is implicitly used by most archeologists. One says that one artifact "looks younger" than another, meaning that because of certain stylistic details it looks more modern. This is as if a person were to study pictures of all the automobiles made by one company in fifty years. It would be very easy to get sequence dates for the cars because the trends of style from early to late would be apparent. However, cars are not quite the same as pots. The mechanical improvement of cars is shown in their size, shape, and ornament. Pottery is seldom improved; it changes according to the whims of its makers. Furthermore, several "types" may be in use at the same time. It is not always clear, therefore, when one has a hundred pots of different ages, which is the earliest and which the latest. Petrie was fortunate in being able to anchor one end of his sequence to pots of known date, but there was much room for error in the earlier periods. At best, sequence dating gives good relative dates. Accurate judgment of the rate of stylistic change is only possible by independent methods.

A final reservation should be mentioned. It is tempting to think of changes in artifacts from simple to complex and to suggest that simple things are older than more complex ones. In this case one might assume that flint arrowheads are older than bullets. In general this may be a correct assumption but it does not take into account technological lag. People having very crude artifacts may live alongside others with a more advanced technology. On typological grounds, the "stone age" aborigines of Australia would be placed much earlier than their "iron age" white Australian neighbors.

CROSS DATING

When one establishes a sequence of artifacts in an area, he then asks how it relates to neighboring sequences. The usual means for establishing relationships between areas is through cross dating (cf. Heizer 1959b, Chap. 10). Unless there has been widespread trade in exotic items, one can only establish general chronological correspondences between areas. Thus an archeologist might recognize an "archaic" site whether it occurred in New York or Arkansas, but he would have no sure way to determine whether the two sites were contemporary; in fact, they might have been occupied several thousand years apart. When trade items can be found it is often possible to state with certainty that the occupation of one of the sites did not occur before a certain date. If coins or pottery or bronze axes of a known date are found as trade items at undated sites, one can say that the sites were occupied no earlier than the date the objects were known to have been made in their homeland. In this way much protohistoric material from Europe can be dated relative to the centers of civilization in the Mediterranean. This extensional dating of European forms whose origin lies further south in the Mediterranean area has been done in detail by V. G. Childe (1957) and Grahame Clark (1952) in their books on the development of European cultures.

Cross dating works best when two groups exchanged easily identifiable objects. If only one-way trade can be discovered because traded artifacts have not been preserved, it is harder to assume close synchronism. That is, if stone axes were traded for sheep or grain, no palpable record of the transaction in the form of vegetal food would remain, or, at least, could be specifically identified. In some instances, perhaps after centuries, axes—being imperishable objects—might find their way a thousand or more miles from their place of origin. The rate of diffusion cannot be easily calculated, but one attempt at calculating the variable speeds at which knowledge of maize agriculture, copper metallurgy, and pottery spread has been made (Edmonson 1961).

The dependability of cross dating increases with the amount of foreign trade in which a group engaged. It is most dependable when one can date special trade artifacts such as coins, beads, or axes to a narrow range of time, especially when there has been reciprocal trade. In exceptional cases, cross dating can help establish absolute chronologies, as in the case of the Minoan sequence that was dated through Egyptian trade items (Kantor 1954:11–12, Fig. 1; Weinberg 1954:90), or in the extension of Puebloan period datings eastward toward the Mississippi Valley (Krieger 1947), but more often it merely places certain stages in one sequence opposite their contemporaries in another sequence.

The reader should keep in mind that imported items may have been carried from distant sources by modern collectors, and their apparent association with archeological sites or in an assumed archeological context (for example, as surface finds) is a special situation. Van Riet Lowe (1954) cites an example of a Neolithic axe from Norway that was found in South Africa but that could be shown to have been brought there by a recent collector, and soapstone carvings of recent Chinese manufacture have been found in Mexican sites (Heizer 1953). Such examples of what have been termed "travellers" or "wayfarers" are, of course, of no value for showing ancient diffusion or cross dating but serve only as traps for the unwary archeologist.

RATE OF ACCUMULATION

Attempts to estimate the rate at which habitation refuse accumulates have been made from the very earliest days of archeology. Petrie estimated that Egyptian sites accumulated about 20 inches a century. Vaillant, excavating the preclassic Mexican site of El Arbolillo, compared its refuse dump with a Pueblo occupation in Pecos, New Mexico. Because the Pueblo trash, amounting to 21 feet, had accumulated in six hundred years, Vaillant (1935:166–167) suggested that the El Arbolillo dumps, which had somewhat more debris, had probably been used for at least as long. In another instance, Braidwood and Howe (1960:159) estimated that a Near Eastern mound might accumulate at the rate of 2 feet in a generation. Lloyd (1963:73) describes how, some years ago, he computed the age of the first occupation of the site of Hassuna, in Iraq, on what he believed to be the rate of accumulation. He learned after a time, during which the radiocarbon dating method came into use, that his early calculation had been a remarkably accurate one.

An amusing case of an archeologist who achieved absolute accuracy of dating by utilizing what are known to be incorrect data is that of

Harrington (1933:171) who calculated the age of the Gypsum Cave culture, associated with extinct ground sloth remains, as 10,500 years (8500 B.C.), or three times that of the age of the Basket Maker culture. He used as his measure the assumed age of the Basket Maker culture at 3500 years (1500 B.C.). Since 1933 the tree-ring chronology has corrected the date of the Basket Maker culture to about A.D. 300, and as Kroeber (1948:681) points out, the age of the Gypsum Cave culture should thereby automatically have been reduced to about 5000 years (3000 B.C.). Radiocarbon age determination of the sloth dung from Gypsum Cave yielded a date of 8505 B.C. (10,505 years old), a figure that checks accurately with the original calculation of 1933!

There is no justification for assuming that the rate of growth of any particular site was constant throughout its occupation. Increase or decrease in population, the use of several debris dumps, the lateral expansion of a site, and similar factors will all skew deductions. An interesting example is that supplied by Fowler (1959:19–20) with reference to Modoc Rock Shelter in Illinois. Total depth of the archeological deposit was 27 feet, and from the several layers eleven charcoal samples were collected and dated by radiocarbon. Fowler, assuming the correctness of most of the radiocarbon dates, has examined the vertical position of each dated sample with reference to the amount of refuse between it and the next higher dated level in an effort to calculate rate of accumulation. He has found that the rate of deposition was constant at about one foot per 500 years for the period between 8000–5000 B.C.; increased to about one foot per 300 years between 5000 and 3600 B.C.; increased to 1.7 feet per 100 years between 3600–3000 B.C.; and decreased to one foot per 400 years between 3300–2700 B.C. These variable rates discourage any attempt in this particular site to apply a single rate of increment, but having discovered the fluctuations, the archeologist is then presented with an intriguing problem of why this occurred. Fowler found it necessary to re-examine his total information to learn whether variable rates of accumulation were due to such factors as climatic conditions, differences over time of number of occupants, variations in living patterns, and so on.

There are times, however, when an archeologist is forced to rely on rate of accumulation because no other means of dating is available to him. The subject is discussed in more detail, with numerous examples cited, in Heizer (1953:24–25; 1959b, Chap. 9) and Laming-Emperaire (1963:137–138). Wheeler (1956:45) says about rate of accumulation dating: "Such calculations have, if any, a purely academic or abstract interest. They make no allowance for the intermittencies and vagaries which, alike in human and in geological history, defy the confines of mathematical formulae." This is a rather positive statement, whose effect is to deny any possible validity or utility in increment dating. Actually Wheeler himself has, in at least one instance, made use of the method in attempting to determine the duration of time involved in the six successive building phases of the platform of the Harappa citadel that he excavated in 1946 (Wheeler 1947:81).

A fair statement about this method of calculating age is that there is no probability that a generally applicable scale or rate of accumulation will be discovered, due to the "intermittencies and vagaries . . . in human and geological history," but this denial of a general method should not beguile us into refusing to attempt to determine the rate of accumulation in particular sites as in restricted regions this information may be helpful in computing the age or duration of occupation of other sites. Merely by way of illustration, we may cite the observation of Yanine (1960) that refuse accumulated in the city of Novgorod 1000 years ago at a rate of about one meter per century. This information might be useful in computing the duration of other, but lesser known, medieval Russian settlements. Atkinson (1956:54–55) calculates the rate of covering by earth of the bluestone chips at the site of Stonehenge at 6 to 8 inches per century. Here again a possibly useful measure for rough dating of nearby but lesser known megalithic remains is available.

GEOGRAPHICAL LOCATION

It is sometimes possible to give a maximum age for a site by noting where it lies in relation to a datable geological feature. The date of the penetration of the Upper Great Lakes area in North America by early hunters using fluted dart points has been estimated in this fashion (Mason 1958). Geologists have calculated the dates when the Wisconsin glacial ice receded and when the various glacial lakes waxed and waned so that it is possible to say that man could not have lived in certain places before a certain time. A relatively well-known example of this is Danger Cave in western Utah (Jennings 1957:85–98) where geological history of Lake Bonneville was judiciously correlated with radiocarbon dates for the lowest levels that mark man's presence in the cave. By similar reasoning it has been possible to date Mousterian occupation of caves on the Italian peninsula (Zeuner 1959:243 ff.). During the Pleistocene, when the level of the Mediterranean Sea rose, some caves that lie close to the water could not have been occupied. Knowledge of sea levels and their approximate dates thus gives archeologists a date before which the caves could not have been lived in.

Many special dating methods give results that may at times appear to be at variance with the archeological-cultural dating. Unless the contradiction can be resolved either by correcting the dating method, or by finding the error in the archeological dating, it is safest to rely upon the less precise but generally dependable archeological dating. Auxiliary sciences do not always provide dates that are correct. An example of conflict between tree-ring dating and archeological dating is provided by Gladwin (1943:55–69), and one between radiocarbon and archeological-geological dating by Heizer (1951c:92).

PART 4

DESCRIBING AND INTERPRETING PREHISTORY

14

PREHISTORIC ECONOMY

WHAT IS ECONOMY?

Economy is multifaceted. What we know as "money-economy" was not known to prehistoric man. His economy consisted of the way in which he hunted, fished, and collected food. In it were included the way he farmed, harvested, and prepared food; the shelters in which he lived and the tools he used. Trading for exotic materials and the manner in which he traveled were included in his economy. In short, prehistoric man's economy was bound up with his everyday necessities. The proper way to begin to understand this economy is to examine the landscape that offered opportunities and set limitations on what man might do (Bennett 1944; Sayce 1961; Sears 1932, 1953; Wedel 1941). The method of viewing prehistoric cultures through their economics is well-illustrated in the works of Grahame Clark (1952, 1953b).

The materials with which man made his living were taken from among those in the natural world around him. This world includes plants, animals, minerals, the soil, weather, and people. In prehistoric times, in any given place, this natural world was often quite a different environment from the present one. One of the prehistorian's first tasks is to learn to know what this past environment was like.

Plants are basic to man's life, and they in turn depend on climate. Vegetation is dispersed in accordance with climatic zones, and the animals that feed on the plants are also restricted in their distribution. In turn,

187

man was limited in what he could hunt and gather by the well-defined distribution of animal species around the world. For most of human history man was not able to move plants and animals from their natural environments into ones better suited to his purposes. Such manipulations were possible only after the domestication of plants and animals.

Even with an environment full of plants and animals man had to be able to use them. He needed the technology for killing, butchering, or otherwise preparing and storing food. Mastery of the first two skills came quickly; even today we have not yet adequately solved the last. Most of the history of prehistoric man is the story of his increasing efficiency in acquiring food. Man still remains at the mercy of his environment to the degree that he can grow only certain crops in any particular area. Where modern man has produced plant hybrids, irrigation, and fertilizer, prehistoric man was largely nonscientific and was forced to get along with what luck and trial-and-error experimentation could produce.

No single environment, delimited by the distance a man might walk in his yearly round of hunting or farming, could supply all the material he might wish to use or might require. In many places this limitation meant that he did without or was forced to settle for a substitute. He might have wished for obsidian to make sharp blades, but have had to settle for flint. In other areas the acquisition of certain materials was a precondition to life. Prehistoric man could not afford to get himself so far out on a limb that he could not get back, but when man settled into farming villages and became more dependent upon one environment, and less mobile as well, he frequently found that he needed to trade for essentials. Salt was prized by farmers who lived exclusively on grain although it may never have been specially sought by hunters who found enough salt in the flesh they ate. Wood for fuel (Heizer 1963) and for houses was sometimes traded into areas where there was none. There are few areas in the world so bountiful in agriculture and so meager in mineral and plant resources as Mesopotamia, where even stone to build with is lacking on the hot desert plain. In fact water for farming here often had to be imported through irrigation.

However, during most of man's past trade was not for necessities because dependence on uncertain supply routes for vital supplies in prehistoric times would often have resulted in death. On the other hand, luxury items were avidly sought and widely traded. Gold, copper, amber, and shells were traded widely and their record provides archeologists with insight into the extent of man's known world. Such trade also tells us something of his acquisitive instincts and esthetic sensibilities. Trade in weapons and luxury goods has left a clear picture of the emergence of class differences and the relation of an "international economy" to the tribal status seekers. For one detailed study of aboriginal intertribal trade in which the particular items exchanged are specified and the complex network of trails is mapped, see the study of trade routes and economic exchange among the Indians of California by J. T. Davis (1961).

A point often overlooked is that trade may consist of more than two people or groups of people exchanging items on an I-will-trade-you-this-for-that basis. Hill's (1948) description of Navajo trade, Berndt's (1951) account of Australian ceremonial exchange, and Malinowski's (1932) classic account of the Trobriand "Kula-ring," illustrate the extraordinary amount of social action that may be involved. Archeologists who find the objects that were exchanged would usually think only of commercial trade, having no idea of the interpersonal aspects that had originally been involved. We are not saying that the social actions can be reconstructed, but familiarity with the fact that they may be involved in trade throws the archeologist's thinking about trade into a quite different perspective. At the minimum it makes him recognize that all trade need not have been commercial in our sense.

There is scarcely a facet of man's life that remains to be uncovered by the archeologist's shovel that is not in some way tied to economy. For this reason prehistorians do best when they write the story of man's economic life. However, even if information on economic life comes easier than other knowledge, it is not always found directly. One must often infer from what is known to what is not known to reconstruct man's economy.

DIET

Most bones found in sites represent animals that were eaten, although an exception is made in the case of some rodents and carnivores. An important job is to identify the bones as to species and, more importantly, the numbers of individuals of each species found (for more details and examples see Chap. 9). Reports of excavations are replete with lists of fauna, but few go further and try to suggest what cultural practices the array of bones can tell. A review of inferences about the cultural significance of animal bones from prehistoric sites may be found in Heizer (1960) and Reed (1963).

Reed (1963) recommends recovering all bones from archeological sites. Later a zoologist can sort them, saving and analyzing only the identifiable pieces. For later interpretation this is far more valuable than having only a casual sample of bones from a site. Recalling this recommendation, we may refer to Coon's (1951) report on the bones from Belt Cave, a stratified site in northern Iran. Coon recovered 14,006 pieces of bone, horn, antler, and teeth. Inferences on species, age, and sex of the animals were made on a sample of 1170 bones—less than ten percent of the total. At first glance it looks as if Coon had been unduly careless and, that in view of the important conclusions he proposes, he was remiss in not analyzing the entire collection of bones. We must recognize, however, that not all fragments of bones are identifiable. Most of the pieces Coon counted were unidentifiable scraps and splinters that are of no value to zoologists.

Identification of the species represented by bones is difficult and requires detailed analysis by persons thoroughly acquainted with comparative anatomy. In many parts of the world there are no collections of fauna that zoologists can use to compare with the ancient bones. In these cases it is usually necessary for the zoologist to begin his work by making his own collection of the modern fauna and preparing the skeletons so that they can be used for comparative purposes. Reed (1963:209) doubts that manuals of bone identification are very useful, especially in the hands of nonzoologists.

Bones that are in bad condition and that are of sufficient interest should be preserved. Reed suggests using some water-soluble glue (gum arabic or carpenter's glue) to harden them. He specifically cautions against the use of shellac, alvar, or celluloid in acetone because these substances do not penetrate well and often cause damage by peeling the surface of the bone. An excellent preservative for routine use is Bedacryl (Imperial Chemicals, Ltd.), a water-soluble resin that can be applied to wet bones or other organic material. Final cleaning can be easily accomplished in a laboratory.

A study of the bones will give some clues about butchering techniques. As for the larger animals, it was common practice for man to kill them away from the site and bring back only the best pieces of meat. By noting which parts of the skeleton are present, one can refine the calculation based upon a hypothetical maximum amount of meat from each species. A series of excellent articles by White (1953a, 1954, 1955b) provides some interesting examples of how an archeologist, working with an osteologist, can reconstruct the method of butchering game animals in the Great Plains area of North America. Furthermore, it is usually possible for the zoologist to tell how old the animals were when they were killed. This information may help him decide at what season the site was occupied and just how good a hunter prehistoric man was.

For example, we know the breeding seasons for most animals. The major skeletal changes in them take place within the first year or two. It is often possible, by noting size and whether or not certain bones were fused, to tell within a few months how old an animal was when it was killed. One can often also tell about the season of the hunt by noting such things as whether deer antlers had been shed because we know at what seasons these animals shed their antlers. In some instances the season can also be inferred if we know the climate. Some animals cannot live in certain places all year round. Migratory animals move between summer and winter pastures, and if the bones of migratory birds are found, one can tell that the site was occupied during the season of migration.

Some examples of inferences about the season in which events happened follow. Wedel (1961:74) notes that mud dauber (wasp) nests, presumably broken open to extract the edible larvae, were common in the trash layers of the Allen site in southern Wyoming. Since the mud dauber makes nests from May to September, a summer occupation by man is thus inferable. Winlock (1942:192) cites the various plant remains found in an Egyptian tomb of the Eighteenth Dynasty, which point to the interment as occurring in the month of November, a botanical conclusion confirmed by the inscribed date on the tomb wall of November 25, 1049 B.C.! One of the first efforts to determine the season in which an ancient event occurred is Parson's opinion of 1758 that fossil fruits from the Isle of Sheppey were "antediluvian" and that since the fruits were ascribable to the autumn of the year, the flood must have occurred at that time (Bowen 1958:135).

While at times it is relatively easy to show that a site was occupied during a particular season, it is not always so easy to say with equal assurance that a site was not occupied during another season. A review of published papers on seasonal occupation of sites as inferred from the age and species of birds and mammals whose bones are found in the refuse deposits may be found in Heizer (1960:112–114).

By observing the ages of animals killed, one may learn something about the skills of the hunters. Very old and very young animals were taken more commonly than mature beasts. We can also learn something of the current practices of meat cutting. Split and broken bones argue for the use of heavy cleavers or choppers, both to break off hunks of meat and to extract the marrow. Slice marks or scorings indicate the use of knives. Burned bones may tell whether animals were roasted. In some instances oil-rich bones were used as a substitute for firewood (Heizer 1963).

Bones also tell what animals were preferred. Some groups specialized in the taking of certain animals. For example, some Neanderthal groups ate little but cattle, others horses, and still others goats. In part this selection was due to availability, but it may also have had to do with what the people thought were good animals to eat. Food taboos are common throughout the world and may have considerable antiquity (Simoons 1961). To give a modern example, we can document the disappearance of the pig from the diet of people in Southwest Asia.

Today, when we find farm animals all over the world, we get the impression that many animals have a wide geographical range. If they have food, protection, and shelter provided by man, this is true, but under natural conditions the range of most species is limited (Reed 1959). For example, pigs and cattle were originally restricted to wooded areas whereas sheep and goats favored hilly or craggy unforested environments. On the other hand, antelopes, horses, and gazelles prefer relatively flat, open grassland. Within certain environments, some animals eat one kind of plants and other animals have quite different diets. These factors, coupled with the fact that many animals migrate seasonally, severely restricted what man found available to hunt in any given area. His specialization on one animal or another might often as well be attributed to availability as to preference. It is just this sort of problem that an archeologist tries to answer, using archeological facts along with knowledge of animal ecology to make his decision. For a summary of ecology and man in prehistoric Africa, see J. D. Clark (1960) and papers by Biberson, Leakey, Howell and Clark, and Hiernaux in Howell and Bourlière (1963).

Until man became adept at special techniques for catching animals, he was geographically restricted. The earliest men had no bows and arrows, or even spears. Men had to rely on the crippled or small animals they might catch by hand, carrion from the kills of carnivores, or animals trapped in bogs. They could not afford to be too choosy about what they ate. Specialization—in the face of varied possibilities—presupposes considerable know-how and the ability to produce on demand what is needed. The earliest men, therefore, must have been largely omnivorous, depending greatly upon plants for food and supplementing their diet with meat when they were lucky. For these people a mouse was important in their diet to a degree that decreased when large game animals could be easily killed.

Man's diet has ranged from almost complete dependence on animal food, as with certain Eskimo groups, to societies, such as Brahman Indians, which place practically complete dependence on vegetal foods; its scope ranges from the extremes of hunting—or better, scrounging—to full domestication and controlled food production.

It is relatively easier to learn about man's meat diet than about his vegetable diet. Plants are seldom preserved—and then rarely ever beyond 10,000 years. On the other hand, the charred remains of plants may last indefinitely. Charred seeds, for example, retain their morphological characteristics so that they can be identified by a specialist and unless they are subjected to mechanical destruction—breaking or crushing— they should last forever. The problem appears to be one of finding the seeds rather than of having them preserved. Recent work by one of us (F. H.) in Iran has demonstrated that a process known as "flotation" is useful even on material 9000 to 10,000 years old and that theoretically we should be able to recover seeds much older. By this method, dirt containing carbonized material is immersed in water or a chemical, such as carbon tetrachloride. Carbonized seeds and other organic remains float to the surface and can easily be collected. Until this and similar techniques are developed and exploited extensively, we will have to depend on our knowledge of the environment for data on what men might have eaten. For these inferences, geology, paleontology, and paleobotany give us the best clues. When pollen can be found, it is an invaluable clue, not to what was actually eaten but to available plants which might have been eaten.

People as well as plants were sometimes preserved in bogs, and the stomachs of these preserved bodies have been analyzed to show that early European farmers ate an amazing variety of plant food. It looks as if they gathered anything that was growing and cooked it into a kind of soupy porridge. H. Helbaek's (1950, 1951) analysis of the stomach contents of the Borremose and Tollund bog bodies shows that weeds were an important part of the diet in Iron Age Denmark, even though the Iron Age culture is classed as agricultural. The intestinal duct of Grauballe Man, a bog body from Denmark, contained fifty-nine species of wild plant remains and seven cultivated plant species (Helbaek 1963: 179). Warren (1911) identified the stomach contents of a Neolithic body preserved in swampy deposits in England and found that just before his death the man had eaten blackberries, rose haws, and *Atriplex* seeds. Emery (1961:243–246) lists the "menu" of a complete meal found preserved in a dry tomb of the Second Dynasty at Sakkara in Egypt. Bird

(1943:222) found a small wooden cup in a grave at the Playa de los Gringos site on the Chilean coast which contained flies and pupae cases. The flies were identified as a species which lives on meat and Bird was thus able to conclude that the cup had been buried with meat in it, perhaps as an offering of food to the deceased. A close parallel is noted by Judd (1954:62) from the site of Pueblo Bonito, New Mexico, where pottery bowls found in graves contained pupae of a muscoid fly (*Calliphoridae*) and body parts of ptinid and darkling beetles (*Niptus* sp.; *Alphitobius* sp.) whose larvae attack stored cereals. Judd concludes that the bowls contained offerings of cornmeal when they were buried. Grahame Clark (1953b:230) cites instances of foods found in Bronze and Iron Age containers in Europe. Carbonized seeds and grains are sometimes found in storage pits of open sites (Fowke 1902:409–410; Parker 1910:Plate 6; Shetrone 1930:58). A careful sifting of fireplace ash will sometimes reveal these. Pottery and clay sometimes trap the impressions of plants and seeds; these casts are indestructible and can be identified by a botanist.

Even though actual seed impressions in clay or carbonized seeds are not preserved, there may be ways to determine whether farming was practiced. Some ways of doing this are by identifying the function of certain tools as farming implements (e.g., hoes, sickles) or by finding prehistoric fields that have survived in the open (Curwen 1946; Delabarre and Wilder 1920; Hubbard 1878; Shetrone 1930, Figs. 25, 26) or that have been buried under earth mounds or refuse deposits (Hatt 1957: 228 ff.; Kelly 1938, Plate 1). Ancient fields buried under mounds might provide unique opportunities to determine whether fertilizers were used, and the amount of mineral depletion that has occurred. In addition, the fields might contain pollen from which the plants grown on the fields could be identified (cf. Cowgill and Hutchinson 1963; Martin and Schoenwetter 1960). Piggott (1959:99) concludes that the Celts of southern England in the fifth century B.C. probably held farms of about twenty acres as judged from the number and size of pit silos used for storing crops. Radford (1936) estimated from the dimensions of the granary of a Roman villa at Ditchley, Oxon, that the estate amounted to about one thousand acres. Such estimates, admittedly only that, are important in giving some idea of the magnitude of land-holdings in antiquity. In some instances ancient fields whose areas can be measured show up clearly in aerial photographs (cf. Bradford 1957).

Fecal remains also provide evidence of diet. In very dry regions feces are preserved in caves and their analysis has demonstrated how omnivorous prehistoric man often was. Along with seeds and plant fibers are found bits of bone from small rodents that were probably eaten whole (for a review see Heizer 1960b:108–109). The size of bone splinters in archeological human feces are often impressive. Callen (1963:194) states that dry feces from caves in Puebla, Mexico, contain bones and bone chips up to 12 by 16 mm. in size. An ethnographer (Scott 1958:326) relates that the Madakuyan of the Philippines "are used to chewing and digesting tough things and in addition to the bones of small fish and very heavy pieces of cartilage, often masticate and swallow some of the bones of a boiled chicken." Remains of plants may be preserved in yet another way. When plants decay or burn they can leave behind silica "ghosts" of their epidermal cells (Helbaek 1963:182–183). If the ground has not been disturbed, it is sometimes possible to recover these silica remains and identify the plants from which they came by microscopic study.

Thus it is often possible to find out something about the vegetal diet, but it is very difficult to tell just how important it was in relation to the animal diet. Unless we can uncover caches that indicate how much food could have been harvested or collected, we have no good way of estimating surplus production or acquisition. The absence of bones, or the presence of only a few, may indicate that vegetal products were more important than meat. In the few instances where quantitative studies have been made on the bones from several sites, it has been possible to distinguish clear-cut differences in the diets of groups of people it might otherwise have been assumed lived on identical foods.

J. T. Davis (1959) has critically reviewed a number of generalizations made by Southwestern archeologists about the relative importance of animal versus vegetal food in the diet of the occupants of specific prehistoric sites, and has shown that these for the most part rest upon very tenuous grounds. The archeologist must not only use judgment in reaching inferences on the basis of what is present, but must also keep in mind that a great deal more evidence has disappeared without any trace. It is this requirement—that the prehistorian balance what is known against an indeterminate amount of information that is not known—that makes the job of interpretation so difficult. As A. L. Kroeber once wrote, the training of anthropology consists of "learning to discriminate between better and worse judgments and better or worse evidence."

Archeologists can get useful clues on the food-getting routine of hunter-gatherers by consulting ethnographic descriptions. McCarthy and McArthur (1960:150–180) have written a detailed event-by-event description of the collection of food by an Australian tribe. The economic routine among the dry-land peoples of the peninsula of Lower California has been presented by Aschmann (1959) and Malkin (1962). Accounts of the food quest of the Ten'a of the Yukon River described by Sullivan (1942), of the Greenland Eskimo (Krogh 1915), the people of Zia Pueblo in New Mexico (Hawley et al. 1943) are cited as examples of the kinds of data available to archeologists that are useful in establishing a framework of reasonable possibilities against which the prehistoric data can be projected.

In areas where animals were painted or pecked on rock surfaces one can gain some idea of the species with which the artists were familiar. The great painted caves of southern France and Spain (Kühn 1955, 1956; Laming 1959; Sieveking 1962; Windels 1949) represent, in one sense, ancient zoological libraries whose main purpose was probably religious, but which also inform us of the kinds of animals the Upper Paleolithic peoples were familiar with. The prehistoric pottery of the Mimbres people of New Mexico is well-known because animals are frequently depicted (Nesbitt 1931). Here it is not so clear that only familiar animals were being painted since in this fishless region piscatorial representations are common (cf. Gladwin 1957:225–230), and there are composite "monsters" that surely never lived. Here the archeologist is faced with the problem of sorting out real from fanciful forms (Taylor 1948:187–189). That fish-forms portrayed on pottery vessels made and used in a fishless region may have been patterned after actual fish is suggested by the fact that Judd (1959:127–128) found scales of the gar pike in a Chaco Canyon (New Mexico) site. Today the nearest occurrence of the pike is in the Rio Grande River over one hundred miles to the east. A parallel is provided by the occurrence of marine forms represented in rock paintings in the interior of South Africa (J. D. Clark 1959:229–230).

A study has been made of the mammalian forms on Assyrian sculpture (Houghton 1877); there is one review of the ancient fauna of Mesopotamia as evidenced in art by Van Buren (1939); an entomologist's identification of arthropods portrayed on prehistoric Mimbres pottery from New Mexico (Rodeck 1932), a study of the domestic and wild animals appearing on cylinder seals (Frankfort 1939), and a review of animals represented on painted Greek pots (Morin 1911). North and South African petroglyphs and pictographs cover a very long time span so that a kind of "zoological dating" is possible by identifying styles and animals represented (Goodall 1946; Wulsin 1941, Chaps. 8, 9). Finally a large number of animals known to the ancient Egyptians were mummified and placed in tombs (Lartet and Gaillard 1907).

	Degree of Wear			
	1 (greatest)	2	3	4 (least)
Tollifero series (18)	1	6	9	2
Dentitions with caries	0	1	3	2
Dentitions with lost teeth	0	1	3	2
Clarksville series (38)	7	17	12	2
Dentitions with caries	7	15	12	2
Dentitions with lost teeth	2	12	12	2

TABLE 3

An interesting example of inference about prehistoric diet is presented by Hoyme and Bass (1962) in their analysis of two prehistoric populations in Virginia. The Tollifero site is late Archaic in time, and its occupants were either pre-agricultural or possibly beginning to practice agriculture. The degree of tooth wear exhibited in the sample of eighteen dentitions shows that the people had a coarse diet that produced rapid tooth wear but relatively little decay or loss of teeth. The Clarksville site is later in time and its occupants subsisted on agricultural products, chiefly maize. Here the teeth, as judged by the sample of thirty-eight dentitions, are in much poorer condition with a high degree of wear, and with correspondingly high incidence of loss of teeth possibly resulting from a soft diet of corn that is high in carbohydrates and that contributes to dental decay and tooth loss. The table above illustrates the situation.

TECHNOLOGY

Studies of diet lead directly into studies of technology. The two are often intimately intertwined. When technology is known in detail, it is possible to infer that certain kinds of hunting or farming were practiced. When an archeologist finds sickles at a settlement, he usually infers agriculture although in some cases sickles have been used to cut plants other than cultivated grain (Heizer 1951a). Bows and arrows indicate hunting of animals and a study of the kinds of points used may indicate what kind of game was being hunted. Bolas (stones tied to long cords for entangling the feet of game) are an old invention and were probably nearly as effective as spears or arrows. However, it is not always possible to tell what was hunted just by looking at the tools; absence of a tool may mean nothing. For example, people who lacked spears tipped with stone may have used perishable bone or wood points. One of the Mousterian skeletons at Mt. Carmel (Skuhl IX) showed evidence of having received a hip wound from a four-sided wooden spear (McCown and Keith 1939:2:74–75, 373), and from this we can verify what has seemed highly probable, namely, that the Mousterians used simple wooden spears. Some people may have preferred to snare animals or to catch them in deadfalls or other traps. Negative evidence does give some clues, however. This is especially true where sites have good preservation and a variety of wooden and bone tools are present.

If people had no bows and arrows, they were limited to trapping or hunting at close range. This might preclude killing certain beasts at all. Without the means for storing food, people had to spend most of their time gathering. This condition probably existed during most of human history. Furthermore, people who had to carry burdens on their backs were limited in the amount they could carry and the distance they could cover (Steward 1938). Sometimes this must have prevented dependence on some kinds of animals. For example, for many Indian groups the bison was only seasonally important before the use of the horse on the Great Plains. After that time Plains Indian economy was revolutionized and the people became almost totally dependent on the bison for the necessities of life (Ewers 1955). Lack of certain tools also prevented people from exploiting rich farm land. Before the mold-board plow was invented, people who could not break the sod were prevented from farming the prairie grasslands.

Such instances serve to illustrate a point—it is difficult to make inferences about diet from technological evidence alone. There are too many imponderables. We know only some of the ways of obtaining food; many others must have been developed and forgotten. Furthermore, we are at the mercy of the vagaries of preservation. We can rarely be sure that we have the total picture. The biggest and ever-present problem in archeology is how to fill the gaps in the record that have been caused by the disappearance of organic materials.

It is probable that remains of organic matter in archeological deposits can be detected, and in many cases identified, through chemical and physical methods so refined that they have not yet been attempted (cf. Cornwall 1958:70–71; Heizer 1960b:99–100). There are methods which are rather gross (in terms of those which are anticipated for the future) now available, such as determining that bone was once present from the presence of phosphate (Heizer 1960b:115); it is practically certain that in the future much more refined methods for detection of organic residues will be devised. The former presence of some feature such as a human corpse or wooden beams in archeological sites may be detectable only as a stain or "silhouette" (G. Clark 1960, Plate 17b; Biek 1963a, 1963b), and special techniques of excavation and recording are required in these situations.

There are many aspects to technology, not all of which relate to the food quest. First and foremost, a study of technology reveals the steady increase of man's skills. Thomsen devised the three-age system—stone, bronze, and iron—and it was applied to describe the cultural evolution of man (Heizer 1962). As Childe (1944b) has pointed out, the three ages each indicated a significant technological advance that allowed man to do many more things than had been possible before. Today most of the stages of prehistory have been defined on the basis of technology. Put into a series, the stages indicate an ever better mastery by man through tools of the world. As man learned to do new things with the resources about him, his economy was enriched. In some instances it meant that he was able to live better, that is, with less worry about food shortages. In other instances he was able to move into new areas, and in still others he was able to surround himself with luxuries. These advances in technology and the fruits derived from them eventually contributed to craft specialization, population increases, large political groupings, and social hierarchies. The culmination was the increasing complexity of society and the increasing technical mastery of the world that led to civilization as we know it. The broad story of the development of culture as it gathered in quantity and quality until civilization emerged has been told by Childe (1951, 1954) and, more recently, in a symposium volume edited by Braidwood and Willey (1962).

The study of technology can lead to inferences about man's cultural progress, but it is also informative about his relations with other people. In more recent prehistoric times it is often possible to trace the spread of technological knowledge into an area and to note the effect it had on the people. For example, a study of sites in Europe indicates that farming was not accepted by all at first and that a hunting and fishing way of life died slowly (J. G. D. Clark 1952). Even though a population tries a particular subsistence economy it may not always be able to count upon its productivity. Thus, the Hamitic herders between the Nile Valley and the Red Sea who depend largely on sheep, will sow a field of barley after one of the occasional rains, settle down and wait for the crop to ripen, and then move on with their flocks (Frankfort 1956:34). Total commitment to a specialized economy by prehistoric men was often hazardous and such dual economies must have been fairly common, but they are difficult to identify from archeological materials.

Study of technology may also reveal where and how objects were made. Metal tools, containers, and ornaments as well as some pottery were manufactured by specialists whose skills were beyond those of the common folk. When especially distinctive wares were made, it is possible to trace their trade throughout an area. When this trade has been charted one must ask what was traded in exchange. Such inquiry may reveal that grain, skins, or raw materials were being exchanged for finished products. Exotic items always imply trade, and trade—as opposed to tribute— usually follows a two-way road.

Caches of an artisan's tools or paraphernalia of a specialist may throw light upon the association of many items that otherwise occur only singly. A few examples may be cited. Mongait (1961:287–288) gives us detailed accounts of the contents of two burned houses in a Russian site, one of an artist, the other of a bead-maker; and Macalister (1949: 134–135) has described in detail an ancient Irish metalworker's hut. Wallace (1954) describes the contents of a basket-maker's kit from eastern California; Elsasser (1961) has collected a great deal of information on medicine-men's kits found in archeological sites in the western United States; prehistoric medicine bags of the Adena culture group of the eastern United States are described by Webb and Baby (1957:72–76); and Emery (1948:65) describes a royal tomb in Nubia containing iron ingots and a set of metal-working tools. Emery (1961:137–139) mentions a number of burials that were deposited on the perimeter of the tomb of a queen of the First Dynasty of Egypt. The bodies in these graves were those of special craftsmen such as sculptors, artists, sailors, butchers, each one accompanied by the characteristic tools of his trade. Dawkins (1880:384–388) provides a list and description of the items in a bronze- smith's hoard found at Larnaud, France. The hoard contained 1485 pieces, of which 163 are items used directly for smelting or working bronze, 266 are tools and implements, 211 are weapons, and the re- maining 845 are personal ornaments.

Mention may also be made of the marvelous models of daily life, activities, and familiar objects that are found in Egyptian royal tombs and from which much specific and detailed interpretation can be ex- tracted (Winlock 1942:25 ff.; 1955). The varied activities such as sowing, reaping, fowling, hunting, warfare, shown on Egyptian tomb paintings provide us with pictorial evidence of what and how things were done in dynastic times, and we can reconstruct from them many aspects of the ethnology of these ancient people. W. S. Smith (1958:138) cautions against assuming that the Egyptian paintings and engraved reliefs are always literally exact when he writes, "Because the Egyptian's pictorial record was unique among his contemporaries, it is now infinitely precious, but his remarkable powers of observation have paradoxically laid him open to criticism for his carelessness. Obviously he was not impelled by a scientific interest in the modern sense and was capable of all sorts of inconsistencies. Hence there is a danger in drawing too exacting conclusions from his work."

TRADE

Trade was undertaken in many ways. The simplest sort must have involved the casual meeting of two groups of people or their representatives who bartered or exchanged goods. This sort of exchange would be expected among nomadic peoples. Before the use of metal or pottery such trade must have been limited, but we know of instances in which certain kinds of flint, calcite crystals, stalactites, sea shells, and obsidian were traded. None of these were necessities to the people who obtained them, although the imported flint and obsidian made better tools. It is worth noting that we do not find evidence of regular trade before the end of the Pleistocene, but sporadic finds indicate that at least a desultory trade in nonsubsistence items was going on. Saint-Perier (1913:49) lists molluscan species that are present in Upper Paleolithic sites in Lespugne, France, and finds that three species come from the Mediterranean and two from the Atlantic. In this case, where there is no other hint of trade relations with these two coastal areas, both of which are about two hundred kilometers distant, one cannot make a definite decision on whether the mollusc shells occur at Lespugne through trade or because the occupants happened in the course of time to visit both coasts and collect the shells.

In addition to the instances where trade in durable items can be proven (as, for example, between coastal Southern California and the Puebloan Southwest—see Brand 1938; Colton 1941; Heizer 1941b; Tower 1945), there must also have been much trade in such perishable materials as feathers and skins. When one finds objects of very distant origin in archeological sites, the logical explanation is that they are the result of intergroup trade. However, an alternative explanation, the possibility that the items have been transported from their area of origin to their outland resting place in the bodies of migratory animals, should be tested. A number of examples of the transport of artifacts (mainly weapon points) by migratory animals are cited by Heizer (1944) and Carneiro (1958).

Objects for decoration and ritual were probably the most favored trade items because prehistoric man was ordinarily self-sufficient as far as his basic food and tool needs were concerned. Probably to be interpreted as imported luxury items are Mesopotamian cylinder seals of the Uruk-Jemdet Nasr period (sometimes called the Protoliterate period and known to date from 3500–2900 B.C.) that have been found in Gerzean (that is, Late Predynastic) period graves in Egypt. The graves cannot be directly dated but are relatively dated as falling between Sequence Dates 50–63 (see above for explanation of S.D. system). These small cylinder seals are therefore highly significant both as evidence of trade and because they permit the fairly precise dating of the Egyptian material just prior to the First Dynasty (Frankfort 1956:122–123; Emery 1961:30; W. S. Smith 1959:19).

One of the earliest well-established trade routes extended for hundreds of miles in Southwest Asia between 7000 and 5000 B.C. During that interval large amounts of obsidian, mostly in the form of blades, were distributed along the Zagros Mountains from eastern Turkey to southern Iran. Most of the stone blades in many of the agricultural sites dating from that period are of obsidian. By contrast, earlier and later peoples did not have obsidian in the same amount (Hole and Flannery 1962: 145–146). The evidence argues for the establishment of a dependable trade route and possibly even the supply of the route by specialists in the art of chipping obsidian. The sources from which the particular raw material came have not yet been identified, although the location of many obsidian fields is known (Esin and Benedict 1963:341). Another problem is to discover what was being traded in return.

Similar trade routes were established in North America to carry copper and shells. The Ohio Hopewell Indians engaged in trade from the Atlantic Ocean to the Rocky Mountains, a distance of some 2000 miles (Griffin 1958:1). Somewhat later more formal land and sea trade routes were established in Meso-America. These came under the protection of the Aztec and Maya rulers and were important in supplying luxury items to them (Cardos 1959; Chapman 1957).

Unless a site is the indisputable place where trade goods were made, it is often difficult to determine that certain items were traded. For example, pottery could be made by almost anyone, and for the most part trade pieces were probably only the finest wares that were made by specialists. However, this need not necessarily be the case. In Meso-America today there are villages where the people make pottery for a whole region. They carry it to market periodically and it is widely distributed. In Crete (Xanthoudides 1927:118) and in Peru (Bruning 1898) there are itinerant potters who travel about the country and settle down for a time where good clay occurs and a profitable market exists for their wares. When their sojourn is no longer profitable, they move on. In antiquity such practices may have occurred and might account for some of the distributions of prehistoric pot forms or styles (cf. K. Dixon 1963). Itinerant bronze age smiths (perhaps like the Sleib or Solubiyeh traveling tinkers of the Syrian desert—Pieper 1923) in Europe have long been recognized as one of the agencies of diffusion of metal-working techniques, as well as weapon and ornament types.

An interesting study by Grace (1961) concerns the ancient wine trade of the Classical period in the Mediterranean as evidenced by two-handled pottery amphoras in which the wine was transported. When pots are not especially distinctive one might not suspect trade. It is here that routine use of technical analysis is important for it can give the clue that trade was practiced and then help find the sources of materials. Shepard (1948) has written a detailed study of the Meso-American trade pottery called plumbate (so named, but incorrectly, on the assumption that it was a lead glaze; however, it proves to be a vitrified surface formed from fine-textured clay of high iron content fired in a reducing atmosphere of about 950 degrees centigrade) which has been found archeologically from Lake Nicaragua in the south to Tepic, Nayarit, in the north. While the place of manufacture still remains unknown, it can be determined from technical analysis of the lustrous vitrified surface and the paste of the pottery that it all derives from a single source.

Shepard (1961) makes a distinction between *intrusive* pottery, which was secured by trade from an outside area of another ceramic tradition, and *trade* pottery, which was traded between settlements within the geographical area of a ceramic tradition. The distinction is a useful one, as intrusive pottery can be used to correlate regional chronologies (for an example see Haury's matching of the Anasazi, Hohokam, and Mogollon cultures of the Southwest in Gladwin *et al.*, 1937:212–219) and trade pottery is useful in correlating local sequences.

STANDARDS OF EXCHANGE

Minted metal coins were not used for exchange in prehistory. For the most part the world was on a barter or exchange system, but there are a few instances in which a form of currency was in use (see Loeb 1936; Bessaignet 1956). The Aztecs and Maya used the cocoa bean (Chapman 1957). Some Indian groups in California measured wealth in tubular sea shells (*Dentalium indianorum*), the longer being the more valuable. We know that today tribal peoples in many countries reckon wealth in the numbers of livestock they own. When they make large purchases a certain number of animals are judged to be an equivalent value. In such systems so many chickens may equal a pig, and so many pigs may equal a cow, and so on. There is an element of barter economy in this, but at the same time quite arbitrary values are given to things and these values need have little relation to the intrinsic worth of an object. Thus a pig with particularly well-developed tusks may bring more than one with small tusks.

Without some system of arbitrary value-units trade would not flourish because it would be limited by the amount of real worth a man could pack on his back. The use of coins relieved man of having to tote a load of bloody hides home in trade for a copper ax—unless, of course, he happened to want hides. The use of coins enabled much more diversified exchange. A man with hides could sell to a man who wanted hides but who did not have axes to trade. The hide seller could in turn buy an ax from a man who did not want hides.

On a surprisingly simple cultural level we note some specialization of labor where certain individuals or families work to produce finished products such as arrowpoints, fishnets, bows and arrows, which they trade to their village mates for other finished items or for food. Ordinarily such craft specialization is found in settled village populations who support themselves by agriculture, but the Indians of central California, whose economy was based upon salmon and acorns and who are therefore nonagricultural, did practice craft specialization. An archeologist who assumes too readily that craft specialists come into existence with farming villagers might thereby overlook the possibility of specialization of labor (for additional discussion, see Heizer 1958).

SHELTER

To the degree that people could shelter themselves they could live in areas that were too hot or too cold for constant exposure. Earliest men were content to lie under a shady bush or tree during the day and to huddle in a burrow during the chill of the night. We do not know when they learned to build shelters or when they learned to clothe themselves with skins. However, once they had done either, they could vastly increase their geographic range. The use of fire not only supplemented their shelter but also enabled them to cook food. What are probably, though not certainly, the most ancient shelters built by man are the curved stone piles found in Olduvai Gorge at the site of the camping spot of *Zinjanthropus* whose age is determined by the Potassium-Argon method as about 1,750,000 years (Curtis 1961; Gentner and Lippolt 1963). The oldest known use of fire by man is at the site of Choukoutien where the bones and tools of Peking Man (*Sinanthropus*), dating from the Second or Mindel Glaciation, were excavated. Use of fire by man in Africa and Europe came somewhat later in Middle Acheulean times just before the Third or Riss Glaciation (Oakley 1955a; Heizer 1963).

In one sense man's houses show his capabilities as a food getter. The camps of hunters are ordinarily small and temporary. Usually impermanent shelters seem to have been favored. There is some evidence, however, that the reindeer hunters who settled so successfully in the rock shelters of France during the Pleistocene may have constructed a sort of shelter under the rock overhang to give additional protection (Peyrony 1939:90). At best this would have been a framework of wood overlain with skins, but it may have lasted from one season to the next. The animal bones in the rock shelter deposits suggest that some of the groups stayed in one place the year round—for all we know, groups may have stayed in one shelter for generations. It is certain that these men could not have carried a shelter very far with them if they migrated because they had no pack animals. Hunters on the loess lands of Central Europe used the bones of mammoths as framework for their houses and probably roofed them over with skins (Klima 1954; Mongait 1961:91–94). Even wood was scarce there and the people burned oil-rich mammoth bones for fuel. If these men had not known how to build houses and to make fires, they could not have lived in these regions.

One of the best adaptations to varied climates is the earth-covered house. In prehistoric times some of these consisted of pits dug into the ground and roofed over with wood and branches covered with mud or skins. The low-lying houses were sheltered from the wind and were well-insulated from heat and cold by the thick layers of dirt on all sides. Of all the houses built in temperate-to-cold climates, these have enjoyed the longest popularity. In fact some of the dwellings of the Paleolithic mammoth hunters of Russia were essentially pit houses and our own pioneers in the West built similar houses of sod.

Many kinds of houses are made from mud. Slabs of mud dried in the sun can be piled on one another as bricks; or, indeed, bricks can be made in wooden forms and baked. Mud can also be layered on a wall, a little bit being added vertically each day, and allowed to dry in the sun. Another system is to build forms for the walls and to tamp mud between them, allowing it to harden in the sun. Still another way is to build a framework of sticks in the form of loose matting and to plaster this with mud to build up a substantial wall. These houses are ordinarily roofed with beams laid across the walls. The beams are then covered with sticks or brush and packed over with mud or earth. The result is an economical house that serves admirably in a hot, dry climate. Rain will eventually ruin such houses, but with reasonable care a mud house will last from fifteen to fifty years. Brick houses, of course, last much longer.

While excavating the floor of the priest's house in the Oval Temple at Khafaje (Iraq) dating from the twenty-sixth century B.C., a number of large mud wasp nests were found. These nests had been built in the angles and joints of the complicated wooden-beam and mat ceiling. From the negative "casts" of the construction elements which were preserved in the attachment surface of the wasp nests, a detailed reconstruction of the wooden ceiling could be made (Lloyd 1963, Plate 25).

The use of stone for building seems to have been a rather late invention, but some of the earliest Mesopotamian and Anatolian mud houses were reinforced, especially at their bases, with stone. However, successful stone construction demanded either careful shaping of the blocks so that they could be laid dry, or else a knowledge of mortar. Stone houses were often plastered on the inside, but where mud was scarce skins could be hung to keep out drafts.

The kinds of houses used depended largely on what building materials were present, but even with limited resources there were alternatives. One of the most unusual villages ever constructed has been excavated at Beersheba in Israel (Perrot 1955a, 1955b). The houses, built entirely underground, resemble an ant colony with passages leading to the rooms. The excavators reported that it was pleasant working underground during the baking heat of the day because there was good ventilation and the heat did not penetrate the earth. In these houses no wood was needed though some passages were lined with stone slabs.

In many parts of the world abandoned houses soon fall down. In Yucatan one finds only a little elevated earth platform on which once stood a thatched house (Bullard 1960). Where there was enough grass or straw and the weather permitted it, houses were built of thatch. These served to keep off the rain and sun, but were of little use for conserving heat. Similar structures are built by nomads whose seasonal migrations take them into warm climates. The same group of people occasionally have winter houses that last from year to year, and seasonal houses that are rebuilt every year.

People who live in tents leave characteristic though easily dispersed remains. There is usually a fireplace, often in the form of a little hollow surrounded by or lined with stones (Wedel 1961:262). The edges of the tent may be ditched to carry off rain water or they may be outlined by a row of rocks that were used to hold down the edges of the tent. Inside the house area one may find a platform or layer of rocks on which the people placed objects that they did not want to expose to rain or dirt, and a fireplace. These remains are on the surface and have little chance of preservation if the land is plowed or otherwise disturbed.

Archeologists can misinterpret archeological features as houses. G. Clark (1960:116–117) explains that the excavators of the Neolithic settlement of Köln-Lindenthal near Cologne interpreted borrow pits (originally dug to secure earth and later filled with garbage) as houses and failed to recognize the rectangular timber structures they found as dwellings. Piggott (1959:84) shows that the same misinterpretation was made in southern England, partly for the reason that inadequate excavation techniques in the early work failed to yield evidence of the presence of timber houses and farm buildings.

As G. Clark (1957:197) has pointed out, there is often a close correspondence between the size of settlement and the kind of economy practiced by prehistoric man. Almost invariably the settlements of farmers are larger than the settlements of hunters (cf. G. Clark 1954:8) because there is a limit to the size of group a purely hunting and gathering economy can support. For some relevant statistics see Table 4. The limit depends largely on the number who can live through the worst season or through a succession of bad years. This, in turn, depends on the amount of game and vegetal food and the efficiency with which the people can get it.

The size of a settlement is also partly a matter of preference. Some people preferred to live in large groups whereas others preferred smaller ones. We see these differing attitudes in the homesteading farmers of the United States as opposed to the pueblo-dwelling Indian farmers of the Southwest. On the one hand each family lives on its plot of land; on the other, all families live in a central village and the farmer walks to his fields. One system stressed independence of action while the other stresses community living.

The size of a settlement may also depend on other preferences. Some areas were probably always more active socially while others were more isolated or frontier areas. Sites at a distance from established trade routes may have seemed less attractive to some peoples even though the level of subsistence may have been equally favorable.

Despite all the sociological reasons for the different sizes of settlements, however, other things being equal there were great inequalities

	Economy		
Site	Hunting-Gathering (Mesolithic)	Early Farming (Neolithic)	Developed Farming and Technology (Bronze Age)
Nørre Sandegaard II, Denmark	100		
Nørre Sandegaard III, Bornholm, Denmark	290		
Oakhanger, Hants, England	160		
Star Carr, England	240		
Teviec, Morbihan, France	240		
Windmill Hill, England		93,080	
Fort Harrouard, France		68,760	
Aichbühl, Germany		6,300	
Moosseedorf, Switzerland		1,000	
Robenhausen, Switzerland		12,100	
Wasserburg Buchau, Germany			15,000
Gournia, Crete			24,280
Gla, Greece			97,120
Los Millares, Spain			50,590
Troy II, Turkey			8,000
Averages	206	36,248	38,998

TABLE 4.
Relation Between Size of Site and Economy
(Area in square meters)

The figures listed above should be taken as general indications only. Precise calculations of sizes of settlements is difficult. Comparisons between sites is hazardous because of particular topographic or environmental conditions, and the kind of houses or shelters present. Reports frequently fail to state sizes of settlements and in cases where sites were occupied over long periods it is hard to state precisely what the size of settlement was for each period. After effective agriculture there begins a great disparity in the size of sites even within one cultural tradition. Some sites, for economic or social reasons, become more important than others and are not strictly comparable with them.

This chart was taken from a much larger list compiled by Ronald Weber, a student at the University of California. It includes the largest and smallest sites of each economy in Weber's list along with three of intermediate size.

between the lives of hunters and farmers. The latter had an assured food supply unless they had settled on poor land. They could readily grow a surplus, and this could be stored against want in the future or traded for goods and services. Population would therefore increase. The history of food producing peoples is one of population expansion and the colonization of "underdeveloped" areas.

TRANSPORTATION AND TRAVEL

Trade, colonization, and migration imply transportation. For most of his history man had to depend on his feet for travel and on his back for transport. This severely restricted his movements. Boats were probably the first improvement in man's means of travel. Simple rafts and dugout canoes were among the first conveyances, and they were followed by vessels with oars and sails. Animal transport, so far as we know, came late although it is conceivable that the dog was used for packing or traction by the end of the Pleistocene. The animals used for transport include the reindeer, elephant, dog, horse, donkey, ass, ox, water buffalo, sheep, goat, and llama.

The extent to which culture change may be effected by adoption of an efficient means of transport is illustrated by the adoption of the horse (from Spanish stock) in the Plains-Plateau area of North America. A careful study of the Blackfoot tribe by Ewers (1955) discusses in detail the cultural changes engendered by the horse. H. Wilson's (1963) analysis of culture change among the Plains Indians leads him to the conclusion that these people developed technologies that are comparable to those of some tribes with agricultural economies. From this he makes the point that there is not, as is often assumed, any precise correlation of social organization and the economic base of a culture.

The use of wheeled vehicles caught on very slowly because they require the services of a draft animal and because most areas require extensive preparation (such as roads) before carts can be moved easily. It was also important to have something worth transporting. Forests, mountains, swamps, and sandy areas are virtually impassable for primitive carts. The hard-packed deserts of Mesopotamia and Egypt were most suitable for traverse, and the animals and the incentive to move goods were present there early. It is likely that the earliest wheeled vehicles in Mesopotamia were reserved for the use of persons with high status and social prerogatives, and not for routine transport of goods. Even today, as the modern traveler to the area is surprised to learn, the rural villager makes little use of the wheel.

By interpreting evidence on climate, geography, plants, animals, and artifacts, the archeologist can learn a great deal about prehistoric man's economy—his struggle to live and improve his lot. However, man's past was not only tied up in technology and in environment; he was also a social being, and by the painstaking and imaginative examination of archeological evidence, we can learn something about the less tangible aspects of his life.

15

DETERMINING THE USE
OF ARTIFACTS

Identifying the use of objects that were made by prehistoric peoples is often a real problem for archeologists. In fact, sometimes it is not even certain whether or not a piece is natural or man made. Even if we are certain that an object is an artifact we must recognize that it may have served many purposes. We cannot always be certain when we identify a chipped, pointed, flint implement as an arrowpoint that it did not also serve as a scarifier, graver, awl, or punch. A hand-stone (mano) used for grinding seeds may on occasion have been used to crack open bones to remove the marrow, to break firewood, to grind a lump of red ocher into red paint powder, to pound a tent-peg into the earth, and so on. Woodbury (1954:92–93) lists many uses of the hammerstone among Indians of the Southwest and then utilizes this list to help him guess the possible uses of archeological examples.

We must also contend with objects that are not clearly one tool or another. For example, flint knives, points, and scrapers may be very similar in shape and size. Finally, and still more difficult, are those objects for which we can make no reasonable guess as to their purpose. Judd (1959:290) has written: "Unusual pieces are the sore thumbs of an archaelogical collection. There is no taxonomic pocket into which they can be dropped conveniently. Their very uniqueness makes them conspicuous and tempts the finder to speculation." As a result of specula-

210

tion one frequently finds these artifacts labeled "ceremonial object" in archeological reports. An example of an artifact of unknown use is illustrated in Fig. 28.

For typological analyses it is not necessary to know the use to which objects were put, but for inferences about the activities of prehistoric peoples it is necessary. Unless the uses of objects are unequivocal—and this is rare—one usually begins by comparing them with similar objects in use today among primitive people (Ascher 1961a; M. Smith 1955; Thompson 1956).

Ethnographic Analogy

Items made and used in a certain fashion by primitive peoples provide the archeologist with an analog of an item that is similar in form and material to one that has been recovered from a prehistoric site. He may thus identify the prehistoric object by its similarity to the more recent one whose function is known. We can gain an understanding of how stone was worked by grinding or chipping; how clay was fashioned and fired to make pottery; how holes were drilled in stone; and how shell, wood, and leather were shaped to produce artifacts by observing modern primitives as they fashion these materials. There are a large number of published ethnographic accounts that contain descriptions of manufacturing processes, but we cite only Te Rangi Hiroa's *Samoan Material Culture* and Blackwood's (1950) monograph on the technology of a stone age New Guinea tribe as examples.

Macalister (1949:99), in a book on the archeology of Ireland, makes excellent use of the method of ethnographic analogy in interpreting prehistoric materials:

> It is not too much to say that a study of the contemporary cultural ethnology of the South Sea Islands must now be regarded as a *necessary* preliminary to any serious study of the cultural ethnology of Ireland down to at least 1500 years ago. A student of Prehistoric Ireland may go to school under the instruction of a lowly Arunta of Central Australia, without the least sense of incongruity; and he will assuredly come back from his teachers enlightened with an illumination which he could never have drawn from any other source.

Père Lafitau in his *Moeurs des Sauvages amèricains comparées aux moeurs des premiers temps* (Paris 1724) produced one of the first attempts at a systematic comparative ethnography by comparing the American Indians' tools and customs with those of "antiquity," by which Lafitau meant mainly the peoples described in Homer's *Odyssey*.

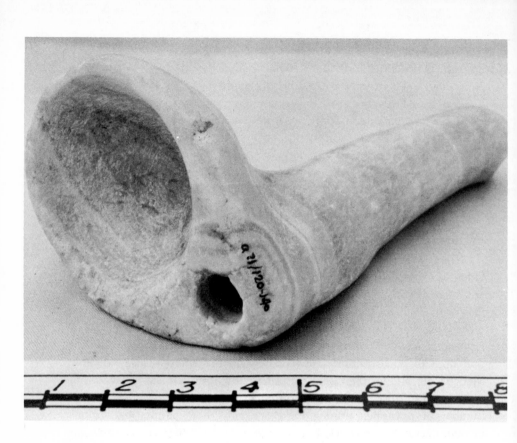

Fig. 28. An object of undetermined use found at Ali Kosh, Iran, dating between about 6500 and 6000 B.C.

Native pottery-making has been frequently observed and recorded in publications—see, for example, Conklin (1953), Fischer (1963), Fontana, et al. (1962), Foster (1955, 1956), Guthe (1925), Hayden (1959), Hill (1937), and Rogers (1936). Attempts to see archeological implications and applications of modern pottery-making techniques have been published by Foster (1948, 1960a), Thompson (1958), and Shepard (1963:14–22).

Our knowledge of flint-chipping comes primarily from first-hand observations of native peoples engaged in the act. The reader is referred to (Hough 1897), Holmes (1919), and Squier (1953) for further information on aboriginal stone-working methods.

Grahame Clark (1953a:355) proposes that identification of prehistoric forms by ethnographic analogy should be restricted to cultures having a similar subsistence level as well as approximately the same ecological background, and Childe (1956:51) and Willey (1953:229) concur. One would not compare prehistoric Eskimo artifacts with those used by the modern desert Bushmen of Southwest Africa and expect to learn the uses of bone snow knives and sea mammal harpoons. Nor would an archeologist compare the tool inventory from a "stone age" prehistoric site in the arid Great Basin with the metal-using cultures of the tropical west coast of Africa for the reasons that the two cultures are too dissimilar in level of technological development and occupy markedly different environments.

We are on much surer grounds in interpreting the way or ways in which a prehistoric object was used or the processes by which it was produced when there has been historical continuity of culture. In Europe the study of prehistory is considerably aided by citing persistences in the modern period of forms or practices in the peasant or folk cultures that are similar to archeological occurrences (E. Evans 1956). J. G. D. Clark (1951, 1952) has applied this method with excellent results, and Gunda (1949) gives us examples of the persistence of plant collecting in the economic life of Eurasia. In the United States the "direct-historical approach" (discussed above) provides the opportunity, by working back in time from historic village sites occupied by identified tribal groups, to determine historical continuity of culture complexes that have been ethnographically identified. An archeological example is Kehoe's (1958) attempt to settle the problem of the function of rings of boulders found in the Great Plains area. By gathering ethnographic examples he is able to demonstrate that these stone circles are tipi rings.

In many instances where traits have persisted in one area over a very long period of time, we may conclude that there has been continuity of culture. Winlock (1942:193, 207) calls attention to the identity of basket forms found in Dynastic Period Egyptian graves and modern baskets made at Edfu in Egypt and Nubia, and the same situation exists in regard to special techniques of hairdress. Emery (1948:17, 44–47) notes an ancient, round leather shield with a central boss found at Qustul, Nubia, which is identical with shields still in use by the modern Beja tribes of the Sudan; a camel saddle with an antiquity of 1500 years, which can be precisely duplicated by modern examples in Nubia; and Nubian graves dating from 2270–1600 B.C. containing pots with water and food, that are exactly like modern Nubian graves. Creel (1937:174) refers to the modern persistence in China of the ancient slate, semilunar knife in the same form but of a different material (iron). The ritual importance of the macaw (*Ara macao, A. militaris*) among the Zuni of New Mexico is abundantly attested on the prehistoric time level in the Puebloan Southwest since the Pueblo III period. Judd (1959:263–267) discusses the persistence of macaws in ritual in the area and gives evidence of their occurrence in archeological sites. A rather similar situation obtains in

California where certain raptorial birds (hawk, condor, eagle) have been employed in a ceremonial context for the past 4000 years (Heizer and Hewes 1940; Wallace and Lathrap 1959).

Context

Once in a while we have the rare good fortune to find artifacts in various stages of completion. When an archeologist finds these, he can arrange them in a series from unshaped raw material to the finished form. As a result of this it is often possible to show that unusual pieces, which might otherwise be put into a separate type, are really unfinished or discarded examples of an abundantly represented type. For example, see a study of the manufacture of C-shaped shell fishhooks by Hamy (1885), and the study of flint tools and steatite bowls by Holmes (1919, esp. Figs. 50, 104).

Sometimes the position of an artifact in the ground gives a clue as to its use. This again points up the need for careful digging and recording. Emery (1948:62, Plate 34) illustrates a specialized kind of tool found in Dynastic Period tombs in Nubia and explains that these were previously thought to be mace heads, but that in fact they were an archer's "arrow loose." He was able to make the identification after he found the artifacts attached to the hand and thumb of skeletons in tombs.

A better knowledge of context might help in the identification of an Upper Paleolithic antler tool, named *"bâton de commandement"* by a French prehistorian of the last century because he believed they were rods of authority possessed by chiefs. They have also been identified as "shaft-straighteners," as "thong-stroppers" (Braidwood 1961:83), as "drumsticks" (Kirchner 1952), and as "twitches" used to hold an animal's lip (Eppel 1958). Actually these are all guesses and we do not know with any certainty what function these artifacts served. On the other hand, the "bannerstones" of eastern United States archeology were once believed to be ceremonial objects, but the finding of these pieces in context in graves in Southeastern sites (Webb and Haag 1939:50–58; Webb 1946: 320–323), associated with antler pieces, allowed them to be correctly identified as parts of throwing-sticks (atlatls, spear-throwers). Whether they were purely decorative or helped to balance the implement when the spear was cast has not yet been decided to everyone's satisfaction.

Experiments

Experiments in duplicating artifacts will provide a rational explanation of how they were made. While the ability of an experimenter today to reproduce an ancient form does not by itself prove that the object was in fact made in just this way, the procedure demonstrates how the artifact may have been produced (Ascher 1961b). We cite the following examples—which are not by any means a complete listing—of experiments to reproduce artifacts or to learn the way in which tools were used, or to learn their degree of efficiency.

Experiments in using stone axes to cut down trees have been performed and reported on by J. Evans (1897:162), Iversen (1956), Jorgensen (1953), Leechman (1950), Morris (1939:137), Nietsch (1939:70), G. V. Smith (1893), and Woodbury (1954:40–42). Stone working by flaking or abrasion (pecking), resulting in the reproduction of "prehistoric" objects, has been carried out in modern times by Skavlem (Pond 1930), Ellis (1940), Kragh (1951), Knowles (1944), McGuire (1891), Neill (1952), Treganza and Valdivia (1955), and Wiltshire (1826). An early experiment by Lovett (1887) attempted to determine the methods of manufacture of prehistoric flint implements by analogy with the recent production of gun flints at Brandon, England. Other kinds of experiments involve earth-oven cooking (Layard 1922); copper smelting (Coghlan 1940); iron smelting (Wynne and Tylecote 1958); stone-drilling methods (Rau 1881); Indian pottery-making (Griffin and Angell 1935); arrowshaft straightening (Cosner 1951); wood-carving with native tools (McEwen 1946); pigments used in South African cave paintings (T. Johnson 1957); efficiency of primitive harvesting implements (Steensberg 1943; Curwen 1930); transport of heavy stones with human labor (Atkinson 1956:99–110; Heyerdahl 1959:132–134); the method of notching atlatl dart foreshafts to seat stone points (Cosgrove 1947:52, Fig. 71a–e); the serviceability of notched animal ribs and scapulae as fiber-extracting tools (Morris and Burgh 1954:61–62); evidences of use-wear on the working edges of stone blades used for digging (Sonnenfeld 1962); experimental production of the glaze on stone walls ("vitrified forts") by burning timbers which were used in their construction (Childe 1937–1938); cutting wood with obsidian-edged wooden saw (Outwater 1957); determination by experiment of the method used to extract the live animal from the conch shell (*Strombus gigas*) by means of a small hole punched in the upper part of the spire (de Booy 1915:79–80); the planned destruction of a mud-hut village in Waziristan (Gordon 1953); reproducing minute drilled holes in stone beads with a shaft drill tipped with a barrel cactus thorn and employing sand abrasive (Haury 1931); reproduction of native copper artifacts (Cushing 1894); testing the belief that bevel-edged arrowpoints turned in flight (T. Wilson 1898). One of the very earliest such experiments was performed by Eduard Lartet (1960; see also Heizer 1962a:107), who reproduced cutting marks on bone made by flint implements and thereby was able to offer proof of the coexistence of man and extinct animals at a time, a century ago, when many were unwilling to accept the idea.

Another way of understanding how an artifact was fashioned is to dissect it. This cannot be done for most solid pieces, but especially for textiles which are woven together of separate pieces this kind of dissection can be performed. In illustration we cite two sling pockets (Heizer and Krieger 1956:102–105; O'Neale 1947) from dry Nevada caves, and O'Neale's (1937) analysis of textiles of the Early Nazca period in Peru. The same technique of analysis can be done with basketry. Occasionally pictorial records of technological processes are found. Childe (1944a) has made excellent use of Egyptian tomb paintings of Egyptian metalworkers at work in a survey of copper and bronze metallurgy in the Old World.

An unusual experiment now being carried out in England is the building of an earthwork in 1960 in Wiltshire (Jewell 1961; Ashbee and Cornwall 1961). The bank and ditch will be studied through future years to determine rates and processes of denudation of the bank and silting-in of the ditch.

Social Correlates

Identifying an object is not the same as understanding its use. Many objects that we regard as mundane and worthy of no special attention are involved in seemingly esoteric rites of which we could have no guess without first-hand knowledge. For most of prehistory these social correlates are, of course, lost to us but we can imagine that they did exist when we read some modern ethnographic accounts. In illustration we cite the paper by Sandin (1962) on the "Whetstone Feast" of the Iban of Sarawak. Among the Iban, after several bad harvests or because new families must have ceremonially blessed whetstones to sharpen iron farming tools, some thirty separate rituals are performed during the ceremony. The events that together form the "feast" include making offerings to the good spirits; bloody sacrifice of pigs and chickens; making small ceremonial huts to store farm tools in; collecting and offering worn-out household tools to the spirits; washing, cleaning, and oiling of old whetstones; playing music; singing and dancing; combing the hair of live pigs; feasting and wine drinking; bathing of pigs; and divining future agricultural success from the whetstones. This ceremony may be taken as one example (how typical it is we do not profess to know) of the complexity of social action that can involve a simple tool which the archeologist would normally assume to be merely utilitarian. At least the complicated ritual of the Iban would not be in the least inferable, either as a general fact or in any detail, from the whetstones as archeological specimens. Only if the institution of blessing whetstones by farming people was widely observed would an archeologist have reason to even suggest the possibility that the Iban whetstones (if they were found as archeological examples) may have been ritually sanctified, but even this would be the sheerest guess. The only hint we would have, and this a very slim one, would be the recorded fact that whetstones are sequestered in the loft of the house after the farming season is over. Archeologically speaking, the association of the whetstone with the housefloor might come about with the abandonment and disintegration of the house, provided, of course, that the occupants of the house did not take with them their sacred whetstone when they moved out.

Natural or Man-Made?

In some instances we must seriously question whether or not an object was made by man. This is a question especially vital to students of very early man who made crude stone tools. Looking at the history of archeology, it is only a little more than a hundred years that the human origin of hand axes found in the gravels of European rivers has been acknowledged. Tools made by relatively modern people, the polished stone axes of Neolithic and later times, found on the surface or dug up by accident in Europe, were until the sixteenth century, thought to have been formed by the action of lightning when it struck the earth (Blinkenberg 1911; Heizer 1962a:61–69). Their true identification came when European explorers found primitive peoples making and using stone axe heads to cut down trees.

The way to recognize an object as an artifact rather than a fortuitously shaped piece produced by natural processes can only be learned from experience. Warren (1914), Barnes (1939), and Leakey (1960:45–48) have tried to set forth the differences between stones flaked by man and those fractured by nature, but written explanations of distinctions that can best be appreciated with a practiced eye do not suffice. Remember, experience is the only proper teacher. Flaking of stone (or more properly, spalling) by lightning is discussed by Farmer (1939) and Laudermilk and Kennard (1938). Harner (1956) has investigated the action of heat in producing spalled rocks or flakes that might be—and in some cases actually have been—taken to be artifacts.

Nature can cause stones to break or chip in such a manner that it is very hard to decide that these pieces are not man-made. Indeed, Leakey's account referred to above admits that in some instances natural and man-make flakes cannot be distinguished. While an experienced archeologist usually can make a definite decision on whether a bone or stone or piece of shell that he digs up has been modified by human action, there will occasionally arise situations where the amount of human interference is so slight that it cannot be clearly differentiated from a flake or groove or scratch or bit of polish that may equally well have been caused by some natural action. It is in these situations that there may arise claims of the existence of very ancient but extremely simple tools. American archeology has had its full share of such claims, usually put forth by sincere but untrained amateurs.

The reader is referred, for studies of naturally fractured stones or bones that have at one time been alleged to be artifacts, to the publications of Breuil (1943), J. D. Clark (1958, 1961), and Watanabe (1949); to Dart's (1949, 1957) claims that *Australopithecus* of South Africa used bone tools (the "osteodontokeratic culture"); Nelson's (1928) demonstration that the alleged bone tools from Pliocene deposits in Nebraska were natural; Pei's (1938) careful analysis of the activities of animals in breaking or otherwise modifying animal bones that might be taken to be implements; and Harrisson and Medway's (1962:336, Plate 1) analysis of broken bones of large mammals from Niah Cave, Sarawak, which do not show signs of grinding, polishing, decoration, or use-wear. Such bones are at times considered to be primitive tool types, but Harrisson and Medway are able to demonstrate convincingly by the experimental smashing of fresh bones with a large stone that similar shapes are readily produced by this means. Dart (1960), on the other hand, reports on the experimental breaking of fresh sheep femora to show that spirally-broken antelope limb bones in the Makapansgat cave were presumably intentionally rather than accidentally produced, and thus sees in these experiments support for the osteodontokeratic culture of the Australopithecines. Dart and Kitching (1958) compare what are undoubtedly human-fractured bones from the Kalkbank site, South Africa, of Middle Stone Age data (ca. 15,000 years old) with the osteodontokeratic tools from the Australopithecine deposits at Makapansgat.

We must be careful *not* to assume that unmodified bones or stones were *not* used as tools because a handy cobble that would serve as a hammer must be considered a universal human tool type. Unmodified lower jaws of ungulates also provide a ready-made implement. Waugh (1916, Plate 6c) illustrates a deer jaw used by the Iroquois for scraping green corn from the cob, and Swanton (1942, Plate 16) illustrates an unmodified deer jaw that has a handle attached at right angles to the ramus. This piece is said to have been used by the Caddo as a sickle, probably for cutting grass. Bison scapulae were widely used as hoes for cultivating maize in the Great Plains area, and these were employed without alteration but show signs of abrasion and polish resulting from use (Dunlevy and Bell 1936:244). Deer antlers used as picks provide us with another example of the utilization of unmodified animal remains.

It should be clear from the foregoing that archeologists must use great care in identifying the uses of artifacts. We should also stress here that many artifacts are not well-made and that archeologists must be careful not to discard them solely because they look natural at first glance. Finally, the absence of prepared tools for certain jobs does not mean that there were no such tools. Unmodified animal jaws, for example, make good scrapers.

PREHISTORIC SOCIETY

Interpreting the economy of prehistoric man is relatively easy, but reconstructing his social organization and determining his numbers require greater use of inference (MacWhite 1956), much of it based on analogy with present-day peoples whose technology is more or less like that of prehistoric man. For help in making inferences about ancient hunters, archeologists turn to ethnographic accounts of today's hunters, hoping to find parallels to a world that is far removed from our own in time, space, and spirit. They must use imagination in thinking out what situations and events may have existed or occurred in the prehistoric past that will enable them to explain the facts they excavate. The process of inference is similar to that described by Herskovits (1950) as a field technique in ethnology, the "hypothetical situation," which serves as a means of eliciting comments and reactions from living informants.

DEMOGRAPHY

Demographic data of variable quality and precision can be obtained in areas that have been well-explored archeologically. There are several ways to find out how many people lived, and where they lived, in an area at a certain time. The direct way is to count the sites of each period and calculate how many people could have lived on them. To compute the population requires inference based on ethnology. If ten houses of a certain size are excavated at one site, it is customary to try to find a parallel situation with present day peoples. If, in a group having a similar economy, a family of five persons ordinarily live in each house, one can assume that about fifty persons lived in the archeological village. Such inferences allow at least a rough estimate of population. Whatever the technique—counting houses or making inferences based on environment and technology—correctness can only be a matter of probability. In the Southwest, where the number of rooms in a Pueblo ruin can be counted, a fairly exact figure can be determined, but for old villages where house counts are not obtainable, one means of calculating the number of inhabitants is through a formula (arrived at from ethnographic data) expressing the relationship of surface area of the site to numbers of occupants. As examples, see the papers of Cook and Treganza (1950), Ascher (1959), and Naroll (1962).

The most extensive survey of vital statistics of primitive peoples is to be found in Kryzwicki's book (1934), but the reader is warned that the data are often treated uncritically and care must be taken in using the figures. Braidwood and Reed (1957; reprinted in Heizer 1959b: 173–185) interpret population densities in the Near East and Europe, and Albright (1957:62) does the same for Transjordan. Densities of American Indian populations are given by Kroeber (1963, Chap. 11); of Australian populations during the Pleistocene, by Birdsell (1957); of California Indians having variable resources of food, by Baumhoff (1963); of groups of hunter-gatherers in the Great Basin, by Steward (1936).

By totaling the populations computed for all the sites in an area, one can get an idea of the density of population. Here again it is often possible to check the reliability of the magnitude of the figure. We have fairly accurate estimates of the population densities of modern people who have various kinds of economy and who live in different environments. Unless the estimate for prehistoric population fits these data tolerably well, an effort must be made to account for the discrepancy. We should bear in mind too that seasonal occupation of sites may influence attempts to compute population since groups which moved their camping spots would occupy two or more sites per year. Citations to published works treating the problem of seasonal occupation of sites may be found in Meighan et al. (1958:9–10) and Heizer (1960b:112–113).

Precise data on population could be obtained from graves if all the persons from a site were buried in one graveyard and if their graves could be dated to within a generation. One could then count the bodies buried during a given time to arrive at the population. Unfortunately, this condition has never been fully realized. We cannot claim that all persons found a common final resting place. Howells (1960) has shown how useful, yet at the same time how limited in significance, prehistoric skeletal data are in an effort to derive exact population numbers. The conditions of life under which people lived is reflected in the figures of the life expectancy. Calculations of length of life (an important matter to archeologists who may wish to know the approximate length of a generation) may be derived from skeletons (Angel 1947; Senyurek 1947; Goldstein 1953; Vallois 1960; Genoves 1963b) or from tombstone inscriptions (Durand 1960). For information on the sex of skeletons, see Genoves (1963a).

Special cultural practices may alter the population as well as the sex ratio. Thus infanticide (usually of females) among the Eskimos (Weyer 1932:123–124, 131–133), human sacrifice in pre-Colonial Mexico (where as many as 15,000 persons were annually sacrificed and thus augmented the normal death rate by about 15 percent—Cook 1946), and the wholesale transfer of captured populations in ancient times (Charanis 1961) are cases in point.

Two unusual attempts at arriving at population numbers may be mentioned. One is Pericot's (1961:210) effort to estimate the population for Mesolithic Spain from numbers of persons represented in group scenes in cave paintings. The second is a speculative essay on the size of the population that occupied the Scripps Estate site on the southern coast of California between 5500–7400 years ago. Here the amount of shell refuse and numbers of manos (grinding stones for reducing seeds to flour) suggest to the authors a population of 30 persons (Shumway, Hubbs, and Moriarty 1961:107–108). Although their estimate may not be precisely accurate, the authors feel confident that they have discovered the general magnitude of the population. Even this amount of precision is useful for making further interpretations.

A useful statistic that does not deal with absolute numbers is that of relative sizes of populations at various periods. A graph of general population density showing increase or decrease through time has been made for the Jeddito Valley region, Arizona, by Hack (1942: 78–80; reprinted in Heizer 1959b:170–173). He assigned a scale of unit values to the lengths of sites to arrive at a curve of population changes. Rather than showing actual population, Hack's curve shows the magnitude of changes. Schwartz (1956, 1963) has made similar attempts to show changes in relative population for the Cohoninna area of western Arizona, and for Nankoweap Canyon in Grand Canyon National Park.

A caution, however, must be observed. If during one period there are ten sites in an area and during another period there are twenty sites, we cannot invariably conclude that there has been a population increase. Such raw figures on number of sites may be misleading because sites differ in size. Ten large sites might have as many people as twenty smaller ones, but if a size difference were discovered, it would have significance for social organization even though the total population in an area remained the same. With larger sites one could look for evidence of a different political structure, perhaps integrated by a chief or temple. One might also wonder whether people were grouped more closely for defense. In addition, differences in the sizes of groups might be related to the way land was used. For example, with slash-and-burn agriculture (Conklin 1961) dispersed settlement is necessary, but with irrigation the settlements can be more concentrated. For ways in which social centralization was possible in the tropical forest region of lowland Mexico and Guatemala (where the Olmec and Maya civilizations developed) under a system of shifting cultivation, see Coe (1961), Cowgill (1961, 1962), Dumond (1961), Heizer (1960), and Meggers (1954). The demographic implications of slash-and-burn farming for the Amazon area have been treated by Carneiro (1956, 1961).

The size of populations depends upon both social and environmental factors. For this reason inferences drawn from present-day peoples are only partially valid. The environmental limitations are clear. With a given population of plants and animals there is a theoretical maximum human population that could be supported. If all the food could be used, one would have only to total up the calories and minerals and vitamins available and calculate how many persons could live on this quantity. However, our knowledge of social factors prevents our even taking the first step in this direction. Man cannot, and may never be able to, use the total food in any environment. In the first place, if he did so there would be nothing left for the next year—we see this today in some places where certain livestock are literally eating themselves out of a future. People could do the same thing. In addition, many plants ripen seasonally so that there is an overabundance of food for a time and a shortage of it later. Without proper storage some food is inevitably lost. Also, animals may migrate in and out of an environment. Distribution of the food governs its use. Not only must there be a steady supply of food—either fresh or preserved—in an area, but it must be obtainable. Migratory birds are of no use if men cannot catch them.

Furthermore, it does no good to have wheat if man does not know how to prepare it for food. What is more basic, even if man can use the grain, lacking the means to get it from the fields to his house he cannot use most of it. Baskets to carry it, sickles to harvest it, grinding stones to prepare it, and fires to cook it are needed for the efficient use of grain. Killing and then eating animals and plants is not always the most efficient way to use them. Sometimes it is better to keep animals for milk and cheese or for wool than for meat.

Man can use the food in an environment only if he can live there. Many areas were too cold for prehistoric man until he had proper shelter. Even though these areas had abundant food it was of no use to man. To this day there are many places where man can shelter himself and food can be found, but where there is too little water to allow so dense a population as he favors.

Still other factors limit the use of food and thus bear on the question of population. All human societies have taboos. We do not know how old taboos are, but we do know that man today willingly restricts his diet and that there are very few people who eat the full range of nourishing food found in their environment (Jensen 1953, Simoons 1961). For the most part the reluctance to make use of everything available stems from beliefs in what is good to eat. For example, pigs, snails, snakes, and insects are not eaten by most persons in Southwest Asia. Such exclusion of good food is not always the result of an abundance of other foods. Many peoples have animals that are clan totems and in some instances members of the clans are forbidden to eat these particular creatures.

Preference rather than taboos also rules out some food except in unusual circumstances. For example, in Southwest Asia sheep and goats are said to be "warm" animals and good to eat, but cattle are "cold" and not so good to eat. We have records of people who abstain from certain foods that are thought to leave persons with a characteristic odor offensive to themselves and detrimental to hunting. Social reasons for particular choices of food could be listed at great length, but these few illustrations should serve to show that any inferences we might make about hypothetical maximum populations, based only upon a simple tally of the available food, are very likely to be wrong.

We must consider another social aspect: minimum population. Several studies have indicated that man prefers to associate with a group larger than the biological family. In some instances twenty-five persons is the lower limit for the size of bands. If this prejudice had prevailed in prehistoric times, many areas would have been uninhabited because they would not have supported a minimum number of people with a primitive technology.

SOCIAL ORGANIZATION

An artifact that is usually present, and from which inferences may reasonably be drawn, is the fireplace or numbers of fireplaces within the walls of a dwelling. By analogy with people today, we reason that when multiple fireplaces are found in one building there was one for each family. It is customary in large houses, especially long houses, for each family to occupy a space along one wall and be divided from other families by screens. In each section there is a fireplace where the family cooking is done.

Again by analogy, we presume that when several families lived under one roof they were related. Thus within one large house there might have lived an old man and his wife, his married sons or daughters, and their families. Another possibility is that all the persons who were related through either the male or female line might have been resident in one house. Rarely we can go a step further and reconstruct even such intangible practices as marriage. For example, marriage customs of the Scythian chiefs could be reconstructed on the basis of evidence from the frozen Altai tombs (Rice 1957:60), but this is an unusual instance. Ordinarily such social practices lie outside the possibility of reasonable inference.

If the houses within a village were clustered into groups of two or three, we suppose that the closest neighbors were related whereas those in separate clusters, while still part of the village, belonged to other lineages (that is, a group of persons who can trace their descent to a common ancestor). It is not so easy to make inferences about single houses evenly dispersed throughout a village. The best evidence in those instances comes from the size of a house. If it is very large it might have held an extended family (that is, one containing three or more generations of kinfolk), whether or not there was more than one fireplace.

Studies of the social organization of people today lead to inferences about the sort of organizations possible under different economic conditions, but it should be stressed that there is no precise relationship between environment, technology, economy, and social order. Nevertheless, the possibilities of organization open to peoples with primitive technologies or poor environments are limited. The hunters and gatherers of the arid Great Basin in the western United States were unable to live in groups larger than extended families except during the winter (Steward 1938). These people were almost continually on the move, and food was obtained most efficiently by individual rather than collective effort.

By contrast, there is no reason why farmers who enjoy sufficient food, permanent settlements, and a large population within a small area should not be able to have a variety of social organizations. In contrast to hunters, some of these people (for example, the Hopi and Iroquois) reckon their inheritance through the female, and it is she who holds property and much civil authority. Among nomadic hunters descent is habitually traced through the men, and it is in them that civil authority is vested (Steward 1936).

Steward's (1936) pioneering work on social organization as influenced by ecology has indicated that there are rules one can follow to infer the kind of organization a people had. Steward (1937:101–102) found that more complex social organization generally goes along with more favorable economic potential. For example, as paraphrased by Eggan (1952: 38), "A low culture and/or unfavorable environment prevents dense population and precludes large population aggregates. It produces groups which, barring special contrary factors, are unilateral, localized, exogamous, and land owning. Descent is male or female largely according to the economic importance of man or woman in that culture."

On the other hand, in attempting to reconstruct social organization, archeologists must beware of falling into the trap of believing that everything has always been as it is now. That is, just because the climate, geography, plants, animals, and house types with a certain number of hearths were present at some time in the past, it does not necessarily follow that the social organization will duplicate that of any living group of people. Social organization is an artifact that depends on the factors just listed as well as on historical influences and internal developments of culture. Every kind of organization had its historical "first" and some of these were unique. We must always remember that present-day peoples have the benefit of a long history. Peoples living 50,000 years ago had less of a history and therefore fewer alternatives from which they might have chosen. Social organization is not a mechanical thing; it is as much an artifact as the shape of a projectile point. With social organization there are many more imponderables than in the decisions people will make before deciding on what kinds of projectile points they will make and use.

Where there is material or other property to be passed on, there will be some rules of inheritance. In fact some items of property may descend through one line and other things through another line. That is, real property might be passed from father to son whereas membership in secret societies might go in the mother's line from her brother to her son. There is infinite diversity and, except under special conditions, it is difficult to infer the precise details with any assurance from archeological evidence.

Differences in status must always have existed because certain persons were looked to for advice and leadership. This is not the same as saying that formal provisions were made for leadership. A stratified society in which certain persons had prerogatives denied others certainly came late in man's history. We have no evidence of hereditary social classes before the beginning of civilizations, but people with a tribal organization did have leaders who were distinguished in dress and certain other artifacts. In a few instances people who were influenced by centers of civilization adopted hereditary classes. For a useful review of ethnographic evidence, see Service (1962).

An excellent summary of archeology in the U.S.S.R. by Mongait (1961) contains numerous statements about the social organization of prehistoric culture groups. Much of this does not seem to derive directly from the archeological data, but from preconceived or ready-made assumptions. Daniel (1962:133) has commented on this aspect of Soviet archeology and we agree with him when he writes, "When I spoke of the Russians and the application of archeology to their schemes of pre-clan, clan, and class society, I did not mean that their schemes were necessarily wrong; merely that it was wrong to pretend that the record of prehistoric archeology proved these schemes." Childe (1951:29) writes, "In fact the Russian scheme of classification [based upon Morgan's sequence of Savagery, Barbarism and Civilization] assumes in advance precisely what archeological facts have to prove."

More useful are a paper by Chang (1958) in which he explores the possibility of making inferences on social organization from archeological data; the reconstruction of the social organization of the Skara Brae village (Childe 1946a:32–33); and Di Peso's (1958:21–22) suggestions on the social organization of a prehistoric Pueblo group in Arizona.

The clearest evidence for status differences in a society comes from graves. Certain graves were larger, or equipped with more luxury goods, weapons, food, and religious objects than others. The Royal Cemetery of Ur, the shaft graves at Mycenae, and King Tutankhamen's tomb are famous examples of the burial of rulers that have their less elaborate parallels in many societies. The mound-building Indians in North America often buried certain people along with what must have been public as well as private wealth (Sears 1954, 1961). Graves of warrior chiefs in Europe and Asia and Central America, which are full of armament, luxury goods, and even servants, indicate the existence of great differences in status. Rice (1957:116) reviewed the historical evidence from Asia and concludes that tattooing was a visible sign of rank. The tattooed chieftain from Pazyryk whom Mongait describes (1961:170–175) corroborates this conclusion. Creel (1937:215) records the discovery, in the seasons of 1934 and 1935, of over one hundred sacrificed humans at the site of the Shang Dynasty capital at Anyang, China. These skeletons, always headless, invariably occurred in groups of ten. Evidence that the wrists were tied together behind the back indicates that the decapitation was involuntary. The repeated occurrence of skeletons, knives, axes, and other items in groups of ten affirms that this was the ritual number of the Shang Chinese of the second millennium B.C.

There must have been differences in religious as well as civil status. The remains of temples and other religious structures are common among civilized peoples; in fact there is reason to believe that civil and religious authority was often vested either in the same person or small groups. Ethnography gives some evidence for religious specialization in the persons of shamans or medicine men. These persons are supposed to have special powers based upon a connection with the supernatural world, but they are ordinarily not exempt from earning their own living. Thus there is no real difference in status between them and other members of the group. Priests who are masters of ritual probably do not appear as a separate social class much earlier than the beginning of civilization.

On the other hand, the right to be a shaman may become hereditary. For instance, a particularly strong man might usurp certain prerogatives for himself, and when it came time for his title to be passed on, the prerogatives might also be transmitted. There are many instances of this occurrence in history where wartime leaders continued to hold civil authority after they "should" have returned it to duly appointed civil leaders.

There have probably always been situations where persons of unusual ability or strength were able to set themselves above others, but without any guarantee that their status would be perpetuated. It was not until such leaders were able to accumulate surpluses to pay and hold allies that they were able to maintain a rigid system of classes.

Several efforts to extract sociological or psychological characteristics of prehistoric peoples have been made, and while none of these is entirely convincing, the attempts are interesting. On Paleolithic sociology see Alonzo del Real (1963); on the social life of Spanish Paleolithic hunters see Pericot (1961); on psychological characteristics of the ancient Maya as inferred from their art see Wallace (1950); and on Maya character as evidenced in archeological remains see Thompson (1954).

IDENTIFYING PREHISTORIC CULTURES

Archeologists working in the United States have a relatively easier time trying to reconstruct prehistoric society because many of the remains they excavate were left by the ancestors of known living people. They can observe the present conditions and infer that these are similar to those in the past. This method, known as the direct historical approach (Steward 1942), involves working back in time from the last known historical or legendary home of the people. This method has been extensively used; for examples from California see Heizer (1941a) and from the Plains, Strong (1940). Linguistic data sometimes help to establish the places from which groups came. Persons speaking a language foreign to that prevalent among the people surrounding them may not be indigenous to the area. A check of the distribution of speakers of various languages may help show their places of origin. In this way the Navajo were shown to have entered the Southwest in relatively recent times; the largest concentration of Athabascan speakers is in Canada and this is assumed to be the place from which the Navajo originally came. Sites dating earlier than the Navajo entry into the Southwest, about 1500 A.D., cannot therefore be ancestral to Navajo (Hester 1962a; Hoijer 1956b; Jett 1964).

With the techniques of glottochronology and lexicostatistics (Bergsland and Vogt 1962; Hoijer 1956a; Hymes 1960; Kroeber 1955; Swadesh 1960), linguists are able, within limits, to tell when groups of people split from other groups by the degrees of divergence that have taken place in their languages. That is, people who were recently together will speak closely related dialects whereas those who have been separated longer will speak more divergent dialects. Attempts have been made to correlate dated archeological cultures with the dates of linguistic separation as determined by glottochronology; see Baumhoff and Olmsted (1963), Hencken (1955), Swadesh (1953, 1959), and Taylor and Rouse (1955). General discussions of the archeological significance of linguistic data have been written by Trager (1955) and Sapir (1916).

Linguistics can also help by finding words in the vocabularies of peoples that do not fit their present environment. In the legends of many peoples there are references to places or things which no living person in the group has seen. Sometimes these places can be found by using leads provided by linguistics. Thus, by comparison of words in the Indo-European languages, Thieme (1958) is able to point out the homeland of the original Indo-European language community as lying between the Vistula and Elbe Rivers in Europe, and by applying archeological dates to certain words (for example, metals and domesticated animals known to the original speakers) can suggest this homeland was occupied toward the end of the fourth millennium B.C. (see also Crossland 1957; Hencken 1955:44 ff.; Pulgram 1959). Provable relationships in the languages of geographically separated populations may be taken as evidence of migration. While this fact is undoubted, it is often difficult to find archeological proof of migrations (MacWhite 1956:16–18).

Instances of migrations in the American Southwest and South America are detailed in articles in the volume edited by Thompson (1958). Rouse (1958:64) proposes five requirements for the demonstration of a prehistoric migration. These are: (1) identify the migrating people as an intrusive unit in the region it has penetrated; (2) trace this unit back to its homeland; (3) determine that all occurrences of the unit are contemporaneous; (4) establish the existence of favorable conditions for migration; (5) demonstrate that some other hypothesis, such as independent invention or diffusion of traits, does not better fit the facts of the situation. Proposed intercontinental diffusions to the New World across the Atlantic or Pacific oceans, such as those of Gladwin (1947), Greenman (1963), Heyerdahl (1963), or Heine-Geldern (1954) and Heine-Geldern and Ekholm (1951) have not met with enthusiastic acceptance by American archeologists who still prefer to envisage man's entry into the New World from Siberia by the Bering Straits route (Byers 1957; Griffin 1960; Hopkins 1959; Linné 1955), although it must be admitted that there is no archeological proof that this route of entry was used (Giddings 1960). Lacking facts, a good deal of interesting speculation has been done on what the climatic conditions and cultural equipment required for the crossing may have been like (Mather 1954), what kind of men came into the New World from northeastern Asia (Stewart 1960), and what light linguistic evidence can throw upon the old migrations (Swadesh 1962). How contacts between prehistoric groups can be detected from archeological evidence is discussed by Willey (1956). Problems such as that of the origin of the American Indians and the source of high cultures in the New World have attracted an unduly large amount of speculative theorizing. Wauchope (1962) has written a thorough review of a number of unacceptable and unsupported theories of origin of the American Indians, which include proposals concerning Alexandrian admirals, Phoenicians, Egyptians, and mythical inhabitants of lost continents of Atlantis and Mu as original migrants or culture-bearers to the supposedly ignorant Indians of the Americas.

RELIGION

We can scarcely hope to discuss with any adequacy the large subject of evidences for religious activity and belief in prehistoric times in this book.

With the advent of civilization ("a high development of society" Kroeber 1962:9), there appear large temples, pyramids, shrines, and the like, and in parts of the Old World, religious writings in the form of epics, myths, temple rituals and accounts. Further back in time, and among less developed societies, evidences of religions may be seen in the manner in which the dead were buried (for the oldest human burials see Hawkes and Woolley 1963:208), or in objects whose primary function was clearly special and presumably religious. The "Venus" figures of the Upper Paleolithic and later times are believed to be symbols of fertility, and the cave paintings of Spain and France are generally thought to have been made as acts of compulsive or imitative magic aimed at success in the hunt. A painting, 12,000 years old, at the cave of Trois Frères in France is said to be a costumed sorcercer. In dry cave sites in western North America there are kits of prehistoric shaman's paraphernalia which are like those used in recent times (Elsasser 1961). Petroglyphs situated along game trails at ambush spots in Nevada are probably explainable as a part of hunting magic (Heizer and Baumhoff 1959). The ritual disposal of bones of game animals is suggested in the disposition of about a thousand wild cattle at an Upper Paleolithic site near Amvrosievskaya in the Stalino region of the Ukraine (Mongait 1961:83), and on a small rock off the coast of northwest California were buried hundreds of skulls of sea lions as part of the ceremonial disposal of bones of game animals (Heizer 1951b). The cave at Bisitun, Iran, was interpreted by Coon (1951:36) as a "shrine" of the Neanderthal people of the area.

A large literature on the religious evidences of prehistoric peoples exists. For examples see Bergounioux and Goetz (1958), Breuil (1951), James (1962), and Maringer (1960).

SPECIALIZATION

As today, there have probably never been skills that could not be mastered by persons of either sex, but it seems likely that in prehistoric times some tasks devolved more upon women and others more upon men. Hunting was probably a man's job if we can believe evidence from modern peoples. This division of labor, of course, has a biological basis in that women find it hard to chase animals when they are pregnant or caring for young children. The result is that tasks that must be done in and around the home—collecting firewood, caring for children, basket making, cooking meals, and so on—are usually female activities. Necessary activities that require hard work and travel, such as animal hunting and aggressive warfare, are customarily male activities. The fact is that in many societies cooking and hunting each take so much time that one person could hardly be expected to do both. Archeologists usually assume that there was some division of labor based on sex, but since it is practically impossible to determine whether a man or woman made a particular artifact in antiquity, detailed interpretation of archeological materials in this regard has not been done. In central California an examination of the artifacts associated with adult male and female skeletons was carried out and it was observed that mortars and pestles (presumably used by women) occurred with about the same frequency in graves of both sexes; the same was true of arrowpoints which were presumably made, owned, and used by men in war and hunting. Students desiring to know more about the sexual division of labor among primitive peoples may consult Brown (1963), Driver and Massey (1957: 312, 314, 371–373, Map 106), Giffen (1930), Heath (1958), Murdock (1937), and Willoughby (1963).

Real specialization, beyond that which is merely sex determined or allocated, involves skills known to only a few persons in any community or area. Such things as metal-working, weaving, mining, specialized pottery-making, and jewelry manufacture were carried out by persons who traded their handicraft for food. These persons might be either men or women. That craft specialization can occur on a very simple cultural level is illustrated by an old Australian man who served as the weapons-repairer for his group and was supported in return for his services (McCarthy and McArthur 1960:148).

Another kind of specialization involves whole communities. There is a traditional division between the farmers and herders in many parts of the world. The two occupations have a symbiotic relationship. People who are solely nomadic may not grow grain, and those who farm in areas where there is little pasture cannot get meat or wool by their own efforts. Trade between the two groups is both necessary and advantageous. Southern Russia, home of the Scythians was, to quote Rice (1957: 51), "one of Greece's granaries." Meat, furs, and wheat were traded from there to Greek colonists on the Black Sea—for shipment to mainland Greece—in exchange for Greek jewelry, metalwork, and fine pottery.

Ewers (1955:11–12) has shown how the spread of horses to the Plains Indians of North America before 1805 was accomplished through trading relations already established between nomadic and horticultural groups. Farm produce was desired by hunting groups and meat and skins were desired by the village farmers. Spencer (1959:28–29, 201, 203) describes the disappearance of the inland Eskimo of the Point Barrow region. These people depended mainly upon caribou for food, but could only survive in the interior region if they could secure whale or seal oil for fuel from the coastal Eskimos. In prehistoric times a two-way trade of caribou hides in return for oil was mutually advantageous. But when clothing could be secured by the coastal peoples from whaling ships or traders, they no longer needed the caribou skins. As a consequence they abandoned trading with their neighbors, leaving the latter in a position where they could not continue to survive. The interior people have thus been forced to migrate to the coast.

If we project this instance into an archeological context, we would see abandonment of sites and perhaps their reoccupation by people who could manage to survive. If the reoccupation did not take place until a more efficient exploitative technology was available to handle the environment, the archeologist would find two different cultures represented in the area. For a collection of information on the enforced abandonment of sites in California, see Heizer (1962c).

17

WRITING
CULTURE HISTORY

Prehistory describes foreign lands and faceless people. It may deal with the culture of a people, a region, or the whole world through time. None of us today has the ability to see the past as it was to those who lived it. We can see the past only in ways that are familiar to us, either through our own experience or through our knowledge of other cultures. We judge the artifacts by what we know today. We can describe prehistoric environments and the tools used to cope with them, but we cannot describe what man thought of himself or of the world. We can deal with the past only on our terms, and our terms are not those of prehistoric man.

Prehistoric men had no real sense of history nor of their place in the world of man, for these imply a conception of the progression of time and events as well as a familiarity with geography and culture. For most men in prehistory tomorrow would expectably be like today and another generation like the last. A prehistorian views the past as a series of changes, and his job becomes one of finding out both what happened and how and why it happened. To learn these things it is first necessary to find out what the chief events of the past were. With this knowledge a prehistorian can see what prehistoric men could not; namely, from whence they came and whither they were going. Having this kind of vision enables an archeologist to begin making guesses as to how and why certain changes in the past occurred. Such guesses depend on a knowledge of the natural environment—its opportunities as well as its changes; of the cultural environment—its pool of technical skill and the possibilities for intercultural exchange; of the interaction between these factors that in the end tell us how cultures change. Knowing how cultures changed is different from knowing why they changed. Ultimate causes are perhaps unobtainable; yet with our scientific predisposition we are led to ask why, and we try to answer it with some statement of cause and effect. It need not invalidate our answer to recognize that prehistoric men would probably not have been able to answer the question. The interpretation of human history is a job for a historian, not for the man who lives, experiences, and inquires about only a small part of it.

Prehistorians try to find reasons not only for the daily life of prehistoric men, but for the existence of the many ways of prehistoric life and how these related to the gradual development of cultures or civilization. Prehistorians are not interested in the annual rainfall and number of frost-free days 20,000 years ago in a valley in France for the sake of this knowledge alone, but for the way changing patterns of weather affected men and their relations with the plants and animals. Prehistorians are interested not in the quarry from which prehistoric men obtained their flint, but in the development of social and technical skills that enabled them to live in and exploit any environment. Prehistorians are interested not in the size of a man buried in an African cave, but in man as a biological organism gradually acquiring the features that we recognize as human. Prehistorians examine the relationships between culture and biology, and how, in the past two million years, man has become king of the beasts. In short, prehistorians are interested in the history of man, not of particular men.

Historians who deal with literate societies are sometimes impressed with the role played by great men and their histories emphasize people. Other historians are more interested in the broad outlines of cultural development and see history as a series of technological or social trends. Still others wonder about the influence of environment on man and write their histories to demonstrate a causal relationship between the two. Prehistorians have different choices. They cannot see particular persons since their human subjects are impersonal, but they can see societies or cultures in the archeological record.

History and prehistory are both based on primary documentation. An archeologist's history will stand or fall on the quality of his basic documents—reports on the excavation of sites. If site reports are adequate it is possible to arrange the data contained in them in a variety of ways depending on the aims of any particular interpreter.

SITE REPORTS

Grahame Clark (1957:107) says that "the archaeologist with little or no experience of excavation is ill qualified to interpret the results of other people's digging." In spite of Clark's pessimism, there are some criteria which identify good and bad reports. Professional archeologists and even students must try to evaluate the reports they read.

A site report should tell what was found in an excavation. It should include a description of the environment, of the methods by which the site was dug, and of the artifacts found. Finally, there should be a synthesis describing the way people at the site lived. An archeologist will usually include a chapter telling how his material relates to that from other sites and how it fits in the history of a region. All reports should begin with a clear statement of what was attempted and what was accomplished. This tells the reader immediately whether the report describes a test excavation, a probing of graves to get a ceramic sequence, the uncovering of a temple complex to determine its development, or the excavation of a whole site, or a portion of it, to get a representative picture of the prehistoric community.

The report should be clear and concise. It should begin with a geographical description and include maps and plans of the site and its environs. The method of excavation should be described in sufficient detail to allow the reader to judge whether, from his knowledge of similar sites, the approach was adequate. It is here that the layman as well as the professional may be seriously misled. The progress of the excavation should be detailed in drawings or photographs and the stratigraphic relationships of one area to another should be clearly shown.

The artifacts and special features—walls, fireplaces, and so on,—should be clearly described and illustrated. Sometimes it is possible to refer to other reports and merely say that certain of the new artifacts are similar to others which have been reported before. Usually artifacts are described in accordance with standardized principles of classification. These results should then be tabulated so that quantities can be readily comprehended.

One can judge a report by the kind of things that are reported. Some things are usually present in sites; for example, bones. These should be mentioned in a report. If they were discarded or not analyzed, the reader can be sure that valuable information was lost. If an archeologist overlooks information of this kind, he may have overlooked other things as well. For example, preoccupation with burials or houses may have blinded the archeologist to the very small but significant objects that can be recovered only by special techniques. Such items as tiny flint tools are often overlooked because the dirt is not screened. Similarly, plant remains are often missed because the archeologist does not recognize the importance of saving them or does not know the techniques for recognizing and recovering them. And, let us emphasize once more, all data must be recorded stratigraphically.

Interpretation of the evidence should be presented apart from the description so that a minimum of bias will have been introduced into the basic data. Interpretations can be personal, and even wholly erroneous ones will not affect the quality of the report if they are kept separate from the basic description. There are, in fact, many archeologists who wish to prove pet theories—and do so—but their reports are written in such a way that their interpretations do not alter their data. Other archeologists are then free to interpret the factual data in their own ways.

This discussion avoids the issue of "objectivity" in reporting the results of any investigation. It is clear that no scientist begins his work with an empty head. His method of work, his choice of a subject, and his reporting of the results all depend on what he considers proper and worthwhile. Some scholars have invented elaborate procedures for recording their data "objectively," but if we examine their position we find that any such attempt represents a sophisticated theoretical bias— the very thing they are trying to avoid. Recognizing this, what we are stressing here is that certain standards of reporting should be observed. These standards are based on what we believe is the most fruitful approach toward prehistory. In any case we cannot conceive of a reasonable defense for sloppy reporting.

REGIONAL HISTORIES

When enough sites in an area have been excavated *and reported,* archeologists can construct the framework of a regional sequence. For this, one only needs the chronological arrangement of assemblages. It is fair to say that most archeology is concerned with this essential task. The size of a "region" varies depending on the archeologist's interests. It may be a little valley, a drainage of a major river such as the Missouri, a major physiographic area such as the American Southwest, or even a nation. Larger regions lend themselves to subdivision, and many archeologists spend their lifetimes studying minor points of larger areas. If there are suitable ways to date sites, it is easy to set up regional sequences. But establishing relative chronologies bears the same relation to history as the arranging of prime numbers in order of ascending size bears to mathematics.

In the long view, change was pervasive throughout prehistory. Regional sequences document this change. Changes, whether in economy, pottery design, or house type, demand an explanation. In fact, were there no change for a considerable period, one would wonder why there had been none. The prehistorian's task is to answer the question of "how" and "why" about his sequences. Explanation of changes depends upon knowing the cultural relations of successive assemblages to one another. That is, how can we account for the differences and similarities in successive assemblages?

Change can result from local invention, influence from another group, or new people bringing in new ideas. If one of these sources can be specified, one might look further to find out the details. Thus, if influences came from another group, it is useful to know from what group and by what means ideas and artifacts were exchanged. Trade, migration, war, or just copying, may account for change. Sometimes ideas are diffused. For example, the idea of the throwing stick (atlatl) or potter's wheel might have been diffused to groups that had never seen such implements.

When ideas about ways of doing things spread, but the precise techniques or artifacts themselves do not move from one culture to another, the results are likely to appear unique. This is what A. L. Kroeber (1940a) had in mind when he described "stimulus diffusion," a situation "where a system or pattern as such encounters no resistance to its spread, but there are difficulties in regard to the transmission of the concrete content of the system. In this case it is the *idea* of the complex system which is accepted, but it remains for the receiving culture to develop a new content." As possible examples of stimulus diffusion, Kroeber discusses the invention of porcelain in Europe in the early eighteenth century, the invention of the Cherokee syllabary, the possible connections between Mesopotamian and Chinese writing systems, and the appearance of fired pottery in the Anasazi culture of the American Southwest. Such possible stimulus diffusions might be proved or disproved by archeological facts; our interest in the matter is primarily to point out that many such problems await solution by archeologists who are aware of them and recover relevant data.

If invention seems the most likely origin of innovation, one might ask under what circumstances it occurred. People have argued that necessity is the mother of invention. The whole subject of "necessity" is complex. What may seem vital to us would not seem so for other people. It is sufficient to say here that events that would seriously impair the ability of a people to survive will usually be counteracted. People do, of course, invent things in time of crisis, but there is good evidence that more changes, or at least a greater variety of changes, will take place when people are relatively secure (Barnett 1953:81–82). Environmental changes that necessitate cultural readaptation are frequently invoked as causes for change (for example, Kelley 1952). For example, increasing aridity might force people to begin irrigation of their crops, or it might result in a shifting of geographical distribution of plants and animals. With the onset of drier conditions, one might find a shift from wood houses to those of stone or mud, and a shift from forest or brush animals to those of grasslands. Prehistory during the Pleistocene records several new adaptations to changing environments.

Explanations of changes in material culture can never hope to discover the motives of particular prehistoric men. Instead they must depend on inference regarding adaptations to environment, preferences to style, invention, trade, and migration of peoples. Regional sequences and histories should provide the substance for more general descriptions and interpretations of culture history.

MODELS OF PREHISTORY

The first attempts to organize and understand man's past were based upon general theories of how culture developed. Throughout the history of archeology most of these theories have been based upon ideas of biological and cultural evolution or progress (Meggers 1959). As archeological data became available they were fitted into the framework allowed by these theories. It is now customary to call these frameworks "models" and "heuristic devices." Whatever they may be called, they are nothing more than constructs of their maker's imagination. For purposes of illustration we cite some extreme examples. For part of history, evolutionary models are the proper skeleton on which to hang the flesh of archeological data, but they do not give the whole possible form to the body. The same can be said of other models. For example, those who believe

that environment determines cultural development may slight consideration of cultural and historical factors which are equally important. Those
who believe in the inevitability of progress sometimes overlook the
adaptive significance of the *status quo*.

Models used with proper understanding of their limitations and of
the limitations of the data do in fact become heuristic devices. Models
which ignore data and themselves become the *modus operandi* of culture
history, blind us to the lessons of the past. A review of some of the most
prominent ways of thinking about prehistory will help the reader understand what he may read in general surveys of history and prehistory.

When Thomsen arranged the museum collections of Denmark into
stone, bronze, and iron he unwittingly provided terms which, set in
chronological sequence, could be used to describe some of culture history.
After excavations showed that in some places people had used stone,
bronze, and iron successively, Thomsen's "Three Ages" became a convenient model of the history of technology (Childe 1944a). Soon, such
terms as "paleolithic," "mesolithic," and "neolithic" were coined to describe subdivisions of the stone age. In all of these there were implications of cultural evolution. In ethnology, models were made that described man's progression from savagery through barbarism to civilization (Morgan 1875). The archeological and ethnological models were
complementary, dealing with technology and culture. All of these early
models, based on very scanty evidence, were "in large part the outcome
of the doctrines of optimism, the inevitability of progress, and the per-
fectibility of man current in the eighteenth century" (Piggott 1960:20).

For some archeologists, the models were viewed as proofs of cultural
laws. To Mortillet (1903) the "law of similar development" was no mere
model, nor would Morgan (1875, 1878:vi) have entertained much doubt
that man had really advanced by his postulated stages. He contended
that "the history of the human race is one in source, one in experience,
and one in progress."

Theories of cultural evolution were confined for the most part to
the Old World where the cultural sequence was long enough to contain
evidence of man's biological as well as his cultural evolution. In the
1930s archeologists began to see that even though there was a general
increase in technological efficiency in prehistoric times, culture did not
everywhere go through precisely the same stages in the same way.

In recent years the trend has been to describe culture history in
terms suitable to each geographic or cultural region. That is, archeological stages are named for the places where sites exist rather than for some

pancontinental or universal stage of development. This sidesteps the issue of assigning every episode in history to one of the theoretical steps in the evolutionary ladder. Unfortunately, it is still customary to call sites "middle paleolithic," "mesolithic," or "archaic" when such terms have long since, by indiscriminate use, lost their original precision. Using terms invented in France to describe sites found in the Gobi Desert is sheer nonsense.

Among a small group of specialists, short-cut terms may be useful, but they only cause confusion for most of us. To take a notorious example, the word "neolithic," in various contexts has meant: a self-sufficient food producing *economy*; an *assemblage* in which pottery is found; an *assemblage* in which polished stone tools are found; and a *culture* in which the people are settled but have no polished stone or pottery. In short, there are several definitions of neolithic, yet many archeologists of sound reputation continue to use the word indiscriminately and wonder what the confusion is all about.

In America there has never been much interest in cultural evolution per se. But if the Americanists have not been interested in evolution, many have been interested in cultural development. Workers in Meso-America and Peru have devised terminologies that describe the events in their region that led to civilization. Such terms as "formative, pre-classic, classic, and post-classic," and "formative, florescent, and militaristic" are used to describe these sequences of development. Outside of the nuclear areas, however, a strong development was never apparent in the data, and most archeologists have preferred to use local place names and noncommittal areal designations.

Terminology has always bothered American archeologists. They soon recognized that what was being called a "culture" by one worker did not correspond to the culture of another. Accordingly, there arose an interest in making more precise systems for classification of artifacts and cultures. The first formal descriptive terminology for use over a wide area reflected this concern for classification, and at the same time the lack of interest in development. This system, labeled the "Midwestern Taxonomic Method," was based entirely upon the degree to which an assemblage from one site resembled that from another (McKern 1939). In other words, there was no implication of time or space in the labels. Beginning with the smallest unit, the system grouped *components* (assemblages of artifacts from one site or cultural level within a site) into *foci*. Foci were said to be somewhat equivalent to what ethnologists call tribes. A grouping of similar foci produced an *aspect*; groups of aspects became *phases*, which in turn were grouped into *patterns,* and these finally into *bases.* A base was the most general classification and patterns were included in it largely on subsistence similarities; for example, "sedentary-fishing base."

A system could hardly be devised that was less directed toward culture history than this one. Even though the sites could be described by this system, its disregard of time and space put the emphasis on classification for the sake of classification. This resulted in arguments over whether something was an aspect or a phase, and, indeed, the designations had to be changed frequently as more was learned.

Alongside the Midwestern Taxonomic Method was a designation of cultures that began with "Paleo Indian," "Early Man," or "Big Game Hunter" and was followed by "Archaic," "Desert Culture," and "Woodland." Again there was no necessary implication of development, although the time and economy were emphasized. For a more extended review see the chapter by J. Bennyhoff in Heizer (1959a:97–101) and Rowe's (1962b) article on stages and periods.

The lack of a sense of cultural development in much American thinking seems odd to many Old World archeologists, but there were reasons for the prevailing attitude. In the first place, in many areas there was no discernible "development" over the whole time of occupation. That is, economy, being in fine adjustment with the physical and cultural environment, remained stable. The changes that could be seen were stylistic, and their causes could hardly be directly related to the broader development of culture.

A second factor was that most American Indians, the descendants of the prehistoric men whose remains were being unearthed, had not advanced much beyond savagery or early barbarism on the ethnographic scale. Any developments seen archeologically would have seemed relatively minor.

A third factor was that archeologists were greatly influenced by ethnographic descriptions. In many instances their aim was to produce for prehistory the kind of description that an ethnologist writes of a present-day tribe. For the most part ethnologists viewed culture without a time dimension. Many archeologists, paralleling the ethnographic use of the "ethnological present," thought of the "prehistoric present" and discounted the importance of historical factors in that momentary slice of life.

A reaction to this kind of thinking began with the direct historical approach that involved working back through time from the known present to the less known prehistoric past. This technique has not yet had the attention it deserves and much valuable insight has been overlooked. However, it is also possible to begin with the earliest cultures and work toward the present by trying to connect successive archeological periods. The first attempts of this sort were made in nuclear America, where the idea of a "co-tradition" was developed (Rouse 1954, 1957). This was a conscious effort to trace the historic development of the Peruvian civilization. Instead of considering Peruvian history as a number of discrete episodes appearing in time, the workers emphasized the continuity of the episodes. In so doing, they discerned parallel sets of traditions. This was an important step in historical reconstruction because it gave a framework which had meaning in culture as well as in time. But an interest in time and culture alone does not lead to historical interpretation.

The next necessary step was to view the separate traditions and try to understand them against a backdrop of environment and the other traditions with which they came in contact. It is out of this kind of study, based on solidly established regional traditions, that archeologists have been able to discern certain regularities in cultural development. To some, these regularities suggest the validity of cultural evolution. The contrast with nineteenth century archeologists is that today the stages are discovered by examining data. They are not a priori theories to which data are fitted.

The stimulus for a nontaxonomic, nonevolutionary approach came largely from the Old World. In America the approach has changed thinking from taxonomy to the process of culture change. The most systematic descriptions of this approach have been made by Braidwood (1958) for Southwest Asia, and Willey (1960) for America, the two later making a joint appraisal (1962) of world-wide evidence. It is worth reviewing these efforts and comparing them with a taxonomic approach (Willey and Phillips 1958) to show how they fit into the general studies of culture history.

All thinking about culture history begins with the obvious assumption that man originally had relatively simple equipment and social organization, and eventually developed the complicated technology and society which we know today. Though some will argue with the use of the term, this change from simple to complex is "progress." It might also be called the "course of culture history," "cultural evolution," or simply "development." Because development is undeniable in the long run, any description of culture history must somehow accommodate and, if possible, help explain it.

The most elaborate summary of New World prehistory to yet appear has been written by Willey and Phillips (1958). They describe culture history by putting all archeological remains into five "stages," which are variously defined on the basis of technology, economy, settlement, society and esthetics. The stages are ahistorical in the sense that their relative chronological placement is not a primary factor in their defintion, yet they are historical in the sense that in some areas they appeared successively. The Willey and Phillips attempt is impressive for its scope, but the fact that its main concern is with classification makes it hard to use for historical interpretation (cf. Caldwell 1959).

While Willey and Phillips were arranging American prehistory into stages, Braidwood was considering the developments which had led to the Old World civilizations. His interest was mainly in Southwest Asia, and the models he devised reflected this interest. In essence he described a series of subsistence-settlement "eras," each of which reflected man's increasing mastery over his environment and his increasing social complexity. The eras were based as much on hindsight as on the evidence at hand. In other words, Braidwood worked from the relatively known to the relatively unknown, but at the same time, as he established each era, he thought of it as a step from the simple to the more complex. Following Braidwood, Willey (1960) described American prehistory in much the same terms. Their jointly edited volume, *Courses Toward Urban Life*, clearly demonstrates that while both see progress—although they do not call it that—they recognize that it took place only when the environmental, social, and historical factors were favorable. In other words, they see culture history resulting from a complex interplay of natural and cultural variables. They stress the "cultural alternates" that man could and did choose.

The result clearly demonstrates that culture history is best seen as a cultural and not as a biological or supernatural phenomenon. It also shows that there is a discernible direction in man's development that can be understood only by taking a dynamic developmental rather than a static taxonomic approach.

In contrast to these works, the most popular and probably the most influential descriptions of prehistory ever written are *Man Makes Himself* (1951) and *What Happened in History* (1954) by the late V. Gordon Childe. Childe's success lies as much in his masterly understanding of Old World prehistory—to a degree unparalleled—as in the sheer volume of his work. It is instructive to consider some of his viewpoints.

Childe described culture history by referring to the major technological and social advances as "revolutions" that enabled man to make better use of his environment. For Childe, man's social evolution went hand in hand with his technology. The first revolution, the "Neolithic" (that is, food-producing), allowed man to amass surpluses that allowed a dramatic increase in population and the support of craft specialists. Childe roughly equated his Neolithic stage with Morgan's (1878) "barbarism," but he subdivided it to allow for the effects of such other technological advances as the use of copper and bronze.

Childe's *Social Evolution* (1951) is an earlier, one-man summary of the same evidence that was compiled by Braidwood and Willey (1962), and the conclusions are essentially the same—that cultures have taken diverse roads but are tending in the same direction. In the sense that man has continuously improved his adaptation to his environment, Childe says that he "progressed," and he calls this progress social evolution. Although their conclusions were similar, Braidwood and Willey were little interested either in progress per se or in revolution.

The descriptive models used by Braidwood, Childe, and Willey attempt to tell what happened in prehistory and how it happened; they do not, except secondarily, try to tell why any particular event occurred.

Most modern archeologists have confined themselves to descriptive models, but other scholars have been less diffident. For example, Arnold Toynbee, in his *Study of History,* contended that cultural progress resulted from man's meeting the challenges placed before him. His point of view has strong religious overtones, and for this and other reasons has not been generally accepted. In many instances he relied on data that are now known to be incorrect, and in others he had no data and only assumed certain challenges where there may have been none. In any event, *ex post facto* it is difficult to know what a "challenge" would have meant to prehistoric man. In short, although Toynbee's work is impressive scholarship, it fails to give much insight into the course of prehistory.

Ellsworth Huntington, a geographer, also made an attempt to organize culture history (1945). He tried to demonstrate the role of environment in determining civilization. In environment he saw opportunities which would be exploited by people who had the proper genetic makeup. Huntington believed vigorous civilizations could only be developed under rigorous climatic conditions. Albright (1957:121) proposes a series of six stages in the history of culture based upon greater or lesser integration and differentiation through time. According to this approach, "the Graeco-Roman civilization of the time of Christ represented the closest approach to a rational unified culture that the world has yet seen and may justly be taken as the culmination of a long period of relatively steady evolution." Culture history has also been written to demonstrate racial superiority. Hitler had his archeologists excavate extensively in Germany to trace the origins of the Aryan race. He had his historians write histories that showed how the Nordics had led the world from the beginning of time.

There remains one important theory that is still viable and will continue to be influential. This is based upon Marx and Engel's incorporation of Morgan's ethnographic data of the late nineteenth century into a picture of the past. It purports to demonstrate the close ties between technology and society. Instead of dividing prehistory into technological stages or economic stages, the communist thinkers have set up a series of social stages wherein society changes from a family based on communism to a matrilineal clan and finally, after techniques of farming are learned, into a series of degenerate class societies. The idea was that the "whole structure of society is determined in the long run by the 'mode (method) of production' which in turn is dependent on the 'means of production'—that is, on the technical forces at the disposal of society for the satisfaction of socially recognized needs" (Childe 1951:10). As Childe goes on to show, such a viewpoint is untenable in the face of evidence. "The Russian scheme of classification assumes in advance precisely what archaeological facts have to prove" (Childe 1951: 29) and hence is foredoomed. Some sort of causal relation between technology and society is not denied; what is denied is that a *kind of technology* inevitably results in a *kind of society*. It is nearer to the truth to say that with a given technology there are certain alternate forms which society may take.

As a general statement we might say that at present there is no wholly adequate model for describing the course of human history. If we go a step farther and inquire about their interpretive value we soon see that none of them goes very far in helping us understand why there are certain trends, let alone particular events in any sequence of cultures. When models emphasize distinctive clusters of artifacts or combinations of artifacts and forms of society, they become cast in an attitude of descriptive typology rather than of interpretation. Probably no scheme of classification can be very useful for purposes of interpretation. But, given an interest in interpretation, there are orderly ways of proceeding toward the discovery of causes. (The following discussion is in some ways similar to that of Steward 1949.)

Students of culture change (for example, Barnett 1953) have pointed out that change is inevitable in the long run. They do not admit, however, that change necessarily takes a continuous path in any particular direction. In fact, there are changes which give all the appearances of being nondirectional although their cyclical nature might be argued.

It is useful to think of changes as being adaptive, or of being the inevitable consequences of certain preconditions. The problem for a prehistorian is to distinguish among the general categories of possible causes. In the instance of directional changes, we may find that there are common situations (for example, raiding and warfare, diffusion of technological innovations) operating in various contexts throughout the world that have the effect of predisposing culture to take certain directions and not others, if only for the sake of survival (adaptation). The causes of unique changes are probably to be found in such factors as are spelled out in great detail by Barnett (1953): in general, the impossibility of duplicating anything because of the uniqueness of every situation; and change breeds change.

Beginning with some rather simple statements—that is, that cultures change and that on a world-wide basis they tend to change from technologically and socially simple to complex—we can suggest orderly ways to approach the answer of why these statements are true.

Clearly we must first find out what happened in the past but just as clearly we cannot do this without taking into account what we want to find out.

We can begin by recognizing that most of any culture's artifacts and activities are likely to be only slightly, if at all, related to the cause for the more general forms that culture has taken. This suggests that, for understanding trends and long-range changes, there may be aspects of culture that are more important than others. Given our interest in the general history of culture, our problem is both to discover which changes were important in the long run and what caused them. By this line of reasoning, for example, we would be more interested in the fact that large groups of laborers were brought together to build the pyramids than in the changes in the architecture of the structures themselves. On the one hand we have a mobilization for common effort, of people who might otherwise have minded their own businesses. On the other hand, we have architectural and artistic changes which, although they may help us identify particular cultures, seem to tell us little about the crucial changes in society itself.

Perhaps we should reemphasize here that we must make our own choices about what is important. For this example we assumed that over the long run, changes in the organization of society were more important than changes in technological efficiency or in style alone. This in no way minimizes any efforts to trace the causes of the technological and artistic changes; it only suggests that for our present example these efforts seem peripheral.

There are a number of aspects of the development of human culture that might be investigated by archeologists, although perhaps not simultaneously. Changes in technology and subsistence are obvious and their causes may be discernible. Changes in the organization of society are not directly observable until graphic art and status symbols announce them, but they are "visible" in such structures as pyramids, which imply the mobilization, direction, and maintenance of laborers drawn from outside the range of any single community. We might consider organized warfare as also being closely related to and an indication of the establishment of an impersonal and complex society.

Still another aspect of human history is the "decline and fall" of some societies and the changing importance relative to neighboring societies of others. The apparent collapse of the Classic Maya is an example of the former, while the emergence of powerful and colorful societies in the Southeast United States or on coastal British Columbia that outstripped their formerly equal neighbors in social organization and wealth is an example of the latter. As archeologists we can ask why these particular changes occurred and, if we can discover their causes, whether our reasons are applicable to general statements about human history. In essence the procedure is to eliminate as many secondary factors as possible so that we can see the more fundamental issues.

Perhaps many will agree with these general aims of archeological research but not understand how we can hope to learn so much. We have only some modest suggestions to make.

As noted above, in the long run, if we are to discover why cultures trended in similar directions or why they changed in particular ways, we must first adequately describe precisely what did happen. This means that we must try to understand particular situations in terms of the situations themselves rather than in terms of some arbitrary set of stages or theories of trends. In any situation there are physical conditions (geographic and demographic) that can be specified. At the same time it is usually possible to specify many of the technical skills of the prehistoric people by observing the tools they used, the things they made, the things they ate, and the things they traded. To this we can add knowledge of social organization and relations to surrounding people. When these factors have been specified, even though we are ignorant of language, customs, and beliefs, we can still make some tentative movements in the direction of understanding by trying to see how each of these elements relates to the others. In this way we begin to see how people in the past acted and interacted with their physical and social environments. When we have done this a number of times we may begin to see recurrent situations. For example, we can cite a rare instance of this sort of inference in the work of Michael Coe (1961) who compared the ancient Maya and Khmer civilizations and found similarities in the environmental situations that suggested possible causes for the form that each society took.

In Coe's view, geographic homogeneity, even distribution of resources, difficulty of travel, and an easily produced surplus of food, predisposed both civilizations to develop "unilineal" societies with a strong religious focus. He contrasts this with highland Mexico and Mesopotamia where, except for abundant food production, opposite factors prevailed and the civilizations were "organic," held together by economic needs. This analysis, incidentally, relieves one of the problem of trying to relate very similar developments to migration or other sorts of influences of one population on another.

Similar studies might be done—not of moments in time—but of sequences where changes are dramatic, and even of sequences where changes are not evident. In these instances we should focus on determining the causes for change or stability. When dependable data covering long periods of change or stability are not available, archeologists have resorted to picking examples from a variety of places, and trying to account for what they find in the various situations. This is exceedingly difficult because of the many variables involved. It would seem more fruitful to concentrate these kinds of analysis on sequences where the basic situations remain relatively unchanging and where the influence of specific factors can be assessed. That is, within an unbroken sequence in one region, it is relatively easy to detect such things as climatic change, the influx of new people, new technology, and the like, and to see reactions by the local people to them.

Most prehistorians have not come to grips with such questions as these but there is no reason why attempts to answer them should not become the goals for serious research. We must emphasize, however, that present data are too few in many places and inadequate in others; for the immediate future, archeologists will have to concentrate on acquiring these data.

It should be clear from the foregoing that major discoveries about the causes for the particular history that culture has had will be made only after a great deal more data have been gathered with this end in mind. In a sense this book is a plea for a long-range approach to archeology, even though its major emphasis has been on what archeology is and what some of the techniques for doing it are.

BIBLIOGRAPHY

Adams, R. M., "Agriculture and Urban Life in Early Southwestern Iran," *Science,* Vol. 136 (1962), pp. 109–122.

Aitken, M. J., "Magnetic Dating," *Archaeometry,* Vol. 3 (1960), pp. 41–44.

———, *Physics and Archaeology.* New York: Interscience, 1961.

———, "Magnetic Location," in D. Brothwell and E. Higgs, eds., *Science in Archaeology.* London: Thames and Hudson, 1963, pp. 555–568.

Albright, W. F., "Ceramics and Chronology in the Near East," in D. D. Brand and F. E. Harvey, eds., *So Live the Works of Men.* Albuquerque, N.M.: University of New Mexico Press, 1939, pp. 49–63.

———, *From the Stone Age to Christianity,* 2d ed. Baltimore: The Johns Hopkins Press, 1957.

Alcock, L., "A Technique for Surface Collecting," *Antiquity,* Vol. 98 (1951), pp. 75–76.

Aldred, C., *The Egyptians.* New York: Praeger, 1961.

Allen, D., "Belgic Coins as Illustrations of Life in the Late Pre-Roman Iron Age in Britain," *Proceedings of the Prehistoric Society,* Vol. 24 (1958), pp. 43–64.

Allen, D. C., "The Predecessors of Champollion," *Proceedings of the American Philosophical Society,* Vol. 104 (1960), pp. 527–547.

Allen, Don, and E. P. Cheatum, "Ecological Implications of Fresh-Water and Land Gastropods in Texas Archeological Studies," *Bulletin of the Texas Archeological Society,* Vol. 31 (1961), pp. 291–316.

Alonso del Real, C., "Notas de Sociologia Paleolitica," *Journal of World History,* Vol. 7 (1963), pp. 675–700.

Andersen, H., "Det Femte Store Mosefund," *Kuml,* Aarhus, (1951a), pp. 9–22.

———, "Tomme Hoje [Empty Tumuli]," *Kuml,* Aarhus, (1951b), pp. 91–135.

Anderson, E. C., and H. Levi, "Some Problems in Radiocarbon Dating," *Det Kongelige Danske Videnskabernes Selskab,* Copenhagen, Vol. 27 (1952), No. 6.

Anderson, R. Y., "Pollen Analysis, A Research Tool for the Study of Cave Deposits," *American Antiquity,* Vol. 21 (1955), pp. 84–85.

Angel, L., "The Length of Life in Ancient Greece," *Journal of Gerontology,* Vol. 2 (1947), pp. 18–24.

Anonymous, *Bibliography of Geochronology.* Cambridge, Mass.: Geochron Laboratories, 1962.

Antevs, E., "Climatic Changes and Pre-White Man," *University of Utah Bulletin,* Vol. 38 (1948), pp. 168–191.

————, "Climatic History and the Antiquity of Man in California," *Report of the University of California Archaeological Survey,* No. 16 (1952), pp. 23–31.

————, "Geochronology of the Deglacial and Neothermal Ages," *Journal of Geology,* Vol. 61 (1953a), pp. 195–230.

————, "Age of the Clovis Fluted Points With the Naco Mammoth," *American Antiquity,* Vol. 19 (1953b), pp. 15–17.

————, "Teleconnection of Varves, Radiocarbon Chronology and Geology," *Journal of Geology,* Vol. 62 (1954), pp. 516–521.

————, "Geological Tests of the Varve and Radiocarbon Chronologies," *Journal of Geology,* Vol. 65 (1957), pp. 129–148.

————, "Geological Age of the Lehner Mammoth Site," *American Antiquity,* Vol. 25 (1959), pp. 31–34.

————, "Transatlantic Climatic Agreement Versus C_{14} Dates," *Journal of Geology,* Vol. 70 (1962), pp. 194–205.

Arnold, J. R., and W. F. Libby, "Age Determinations by Radiocarbon Content: Checks with Samples of Known Age," *Science,* Vol. 110 (1949), pp. 678–680.

Ascher, R., "A Prehistoric Population Estimate Using Midden Analysis and Two Population Models," *Southwestern Journal of Anthropology,* Vol. 15 (1959), pp. 168–178.

————, "Analogy in Archaeological Interpretation," *Southwestern Journal of Anthropology,* Vol. 17 (1961a), pp. 317–325.

————, "Experimental Archeology," *American Anthropologist,* Vol. 63 (1961b), pp. 793–816.

Aschmann, H., *The Central Desert of Baja California: Demography and Ecology.* Berkeley: Calif. Ibero-Americana, No. 42, 1959.

Ashbee, P., and I. W. Cornwall, "An Experiment in Field Archaeology," *Antiquity,* Vol. 35 (1961), pp. 129–134.

Atkinson, R. J. C., *Field Archaeology.* London: Methuen, 1946.

————, *Stonehenge.* London: Hamish Hamilton, 1956.

————, "Worms and Weathering," *Antiquity,* Vol. 33 (1957), pp. 219–233.

Baker, R. G., "The Recarving and Alteration of Maya Monuments," *American Antiquity,* Vol. 27 (1962), pp. 281–302.

Balfet, H., "Basketry: A Proposed Classification," *L'Anthropologie,* Vol. 56 (1952), pp. 259–280. Reprinted in English translation in *Reports of the University of California Archaeological Survey,* No. 37, pp. 1–21.

Ball, S. H., "The Mining of Gems and Ornamental Stones by American Indians," *Bureau of American Ethnology,* Bulletin 128 (1941), pp. 1–77.

Bannister, B., "The Interpretation of Tree-Ring Dates," *American Antiquity,* Vol. 27 (1962), pp. 508–514.

————, "Dendrochronology," in D. Brothwell and E. Higgs, eds., *Science in Archaeology.* London: Thames and Hudson, 1963, pp. 162–176.

————, and T. L. Smiley, "Dendrochronology," in T. L. Smiley, ed., *Geochronology, with Special Reference to the Southwestern United States.* Tucson, Ariz.: University of Arizona Bulletin, Vol. 26 (1955), pp. 177–195.

Barnes, A. S., "The Difference Between Natural and Human Flaking in Prehistoric Flint Implements," *American Anthropologist,* Vol. 41 (1939), pp. 99–112.

Barnett, H. G., *Innovation*. New York: McGraw-Hill, 1953.

Barrington, D., "Particulars relative to a human skeleton and the garments that were found thereon when dug out of a bog at the foot of Drumkeragh, a mountain in the county of Down and barony of Kinelearty, on Lord Moira's estate, in the autumn of 1780," *Archaeologia*, Vol. 7 (1783), pp. 90–110.

Bass, G. F., "Underwater Archeology: Key to History's Warehouse," *National Geographic*, Vol. 124 (1963), pp. 138–156.

Bastian, T., "Trace Element and Metallographic Studies of Prehistoric Copper Artifacts in North America: A Review," *Anthropological Papers of the Museum of Anthropology*, University of Michigan, No. 17 (1961), pp. 151–189.

Baud, C. A., "Dating of Prehistoric Bones by Radiological and Optical Methods," *Viking Fund Publications in Anthropology*, No. 28 (1960), pp. 246–264.

Baumhoff, M. A., "Ecological Determinants of Aboriginal California Populations," *University of California Publications in American Archaeology and Ethnology*, Vol. 49 (1963), No. 2, pp. 155–236.

———, and R. F. Heizer, "Some Unexploited Possibilities in Ceramic Analysis," *Southwestern Journal of Anthropology*, Vol. 15 (1959), pp. 308–316.

———, and D. L. Olmsted, "Palaihnihan: Radiocarbon Support for Glottochronology," *American Anthropologist*, Vol. 65 (1963), pp. 278–284.

Belzoni, G., *Narrative of the Operations and Recent Discoveries Within the Pyramids, Temples, Tombs and Excavations in Egypt and Nubia*, 2 Vols. London: J. Murray, 1820.

Bennett, H. G., "An account of the ancient rolls of papyrus, discovered at Herculaneum, and the method employed to unroll them," *Archaeologia*, Vol. 15 (1806), pp. 114–117.

Bennett, J. W., "The Interaction of Culture and Environment in the Smaller Societies," *American Anthropologist*, Vol. 46 (1944), pp. 461–478.

Bennett, W. C., "Excavations at Wari, Ayacucho, Peru," *Yale University Publications in Anthropology*, No. 49 (1953).

Bennyhoff, J. A., and A. B. Elsasser, "Sonoma Mission: An Historical and Archaeological Study of Primary Constructions, 1823–1913," *Reports of the University of California Archaeological Survey*, Vol. 27 (1954).

Berger, R., A. G. Horney, and W. F. Libby. "Radiocarbon Dating of Bone and Shell from their Organic Components." *Science*, Vol. 144 (1964), pp. 999–1001.

Bergounioux, F.-M., and J. Goetz, *Les Religions des Préhistoriques et des Primitifs*. Paris: Artheime Fayard, 1958.

Bergsland, K., and H. Vogt, "On the Validity of Glottochronology," *Current Anthropology*, Vol. 3 (1962), pp. 115–153.

Berndt, R. M., "Ceremonial Exchange in Western Arnhem Land," *Southwestern Journal of Anthropology*, Vol. 7 (1951), pp. 156–176.

Bessaignet, P., "An Alleged Case of Primitive Money (New Caledonia Beads)," *Southwestern Journal of Anthropology*, Vol. 12 (1956), pp. 333–345.

Bibby, G., *The Testimony of the Spade*. New York: Knopf, 1956.

Biek, L., "Soil Silhouettes," in D. Brothwell and E. Higgs, eds., *Science in Archaeology*. London: Thames and Hudson, 1963a, pp. 108–112.

———, *Archaeology and the Microscope*. London: Lutterworth Press, 1963b.

Binford, L. R., "A Proposed Attribute List for the Description and Classification of Projectile Points," *Anthropological Papers of the Museum of Anthropology*, University of Michigan, No. 19 (1963), pp. 193–221.

Bird, J. B., "Excavations in Northern Chile," *Anthropological Papers of the American Museum of Natural History*, Vol. 38 (1943), part 4.

Birdsell, J. B., "Some Population Problems Involving Pleistocene Man," *Cold Spring Harbor Symposia on Quantitative Biology*, Vol. 22 (1957), pp. 47–69.

Black, G. A., and R. B. Johnston, "A Test of Magnetometry as an Aid to Archaeology," *American Antiquity*, Vol. 28 (1962), pp. 199–205.

Blackwood, B., "The Technology of a Modern Stone Age People in New Guinea," *Pitt Rivers Museum, Oxford University, Occasional Papers on Technology*, No. 3, 1950.

Blanc, A. C., "The Finest Paleolithic Drawings of the Human Figure—Revealed by the Demolition of Artillery Shells in a Sicilian Cave," *Illustrated London News*, Vol. 223 (1953), pp. 187–189.

———, and L. Pales. "Le Vestigia Umane nella Grotta della Bàsura a Toirano." *Rivista di Studi Liguri*, Anno XXVI (1960), pp. 1–90. Instituto Internazionale di Studi Liguri, Bordighera, Italy.

Blinkenberg, C., *The Thunder Weapon in Religion and Folklore: A Study in Comparative Folklore*. London: Cambridge University Press, 1911.

Bohmers, A., "Statistics and Graphs in the Study of Flint Assemblages," *Palaeohistoria*, Vol. 5 (1956), pp. 1–5, 7–25, 27–38.

———, "A Statistical Analysis of Flint Artifacts," in D. Brothwell and E. Higgs, eds., *Science in Archaeology*. London: Thames and Hudson, 1963, pp. 469–481.

de Booy, T., "Pottery from Certain Caves in Eastern Santo Domingo, West Indies," *American Anthropologist*, Vol. 17 (1915), pp. 69–97.

Borden, C. E., "A Uniform Site Designation Scheme for Canada," British Columbia Provincial Museum, *Anthropology in British Columbia*, No. 3 (1952), pp. 44–48.

Bordes, F., "Les Limons Quaternaires du Bassin de la Seine," *Archives de l'Institut de Paléontologie Humaine*, Mémoire No. 26, 1954.

———, *Typologie du Paléolithique Ancien et Moyen*, Mémoire No. 1, de l'Institut de Préhistoire de l'Université de Bordeaux, 1961.

Bouchud, J., "Dents de Rennes, Bois de Rennes, et migrations," *Bulletin Société Préhistorique Française*, Vol. 51 (1954), pp. 340–345.

Bowen, R. N. C., *The Exploration of Time*. London: G. Lewnes, 1958.

Bowie, S. H. U., and C. F. Davidson, "The Radioactivity of the Piltdown Fossils," *Bulletin of the British Museum of Natural History, Geology*, Vol. 2 (1955), No. 6, pp. 276–282.

Bradford, J., *Ancient Landscapes: Studies in Field Archaeology*. London: G. Bell, 1957.

Braidwood, L., *Digging Beyond the Tigris*. New York: Abelard-Schuman, 1953.

Braidwood, R. J., "The Order of Incompleteness of the Archeological Record," in *Human Origins: Selected Readings*, 2d ed. Chicago: University of Chicago Bookstore, 1946, pp. 108–112.

———, *Archeologists and What They Do*. New York: Watts, 1960.

———, "Prehistoric Men," rev. ed., *Chicago Natural History Museum Popular Series, Anthropology*, No. 37, 1961.

————, and C. A. Reed, "The Achievement and Early Consequences of Food-Production: A Consideration of the Archeological and Natural-Historical Evidence," *Cold Spring Harbor Symposia on Quantitative Biology,* Vol. 22 (1957), pp. 19–32.

————, and B. Howe, "Prehistoric Investigations in Iraqi Kurdistan," Oriental Institute of the University of Chicago, *Studies in Oriental Civilization,* No. 31, 1960.

————, and G. Willey, *Courses Toward Urban Life.* Chicago: Viking Fund Publications in Anthropology, No. 32, 1962.

Brainerd, G. W., "The Place of Chronological Ordering in Archaeological Analysis," *American Antiquity,* Vol. 16 (1951), pp. 301–313.

Brand, D. D., "Aboriginal Trade Routes for Sea Shells in the Southwest," *Association of Pacific Coast Geographers,* Vol. 4 (1938), pp. 3–10.

Breasted, C., *Pioneer to the Past; The Story of James Henry Breasted, Archaeologist.* London: Jenkins, 1947.

Breuil, H., *The Discovery of the Antiquity of Man.* London: Royal Anthropological Institute of Great Britain and Ireland, 1941.

————, "Pratiques religieuses chez les humanités quaternaires," *Scienza e Civilta* (1951), pp. 45–75.

————, *Four Hundred Centuries of Cave Art,* trans. by M. E. Boyle. Montignac, Dordogne: Centre d'Etudes et de Documentation Préhistoriques, 1952.

Brew, J. O., "The Threat to Nubia," *Archaeology,* Vol. 14 (1961), pp. 268–276.

Briggs, L. J., and K. F. Weaver, "How Old Is It?" *The National Geographic Magazine,* Vol. 114 (1958), pp. 234–255.

Brill, R. H., "The Record of Time in Weathered Glass," *Archaeology,* Vol. 14 (1961), pp. 18–22.

Brisse A., and L. Routrou, *The Draining of Lake Fucino Accomplished by Prince Alexander Torlonia,* 2 vols. Rome: Propaganda Press, 1876.

Broecker, W., "Radiocarbon Dating: A Case Against the Proposed Link Between River Mollusks and Soil Humus," *Science,* Vol. 143 (1964), pp. 596–597.

————, and J. L. Kulp, "The Radiocarbon Method of Age Determination," *American Antiquity,* Vol. 22 (1956), pp. 1–11.

Broholm, H. C., and M. Hald, *Costumes of the Bronze Age in Denmark.* Copenhagen: Gyldendal, 1940.

Brothwell, D., and E. Higgs, eds., *Science in Archaeology.* London: Thames and Hudson, 1963.

Brown, J. K., "A Cross-Cultural Study of Female Initiation Rites," *American Anthropologist,* Vol. 65 (1963), pp. 837–853.

Bruce-Mitford, R. L. S., ed., *Recent Archaeological Excavations in Britain.* London: Routledge, 1956.

Bruning, H. H., "Moderne Topferei der Indianer Perus," *Globus,* Vol. 74 (1898), pp. 259–260.

Bryan, K., "Flint Quarries—the Sources of Tools and, at the Same Time, the Factories of the American Indian," *Papers of the Peabody Museum,* Cambridge, Mass., Vol. 17, No. 3, 1950.

Buettner-Janusch, J., "Use of Infrared Photography in Archaeological Field Work," *American Antiquity,* Vol. 20 (1954), pp. 84–87.

Burchell, J. P. T., "Land Shells and Their Role in Dating Deposits of Postglacial Times in Southeast England," *Archaeological News Letter*, London, Vol. 7 (1961), pp. 34–38.

Burkitt, M. C., *The Old Stone Age*. London: Cambridge University Press, 1933.

Burton, D., J. B. Poole, and R. Reed, "A New Approach to the Dating of the Dead Sea Scrolls," *Nature*, Vol. 184 (1959), pp. 533–534.

Byers, D. S., "The Bering Bridge—Some Speculations," *Ethnos* (1957), pp. 20–26.

———, and F. Johnson, "Two Sites on Martha's Vineyard," *Papers of the R. S. Peabody Foundation for Archaeology*, Vol. 1, 1940.

Caldwell, J. R., "The New American Archeology," *Science*, Vol. 129 (1959), pp. 303–307.

Caley, E. R., "Archaeological Chemistry," *Chemical and Engineering News*, Vol. 27 (1949), pp. 2140–2142.

Callen, E. O., "Diet as Revealed by Coprolites," in D. Brothwell and E. Higgs, eds., *Science in Archaeology*. London: Thames and Hudson, 1963, pp. 186–194.

———, and T. W. M. Cameron, "A Prehistoric Diet Revealed by Coprolites," *The New Scientist*, (July 7, 1960), pp. 35–40.

Cardos de M., A., *El Commercio de los Mayas Antiguos*. Mexico City: Acta Anthropologica, Epoca 2, Vol. 2; No. 1, 1959.

Carneiro, R., "Slash-and-Burn Agriculture: A Closer Look at its Implications for Settlement Patterns," *Selected Papers of the Fifth International Congress of Anthropological and Ethnological Sciences*. Philadelphia: The University of Pennsylvania Press, 1956, pp. 229–234.

———, "An Instance of the Transport of Artifacts by Migratory Animals in South America," *American Antiquity*, Vol. 24 (1958), pp. 192–193.

———, "Slash-and-Burn Cultivation Among the Kuikuru and Its Implications for Cultural Developments in the Amazon Basin," *Antropologica* (Supplement No. 2), Caracas, Venezuela, 1961, pp. 47–67.

Carr, D. R., and J. L. Kulp, "Potassium-Argon Method of Geochronometry," *Bulletin of the Geological Society of America*, Vol. 68 (1957), pp. 763–784.

Casson, S., *The Discovery of Man: The Story of the Inquiry Into Human Origins*. New York: Harper & Row, 1939.

Catch, J. R., *Carbon-14 Compounds*. Toronto: Butterworth, 1961.

Caton-Thompson, G., and E. W. Gardner, *The Desert Fayum*. London: The Royal Anthropological Institute of Great Britain and Ireland, 1934.

Ceram, C. W., *The March of Archaeology*. New York: Knopf, 1958.

Chadwick, J., "A Prehistoric Bureaucracy," *Diogenes*, No. 26 (1959), pp. 7–18.

———, *The Decipherment of Linear B*. Baltimore: Penguin Books A340, 1961.

Chapman, A. M., "Trade Enclaves in Aztec and Maya Civilizations," in K. Polanyi, C. M. Arensberg, and H. W. Pearson, eds., *Trade and Market in the Early Empires*. New York: Free Press, 1957, pp. 114–153.

Chang, Kwang-Chih, "Study of the Neolithic Social Grouping: Examples from the New World," *American Anthropologist*, Vol. 60 (1958), pp. 298–334.

Charanis, P., "The Transfer of Population as a Policy in the Byzantine Empire," *Comparative Studies in History and Sociology*, Vol. 3 (1961), pp. 140–154.

Childe, V. G., "The Experimental Production of the Phenomena Distinctive of Vitrified Forts," *Proceedings of the Society of Antiquaries of Scotland*, Vol. 72 (1937–1938), pp. 23–50.

——, "Historical Analysis of Archaeological Method (a Review of G. Daniel, *The Three Ages*.)," *Nature*, Vol. 153 (1944a), pp. 206–207.

——, *Archaeological Ages as Technological Stages*. London: Royal Anthropological Institute of Great Britain and Ireland, Huxley Lecture, 1944b.

——, *Scotland Before the Scots*. London: Methuen, 1946.

——, *Man Makes Himself*, rev. ed. New York: New American Library, 1951.

——, *Social Evolution*. London: Watts, 1951.

——, *What Is History?*. New York: Abelard-Schuman, 1953.

——, *What Happened in History*, rev. ed. Baltimore: Penguin Books, 1954.

——, *Piecing Together the Past*. New York: Praeger, 1956.

——, *The Dawn of European Civilization*, 6th ed., rev. New York: Knopf, 1957.

——, *The Prehistory of European Society*. Baltimore: Penguin Books, 1958.

——, *A Short Introduction to Archaeology*. New York: Collier, 1962.

Clair, C., *Strong Man Egyptologist*. London: Olbourne Press, 1957.

Clark, D. L., "The Obsidian Dating Method," *Current Anthropology*, Vol. 2 (1961), pp. 111–116.

Clark, J. G. D., "Folk-Culture and the Study of European Prehistory," in W. Grimes, ed., *Aspects of Archaeology in Great Britain and Beyond*. London: H. W. Edwards, 1951, pp. 49–65.

——, *Prehistoric Europe: The Economic Basis*. London: Methuen, 1952.

——, "Archaeological Theories and Interpretations," in A. L. Kroeber, chairman, *Anthropology Today*. Chicago: University of Chicago Press, 1953a, pp. 343–360.

——, "The Economic Approach to Prehistory," *Proceedings of the British Academy*, Vol. 39 (1953b), pp. 215–238.

——, *Excavations at Star Carr*. London: Cambridge University Press, 1954.

——, *Archaeology and Society*. Cambridge, Mass.: Harvard University Press, 1957.

——, *Archaeology and Society*. London: Methuen, University Paperbacks, 1960.

Clark, J. Desmond, "The Natural Fracture of Pebbles from the Batoka Gorge, Northern Rhodesia, and its Bearing on the Kafuan Industries of Africa," *Proceedings of the Prehistoric Society*, Vol. 24 (1958), pp. 64–77.

——, *The Prehistory of Southern Africa*. Baltimore: Pelican Books, 1959.

——, "Human Ecology During Pleistocene and Later Times in Africa South of the Sahara," *Current Anthropology*, Vol. 1 (1960), pp. 307–324.

——, "Fractured Chert Specimens From the Lower Pleistocene Bethlehem Beds, Israel," *Bulletin of the British Museum of Natural History (Geology)*, Vol. 5 (1961), No. 4.

Clark, T. and T., *Explorations in Bible Lands*. Edinburgh: T. and T. Clark, 1903.

Cleator, P. E., *Lost Languages*. New York: Mentor Books MT 427, 1962.

Coe, M. D., "The Funerary Temple Among the Classic Maya," *Southwestern Journal of Anthropology*, Vol. 12 (1956), pp. 387–394.

——, "Social Typology and the Tropical Forest Civilizations," *Comparative Studies in Society and History*, Vol. 4 (1961), pp. 65–85.

Coe, W. R., *Piedras Negras Archaeology: Artifacts, Caches and Burials.* Philadelphia: Museum Monographs, University of Pennsylvania Museum, 1959.

Coghlan, H. H., "Prehistoric Copper and Some Experiments in Smelting," *Transactions of the Newcomen Society,* Vol. 20 (1940), pp. 49–65.

———, "Metallurgical Analysis of Archaeological Materials: I," *Viking Fund Publications in Anthropology,* No. 28 (1960), pp. 1–20.

Cole, F.-C., and T. Deuel, *Rediscovering Illinois.* Chicago: University of Chicago Press, 1937.

Colton, H. S., "Sunset Crater; the Effect of a Volcanic Eruption on an Ancient People," *Geographical Review,* Vol. 22 (1932), pp. 582–590.

———, "Prehistoric Trade in the Southwest," *Scientific Monthly,* Vol. 52 (1941), pp. 308–319.

———, *The Sinagua.* Flagstaff, Ariz.: Museum of Northern Arizona, Bulletin 22, 1946.

———, *Potsherds.* Flagstaff, Ariz.: Museum of Northern Arizona, Bulletin 25, 1953.

Conklin, H. C., "Buhid Pottery," *University of Manila Journal of East Asiatic Studies,* Vol. 3 (1953), pp. 1–12.

———, "The Study of Shifting Cultivation," *Current Anthropology,* Vol. 2 (1961), pp. 27–61.

Cook, R. M., "Archaeomagnetism," in D. Brothwell and E. Higgs, eds., *Science in Archaeology.* London: Thames and Hudson, 1963, pp. 59–71.

———, and J. C. Belshe, "Dating by Archaeomagnetism," *Archaeology,* Vol. 12 (1959), pp. 158–162.

Cook, S. F., "Human Sacrifice and Warfare as Factors in the Demography of Pre-Colonial Mexico," *Human Biology,* Vol. 18 (1946), pp. 81–102.

———, "Dating Prehistoric Bone by Chemical Analysis," *Viking Fund Publications in Anthropology,* No. 28 (1960), pp. 223–245.

———, "Erosion Morphology and Occupation History in Western Mexico," *University of California Anthropological Records,* Vol. 17 (1963), No. 3, pp. 281–334.

———, and H. C. Ezra-Cohn, "An Evaluation of the Fluorine Dating Method," *Southwestern Journal of Anthropology,* Vol. 15 (1959), pp. 276–290.

———, and A. E. Treganza, "The Quantitative Investigation of Indian Mounds," *University of California Publications in American Archaeology and Ethnology,* Vol. 40 (1950), No. 5.

———, and R. F. Heizer, "The Fossilization of Bone: Organic Components and Water," *Reports of the University of California Archaeological Survey,* No. 17 (1952).

———, and ———, "Archaeological Dating by Chemical Analysis of Bone," *Southwestern Journal of Anthropology,* Vol. 9 (1953), pp. 231–238.

———, and ———, "The Chemical Analysis of Fossil Bone: Individual Variation," *American Journal of Physical Anthropology,* Vol. 17 (1959), pp. 109–115.

———, and ———, "Chemical Analysis of the Hotchkiss Site," *Reports of the University of California Archaeological Survey,* No. 57 (1962), Part I, pp. 1–24.

Cookson, M. B., *Photography for Archaeologists*. London: Parrish, 1954.

Coon, C. S., *Cave Explorations in Iran, 1949*. Philadelphia: Museum Monographs, University of Pennsylvania Museum, 1951.

———, *The Seven Caves*. New York: Knopf, 1957.

Cooney, J. D., "Assorted Errors in Art Collecting," *Expedition*, Vol. 6 (1963), No. 1, pp. 20–27.

Cornwall, I. W., *Bones for the Archaeologist*. London: Phoenix House, 1956.

———, *Soils for the Archaeologist*. London: Phoenix House, 1958.

———, "Soil Investigations in the Service of Archaeology," *Viking Fund Publications in Anthropology*, No. 28 (1960), pp. 265–299.

———, "Soil-Science Helps the Archaeologist," in E. Pyddoke, ed., *The Scientist and Archaeology*. London: Phoenix House, 1963, pp. 31–55.

Cosgrove, C. B., "Caves of the Upper Gila and Hueco Areas in New Mexico and Texas," *Papers of the Peabody Museum*, Cambridge, Mass., Vol. 24, No. 2, 1947.

Cosner, A. J., "Arrowshaft Straightening with a Grooved Stone," *American Antiquity*, Vol. 17 (1951), pp. 147–148.

Cotter, J. L., *Archeological Excavations at Jamestown, Virginia*. Washington, D.C., National Park Service, Archeological Research Series, No. 4, 1958.

Cowgill, U. M., "Soil Fertility and the Ancient Maya," *Transactions of the Connecticut Academy of Arts and Sciences*, Vol. 42 (1961), pp. 1–56.

———, "An Agricultural Study of the Southern Maya Lowlands," *American Anthropologist*, Vol. 64 (1962), pp. 273–286.

———, and G. E. Hutchinson, "Ecological and Geochemical Archaeology in the Southern Maya Lowlands," *Southwestern Journal of Anthropology*, Vol. 19 (1963), pp. 267–286.

Craig, H., "Carbon-13 in Plants and Relationships Between Carbon-13 and Carbon-14 Variations in Nature," *Journal of Geology*, Vol. 62 (1954), pp. 115–149.

Crawford, O. G. S., *Archaeology in the Field*. New York: Praeger, 1953.

———, *Said and Done; the Autobiography of an Archaeologist*. London: Weidenfeld and Nicolson, 1955.

Creel, H. G., *Studies in Early Chinese Culture*. American Council of Learned Societies, Studies in Chinese and Related Civilizations, Washington, D.C., No. 3, 1937.

Crossland, R. A., "Indo-European Origins: the Linguistic Evidence," *Past and Present*, No. 12 (1957), pp. 16–46.

Cummings, B., "Cuicuilco and the Archaic Culture of Mexico," *University of Arizona Bulletin*, Vol. 4 (1933), No. 8.

Curtis, G. H., "A Clock for the Ages: Potassium-Argon," *National Geographic Magazine*, Vol. 120 (1961), pp. 590–592.

Curwen, E. C., "Prehistoric Flint Sickles," *Antiquity*, Vol. 4 (1930), pp. 179–186.

———, "The Furrows in Prehistoric Fields in Denmark," *Antiquity*, Vol. 20 (1946), pp. 38–39.

Cushing, F. H., "Primitive Copper Working: An Experimental Study," *American Anthropologist*, Old Series, Vol. 7 (1894), pp. 93–117.

Daniel, G. E., *The Three Ages*. London: Cambridge University Press, 1943.

———, *A Hundred Years of Archaeology*. London: Macmillan, 1950.

——, "Prehistory and Protohistory in France," *Antiquity,* Vol. 29 (1955), pp. 209–214.

——, "The Idea of Man's Antiquity," *Scientific American,* Vol. 201 (1959), pp. 167–176.

——, *The Prehistoric Chambered Tombs of France.* London: Longmans, 1960.

——, *The Idea of Prehistory.* London: Watts, 1962.

Dannenfeldt, K., "Egypt and Egyptian Antiquities in the Renaissance," *Studies in the Renaissance,* Vol. 6 (1959), pp. 7–27.

Dart, R. A., "The Predatory Implement Technique of *Australopithecus,*" *American Journal of Physical Anthropology,* New Series, Vol. 7 (1949), pp. 1–38.

——, *The Osteodontokeratic Culture of Australopithecus Prometheus.* Transvaal Museum Memoir, No. 10, 1957.

——, "The Persistence of Some Tools and Utensils Found First in the Makapansgat Grey Breccia," *South African Journal of Science,* Vol. 56 (1960), pp. 71–74.

——, and J. W. Kitching, "Bone Tools at the Kalkbank Middle Stone Age Site and the Makapansgat Australopithecine Locality, Central Transvaal. Part 2, The Osteodontokeratic Contribution," *South African Archaeological Bulletin,* Vol. 13 (1958), pp. 94–116.

Daux, G., *Les Étapes de l'Archéologie.* Paris: Presses Universitaires de France, 1948.

Davis, J. T., "Trade Routes and Economic Exchange Among the Indians of California," *Reports of the University of California Archaeological Survey,* No. 61, 1961, Berkeley, Calif.

Dawkins, W. B., *Early Man in Britain and His Place in the Tertiary Period.* London: Macmillan, 1880.

Debenham, F., *Map Making.* Glasgow: Blackie, 1947.

de Borhegyi, S., *Ships, Shoals and Amphoras: The Story of Underwater Archaeology.* New York: Holt, Rinehart and Winston, Inc., 1961.

Deevey, E. S., Jr., "Pollen Analysis and Mexican Archaeology," *American Antiquity,* Vol. 10 (1944), pp. 135–149.

——, "On the Date of the Last Rise of Sea Level in Southern New England with Remarks on the Grassy Island Site," *American Journal of Science,* Vol. 246 (1948), pp. 329–352.

——, "Late Glacial and Postglacial Pollen Diagrams From Maine," *American Journal of Science,* Vol. 249 (1951), pp. 177–207.

Deetz, J., and E. Dethlefsen, "Soil pH as a Tool in Archaeological Site Interpretation," *American Antiquity,* Vol. 29 (1963), pp. 242–243.

De Geer, G., "A Geochronology of the Last 12,000 Years," *11th International Geological Congress, Stockholm (1910), Compte Rendu,* Vol. 1 (1912), pp. 241–258.

DeLaet, S. J., *Archaeology and its Problems.* London: Phoenix House, 1957.

DeLabarre, E. B., and H. H. Wilder, "Indian Corn-Hills in Massachusetts," *American Anthropologist,* Vol. 22 (1920), pp. 203–225.

De Laguna, F., "Geological Confirmation of Native Traditions, Yakutat, Alaska," *American Anthropologist,* Vol. 23 (1958), p. 434.

Delougaz, P., "The Treatment of Clay Tablets in the Field," Oriental Institute, *Studies in Ancient Oriental Civilizations,* No. 7, Part 2 (1933), pp. 39–57.

Dempsey, P., and M. Baumhoff, "The Statistical Use of Artifact Distributions to Establish Chronological Sequence," *American Antiquity,* Vol. 28 (1963), pp. 496–509.

Detweiler, A. H., *Manual of Archaeological Surveying.* New Haven, Conn.: American Schools of Oriental Research, Publications of the Jerusalem School, Archaeology, Vol. 2, 1948.

Dietz, E. F., "Natural Burial of Artifacts," *American Antiquity,* Vol. 20 (1955), pp. 273–274.

———, "Phosphorus Accumulation in Soil of an Indian Habitation Site," *American Antiquity,* Vol. 22 (1957), pp. 405–409.

Dimbleby, G. W., "Pollen Analysis," in D. Brothwell and E. Higgs, eds., *Science in Archaeology.* London: Thames and Hudson, 1963, pp. 139–149.

Di Peso, C. C., *The Reeve Ruin of Southeastern Arizona.* Dragoon, Arizona: Amerind Foundation, Publication No. 8, 1958.

Dittert, A. E., Jr., and F. Wendorf, *Procedural Manual for Archeological Field Research Projects of the Museum of New Mexico.* Santa Fe, N.M.: Museum of New Mexico Press, Papers in Anthropology No. 12 (1963).

Dixon, K. A., "The Interamerican Diffusion of a Cooking Technique: The Culinary Shoe-Pot," *American Anthropologist,* Vol. 65 (1963), pp. 593–619.

Dixon, R. B., "The Northern Maidu," Bulletin of the *American Museum of Natural History,* Vol. 17 (1903), Part 3.

———, and J. B. Stetson, "Analysis of Pre-Columbian Pipe Dottels," *American Anthropologist,* Vol. 24 (1922), No. 2, pp. 245–246.

Doblhofer, E., *Le Déchiffrement des Écritures, Collection Signes des Temps.* Paris: Arthaud, 1959.

Dreimanis, A., "Depths of Leaching in Glacial Deposits," *Science,* Vol. 126 (1957), pp. 403–404.

Drier, R. W., "Archaeology and Some Metallurgical Investigative Techniques," *Anthropological Papers of the Museum of Anthropology,* University of Michigan, No. 17 (1961), pp. 134–147.

Driver, H. E., "Introduction to Statistics for Comparative Research," in F. W. Moore, ed., *Readings on Cross-Cultural Methods.* New Haven, Conn.: HRAF Press, 1961, pp. 303–331.

———, *The Contribution of A. L. Kroeber to Culture Area Theory and Practice.* Indiana University Publications in Anthropology and Linguistics, Memoir No. 18, 1962.

———, and W. C. Massey, "Comparative Studies of North American Indians," *Transactions of the American Philosophical Society,* Vol. 47 (1957), Part 2.

Drucker, P., "The La Venta Olmec Support Area," *Kroeber Anthropological Society Papers,* No. 25 (1961), pp. 59–72.

———, R. F. Heizer, and R. J. Squier, *Excavations at La Venta, 1955.* Bureau of American Ethnology, Bulletin 170, 1959.

Duignan, Peter, "Early Jesuit Missionaries: A Suggestion for Further Study," *American Anthropologist,* Vol. 60 (1958), No. 4, pp. 725–732.

Dumas, F., *Deep Water Archaeology.* London: Routledge, 1962.

Dumond, D. E., "Swidden Agriculture and the Rise of Maya Civilization," *Southwestern Journal of Anthropology,* Vol. 17 (1961), pp. 301–316.

———, "A Practical Field Method for the Preservation of Soil Profiles from Archaeological Cuts," *American Antiquity,* Vol. 29 (1963), pp. 116–118.

Dunlevy, M. L., and E. H. Bell, "A Comparison of the Cultural Manifestations of the Burkett and the Gray Wolf Sites," in E. H. Bell, ed., *Chapters in Nebraska Archaeology*. Lincoln, Neb.: University of Nebraska Press, 1936, pp. 151–247.

Durand, J. D., "Mortality Estimates from Roman Tombstone Inscriptions," *American Journal of Sociology*, Vol. 65 (1960), pp. 365–373.

Dyson, J. L., *The World of Ice*. New York: Knopf, 1962.

Edmonson, M. S., "Neolithic Diffusion Rates," *Current Anthropology*, Vol. 2 (1961), pp. 71–102.

Eggan, F., "The Ethnological Cultures [of Eastern United States] and Their Archaeological Backgrounds," in J. B. Griffin, ed., *Archeology of Eastern United States*. Chicago: University of Chicago Press, 1952, pp. 35–45.

Ellis, H. H., *Flint-Working Techniques of the American Indian: An Experimental Study*. Columbus, Ohio: Ohio State Museum Lithic Laboratory, 1940.

Ellis, Henry, "On the Ruins of a City Submerged in the Sea on the Coast of Pomerania," *Archaeologia*, Vol. 32 (1847), pp. 419–422.

Elsasser, A. B., "Archaeological Evidence of Shamanism in California and Nevada," *Kroeber Anthropological Society Papers*, No. 24 (1961), pp. 38–48.

Emery, W. B., *Nubian Treasure*. London: Methuen, 1948.

——, *Archaic Egypt*. Baltimore: Penguin Books A462, 1961.

Eppel, F., "Funktion und Bedeutung der Lochstäbe aus dem Magdalénien," *Praehistorisches Zeitschrift*, Berlin, Vol. 36 (1958), pp. 220–223.

Esin, U., and P. Benedict, "Recent Developments in the Prehistory of Anatolia," *Current Anthropology*, Vol. 4 (1963), pp. 339–346.

Evans, A., *The Palace of Minos*, Vol. 4. London: Macmillan, 1921–1935.

Evans, C., and B. J. Meggers, "A New Dating Method Using Obsidian: II, an Archaeological Evaluation of the Method," *American Antiquity*, Vol. 25 (1960), pp. 523–537.

Evans, E. E., "The Ecology of Peasant Life in Western Europe," in W. L. Thomas, ed., *Man's Role in Changing the Face of the Earth*. Chicago: University of Chicago Press, 1956, pp. 217–239.

Evans, J., *Ancient Stone Implements, Weapons and Ornaments of Great Britain*, 2d ed. London: Longmans, 1897.

——, *Time and Chance; the Story of Arthur Evans and his Forebears*. New York: David McKay, 1943.

Ewers, J. C., *The Horse in Blackfoot Culture*. Washington, D.C.: Bureau of American Ethnology, Bulletin 159, 1955.

Fairbridge, R. W., "Dating the Latest Movements of the Quaternary Sea Level," *Transactions of the New York Academy of Sciences*, Series II, Vol. 20 (1958), pp. 471–482.

Farabee, W. C., "Indian Children's Burial Place in Western Pennsylvania," University of Pennsylvania, *Museum Journal*, Vol. 10 (1919), pp. 102–116.

Farmer, M. F., "Lightning Spalling," *American Antiquity*, Vol. 4 (1939), pp. 346–348.

Fischer, E., "Die Töpferei bei den Westlichen Dan [of Liberia]," *Zeitschrift für Ethnologie*, Vol. 88 (1963), pp. 100–115.

Flint, R. F., *Glacial and Pleistocene Geology*. New York: Wiley, 1957.

——, "Pleistocene Climates in Eastern and Southern Africa," *Bulletin of the Geological Society of America*, Vol. 70 (1959), pp. 343–374.

———, and E. S. Deevey, Jr., "Radiocarbon Dating of Late-Pleistocene Events," *American Journal of Science,* Vol. 249 (1951), pp. 257–300.

Fontana, B. L., W. J. Robinson, C. W. Cormack, and E. E. Leavitt, Jr., *Papago Indian Pottery.* Seattle: University of Washington Press, 1962.

Forbis, R. G., "Early Man and Fossil Bison," *Science,* Vol. 123 (1956), pp. 327–328.

Ford, J. A., "A Surface Survey of the Viru Valley, Peru," *American Museum of Natural History, Anthropological Papers,* Vol. 43 (1949), Part 1.

———, "Greenhouse: A Troyville-Coles Creek Period Site in Avoyelles Parish, Louisiana," *American Museum of Natural History, Anthropological Papers,* Vol. 44 (1951), Part 1.

———, "Comment on A. C. Spaulding, 'Statistical Techniques for the Discovery of Artifact Types,' " *American Antiquity,* Vol. 19 (1954a), pp. 390–391.

———, "On the Concept of Types," *American Anthropologist,* Vol. 56 (1954b), pp. 42–54.

———, "Eskimo Prehistory in the Vicinity of Point Barrow," *American Museum of Natural History, Anthropological Papers,* Vol. 47 (1959), Part 1.

———, *A Quantitative Method for Deriving Cultural Chronology.* Pan American Union, Technical Manual, No. 1, 1962.

———, and C. H. Webb, "Poverty Point, a Late Archaic Site in Louisiana," *American Museum of Natural History, Anthropological Papers,* Vol. 46 (1956), pp. 5–136.

Foster, G. M., "Some Implications of Modern Mold-Made Pottery," *Southwestern Journal of Anthropology,* Vol. 4 (1948), pp. 356–370.

———, "Contemporary Pottery Techniques in Southern and Central Mexico," *Middle American Research Institute, Publication* No. 22 (1955), pp. 1–48.

———, "Pottery-Making in Bengal," *Southwestern Journal of Anthropology,* Vol. 12 (1956), pp. 395–405.

———, "Archaeological Implications of the Modern Pottery of Acatlán, Puebla, Mexico," *American Antiquity,* Vol. 26 (1960a), pp. 205–214.

———, "Life-Expectancy of Utilitarian Pottery in Tzintzuntzan, Michoacán, Mexico," *American Antiquity,* Vol. 25 (1960b), pp. 606–609.

Fowke, G., *Archaeological History of Ohio.* Columbus, Ohio: Ohio State Historical Society, 1902.

Fowler, M. L., "Summary Report of Modoc Rockshelter 1952, 1953, 1955, 1956," *Illinois State Museum, Report of Investigations,* No. 8 (1959).

Fox, C., *The Personality of Britain.* Cardiff, Wales: National Museum of Wales, 1938.

Frankfort, H., *Cylinder Seals.* London: Macmillan, 1939.

———, *The Birth of Civilization in the Near East.* Garden City, N.Y.: Doubleday Anchor Books A89, 1956.

Frantz, A., "Truth Before Beauty; or The Incompleat Photographer," *Archaeology,* Vol. 3 (1950), pp. 202–215.

Friedman, I., and R. L. Smith, "A New Dating Method Using Obsidian: I, The Development of the Method," *American Antiquity,* Vol. 25 (1960), pp. 476–493.

———, ———, and D. Clark, "Obsidian Dating," in D. Brothwell and E. Higgs, eds., *Science in Archaeology.* London: Thames and Hudson, 1963, pp. 47–58.

Frost, H., *Under the Mediterranean.* Englewood Cliffs, N.J.: Prentice-Hall, 1963.

Fryxell, R., and R. D. Daugherty, *Late Glacial and Post Glacial Geological and Archaeological Chronology of the Columbia Plateau, Washington.* Laboratory of Anthropology, Washington State University, Report of Investigations, No. 23, 1963.

Gadow, H., *Through Southern Mexico.* London: Witherby and Co., 1908.

Gardin, Jean-Claude, "Four Codes for the Description of Artifacts: An Essay in Archeological Technique and Theory," *American Anthropologist,* Vol. 60 (1958), pp. 335–357.

Garrod, D. A. E., *Environment, Tools, and Man.* London: Cambridge University Press, 1946.

Gebhard, D., *Prehistoric Paintings of the Diablo Region of Western Texas.* Roswell Museum and Art Center, Publications in Art and Science, No. 3, 1960.

Genovés, S., "Sex Determination in Earlier Man," in D. Brothwell and E. Higgs, eds., *Science in Archaeology.* London: Thames and Hudson, 1963a, pp. 343–352.

——, "Estimation of Age and Mortality," in D. Brothwell and E. Higgs, eds., *Science in Archaeology.* London: Thames and Hudson, 1963b, pp. 353–364.

Gentili, G. V., and D. Edwards, "Roman Life in 1600-Year-Old Color Pictures," *National Geographic Magazine,* Vol. 111 (1957), pp. 211–229.

Gentner, W., and H. J. Lippolt, "The Potassium-Argon Dating of Upper Tertiary and Pleistocene Deposits," in D. Brothwell and E. Higgs, eds., *Science in Archaeology.* London: Thames and Hudson, 1963, pp. 72–84.

Geoffrey, A., "Archéologie du lac Fucin," *Revue Archéologique,* New Series, Paris, Vol. 36 (1876), pp. 1–18.

Gettens, R. J., and B. M. Usilton, *Abstracts of Technical Studies in Art and Archaeology.* Washington, D.C.: Smithsonian Institution, Freer Gallery of Art, Occasional Papers, Vol. 2, No. 2, 1955.

Ghirshman, R., *Iran.* Baltimore: Penguin Books A239, 1961.

Giddings, J. L., "The Archeology of Bering Strait," *Current Anthropology,* Vol. 1 (1960), pp. 121–130.

——, "Development of Tree-Ring Dating as an Archeological Aid," in T. T. Kozlowski, ed., *Tree Growth.* New York: Ronald, 1962, pp. 119–132.

Giehlow, K., "Die Hierglyphenkunder des Humanismus in der Allegorei der Renaissance," *Jahrbuch der Kunsthistorischen Sammlungen,* Vol. 32 (1915), pp. 1–218.

Giffen, N. M., *The Roles of Men and Women in Eskimo Culture.* University of Chicago Publications in Anthropology, Ethnological Series, Vol. 13, 1930.

Gifford, E. W., *Composition of California Shellmounds.* University of California Publications in American Archaeology and Ethnology, Vol. 12, No. 1, 1916.

——, *Archaeological Investigations in Fiji.* University of California Anthropological Records, Vol. 13 (1951), No. 3.

Gifford, J. C., "The Type-Variety Method of Ceramic Classification as an Indicator of Cultural Phenomena," *American Antiquity,* Vol. 25 (1960), pp. 341–347.

Gladwin, H. S., *A Review and Analysis of the Flagstaff Culture.* Globe, Ariz.: Gila Pueblo Medallion Papers, No. 31, 1943.

——, *Men Out of Asia.* New York: McGraw-Hill, 1947.

——, *A History of the Ancient Southwest*. Portland, Maine: Bond Wheelwright, 1957.

Gladwin, W., and H. S. Gladwin, *The Use of Potsherds in an Archaeological Survey of the Southwest*. Globe, Ariz.: Gila Pueblo Medallion Papers, No. 2, 1928a.

——, and ——, *A Method for the Designation of Cultures and Their Variations*. Globe, Ariz.: Gila Pueblo Medallion Papers, No. 15, 1928b.

Gladwin, H. S., E. W. Haury, E. B. Sayles, and N. Gladwin, *Excavations at Snaketown: Material Culture*. Globe, Ariz.: Gila Pueblo Medallion Papers, No. 25, 1937.

Glemser, M. S.. "Palaeoserology," in D. Brothwell and E. Higgs, eds., *Science in Archaeology*. London: Thames and Hudson, 1963, pp. 437–446.

Glob, P., "Lifelike Man Preserved 2,000 Years in Peat," *National Geographic Magazine*, Vol. 105 (1954), pp. 419–430.

Glock, W. S., *Principles and Methods of Tree-Ring Analysis*. Washington, D.C.: Carnegie Institution of Washington, Publication No. 486, 1937.

——, "Tree Growth: Growth Rings and Climate," *The Botanical Review*, Vol. 21 (1955), pp. 73–188.

Goggin, J. M., "Underwater Archaeolgy: Its Nature and Limitation," *American Antiquity*, Vol. 25 (1960), pp. 348–354.

Goldstein, M. S., "Some Vital Statistics Based on Skeletal Material," *Human Biology*, Vol. 25 (1953), pp. 3–10.

Goodall, E., "Domestic Animals in Rock Art," *Transactions of the Rhodesian Science Association*, Salisbury, Vol. 41 (1946), pp. 57–62.

——, C. K. Cooke, and J. D. Clark, *Prehistoric Rock Art of the Federation of Rhodesia and Nyasaland*. Rhodesia and Nyasaland: National Publication Trust, 1959.

Goodwin, A. J. H., "Chemical Alteration (Patination) of Stone," *Viking Fund Publications in Anthropology*, No. 28 (1960), pp. 300–312.

Gordon, D. H., "Fire and the Sword: The Technique of Destruction," *Antiquity*, Vol. 27 (1953), pp. 149–153.

Grace, V. R., *Amphoras and the Ancient Wine Trade*. Princeton, N.J.: American School of Classical Studies at Athens, 1961.

Grant, C., *The Chumash Indians and Their Rock Paintings*. Berkeley, Calif.: University of California Press, 1964.

Grant, M., *Roman History from Coins*. London: Cambridge University Press, 1958.

Greengo, R., "Archaeological Marine Shells [from the Monagrillo Site, Panama]," *Papers of the Peabody Museum*, Cambridge, Mass., Vol. 49 (1954), pp. 141–150.

Greenman, E. F., "The Upper Paleolithic in the New World," *Current Anthropology*, Vol. 4 (1963,) pp. 41–91.

Griffin, J. B., "Chronology and Dating Processes," in *Yearbook of Anthropology*. New York: Wenner-Gren Foundation, 1955, pp. 133–148.

——, "The Chronological Position of the Hopewellian Culture in the Eastern United States," *Anthropological Papers of the Museum of Anthropology*, University of Michigan, No. 12 (1958).

——, "Some Prehistoric Connections Between Siberia and America," *Science*, Vol. 131 (1960), pp. 801–812.

———, and C. W. Angell, "An Experimental Study of the Techniques of Pottery Making," *Papers of the Michigan Academy of Science, Arts and Letters*, Vol. 20 (1935), pp. 1–6.

Griffiths, J. G., "Archaeology and Hesiod's Five Ages," *Journal of the History of Ideas*, Vol. 17 (1956), pp. 109–119.

Grimes, W. F., "The Scientific Bias of Archaeology," *The Advancement of Science*, London, Vol. 10 (1954), pp. 343–346.

Grinnell, J., "The Burrowing Rodents of California as Agents in Soil Formation," *Smithsonian Institution, Annual Report for 1923* (1924), pp. 339–350.

Grüss, J., "Die beiden ältesten Weine unserer Kulturwelt," *Forschungen und Fortschritte*, Vol. 8 (1932), No. 2, pp. 23–24.

Gunda, B., "Plant Gathering in the Economic Life of Eurasia," *Southwestern Journal of Anthropology*, Vol. 5 (1949,) pp. 369–378.

Guthe, C. E., *Pueblo Pottery Making: A Study at the Village of San Ildefonso.* New Haven, Conn.: Yale University Press, 1925.

Hack, J. T., "The Changing Physical Environment of the Hopi Indians of Arizona," *Papers of the Peabody Museum*, Cambridge, Mass., Vol. 35, No. 1, 1942.

Hall, E. T., "Dating Pottery by Thermo-luminescence," in D. Brothwell and E. Higgs, eds., *Science in Archaeology*. London: Thames and Hudson, 1963, pp. 90–92.

———, "Physical Methods of Chemical Analysis," in E. Pyddoke, ed., *The Scientist and Archaeology*. London: Phoenix House, 1963, pp. 168–192.

Halseth, O. S., "Archaeology in the Making," *Masterkey*, Vol. 7 (1933), pp. 37–41.

Hamy, E. T., *Précis de paléontologie humaine.* Paris: J.-B. Ballière, 1870.

———, "The Fishhook Industry of the Ancient Inhabitants of the Archipelago of California," *Revue d'Ethnographie*, Vol. 4 (1885), pp. 6–13. Reprinted in English trans., in the *Reports of the University of California Archaeological Survey*, No. 59 (1963), pp. 61–69.

Haring, A., A. E. De Vries, and H. De Vries, "Radiocarbon Dating Up to 70,000 Years by Isotopic Enrichment," *Science*, Vol. 128 (1958), pp. 472–473.

Harner, M. J., "Gravel Pictographs of the Lower Colorado River Region," *Reports of the University of California Archaeological Survey*, No. 20 (1953), pp. 1–32.

———, "Thermo-facts vs. Artifacts: An Experimental Study of the Malpais Industry," *Reports of the University of California Archaeological Survey*, No. 33 (1956), pp. 39–43.

Harrington, J. C., "Historic Site Archeology in the United States," in J. B. Griffin, ed., *Archeology of Eastern United States*, Chicago: University of Chicago Press, 1952, pp. 335–344.

———, "Archeology as an Auxiliary Science to American History," *American Anthropologist*, Vol. 57 (1955), pp. 1121–1130.

Harrington, M. R., *Gypsum Cave, Nevada.* Los Angeles, Calif.: Southwest Museum Papers, No. 8, 1933.

Harrisson, T., and L. Medway, "A First Classification of Prehistoric Bone and Tooth Artifacts (Based on Material from Niah Great Cave)," *Sarawak Museum Journal*, Vol. 10 (1962), pp. 335–362.

Hatt, G., *Nørre Fjand, an Early Iron Age Village Site in West Jutland,* Arkae-ologisk-kunsthistoriske Skrifter udgivet af Det Kongelige Danske Videnska-bernes Selskab, Bind 2 (1957), No. 2.

Haury, E. W., "Minute Beads from Prehistoric Pueblos," *American Anthro-pologist,* Vol. 33 (1931), pp. 80–87.

——, "An Alluvial Site on the San Carlos Indian Reservation, Arizona," *American Antiquity,* Vol. 23 (1957), pp. 2–27.

——, E. Antevs, and J. F. Lance, "Artifacts with Mammoth Remains, Naco, Arizona," *American Antiquity,* Vol. 19 (1953,) pp. 1–24.

Hawkes, C., "Archeological Theory and Method: Some Suggestions from the Old World," *American Anthropologist,* Vol. 56 (1954), pp. 155–168.

Hawkes, J., and L. Woolley, *History of Mankind;* Vol. I, *Prehistory and the Beginnings of Civilization.* New York: Harper & Row, 1963.

Hawley, F. M., *The Significance of the Dated Prehistory of Chetro Ketl.* Al-buquerque, N.M.: University of New Mexico Bulletin, Monograph Series, Vol. 1, No. 1, 1934.

——, "Reversed Stratigraphy," *American Antiquity,* Vol. 2 (1937), pp. 297–299.

——, M. Pijoan, and C. A. Elkin, "An Inquiry Into the Food Economy of Zia Pueblo," *American Anthropologist,* Vol. 45 (1943), pp. 547–556.

Hayden, J. D., "Notes on Pima Pottery Making," *The Kiva,* Vol. 24 (1959), pp. 10–16.

Heath, D. W., "Sexual Division of Labor and Cross-Cultural Research," *Social Forces,* Vol. 37 (1958), pp. 77–79.

Heer, O., *Die Urwelt der Schweiz.* Zürich: F. Schulthess, 1863.

Heinè-Geldern, R., "Die Asiatische Herkunft der Südamerikanischen Metalltech-nik," *Paideuma,* Vol. 5 (1954), pp. 347–423.

——, and G. Ekholm, "Significant Parallels in the Symbolic Arts of Southern Asia and Middle America," in *The Civilizations of Ancient America.* Selected Papers of the 29th International Congress of Americanists, pp. 299–309, 1951.

Heizer, R. F., "The Direct-Historical Approach in California Archaeology," *American Antiquity,* Vol. 7 (1941a), pp. 98–122.

——, "Aboriginal Trade Between the Southwest and California," *Southwest Museum Masterkey,* Vol. 15 (1941b), pp. 185–188.

——, "Artifact Transport by Migratory Animals and Other Means," *American Antiquity,* Vol. 9 (1944), pp. 395–400.

——, "The Sickle in Aboriginal Western North America," *American Antiquity,* Vol. 16 (1951a), pp. 247–252.

——, "A Prehistoric Yurok Ceremonial Site (Hum-174)," *Reports of the Uni-versity of California Archaeological Survey,* No. 11 (1951b), pp. 1–4.

——, "Preliminary Report on the Leonard Rockshelter Site, Pershing County, Nevada," *American Antiquity,* Vol. 17 (1951c), pp. 89–98.

——, "Long-Range Dating in Archaeology," in *Anthropology Today.* Chicago: University of Chicago Press, 1953, pp. 3–42.

——, "Primitive Man as an Ecologic Factor," *Kroeber Anthropological So-ciety Papers,* No. 13 (1955), pp. 1–31.

——, "Prehistoric Central California: A Problem in Historical-Developmental Classification," *Reports of the University of California Archaeological Survey*, No. 41 (1958), pp. 19–26.

———, ed., *A Guide to Archaeological Field Methods*, 3d rev. ed. Millbrae, Calif.: National Press, 1959a.

———, ed., *The Archaeologist at Work*. New York: Harper & Row, 1959b.

———, "Agriculture and the Theocratic State in Lowland Southeastern Mexico," *American Antiquity*, Vol. 26 (1960a), pp. 215–222.

———, "Physical Analysis of Habitation Residues," *Viking Fund Publications in Anthropology*, No. 28 (1960b), pp. 93–142.

———, "Inferences on the Nature of Olmec Society Based on Data from the La Venta Site," *Kroeber Anthropological Society Papers*, No. 25 (1961), pp. 43–57.

———, *Man's Discovery of his Past: Literary Landmarks in Archaeology*. Englewood Cliffs, N.J.: Prentice-Hall, 1962a.

———, "The Background of Thomsen's Three Age System," *Technology and Culture*, Vol. 3 (1962b), pp. 259–266.

———, "Village Shifts and Tribal Spreads in California Prehistory," *Southwest Museum Masterkey*, Vol. 36 (1962c), pp. 60–67.

———, "Domestic Fuel in Primitive Society," *Journal of the Royal Anthropological Institute*, Vol. 93, (1963), pp. 186–193.

———, and editors, "Physical Analysis of Habitation Residues," in *The Application of Quantitative Methods in Archaeology*. Viking Fund Publications in Anthropology, No. 28, 1960, pp. 93–157.

———, and M. A. Baumhoff, "Great Basin Petroglyphs and Prehistoric Game Trails," *Science*, Vol. 129 (1959), pp. 904–905.

———, and ———, *Prehistoric Rock Art of Nevada and Eastern California*. Berkeley, Calif.: University of California Press, 1962.

———, and S. F. Cook, "Fluorine and Other Chemical Tests of Some North American Human and Fossil Bones," *American Journal of Physical Anthropology*, Vol. 10 (1952), pp. 289–304.

———, and G. W. Hewes, "Animal Ceremonialism in Central California in the Light of Archaeology," *American Anthropologist*, Vol. 42 (1940), pp. 587–603.

———, and A. D. Krieger, "The Archaeology of Humboldt Cave, Churchill County, Nevada," *University of California Publications in American Archaeology and Ethnology*, Vol. 47 (1956), pp. 1–190.

———, and A. E. Treganza, "Mines and Quarries of the Indians of California," *California Journal of Mines and Geology*, Vol. 40 (1944), pp. 291–351.

Helbaek, H., "Tollund Manden Sidste Maaltid," *Aarböger for Nordisk Oldkyndighed og Historie*, 1950, pp. 311–314.

———, "Seeds of Weeds as Food in the Pre-Roman Iron Age," *Kuml*, Aarhus, (1951), pp. 65–74.

———, "Archaeology and Agricultural Botany," University of London, *Institute of Archaeology, Ninth Annual Report* (1953), pp. 44–59.

———, "Paleo-Ethnobotany," in D. Brothwell and E. Higgs, eds., *Science in Archaeology*. London: Thames and Hudson, 1963, pp. 177–185.

Helm, J., "The Ecological Approach in Anthropology," *American Journal of Sociology*, Vol. 47 (1962), pp. 630–639.

Hencken, H. C., "Indo-European Languages and Archeology," *American Anthropological Association*, Memoir No. 84, 1955.

Herskovits, M. J., "The Hypothetical Situation: A Technique of Field Research," *Southwestern Journal of Anthropology*, Vol. 6 (1950), pp. 32–40.

Hester, J. J., "Late Pleistocene Extinction and Radiocarbon Dating," *American Antiquity*, Vol. 26 (1960), pp. 58–77.

———, *Early Navajo Migrations and Acculturation in the Southwest*. Santa Fe, N.M.: Museum of New Mexico Papers in Anthropology, No. 6, 1962.

Heusser, C. J., *Late-Pleistocene Environments of North Pacific North America*. New York: American Geographic Society, Special Publication No. 35, 1960.

Heyerdahl, T., *Aku-Aku*. New York: Cardinal Giant Pocket Book No. GC-758, 1959.

———, "Feasible Ocean Routes to and from the Americas in Pre-Columbian Times," *American Antiquity*, Vol. 28 (1963), pp. 482–488.

Higgs, Eric, "Excavations at a Mesolithic Site at Downton near Salisbury, Wiltshire," *Proceedings of the Prehistoric Society*, New Series, Vol. 25 (1959), pp. 209–232.

Hill, W. W., *Navajo Pottery Manufacture*. University of New Mexico Bulletin, Anthropology Series, Vol. 2, No. 3, 1937.

———, "Navajo Trading and Trading Ritual: A Study of Cultural Dynamics," *Southwestern Journal of Anthropology*, Vol. 4 (1948), pp. 371–396.

Hockett, C. F., *A Course in Modern Linguistics*. New York: Macmillan, 1958.

Hodge, F. W., *History of Hawikuh, New Mexico*. Los Angeles, Calif.: Southwest Museum, 1937.

Hodgson, J., "On the Study of Antiquities," *Archaeologia Aeliana*, Vol. 1 (1822), pp. 9–19.

Hoijer, H., "Lexicostatistics: A Critique," *Language*, Vol. 32 (1956a), pp. 49–60.

———, "The Chronology of the Athapaskan Languages," *International Journal of American Linguistics*, Vol. 22 (1956b), pp. 219–232.

Hole, F., and K. V. Flannery, "Excavations at Ali Kosh, Iran, 1961," *Iranica Antiqua*, Vol. 2 (1962), pp. 97–148.

Holland, W. R., and R. J. Weitlaner, "Modern Cuicatec Use of Prehistoric Sacrificial Knives," *American Antiquity*, Vol. 25 (1960), pp. 392–396.

Holmes, G. W., "The Regional Significance of the Pleistocene Deposits in the Eden Valley, Wyoming," *Museum Monographs, University of Pennsylvania Museum*, 1951, pp. 95–102.

Holmes, W. H., "Prehistoric Textile Fabrics of the United States, Derived from Impressions in Pottery," *Bureau of American Ethnology, Annual Report* No. 3 (1881), pp. 393–425.

———, "Vestiges of Early Man in Minnesota," *The American Geologist*, Vol. 11 (1893), pp. 219–240.

———, *Archeological Studies Among the Ancient Cities of Mexico*. Chicago: Field Columbian Museum, Publication No. 16, Anthropological Series, Vol. 1, No. 1, 1897.

———, *Handbook of Aboriginal American Antiquities*. Bureau of American Ethnology, Bulletin 60, 1919.

Hopkins, D. M., "Cenozoic History of the Bering Land Bridge," *Science*, Vol. 129 (1959), pp. 1519–1528.

Hough, W., "Stone-Working at Tewa," *American Anthropologist,* Vol. 10, Old Series (1897), p. 191.

Houghton, W., "On the Mammalia of the Assyrian Sculptures," *Transactions of the Society of Biblical Archaeology,* Vol. 5 (1877), pp. 229–383.

Howell, F. C., "Upper Pleistocene Stratigraphy and Early Man in the Levant," *Proceedings of the American Philosophical Society,* Vol. 103 (1959), pp. 1–65.

———, "Potassium-Argon Dating at Oludvai Gorge," *Current Anthropology,* Vol. 3 (1962a), pp. 306–308.

———, ed., "Early Man and Pleistocene Stratigraphy in the Circum-Mediterranean Regions," *Quaternaria,* Vol. 6 (1962b).

———, and F. Bourlière, eds., *African Ecology and Human Evolution.* Viking Fund Publications in Anthropology, No. 36, 1963.

Howells, W. W., "Estimating Population Numbers Through Archaeological and Skeletal Remains," *Viking Fund Publications in Anthropology,* No. 28 (1960), pp. 158–180.

Hoyme, L. E., and W. M. Bass, "Human Skeletal Remains from Tollifero (Ha-6) and Clarksville (Mc-14) Sites, John H. Kerr Reservoir Basin, Virginia," *Bureau of American Ethnology,* Bulletin 182 (1962), pp. 329–400.

Hubbard, B., "Ancient Garden Beds in Michigan," *American Antiquarian,* Vol. 1 (1878), pp. 1–9.

Huntington, E., *Mainsprings of Civilization.* New York: Wiley, 1945. (Reprinted as a Mentor Book, 1959).

Hurst, V. J., and A. R. Kelly, "Patination of Cultural Flints," *Science,* Vol. 134 (1961), pp. 251–256.

Hymes, D. H., "Lexicostatistics So Far," *Current Anthropology,* Vol. 1 (1960), pp. 3–44.

———, "Conference in the Use of Computers in Anthropology," *Current Anthropology,* Vol. 4 (1963), pp. 123–129.

Iversen, J., "Forest Clearance in the Stone Age," *Scientific American,* Vol. 194 (1956), pp. 36–41.

Jackson, A. T., *Picture-Writing of Texas Indians.* Austin, Texas: University of Texas, Bureau of Research in the Social Sciences, Study No. 27, 1938.

Jacobsen, T., and R. M. Adams, "Salt and Silt in Ancient Mesopotamian Agriculture," *Science,* Vol. 128 (1958), pp. 1251–1258.

James, E. O., *Prehistoric Religion: A Study in Prehistoric Archaeology.* New York: Barnes & Noble, University Paperbacks UP-42, 1962.

Jelinek, A. J., "Pleistocene Faunas and Early Man," *Papers of the Michigan Academy of Science, Arts and Letters,* Vol. 42 (1957), pp. 225–237.

———, "Use of the Cumulative Graph in Temporal Ordering," *American Antiquity,* Vol. 28 (1962a), No. 2, pp. 241–243.

———, "An Index of Radiocarbon Dates Associated with Cultural Materials," *Current Anthropology,* Vol. 3 (1962b), pp. 451–477.

———, and J. E. Fitting, "Some Studies of Natural Radioactivity in Archaeological and Paleontological Materials," *Papers of the Michigan Academy of Sciences, Arts and Letters,* Vol. 48 (1963), pp. 531–540.

Jennings, J. D., *Danger Cave.* Salt Lake City: University of Utah Press, Memoirs of the Society for American Archaeology, No. 14, 1957.

———, "Administration of Contract Emergency Archaeological Programs," *American Antiquity,* Vol. 28 (1963), pp. 282–285.

———, and E. Norbeck, eds., *Prehistoric Man in the New World*. Chicago: University of Chicago Press, 1964.

Jensen, L. B., *Man's Foods*. Champaign, Ill.: Garrard Press, 1953.

Jessup, R., *Curiosities of British Archaeology*. Toronto: Butterworth, 1961.

Jett, S. C., "Pueblo Indian Migrations: An Evaluation of the Possible Physical and Cultural Determinants," *American Antiquity*, Vol. 29 (1964), pp. 281–299.

Jewell, P. A., "Buzzards and Barrows," *The South African Archaeological Bulletin*, Vol. 13 (1958), pp. 153–155.

———, "An Experiment in Field Archaeology," *Advancement of Science*, London, Vol. 17 (1961), pp. 106–109.

Johnson, T., "An Experiment with Cave-Painting Media," *The South African Archaeological Bulletin*, Vol. 47 (1957), pp. 98–101.

Johnson, Frederick, *The Boylston Street Fishweir*. Papers of the Robert S. Peabody Foundation for Archaeology, Vol. 2, 1942.

Johnston, D. W., "Problems of Terrace Correlation," *Bulletin of the Geological Society of America*, Vol. 55 (1944), pp. 793–818.

Johnston, F. J., and P. H. Johnston, "An Indian Trail Complex of the Central Colorado Desert," *Reports of the University of California Archaeological Survey*, No. 37 (1957), pp. 22–39.

Johnston, R. B., *Proton Magnetometry and its Application to Archaeology; an Evaluation at Angel Site*. Indianapolis: Indiana Historical Society, Prehistory Research Series, Vol. IV, No. 2, 1964.

Jope, M., "The Mollusca and Animal Bones from the Excavations at Ringneill Quay," in N. Stephens and A. E. P. Collins, *The Quaternary Deposits at Ringneill Quay and Ardmillan, County Down*, Proceedings of the Royal Irish Academy, Vol. 61 (1960), Section 6, No. 3, pp. 41–77.

Jorgensen, S., "Skovryoning med Flintokse [Forest Clearance with Flint Axes]," *Fra Nationalmuseets Arbejdsmark*, 1953, pp. 36–43, 109–110.

Judd, N. M., "The Excavation and Repair of Betatakin," *Proceedings of the United States National Museum*, Vol. 77 (1930), Article 5, pp. 1–77.

———, *The Material Culture of Pueblo Bonito*. Washington, D.C.: Smithsonian Institution, Miscellaneous Collections, Vol. 124, 1954.

———, *Pueblo del Arroyo, Chaco Canyon, New Mexico*. Washington, D.C.: Smithsonian Institution, Miscellaneous Collections, Vol. 138, No. 1, 1959.

Judson, S., *Geology of the San Jon Site, Eastern New Mexico*. Washington, D.C.: Smithsonian Institution, Miscellaneous Collections, Vol. 121, No. 1, 1953.

———, "Archaeology and the Natural Sciences," *American Scientist*, Vol. 49 (1961), pp. 410–414.

Kamen, M. D., "Early History of Carbon-14," *Science*, Vol. 140 (1963), pp. 584–590.

Kantor, H. J., "The Chronology of Egypt and Its Correlation with That of Other Parts of the Near East in the Periods before the Late Bronze Age," in R. W. Ehrich, ed., *Relative Chronologies in Old World Archaeology*. Chicago: University of Chicago Press, 1954, pp. 1–27.

Kurtén, B., and Y. Vasari, *On the Date of Peking Man*. Helsingfors: Societas Scientiarum Fennica, Commentationes Biological, Vol. 23, No. 7, 1960.

Kay, G. F., "Classification and Duration of the Pleistocene Period," *Bulletin of the Geological Society of America*, Vol. 48 (1931), pp. 425–466.

Kehoe, T. F., "Tipi Rings: The 'Direct Ethnological' Approach Applied to an Archeological Problem," *American Anthropologist,* Vol. 60 (1958), pp. 861–873.

———, and A. B. Kehoe, "Observations on the Butchering Technique at a Prehistoric Bison Kill in Montana," *American Antiquity,* Vol. 25 (1960), pp. 420–423.

Keiller, A., S. Piggott, and F. S. Wallis, "First Report of the Sub-Committee of the South-Western Group of Museums and Art Galleries on the Petrological Identification of Stone Axes," *Proceedings of the Prehistoric Society,* Vol. 7 (1941), pp. 50–72. (Reprinted in part in Heizer, 1959, pp. 450–456.)

Keith, M. L., and G. M. Anderson, "Radiocarbon Dating: Fictitious Results with Mollusk Shells," *Science,* Vol. 141 (1963), pp. 634–636.

Kelly, A. R., *A Preliminary Report on Archeological Explorations at Macon, Georgia.* Bureau of American Ethnology, Bulletin 119, Anthropological Paper No. 1, 1938.

———, and V. J. Hurst, "Patination and Age Relationship in South Georgia Flint," *American Antiquity,* Vol. 22 (1956), pp. 193–194.

Kennedy, G., and L. Knopff, "Dating by Thermoluminescence," *Archaeology,* Vol. 13 (1960), pp. 147–148.

Kenyon, K., *Digging Up Jericho.* London: E. Benn, 1957.

———, *Archaeology in the Holy Land.* New York: Praeger, 1960.

———, *Beginning in Archaeology,* Rev. Ed. New York: Praeger, 1961.

Kidder, A. V., *Pottery of the Pajarito Plateau and of Some Adjacent Regions in New Mexico.* American Anthropological Association, Memoirs, Vol. 2, part 6, 1915.

———, *Pecos, New Mexico: Archaeological Notes.* Andover, Mass.: Papers of the Robert S. Peabody Foundation for Archaeology, Vol. 5, 1958.

———, J. D. Jennings, and E. M. Shook, *Excavations at Kaminaljuyu, Guatemala.* Washington, D.C.: Carnegie Institute of Washington, 1946.

Kirchner, H., "Ein archaeologischer Beitrag zur Urgeschichte des Shamanismus," *Anthropos,* Vol. 47 (1952), pp. 244–286.

Kleindienst, M. R., "Components of the East African Acheulian Assemblage: an Analytic Approach," *Acts 4e Pan-African Congrès Préhistoire,* Leopoldville, 1959, pp. 81–111.

———, "Variability Within the Late Acheulian Assemblage in Eastern Africa," *South African Archaeological Bulletin,* Vol. 16 (1961), pp. 35–52.

Klima, B., "Paleolithic Huts at Dolní Věstonice, Czechoslovakia," *Antiquity,* Vol. 28 (1954), pp. 4–14.

Kloiber, A., *Die Gräberfelder von Lauriacum; das Ziegelfeld.* Linz und Donau Austria: Oberosterreichischer Landesverlag, 1957.

Knowles, F. H. S., *The Manufacture of a Flint Arrowhead by a Quartzite Hammer Stone.* Oxford University, Pitt-Rivers Museum, Occasional Papers on Technology, No. 1, 1944.

Kosok, P., and M. Reiche, "Ancient Drawings on the Desert of Peru," *Archaeology,* Vol. 2 (1949), pp. 206–215.

Kragh, A., "Stenalderens Flintteknik," *Kuml,* 1951, pp. 49–64.

Krieger, A. D., "The Eastward Extension of Puebloan Datings Toward Cultures of the Mississippi Valley," *American Antiquity,* Vol. 12 (1947), pp. 141–148.

———, "Archaeological Typology in Theory and Practice," in *Selected Papers of the Fifth International Congress of Anthropology and Ethnological Sciences.* Philadelphia, 1960, pp. 141–151.

Kroeber, A. L., *Zuni Potsherds.* American Museum of Natural History, Anthropological Papers, Vol. 18, No. 1, 1916.

———, *Handbook of the Indians of California.* Bureau of American Ethnology, Bulletin 78, 1925.

———, *Culture Element Distributions: III, Area and Climax.* University of California Publications in American Archaeology and Ethnology, Vol. 37, No. 3, 1936.

———, "Stimulus Diffusion," *American Anthropologist,* Vol. 42 (1940a), pp. 1–20.

———, "Statistical Classification," *American Antiquity,* Vol. 6 (1940b), pp. 29–44.

———, *Anthropology.* New York: Harcourt, 1948.

———, "Linguistic Time Depth Results So Far and Their Meaning," *International Journal of American Linguistics,* Vol. 21 (1955), pp. 91–104.

———, "An Anthropologist Looks at History," *Pacific Historical Review,* Vol. 26 (1957), pp. 281–287.

———, *A Roster of Civilizations and Culture.* Chicago: Viking Fund Publications in Anthropology, No. 33, 1962.

———, *Cultural and Natural Areas of Native North America.* Berkeley, Calif.: University of California Press, 1963. Originally published in *University of California Publications in American Archaeology and Ethnology,* Vol. 38.

———, and W. D. Strong, *The Uhle Pottery Collection from Ica.* University of California Publications in American Archaeology and Ethnology, Vol. 21, No. 3, 1924.

Krogh, A., and M. Krogh, "A Study of the Diet and Metabolism of Eskimo Undertaken in 1908 on an Expedition to Greenland," *Meddelelser om Grönland,* Vol. 2 (1915), pp. 1–52.

Kryzwicki, L., *Primitive Society and Its Vital Statistics.* London: Macmillan, 1934.

Kuhn, E., "Zur Quantitativen Analyse der Haustierwelt der Pfahlbauten der Schweiz," *Vierteljahrsschrift der Naturforschenden Gesellschaft Zürich,* Vol. 83, (1938), pp. 253–263.

Kühn, H., *The Rock Pictures of Europe.* London: Sidgwick & Jackson, 1956.

———, *On the Track of Prehistoric Man.* London: Hutchinson, 1955.

Kurtz, E. B., Jr., and R. Y. Anderson, "Pollen Analysis," University of Arizona, Tucson, *Physical Science Bulletin* No. 2 (1955), pp. 113–125.

Lais, R., "Molluskenkunde und Vorgeschichte," Berlin, Deutches Archäol. Institut., *Römisch-Germanisch Komm.,* Ber. 26 (1936), pp. 5–23.

Lambert, R. J., "Review of the Literature of Ethno-conchology Pertinent to Archaeology," *Sterkiana,* Vol. 2 (1960), pp. 1–8.

Laming, A., "L'aimentation thermoremanente des terres cuites," in A. Laming, ed., *La Découverte du Passé.* Paris: A. and J. Picard, 1952, Chap. 10.

———, *Lascaux: Paintings and Engravings.* Baltimore: Penguin Books A-419, 1959.

Laming-Emperaire, A., *L'archéologie préhistorique.* Paris: Editions du Seuil, 1963.

Lancaster, O., *Draynefleete Revisited.* London: J. Murray, 1949.

Lang, A., "Homer and Anthropology," in R. R. Marett, ed., *Anthropology and the Classics*. Oxford: Clarendon Press, 1908.

Lartet, E., "Sur l'ancienneté géologique de l'espéce humaine," *Comptes Rendus de l'Academie des Sciences*, Vol. 50 (1860), pp. 790–791.

——, and C. Gaillard, "La Faune momifée de l'ancienne Egypte," *Archives de Musée Histoire Naturelle de Lyon*, Vol. 9 (1907), pp. 1–130.

Lasker, G. W., *The Evolution of Man*. New York: Holt, Rinehart and Winston, Inc., 1961.

Laudermilk, J. D., and T. G. Kennard, "Concerning Lightning Spalling," *American Journal of Science*, Series 5, Vol. 25 (1938), pp. 104–122.

Layard, A. H., *Nineveh and Its Remains*. New York: Putnam, 1849.

——, *Discoveries in the Ruins of Nineveh and Babylon*. New York: Putnam, 1853.

——, *Sir A. Henry Layard, G.C.B.; D.C.L.; Autobiography and Letters*. London: J. Murray, 1903.

Layard, N. F., "Prehistoric Cooking Places in Norfolk," *Proceedings of the Prehistoric Society of East Anglia*, Vol. 3 (1922), Part 4, pp. 483–498.

Leakey, L. S. B., *Adam's Ancestors*, 4th ed. New York: Harper Torchbooks TB-1019, 1960.

——, and H. van Lawick, "Adventures in the Search for Man," *National Geographic Magazine*, Vol. 123 (1963), pp. 132–152.

Leechman, D., "Technical Methods in the Preservation of Anthropological Museum Specimens," Ottawa: *National Museum of Canada, Annual Report for 1929* (1931), pp. 127–158.

——, *Aboriginal Tree-Felling*. Ottawa: National Museum of Canada, Bulletin 118, 1950.

Lehmer, D. J., *Archeological Investigations in the Oahe Dam Area, South Dakota, 1950-51*. Bureau of American Ethnology, Bulletin 158, 1954.

Lerici, C. M., "Periscope Camera Pierces Ancient Tombs to Reveal 2,500 Year Old Frescoes," *National Geographic Magazine*, Vol. 116 (1959), pp. 336–351.

Libby, W. F., *Radiocarbon Dating*. Chicago: University of Chicago Press, 2d ed., 1955.

——, "Radiocarbon Dating," *Science*, Vol. 133 (1961), pp. 621–629.

——, "Radiocarbon Dating," *Science*, Vol. 140 (1963), pp. 278–280.

Linington, R. E., "Physics and Archaeological Salvage," *Archaeology*, Vol. 14 (1961), pp. 287–292.

——, "The Application of Geophysics to Archaeology," *American Scientist*, Vol. 51 (1963), pp. 48–70.

Lloyd, S., *Foundations in the Dust*. Baltimore: Penguin Books, 1955.

——, *Mounds of the Near East*. Edinburgh: Edinburgh University Press, 1963.

Locke, L. L., "The Ancient Quipu, a Peruvian Knot Record," *American Anthropologist*, Vol. 14 (1912), pp. 325–332.

Loeb, E. M., "The Distribution and Function of Money in Early Societies," in *Essays in Anthropology*. Berkeley, Calif.: University of California Press, 1936, pp. 153–168.

Loftus, W. K., "Warkah: Its Ruins and Remains," *Transactions of the Royal Society of Literature*, Series 2, Vol. 6 (1858), pp. 1–64.

Lothrop, E. B., *Throw Me a Bone; What Happens When You Marry an Archaeologist*. New York: Whittlesey, 1948.

Lotspeich, F. B., "Soil Science in the Service of Archaeology," *Fort Burgwin Research Center, Publication* No. 1 (1961), pp. 137–144, Sante Fe, N.M.

Lovett, E., "Notice of the gun flint manufactory at Brandon, with reference to the bearing of its processes upon the modes of flint-working practiced in prehistoric times," *Proceedings of the Society of Antiquaries of Scotland,* Vol. 21 (1887), pp. 206–212.

Lucas, A., *Ancient Egyptian Materials and Industries.* London: E. Arnold, 1934.

Lyell, C., *Principles of Geology.* 2 Vols., 11th ed. New York: Appleton, 1872.

Lyne, W. C., "The Significance of the Radiographs of the Piltdown Teeth," *Proceedings of the Royal Society of Medicine,* Vol. 9 (1916), Part 3, pp. 33–62.

McCarthy, F. D., and M. McArthur, "The Food Quest and the Time Factor in Aboriginal Economic Life," *Records of the American-Australian Scientific Expedition,* University of Melbourne Press, Vol. 2 (1960), pp. 145–194.

McConnell, D., "Dating of Fossil Bones by the Fluorine Method," *Science,* Vol. 136 (1962), pp. 241–244.

McCown, T. D., and A. Keith, *The Stone Age of Mt. Carmel.* Oxford: Clarendon Press, Vol. 2, 1939.

McDowell, B., and J. E. Fletcher, "Avalanche! 3500 Peruvians Perish in Seven Minutes," *National Geographic Magazine,* Vol. 121 (1962), pp. 855–880.

McEwen, J. M., "An Experiment with Primitive Maori Carving Tools," *The Journal of the Polynesian Society,* Vol. 55 (1946), pp. 111–116.

McGinnies, W. G., "Dendrochronology," *Journal of Forestry,* Vol. 61 (1963), pp. 5–11.

McGuire, J. D., "The Stone Hammer and Its Various Uses," *American Anthropologist,* Vol. 4 (1891), pp. 301–312.

McKern, W. C., "The Midwestern Taxonomic Method as an Aid to Archaeological Culture Study," *American Antiquity,* Vol. 4 (1939), pp. 301–313.

MacAdam, W. I., "On the results of a chemical investigation into the composition of the "bog butters" and of "adipocere" and the "mineral resins" with notice of a cask of bog butter found in Glen Gell, Morvern, Argyllshire," *Proceedings of the Society of Antiquaries of Scotland,* New Series, Vol. 4 (1882), pp. 204–223.

———, "Notes on the analysis of samples of bog butter found in different parts of Scotland," *Proceedings of the Society of Antiquaries of Scotland,* Vol. 23 (1889), pp. 433–434.

MacAlister, R. A. S., *The Archaeology of Ireland.* London: Methuen, 1949.

MacNeish, R. S., "Preliminary Archaeological Investigations in the Sierra de Tamaulipas, Mexico," *Transactions of the American Philosophical Society,* New Series, Vol. 48 (1958), Part 6.

———, "Ancient Mesoamerican Civilization," *Science,* Vol. 143 (1964), pp. 531–537.

MacWhite, E., "On the Interpretation of Archeological Evidence in Historical and Sociological Terms," *American Anthropologist,* Vol. 58 (1956), pp. 3–25.

Maiuri, A., P. V. Bianchi, and L. E. Battaglia, "Last Moments of the Pompeians," *National Geographic Magazine,* Vol. 120 (1961), pp. 651–670.

Malinowski, B., *Argonauts of the Western Pacific.* New York: Dutton, 1932.

Malkin, B., *Seri Ethnozoology*. Pocatello, Idaho: Occasional Papers of the Idaho State College Museum, No. 7, 1962.

March, B., *Standards of Pottery Description*. Ann Arbor, Mich.: Occasional Contributions from the Museum of Anthropology of the University of Michigan, No. 3, 1934.

Maringer, J., *The Gods of Prehistoric Man*. New York: Knopf, 1960.

Martin, P. S., J. B. Rinaldo, E. Bluhm, H. C. Cutler, and R. Grange, *Mogollon Cultural Continuity and Change: The Stratigraphic Analysis of Tularosa and Cordova Caves*. Chicago: Fieldiana, Anthropology, Chicago Natural History Museum, 1952.

Martin, P. S., and J. Schoenwetter, "Arizona's Oldest Cornfield," *Science*, Vol. 132 (1960), pp. 33–34.

——, B. E. Sabels, and D. Shutler, "Rampart Cave Coprolite and Ecology of the Shasta Ground Sloth," *American Journal of Science*, Vol. 259 (1961), pp. 102–127.

——, and J. Gray, "Pollen Analysis and the Cenozoic," *Science*, Vol. 137 (1962), pp. 103–111.

Marquina, I., *Arquitectura Prehispanica*. Mexico City: Memorias del Instituto de Antropologia e Historia, No. 1, 1951.

Mason, R. J., *Late Pleistocene Geochronology and the Paleo-Indian Penetration Into the Lower Michigan Peninsula*. Ann Arbor, Mich.: Anthropological Papers, Museum of Anthropology, University of Michigan, No. 11, 1958.

Mather, J. R., "The Effect of Climate on the New World Migration of Primitive Man," *Southwestern Journal of Anthropology*, Vol. 10 (1954), pp. 304–321.

Mathiassen, T., "Blubber Lamps in the Ertebølle Culture?" *Acta Archaeologica*, Vol. 9 (1935), pp. 224–228.

Matson, F. R., "Ceramic Technology as an Aid to Cultural Interpretation: Techniques and Problems," *Anthropological Papers of the University of Michigan*, No. 8 (1951), pp. 102–116.

——, "The Quantitative Study of Ceramic Materials," *Viking Fund Publications in Anthropology*, No. 28 (1960), pp. 34–51.

Matteson, M. R., "Land Snails in Archeological Sites," *American Anthropologist*, Vol. 61 (1959), pp. 1094–1096.

——, "Reconstruction of Prehistoric Environments through the Analysis of Molluscan Collections from Shell Middens," *American Antiquity*, Vol. 26 (1960), pp. 117–120.

Matthes, F. E., *The Incomparable Valley*. Berkeley, Calif.: University of California Press, 1956.

Mayes, S., *The Great Belzoni (Archaeologist Extraordinary)*. New York: Walker and Company, 1961.

Meggers, B. J., "Environmental Limitation on the Development of Culture," *American Anthropologist*, Vol. 56 (1954), pp. 801–824.

——, ed., *Evolution and Anthropology: A Centennial Appraisal*. Washington, D.C.: Anthropological Society of Washington, 1959.

Meighan, C. W., and others, "Ecological Interpretation in Archaeology," *American Antiquity*, Vol. 24 (1958), pp. 1–23, 131–150.

Mellaart, J., "The Neolithic Obsidian Industry of Ilicapinar and Its Relations," *Istanbuler Mitteilungen*, Vol. 8 (1958), pp. 82–92.

Merrill, R. H., "Photo-surveying Assists Archaeologists," *Civil Engineering*, Vol. 11 (1941a), pp. 233–235.

———, "Photographic Surveying," *American Antiquity*, Vol. 6 (1941b), pp. 343–346.

Miller, W. C., "Uses of Aerial Photographs in Archaeological Field Work," *American Antiquity*, Vol. 23 (1957), pp. 46–62.

Millon, R., and B. Drewitt, "Earlier Structures Within the Pyramid of the Sun at Teotihuacan," *American Antiquity*, Vol. 26 (1961), pp. 371–380.

Miner, H. C., "The Importance of Textiles in the Archaeology of the Eastern United States," *American Antiquity*, Vol. 1 (1936), pp. 181–192.

Moberg, C-A., "Mängder av Fornfynd (with English summary: Trends in the Present Development of Quantitative Methods in Archaeology)," *Acta Universitatis Göthoburgensis*, Göteborg, Göteborgs Universitets Arsskrift, Vol. 47, No. 1, 1961.

Mongait, A. L., *Archaeology in the U.S.S.R.*, Baltimore: Penguin Books, 1961.

Montgomery, R. G., W. Smith, and J. O. Brew, *Franciscan Awatovi*. Cambridge, Mass.: Harvard University, Peabody Museum Papers, Vol. 36, 1949.

Moorehead, A., "A Reporter at Large: The Temples of the Nile," *The New Yorker*, September 23, 1961, pp. 106–137.

Morgan, L. H., "Ethnical Periods," *Proceedings of the American Association for the Advancement of Science*, Vol. 24 (1875), pp. 266–274.

———, *Ancient Society*. New York: Holt, Rinehart and Winston, Inc., 1878.

Morin, J., *Les dessins des animaux en Grèce d'aprés les vases peints*. Paris, 1911.

Morley, S. G., *The Ancient Maya*. Palo Alto, Calif.: Stanford University Press, 1946.

Morris, E. H., *Archaeological Studies in the La Plata District*. Carnegie Institute of Washington, Publication 519, 1939.

———, and R. F. Burgh, *Basket Maker II Sites Near Durango, Colorado*. Carnegie Institute of Washington, Publication 604, 1954.

Mortillet, G. de, *Le Préhistorique Antiquité de l'Homme*, 3d ed. Paris: Reinwald, 1903.

Moss, J. H., "Glaciation in the Wind River Mountains and its Relation to Early Man in the Eden Valley, Wyoming," *Museum Monographs, University of Pennsylvania Museum*, 1951a, pp. 9–94.

———, *Early Man in the Eden Valley*. Philadelphia: University of Pennsylvania Museum Monographs, 1951b.

Moss, R. J., "Chemical Notes on a Stone Lamp from Ballyetagh and Other Similar Stone Vessels in the Royal Irish Academy Collection," *Proceedings of the Royal Irish Academy*, Vol. 28 (1910), pp. 162–168.

Movius, H. L., Jr., "A Wooden Spear of Third Interglacial Age from Lower Saxony," *Southwestern Journal of Anthropology*, Vol. 6 (1950), pp. 139–142.

———, "Radiocarbon Dates and Upper Paleolithic Archaeology in Central and Western Europe," *Current Anthropology*, Vol. 1 (1960), pp. 355–391.

———, "The Proto-Magdalenian of the Abri Pataud, Les Eyzies (Dordogne)," *Fifth International Congress for Pre- and Proto-History*, Hamburg, 1958, (1961), pp. 561–566.

———, "L'age du périgordien, de l'aurignacien et du proto-magdalenien en France sur la base des datations au carbone 14," *Bulletin de la Société méridionale de Spéologie et de Préhistoire.* Centenaire des fouilles d'Edouard Lartet, 1963, pp. 131–142.

Müller-Beck, H., *Das Obere Altpaläolithikum in Süddeutschland.* Bonn: Rudolf Habelt Verlag, 1957.

Munger, P., and R. M. Adams, "Fabric Impressions of Pottery From the Elizabeth Herrell Site, Missouri," *American Antiquity,* Vol. 7 (1941), pp. 166–171.

Murdock, G. P., "Comparative Data on Division of Labor by Sex," *Social Forces,* Vol. 15 (1937), pp. 551–553.

Myres, J. L., "Herodotus and Anthropology," in R. R. Marett, ed., *Anthropology and the Classics.* Oxford: Clarendon Press, 1908.

Naroll, R., "Floor Area and Settlement Pattern," *American Antiquity,* Vol. 27 (1962), pp. 587–589.

Nathan, R., *The Weans.* New York: Knopf, 1960.

Neill, W. T., "The Manufacture of Fluted Points," *The Florida Anthropologist,* Vol. 5 (1952), pp. 9–16.

Nelson, N. C., "Chronology of the Tano Ruins, New Mexico," *American Anthropologist,* Vol. 18 (1916), pp. 159–180.

———, "Pseudo-Artifacts from the Pliocene of Nebraska," *Science,* Vol. 67 (1928), pp. 316–317.

Nesbitt, P. H., *The Ancient Mimbreños.* Beloit, Wis.: Beloit College, Logan Museum Bulletin, No. 4, 1931.

Newell, H. P., and A. D. Krieger, "The George C. Davis Site, Cherokee County, Texas," *American Antiquity,* Vol. 14 (1949), No. 4, Part 2.

Nietsch, H., *Wald und Siedlung im vorgeschichtlichen Mitteleuropa.* Leipzig: Mannus-Bücherei, 1939.

North, F. J., "Geology for Archaeologists," *Archaeological Journal,* Vol. 94 (1937), pp. 73–115.

Oakley, K. P., "The Fluorine-Dating Method," *Yearbook of Physical Anthropology,* Vol. 5 (1951), pp. 44–52.

———, "Dating Fossil Human Remains," in *Anthropology Today.* Chicago: University of Chicago Press, 1953, pp. 43–57.

———, "Fire as a Paleolithic Tool and Weapon," *Proceedings of the Prehistoric Society,* Vol. 21 (1955a), pp. 36–48.

———, *Further Contributions to the Solution of the Piltdown Problem.* London: Bulletin of the British Museum of Natural History, Vol. 2, No. 6, 1955b.

———, "Radiocarbon Dating of the Piltdown Skull and Jaw," *Nature,* Vol. 184 (1959), pp. 224–226.

———, "Radiometric Assays [of uranium content of bones from Llano Estacado region]," in F. Wendorf, ed., *Paleoecology of the Llano Estacado.* Santa Fe, N.M.: Fort Burgwin Research Center, Publication No. 1, 1961, p. 136.

———, "Relative Dating of Arlington Springs Man," *Science,* Vol. 141 (1963a), p. 1172.

———, "Analytical Methods of Dating Bones," in D. Brothwell and E. Higgs, eds., *Science in Archaeology.* London: Thames and Hudson, 1963b, pp. 25–34.

———, "Dating Skeletal Material," *Science,* Vol. 140 (1963c), p. 488.

———, *The Problem of Man's Antiquity; an Historical Survey.* London: Bulletin of the British Museum (Natural History), Geology, Vol. 9, No. 5, 1964.

———, and J. S. Weiner, "Piltdown Man," *American Scientist,* Vol. 43 (1955), pp. 573–583.

———, and A. E. Rixon, "The Radioactivity of Materials from the Scharbauer Site Near Midland, Texas," *American Antiquity,* Vol. 24 (1958), pp. 185–187.

———, and W. W. Howells, "Age of the Skeleton from the Lagow Sand Pit, Texas," *American Antiquity,* Vol. 26 (1961), pp. 543–545.

O'Bryan, D., "Methods of Felling Trees and Tree-Ring Dating in the Southwest," *American Antiquity,* Vol. 15 (1949), pp. 155–156.

Olsen, S. J., "A Basic Annotated Bibliography to Facilitate the Identification of Vertebrate Remains from Archeological Sites," *Bulletin of the Texas Archeological Society,* Vol. 30 (1961a), pp. 219–222.

———, "The Relative Value of Fragmentary Mammalian Remains," *American Antiquity,* Vol. 26 (1961b), pp. 538–540.

———, "Metal Detectors as Archaeological Aids," *Curator,* Vol. 6 (1963), pp. 321–324.

O'Neale, L. M., *Archaeological Explorations in Peru. Part III, Textiles of the Early Nazca Period.* Chicago: Field Museum of Natural History, Anthropology, Memoirs, Vol. 2, No. 3 (1937), pp. 117–218.

———, "Note on an *Apocynum* Fabric," *American Antiquity,* Vol. 13 (1947), pp. 179–180.

Outwater, J. O., "Pre-Columbian Wood-Cutting Techniques," *American Antiquity,* Vol. 22 (1957), pp. 410–411.

Page, D., *History and the Homeric Iliad.* Berkeley, Calif.: The University of California Press, 1959.

Parker, A. C., *Iroquois Uses of Maize and Other Food Plants.* New York: State Museum, Bulletin 144, 1910.

Parkinson, A. E., "The Preservation of Cuneiform Tablets by Heating to a High Temperature," *Museum News,* Vol. 27 (1951), pp. 6–8.

Parrot, A., *Malédictions et Violations des Tombes.* Paris: P. Geuthner, 1939.

Parsons, R. B., *Indian Mounds of Northeast Iowa as Soil Genesis Benchmarks.* Journal of the Iowa Archeological Society, Vol. 12, No. 2, 1962.

Partington, J. R., "History of Alchemy and Early Chemistry," *Nature,* Vol. 159 (1947), pp. 81–85.

Peake, H. J. E., "The Study of Prehistoric Times," *Journal of the Royal Anthropological Institute,* Vol. 70 (1940), pp. 103–146.

Peet, T. E., *The Great Tomb Robberies of the Twentieth Egyptian Dynasty.* Oxford: Clarendon Press, 1943.

Pei, W. C., *Le rôle des animaux et des causes naturelles dans la cassure des os.* Nanking: Paleontologica Sinica, n.s.d., No. 7, Whole Series No. 118 (1938), Geological Survey of China.

Pericot, L., "The Social Life of Spanish Paleolithic Hunters as Shown in Levantine Art," *Viking Fund Publications in Anthropology,* No. 31 (1961), pp. 194–213.

Perrot, J., "The Excavations at Tell Abu Matar, Near Beersheba," *Israel Exploration Journal,* Vol. 5 (1955a), pp. 17–189.

———, "Les Fouilles d'Abu Matar," *Syria,* Vol. 34 (1955b), pp. 1–38.

Petrie, W. M. F., *Diospolis Parva.* London: Egyptian Exploration Fund Memoirs, No. 20, 1901.

———, *Tell el-Hesy (Lachish).* London: Palestine Exploration Fund, 1891.

———, "Sequences in Prehistoric Remains," *Journal of the Royal Anthropological Institute,* Vol. 29 (1899), pp. 295–301.

———, *Seventy Years in Archaeology.* London: S. Low, Marston and Co., 1931.

Pewe, T. L., "The Geological Approach to Dating Archaeological Sites," *American Antiquity,* Vol. 20 (1954), pp. 51–61.

Peyrony, D., "La Ferrassie," *Préhistoire,* Paris, 1939.

Phillips, P., J. A. Ford, and J. B. Griffin, "Archaeological Survey in the Lower Mississippi Alluvial Valley, 1940–1947," *Papers of the Peabody Museum of American Archaeology and Ethnology,* Cambridge, Mass., Vol. 25, 1951.

Pieper, W., "Der Pariastamm der Ṣlêb," *Le Monde Orientale,* Vol. 17 (1923), pp. 1–75.

Piggott, S., *Approach to Archaeology.* Cambridge, Mass.: Harvard University Press, 1959.

———, "Prehistory and Evolutionary Theory," in Sol Tax, ed., *Evolution After Darwin.* Chicago: University of Chicago Press, 1960, pp. 85–98.

Pittioni, R., "Metallurgical Analysis of Archaeological Materials: II," *Viking Fund Publications in Anthropology,* No. 28 (1960), pp. 21–33.

Plenderleith, H. J., "Fakes and Forgeries in Museums," *The Museum Journal,* Vol. 52 (1952), pp. 143–148.

———, *The Conservation of Antiquities and Works of Art.* London: Oxford University Press, 1956.

Pond, A., *Primitive Methods of Working Stone Based on Experiments by Halvor L. Skavlem.* Beloit, Wis.: Beloit College, Logan Museum Bulletin, Vol. 2, No. 1, 1930.

Posnansky, A., *Tihuanacu, the Cradle of American Man,* trans. by James F. Shearer. New York: J. J. Augustin, 1945–1957.

Powell, J. W., *The Colorado River and Its Canyons.* New York: Dover Books, T94, 1961.

Pulgram, E., "Proto-Indo-European; Reality and Reconstruction," *Language,* Vol. 35 (1959), No. 3, pp. 421–426.

Pyddoke, E., *Stratification for the Archaeologist.* London: Phoenix House, 1961.

Quimby, G. I., "Rates of Culture Change in Archaeology," *American Antiquity,* Vol. 25 (1960), pp. 416–417.

Rachlin, C. K., "The Rubber Mold Technic for the Study of Textile-Impressed Pottery," *American Antiquity,* Vol. 20 (1955), pp. 394–396.

Radford, C. A. R., "The Roman Villa at Ditchley, Oxon," *Oxoniensia,* Vol. 1 (1936).

Ragir, S., *Field Sampling Methods.* Reports of the University of California Archaeological Survey, No. 63, 1964.

Rassam, H., *Asshur and the Land of Nimrod.* Cincinnati: Curts and Jennings, 1897.

Rau, C., "Aboriginal Stone Drilling," *American Naturalist,* Vol. 15 (1881), pp. 536–542.

Rawlinson, H. C., "Notes on the Inscriptions of Assyria and Babylonia," *Journal of the Royal Asiatic Society of Great Britain and Ireland,* Vol. 12 (1850), Article 10, pp. 402–410.

Reed, C. A., "Animal Domestication in the Prehistoric Near East," *Science,* Vol. 130 (1959), pp. 1629–1639.

——, "Osteo-Archaeology," in D. Brothwell and E. Higgs, eds., *Science in Archaeology.* London: Thames and Hudson, 1963, pp. 204–216.

Reeves, D. M., "Aerial Photography and Archaeology," *American Antiquity,* Vol. 2 (1936), pp. 102–107.

Reiche, M., *Los Dibujos Gigantescos en el Suelo de las Pampas de Nazca y Palpa.* Lima: Editoria Medica Peruana, 1949.

Ricard, R., "La 'conquete spirituelle' du Mexique," Paris, *Mémoirs, Institut d'Ethnologie,* Vol. 2 (1933), pp. 196–199.

Rice, T. T., *The Scythians.* New York: Praeger, 1957.

Rich, C. J., *Second Memoir on Babylon.* London, 1819.

Ricketson, O. G., and E. B. Ricketson, *Uaxactun, Guatemala: Group E—1926–1931.* Carnegie Institute of Washington, Publication 477, 1937.

Riesenfeld, A., *The Megalithic Culture of Melanesia.* Leiden: E. J. Brill, 1950.

Ritchie, W. A., *Dutch Hollow, an Early Historic Period Seneca Site in Livingston County, New York.* Transactions and Researches of the New York State Museum, Circular No. 40, 1954.

Robinson, W., "A Method for Chronologically Ordering Archaeological Deposits," *American Antiquity,* Vol. 16 (1951), pp. 293–301.

Rodeck, H. G., Arthropod Designs on Prehistoric Mimbres Pottery. *Annals of the Entomological Society of America,* Vol. 25 (1932), pp. 688–693

Rogers, M. J., *Yuman Pottery Making.* San Diego Museum Papers, No. 2, 1936.

Rouse, I., "The Strategy of Culture History," in A. L. Kroeber, ed., *Anthropology Today.* Chicago: University of Chicago Press, 1953, pp. 57–76.

——, "On the Use of the Concept of Co-Tradition," *American Antiquity,* Vol. 19 (1954), pp. 221–225.

——, "On the Correlation of Phases of Culture," *American Anthropologist,* Vol. 57 (1955), pp. 713–722.

——, "Culture Area and Co-Tradition," *Southwestern Journal of Anthropology,* Vol. 13 (1957), pp. 123–133.

——, "The Inference of Migrations from Anthropological Evidence," *University of Arizona, Social Science Bulletin* No. 27 (1958), pp. 63–68.

——, "The Classification of Artifacts in Archaeology," *American Antiquity,* Vol. 25 (1960), pp. 313–323.

Rowe, J. H., *An Introduction to the Archaeology of Cuzco.* Cambridge, Mass.: Papers of the Peabody Museum, Vol. 27, No. 2, 1944.

——, "Absolute Chronology in the Andean Area," *American Antiquity,* Vol. 10 (1945a), pp. 265–284.

——, "Inca Culture at the Time of the Spanish Conquest," *Bureau of American Ethnology,* Bulletin 143, Vol. 2 (1945b), pp. 183–330.

——, "Technical Aids in Anthropology: A Historical Survey," in *Anthropology Today.* Chicago: University of Chicago Press, 1953, pp. 895–941.

——, "Archaeology as a Career," *Archaeology,* Vol. 7 (1954), pp. 229–236.

——, "Archaeological Dating and Cultural Process," *Southwestern Journal of Anthropology,* Vol. 15 (1959), pp. 317–324.

———, "Stratigraphy and Seriation," *American Antiquity,* Vol. 26 (1961), pp. 324–330.

———, "Worsaae's Law and the Use of Grave Lots for Archaeological Dating," *American Antiquity,* Vol. 28 (1962a), pp. 129–137.

———, "Stages and Periods in Archaeological Interpretation," *Southwestern Journal of Anthropology,* Vol. 18 (1962b), pp. 40–54.

Ruz Lhuillier, A., "Exploraciones in Palenque, 1950, 1951," *Anales del Instituto Nacional de Antropologia e Historia,* Vol. 5 (1952), pp. 25–66.

Russell, R. J., "Instability of Sea Level," *American Scientist,* Vol. 45 (1957), pp. 414–430.

Ryan, E. J., and G. F. Bass, "Underwater Surveying and Draughting—a Technique," *Antiquity,* Vol. 36 (1962), No. 144, pp. 252–261.

Saint David's, Lord Bishop of, "On some traditions relating to the submersion of ancient cities," *Transactions of the Royal Society of Literature,* 2d Series, Vol. 6 (1859), pp. 387–415.

Saint-Perier, R. de, "Gravure à contours decoupés en os et coquilles perforées de l'époque magdalénienne," *Bulletin et Mémoires, Société d'Anthropologie,* Paris, Series 6, Vol. 4 (1913), pp. 47–52.

Salim, S. M., *Marsh Dwellers of the Euphrates Delta.* London: London School of Economics, Monographs on Social Anthropology, No. 23, 1962.

Salisbury, R., *From Stone to Steel.* Melbourne: Melbourne University Press, 1962.

Sandford, K. S., and W. J. Arkell, *Prehistoric Survey of Egypt and Western Asia,* Vol. 1–4. Chicago: Oriental Institute Publications, Vols. 10, 17, 18, 46, 1929–39.

Sandin, B., "Gawai Batu: The Iban Whetstone Feast," *Sarawak Museum Journal,* Vol. 10 (1962), pp. 392–408.

Sapir, E., *Time Perspective in Aboriginal American Culture: A Study in Method.* Ottawa: Canada Department of Mines, Geological Survey, Memoir No. 90, 1916. Reprinted in D. G. Mandelbaum, ed., *Selected Writings of Edward Sapir.* Berkeley, Calif.: University of California Press, 1949.

Satterthwaite, L., and E. Ralph, "New Radiocarbon Dates and the Maya Correlation Problem," *American Antiquity,* Vol. 26 (1960), pp. 165–184.

Sayce, R. U., "The Ecological Study of Culture," in G. A. Theodorson, ed., *Studies in Human Ecology.* New York: Harper & Row, 1961.

Sayre, E. V., A. Murrenhoff, and C. F. Weick, *The Nondestructive Analysis of Ancient Potsherds Through Neutron Activation Analysis.* Brookhaven National Laboratory, Report No. 508, 1958.

Schlabow, K., and others, "Zwei Moorleichenfunde aus dem Domlandsmoor," Berlin, *Praehistorische Zeitschrift,* Vol. 36 (1958), pp. 118–219.

Schmalz, R. F., "Flint and the Patination of Flint Artifacts," *Proceedings of the Prehistoric Society,* Vol. 26 (1960), pp. 44–49.

Schmid, E., "Cave Sediments and Prehistory," in D. Brothwell and E. Higgs, eds., *Science in Archaeology.* London: Thames and Hudson, 1963, pp. 123–138.

Schmidt, E. F., *Time-Relations of Prehistoric Pottery Types in Southern Arizona.* Anthropological Papers of the American Museum of Natural History, Vol. 30, Part 4, 1928.

Schoenwetter, J., *The Pollen Analysis of Eighteen Archaeological Sites in Arizona and New Mexico.* Chicago: Fieldiana, Anthropology, Chicago Natural History Museum, Vol. 53, 1962.

Schoute-Vanneck, C. A., "A Chemical Aid for the Relative Dating of Coastal Shell Middens," *South African Journal of Science,* Vol. 56 (1960), pp. 67–70.

Schroeder, A., *A Brief Survey of the Lower Colorado River from Davis Dam to the International Border.* Boulder City, Nev.: U. S. Bureau of Reclamation, 1952.

Schulman, E., "Bristlecone Pine, Oldest Known Living Thing," *National Geographic Magazine,* Vol. 113 (1958), pp. 353–372.

Schultz, G. B., G. C. Lueninghoener, and W. D. Frankforter, "Preliminary Geomorphological Studies of the Lime Creek Area," *Bulletin of University of Nebraska State Museum,* Vol. 3 (1948), pp. 31–42.

Schwartz, D. W., Demographic Changes in the Early Periods of Cohoninna Prehistory," *Viking Fund Publications in Anthropology,* No. 23 (1956), pp. 26–31.

———, "An Archaeological Survey of Nankoweap Canyon, Grand Canyon National Park," *American Antiquity,* Vol. 28 (1963), pp. 289–302.

Scott, W. H., "Economic and Material Culture of the Kalingas of Madukayan," *Southwestern Journal of Anthropology,* Vol. 14 (1958), pp. 318–337.

Sears, P. B., "The Archaeology of Environment in Eastern North America," *American Anthropologist,* Vol. 34 (1932), pp. 610–622.

———, "Palynology in Southern North America. I: Archaeological Horizons in the Basin of Mexico," *Bulletin of the Geological Society of America,* Vol. 63 (1952), pp. 225–240.

———, "The Interdependence of Archaeology and Ecology, with Examples from Middle America," *Transactions of the New York Academy of Science,* Series 2, Vol. 15 (1953), pp. 113–117.

———, "Vegetation, Climate, and Coastal Submergence in Connecticut," *Science,* Vol. 140 (1963), pp. 59–60.

———, and A. Roosma, "A Climatic Sequence from Two Nevada Caves," *American Journal of Science,* Vol. 259 (1961), pp. 669–678.

Sears, W, H., "The Sociopolitical Organization of Pre-Columbian Cultures on the Gulf Coastal Plain," *American Anthropologist,* Vol. 56 (1954), pp. 339–346.

———, "The Study of Social and Religious Systems in North American Archaeology," *Current Anthropology,* Vol. 2 (1961), pp. 223–231.

Seborg, R. M., and R. B. Inverarity, "Preservation of Old, Waterlogged Wood by Treatment with Polyethylene Glycol," *Science,* Vol. 136 (1962), pp. 649–650.

Senyurek, M. S., "Duration of Life of the Ancient Inhabitants of Anatolia," *American Journal of Physical Anthropology,* Vol. 5 (1947), pp. 55–66.

Service, E. R., *Primitive Social Organization.* New York: Random House, 1962.

Setzler, F. M., "Seeking the Secret of the Giants," *National Geographic Magazine,* Vol. 102 (1952), pp. 390–404.

Shaeffer, J. B., "The County Grid System of Site Designation," *Plains Anthropologist,* Vol. 5 (1960), No. 9, pp. 29–31.

Shepard, A. O., *Plumbate: A Mesoamerican Trade Ware*. Carnegie Institute of Washington, Publication No. 573, 1948.

———, *Ceramics for the Archaeologist*. Carnegie Institute of Washington, Publication No. 609, 1956.

———, *Beginnings of Ceramic Industrialization: An Example from the Oaxaca Valley*. Carnegie Institute of Washington, Notes from a Ceramic Laboratory, No. 2, 1963.

Shetrone, H. C., *The Mound Builders*. New York: Appleton, 1930.

Shorr, P., "The Genesis of Prehistorical Research," *Isis*, Vol. 23 (1935), pp. 425–443.

Shumway, G., C. L. Hubbs, and J. R. Moriarty, "Scripps Estate Site, San Diego, California: A La Jolla Site Dated 5640 to 7370 Years Before the Present," *Annals of the New York Academy of Sciences*, Vol. 93 (1961), Article 3, pp. 37–132.

Sieveking, A. and G., *The Caves of France and Northern Spain: A Guide*. London: Vista Books, 1962.

Silverberg, R., *Sunken History: The Story of Underwater Archeology*. Philadelphia: Chilton, 1963.

Simoons, F. J., *Eat Not This Flesh*. Madison, Wis.: University of Wisconsin Press, 1961.

Sinex, F. M., and B. Faris, "Isolation of Gelatin from Ancient Bones," *Science*, Vol. 129 (1959), p. 969.

Slosson, E. E., "The Science of the City Dump," in *Snapshots in Science*, New York: Appleton, 1928.

Smiley, T. L., "Varve Studies," *University of Arizona Bulletin*, Series No. 26 (1955a), pp. 135–150.

———, ed., *Geochronology*. Tucson, Ariz.: University of Arizona Press, 1955b.

Smith, A. L., "Report on the Investigation of Stelae," *Carnegie Institute of Washington*, Vol. 28 (1929), pp. 323–325.

Smith, G. V., "The Use of Flint Blades to Work Pine Wood," *Smithsonian Report*, 1893, pp. 601–605.

Smith, H. W., and C. D. Moodie, "Collection and Preservation of Soil Profiles," *Soil Science*, Vol. 64 (1947), pp. 61–69.

———, R. A. McCreery, and C. D. Moodie, "Collection and Preservation of Soil Profiles: II," *Soil Science*, Vol. 73 (1952), p. 243.

Smith, M., "Blood Groups of the Ancient Dead," *Science*, Vol. 131 (1960), pp. 699–702.

Smith, M. A., "The Limitations of Inference in Archaeology," *The Archaeological Newsletter*, Vol. 6 (1955), pp. 1–7.

Smith, R. E., *Ceramic Sequences at Uaxactun*. New Orleans, La.: Tulane University, Middle American Research Institute, Publication No. 20, 1955.

Smith, W., *Kiva Mural Decorations at Awatovi and Kawaika-a*. Cambridge, Mass.: Peabody Museum Papers, Vol. 37, 1952.

Smith, W. S., *The Art and Architecture of Ancient Egypt*. Baltimore: Pelican History of Art Series, Penguin Books, 1958.

Solecki, R., "Exploration of an Adena Mound at Natrium, West Virginia," *Bureau of American Ethnology, Bulletin 151*, Anthropological Paper No. 40 (1953), pp. 313–396.

———, "Practical Aerial Photography for Archaeologists," *American Antiquity,* Vol. 22 (1957), pp. 337–351.

Sonnenfeld, J., "Interpreting the Function of Primitive Implements," *American Antiquity,* Vol. 28 (1962), pp. 56–65.

Sonneville-Bordes, D. de "Le Paléolithique supérieur du plateau Baillart à Gavaudun (Lot-et-Garonne)," *Bulletin de la Société Française Préhistorique,* Vol. 50 (1953), pp. 356–364.

———, *La Paléolithique Supérieur en Périgord.* 2 Vols. Bordeaux: Imprimeries Delmas, 1960.

South, S., "Evolutionary Theory in Archaeology," *Southern Indian Studies,* Chapel Hill, N.C., Vol. 7 (1955), pp. 10–32.

Sparks, B. W., "Non-Marine Mollusca and Archaeology," in D. Brothwell and E. Higgs, eds., *Science in Archaeology.* London: Thames and Hudson, 1963, p. 313–323.

Spaulding, A. C., "Statistical Techniques for the Discovery of Artifact Types," *American Antiquity,* Vol. 18 (1953), pp. 305–313; 391–393.

———, "The Significance of Differences Between Radiocarbon Dates," *American Antiquity,* Vol. 23 (1958), pp. 309–311.

———, "Statistical Description and Comparison of Artifact Assemblages," in *Viking Fund Publications in Anthropology,* No. 28 (1960), pp. 60–92.

Spencer, R. F., *The North Alaskan Eskimos.* Washington, D.C.: Smithsonian Institution, Bureau of American Ethnology, Bulletin 171, 1959.

Spier, L., "An Outline for a Chronology of Zuni Ruins," *Anthropological Papers of the American Museum of Natural History,* Vol. 18 (1917), pp. 209–331.

Squier, R. J., "The Manufacture of Flint Implements by the Indians of Northern and Central California," *Reports of the University of California Archaeological Survey,* No. 19 (1953), pp. 15–32.

Staub, G., "Die Geographische Fixierung historischer Objekte und Örtlichkeiten," *Jahrbuch 41 der Schweizerischen Gesellschaft für Urgeschichte,* 1951, pp. 191–195.

Steensberg, A., *Ancient Harvesting Implements: A Study in Archaeology and Human Geography.* Copenhagen: Nationalmuseets Skrifter, Arkeologisk-Historisk Raekke 1, 1943.

Stein, M. A., *Ancient Khotan: Detailed Report of Archaeological Explorations in Chinese Turkestan,* 2 Vols. Oxford: Clarendon Press, 1907.

Stein, W. T., "Mammal Remains from Archaeological Sites in the Point of Pines Region, Arizona," *American Antiquity,* Vol. 29 (1963), pp. 213–220.

Stephens, J. L., *Incidents of Travel in Central America, Chiapas and Yucatan,* 2 Vols. New York: Harper & Row, 1842.

Steward, J. H., *Petroglyphs of California and Adjoining States.* University of California Publications in American Archaeology and Ethnology, Vol. 24, No. 2, 1929.

———, "The Economic and Social Basis of Primitive Bands," in *Essays in Anthropology Presented to A. L. Kroeber.* Berkeley, Calif.: University of California Press, 1936, pp. 331–350.

———, "Ecological Aspects of Southwestern Society," *Anthropos,* Vol. 32 (1937), pp. 87–104.

————, *Basin-Plateau Aboriginal Sociopolitical Groups.* Washington, D.C.: Bureau of American Ethnology, Bulletin 120, 1938.

————, "The Direct Historical Approach in Archaeology," *American Antiquity,* Vol. 7 (1942), pp. 337–343.

————, "Cultural Causality and Law: A Trial Formulation of the Development of Early Civilizations," *American Anthropologist,* Vol. 51 (1949), pp. 1–27.

————, *Theory of Culture Change.* Urbana, Ill.: University of Illinois Press, 1955.

Stewart, T. D., "A Physical Anthropologist's View of the Peopling of the New World," *Southwestern Journal of Anthropology,* Vol. 16 (1960), pp. 259–273.

Stone, J. F. S., *Wessex Before the Celts.* New York: Praeger, 1958.

————, and L. C. Thomas, "The Use and Distribution of Faience in the Ancient East and Prehistoric Europe," *Proceedings of the Prehistoric Society,* Vol. 22 (1956), pp. 37–85.

Strong, W. D., "From History to Prehistory in the Northern Great Plains," *Smithsonian Institution, Miscellaneous Collections,* Vol. 100 (1940), pp. 353–394.

————, and J. M. Corbett, *A Ceramic Sequence at Pachacamac.* Columbia University Studies in Archeology and Ethnology, Vol. 1, No. 2, 1943.

Stross, F. H., "Authentication of Antique Stone Objects by Physical and Chemical Means," *Analytical Chemistry,* Vol. 32 (1960), pp. 17A–24A.

Studhalter, R. A., "Tree Growth: Some Historical Chapters," *The Botanical Review,* Vol. 24 (1955), pp. 1–72.

Struever, S., "Implications of Vegetal Remains from an Illinois Hopewell Site," *American Antiquity,* Vol. 27 (1962), pp. 584–587.

Sturtevant, W. C., *Anthropology as a Career.* Washington, D.C.: Smithsonian Institution, 1958.

Sullivan, R. J., *The Ten'a Food Quest.* Washington, D.C.: Catholic University of America, Anthropological Series, No. 11, 1942.

Swadesh, M., "Archeological and Linguistic Chronology of Indo-European Groups," *American Anthropologist,* Vol. 55 (1953), pp. 349–352.

————, "Linguistics as an Instrument of Prehistory," *Southwestern Journal of Anthropology,* Vol. 15 (1959), pp. 20–35.

————, *Estudios Sobre Lengua y Cultura.* Mexico City: Acta Anthropologica, Epoca 2, Vol. 2, No. 2. 1960.

————, "Linguistic Relations Across Bering Strait," *American Anthropologist,* Vol. 64 (1962), pp. 1262–1291.

Swanton, J. R., *Source Material on the History and Ethnology of the Caddo Indians.* Bureau of American Ethnology, Bulletin 132, 1942.

Tanzer, H. H., *The Common People of Pompeii.* Johns Hopkins University Studies in Archaeology, No. 29, 1939.

Tauber, H., "Difficulties in the Application of C_{14} Results in Archaeology," *Archaeologia Austriaca,* Vol. 24 (1958), pp. 59–69.

Taylor, D., and I. Rouse, "Linguistic and Archaeological Time Depth in the West Indies," *International Journal of American Linguistics,* Vol. 21 (1955), pp. 105–115.

Taylor, W. W., *A Study of Archeology.* American Anthropological Association, Memoir No. 69, 1948.

Thieme, F. P., "The Indo-European Language," *Scientific American*, Vol. 199 (1958), pp. 63–74.

———, and C. M. Otten, "The Unreliability of Blood Typing Aged Bone," *American Journal Of Physical Anthropology*, Vol. 15 (1957), pp. 387–398.

Thomas, D. W., *Documents from Old Testament Times*. New York: Harper Torchbooks TB 85, 1961.

Thomas, W. L., ed., *Man's Role in Changing the Face of the Earth*. Chicago: University of Chicago Press, 1956.

Thompson, J. E. S., *Maya Hieroglyphic Writing*. Carnegie Institute of Washington, Publication No. 589, 1950.

———, "The Character of the Maya," *Proceedings of the 30th International Congress of Americanists*, 1954, pp. 36–40.

Thompson, R. H., "Review of R. E. M. Wheeler, *Archaeology from the Earth*," *American Antiquity*, Vol. 21 (1955), pp. 188–189.

———, "The Subjective Element in Archaeological Inference," *Southwestern Journal of Anthropology*, Vol. 12 (1956), pp. 327–332.

———, *Modern Yucatecan Maya Pottery Making*. Society for American Archaeology, Memoir No. 15, 1958.

———, ed., *Migrations in New World Culture History*. Tucson, Ariz.: University of Arizona Social Science Bulletin, No. 27, 1958.

Thorvildsen, E., "Menneskeofringer i Oldtiden [Human Offerings in Antiquity]," *Kuml*, Aarhus (1952), pp. 32–48.

Throckmorton, P., and J. M. Bullitt, "Underwater Surveys in Greece: 1962," *Expedition*, University of Pennsylvania Museum, Vol. 5 (1963), pp. 17–23.

Tilton, G. R., and S. R. Hart, "Geochronology," *Science*, Vol. 140 (1963), pp. 357–366.

Tite, M. S., and J. Waine, "Thermoluminescent Dating: A Re-appraisal," *Archaeometry*, Vol. 5 (1962), pp. 53–79.

Tolstoy, P., *Surface Survey of the Northern Valley of Mexico: The Classic and Post-Classic Periods*. Transactions of the American Philosophical Society, Vol. 48, Part 5, 1958.

Toulouse, J. H., Jr., *The Mission of San Gregorio de Abó*, Santa Fe, N.M.: School of American Research, Monograph No. 13, 1949.

Tower, D. B., *The Use of Marine Mollusca and Their Value in Reconstructing Prehistoric Trade Routes in the American Southwest*. Cambridge, Mass.: Papers of the Excavators' Club, Vol. 2, No. 3, 1945.

Toynbee, A. J., *A Study of History*. 12 vols. London: Oxford University Press, 1934–1960.

Trager, G. L., "Linguistics and the Reconstruction of Culture History," in *New Interpretations of Aboriginal American Culture History*. Washington, D. C.: Anthropological Society of Washington, 1955, pp. 110–115.

Treganza, A. E., "Sonoma Mission: An Archaeological Reconstruction of the Mission San Francisco de Solano Quadrangle," *Kroeber Anthropological Society Papers*, No. 14 (1956), pp. 1–18.

———, and L. L. Valdivia, "The Manufacture of Pecked and Ground Stone Artifacts: A Controlled Study," *Reports of the University of California Archaeological Survey*, No. 32 (1955), pp. 19–29.

Troels-Smith, J., "The Muldbjerg Dwelling Place: An Early Neolithic Archaeological Site in the Aamosen Bog, West Zealand, Denmark," *Annual Report, Smithsonian Institution for 1959*, (1960), pp. 577–601.

Vaillant, G. C., "Excavations at El Arbolillo," *Anthropological Papers, American Museum of Natural History*, Vol. 35 (1935), Part 2.

Vallois, H. V., "Etude des empreintes de pieds humains du Tuc d'Audoubert, de Cabrerets et de Ganties." Institut Internationale d'Anthropologie, 3ᵉ session, Amsterdam, Sept. 20–29, 1927 (1928).

———, "Vital Statistics in Prehistoric Populations as Determined from Archaeological Data," *Viking Fund Publications in Anthropology*, No. 28 (1960), pp. 181–222.

Van Buren, E. D., "The Fauna of Ancient Mesopotamia as Represented in Art," *Analecta Orientalia*, Vol. 18 (1939), pp. 1–113.

Van Riet Lowe, C., "Pitfalls in Prehistory," *Antiquity*, Vol. 28 (1954), pp. 85–90.

———, *The Distribution of Prehistoric Rock Engravings and Paintings in South Africa*. Pretoria: Archaeological Series, No. 7, 1956.

Van Zeist, W., and H. E. Wright, Jr., "Preliminary Pollen Studies at Lake Zeribar, Zagros Mountains, Southwestern Iran," *Science*, Vol. 140 (1963), pp. 65–69.

Van Zinderen Bakker, E. M., ed., *Palynology in Africa*, Sixth Report. Bloemfontein, S.A.: University of the Orange Free State, 1960.

Vescelius, G., "Archaeological Sampling: A Problem in Statistical Inference," in G. E. Dole and R. L. Carneiro, eds., *Essays in the Science of Culture*. New York: Crowell, 1955, pp. 457–470.

Von Bothmer, D., and J. V. Noble, *An Inquiry into the Forgery of the Etruscan Terracotta Warriors in the Metropolitan Museum of Art*. New York: Metropolitan Museum of Art, Occasional Papers, No. 11, 1961.

Von Hagen, V. W., "The Highways of the Inca," *Archaeology*, Vol. 5 (1952), pp. 104–109.

———, *Highway of the Sun*. London: Gollancz, 1955.

Von Koenigswald, G. H. R., *Meeting Prehistoric Man*. New York: Harper & Row, 1956.

Wace, A. J. B., "The Greeks and Romans as Archaeologists," Societé Royale d'Archéologie d'Alexandrie, Bulletin No. 38, 1949. (Reprinted in R. F. Heizer, *Man's Discovery of his Past: Literary Landmarks in Archaeology*, 1962a, pp. 152–165.)

Wakeling, T. G., *Forged Egyptian Antiquities*. London: Adam and Charles Black, 1912.

Wallace, A. F., "A Possible Technique for Recognizing Psychological Characteristics of the Ancient Maya from an Analysis of their Art," *American Imago*, Vol. 7 (1950), pp. 239–258.

Wallace, W. J., "A Basket-Weaver's Kit from Death Valley," *Southwest Museum Masterkey*, Vol. 28 (1954), pp. 216–221.

———, and D. Lathrap, "Ceremonial Bird Burials in San Francisco Bay Shellmounds," *American Antiquity*, Vol. 25 (1959), pp. 262–264.

Warren, S. H., "On a Prehistoric Interment Near Walton-on-Naze," *Essex Naturalist*, Vol. 16 (1911), pp. 198–208.

———, "The Experimental Investigation of Flint Fracture and its Application to Problems of Human Implements," *Journal of the Royal Anthropological Institute*, Vol. 44 (1914), pp. 412–450.

Washburn, S. L., "Speculations on the Interrelations of the History of Tools and Biological Evolution," *Human Biology,* Vol. 31 (1959), pp. 21–31.

———, "Tools and Human Evolution," *Scientific American,* Vol. 203 (1960), pp. 3–15.

———, and F. C. Howell, "Human Evolution and Culture," in Sol Tax, ed., *Evolution After Darwin,* Vol. II. Chicago: University of Chicago Press, 1960, pp. 33–56.

Watanabe, H., "Natural Fracture of Pebbles From the Fossil-Bearing Pleistocene Deposits Near Akashi," Tokyo, *Zinruigaku Zassi,* Vol. 60 (1949), pp. 121–142.

———, "The Direction of Remanent Magnetism of Baked Earth and Its Application to Chronology for Anthropology and Archaeology in Japan," University of Tokyo, *Journal of the Faculty of Science,* Section 2, Vol. 2 (1959), pp. 1–188.

Watson, V., "Archaeology and Proteins," *American Antiquity,* Vol. 20 (1955), p. 288.

Wauchope, R., *Lost Tribes and Sunken Continents.* Chicago: University of Chicago Press, 1962.

Waugh, F. W., *Iroquois Foods and Food Preparation.* Ottawa, Can.: Department of Mines, Geological Survey, Memoir 86, Anthropological Series, No. 12, 1916.

Webb, W. S., *Indian Knoll.* Lexington, Ky.: University of Kentucky Reports in Anthropology, Vol. 4, No. 3, 1946.

———, and W. G. Haag, *The Chiggerville Site.* Lexington, Ky.: University of Kentucky Reports in Anthropology, Vol. 4, 1939.

———, and D. L. De Jarnette, *An Archeological Survey of Pickwick Basin in the Adjacent Portions of the States of Alabama, Mississippi, and Tennessee.* Bureau of American Ethnology, Bulletin 129, 1942.

———, and R. S. Baby, *The Adena People: No. 2.* Columbus, Ohio: The Ohio Historical Society, Ohio State University Press, 1957.

Wedel, W. R., *Environment and Native Subsistence Economies in the Central Great Plains.* Washington, D.C.: Smithsonian Institution, Miscellaneous Collections, Vol. 101, No. 3, 1941.

———, "The Use of Earth-Moving Machinery in Archaeological Excavation," *Anthropological Papers of the Museum of Anthropology,* University of Michigan, No. 8 (1951), pp. 17–33.

———, *Prehistoric Man on the Great Plains.* Norman, Okla.: University of Oklahoma Press, 1961.

Weinberg, S. S., "The Relative Chronology of the Aegean in the Neolithic Period and the Early Bronze Age," in R. W. Ehrich, ed., *Relative Chronologies in Old World Archaeology.* Chicago: University of Chicago Press, 1954, pp. 86–107.

Weiner, J. S., *The Piltdown Forgery.* London: Oxford University Press, 1955.

Weiss, L. E., "Fabric Analysis of Some Greek Marbles and Its Application to Archaeology," *American Journal of Science,* Vol. 252 (1954), pp. 641–662.

Wendorf, F., *Paleoecology of the Llano Estacado,* Santa Fe, N.M.: Fort Burgwin Research Center, Publication No. 1, 1961.

———, *A Guide for Salvage Archaeology.* Santa Fe, N.M.: Museum of New Mexico Press, 1962.

Wertenbaker, T. J., "The Archaeology of Colonial Williamsburg," *Proceedings of the American Philosophical Society,* Vol. 97 (1953), pp. 44–50.

Wettstein, E., "Die Tierreste aus dem Pfahlbau am Alpenquai in Zürich," *Vierteljahrschrift der Naturforschenden Gesellschaft Zürich,* Vol. 69 (1924), pp. 78–127.

Weyer, E. M., *The Eskimos.* New Haven, Conn.: Yale University Press, 1932.

Wheeler, M., *Still Digging.* London: M. Joseph, 1955.

——, *Archaeology From the Earth.* Baltimore: Pelican Book A356, 1956.

Wheeler, R. E. M., "Harappa 1946: The Defences and Cemetery R 37," *Ancient India,* No. 3 (1947), pp. 59–130.

White, L. A., "Evolutionary Stages, Progress, and the Evaluation of Cultures," *Southwestern Journal of Anthropology,* Vol. 3 (1947), pp. 165–192.

White, T. E., "Observations on the Butchering Techniques of Some Aboriginal Peoples, No. 1," *American Antiquity,* Vol. 17 (1952), pp. 337–338.

——, "Observations on the Butchering Techniques of Some Aboriginal Peoples, No. 2," *American Antiquity,* Vol. 19 (1953a), pp. 160–164.

——, "A Method for Calculating the Dietary Percentage of Various Food Animals Utilized by Aboriginal Peoples," *American Antiquity,* Vol. 18 (1953b), pp. 396–398.

——, "Observations on the Butchering Techniques of Some Aboriginal Peoples, Nos. 3, 4, 5, 6," *American Antiquity,* Vol. 19 (1954), pp. 254–264.

——, "Observations on the Butchering Techniques of Some Aboriginal Peoples, Nos. 7, 8, 9," *American Antiquity,* Vol. 21 (1955), pp. 170–178.

Whiteford, A. H., "Description for Artifact Analysis," *American Antiquity,* Vol. 12 (1947), pp. 226–239.

Wickman, F. E., "Variations in the Relative Abundance of the Carbon Isotopes in Plants," *Geochimica et Cosmochimica Acta,* London, Vol. 2 (1952), pp. 243–254.

Willey, G. R., "Ceramic Stratigraphy in a Georgia Village Site," *American Antiquity,* Vol. 5 (1939), pp. 140–147.

——, Participant in discussion session, International Symposium on Anthropology. S. Tax, L. Eiseley, I. Rouse, and C. F. Vogelin, eds., *Appraisal of Anthropology Today.* Chicago: University of Chicago Press, 1953.

——, "Prehistoric Settlement Patterns in the Virú Valley, Peru," *Bureau of American Ethnology,* Bulletin 153, 1953.

——, "The Prehistoric Civilizations of Nuclear America," *American Anthropologist,* Vol. 57 (1955), pp. 571–613.

——, "An Archaeological Classification of Culture Contact Situations," *Society for American Archaeology,* Memoir No. 11, (1956), pp. 1–30.

——, "New World Prehistory," *Science,* Vol. 131 (1960), pp. 73–86.

——, and C. R. McGimsey, *The Monagrillo Culture of Panama.* Cambridge, Mass.: Peabody Museum Papers, Vol. 49, No. 2, 1954.

——, and P. Phillips, *Method and Theory in American Archaeology.* Chicago: University of Chicago Press, 1958.

Williams, H., "Petrographic Notes on Tempers of Pottery from Chupicuaro, Cerro del Tepelcate and Ticoman, Mexico," *Transactions of the American Philosophical Society,* Vol. 46 (1956), Part 5, pp. 576–580.

Willis, E. H., "Radiocarbon Dating," in D. Brothwell and E. Higgs, eds., *Science in Archaeology.* London: Thames and Hudson, 1963, pp. 35–46.

Willoughby, N. C., "Division of Labor Among the Indians of California," *Reports of the University of California Archaeological Survey*, No. 60 (1963), pp. 7–79.

Wilson, H. C., "An Inquiry into the Nature of Plains Indian Cultural Development," *American Anthropologist*, Vol. 65 (1963), pp. 355–369.

Wilson, J. A., *The Culture of Ancient Egypt*. Chicago: University of Chicago Press, 1951.

———, *The Culture of Ancient Egypt*. Chicago: Phoenix Books P11, 1956.

Wilson, T., "The Beginnings of the Science of Prehistoric Anthropology," *Proceedings of the American Association for the Advancement of Science*, Vol. 48 (1899), pp. 309–353.

———, "Beveled Arrow Heads," *American Archaeologist*, Vol. 2 (1898).

Wiltshire, T., "On the ancient flint implements of Yorkshire, and the modern fabrications of similar specimens," *Geological Society of London*, Vol. 1 (1826), pp. 215–226.

Windels, F., *The Lascaux Cave Paintings*. London: Faber, 1949.

Winlock, H. S., *Excavations at Deir el Bahri*. New York: Macmillan, 1942.

———, *Models of Daily Life in Ancient Egypt*. Cambridge, Mass.: Harvard University Press, 1955.

Witherspoon, Y. T., "A Statistical Device for Comparing Trait Lists," *American Antiquity*, Vol. 26 (1961), pp. 433–436.

Wood, E. S., *Collins Field Guide to Archaeology*. London: Collins, 1963.

Woodbury, R. B., *Prehistoric Stone Implements from Northeastern Arizona*. Cambridge, Mass.: Papers of the Peabody Museum, Vol. 34, 1954.

———, "Nels C. Nelson and Chronological Archaeology," *American Antiquity*, Vol. 25 (1960), pp. 400–407.

Woodward, A., "Ancient Houses of Modern Mexico," *Bulletin of the Southern California Academy of Sciences*, Vol. 32 (1933), pp. 79–98.

Woolley, L., *Spadework: Adventures in Archaeology*. London: Lutterworth Press, 1953.

———, *History Unearthed*. London: Benn, 1958.

———, *Digging Up the Past*, 2d ed. Baltimore: Pelican Books A4, 1960.

Wormington, H. M., *Ancient Man in North America*. Denver, Colo.: Denver Museum of Natural History, Popular Series, No. 4, 1949.

Wright, H. E., Jr., "Late Pleistocene Climate of Europe: A Review," *Bulletin of the Geological Society of America*, Vol. 72 (1961), pp. 933–984.

———, "Late Pleistocene Geology of Coastal Lebanon," *Quaternaria*, Vol. 6 (1962), pp. 525–539.

Wright, T., "On Antiquarian Excavations and Researches in the Middle Ages," *Archaeologia*, Vol. 30 (1844), Article No. 30, pp. 438–457.

Wulsin, F., *The Prehistoric Archaeology of Northwest Africa*. Cambridge, Mass.: Papers of the Peabody Museum, Vol. 19, No. 1, 1941.

Wylie, J. C., *The Wastes of Civilization*. London: Faber, 1959.

Wynne, E. J., and R. F. Tylecote, "An Experimental Investigation into Primitive Iron-Smelting Technique," *Journal of the Iron and Steel Institute*, Vol. 191 (1958), pp. 339–348.

Xanthoudides, S., "Some Minoan Potter's-Wheel Discs," in C. S. Casson, ed., *Essays in Aegean Archaeology Presented to Sir Arthur Evans in Honour of His 75th Birthday*. Oxford: Clarendon Press, 1927, pp. 111–128.

Yanine, V. L., "Modern Methods in Archaeology: The Novgorod Excavation," *Diogenes,* Vol. 29 (1960), pp. 82–101.

Zeiner, H. M., "Botanical Survey of the Angel Mounds Site, Evansville, Indiana," *American Journal of Botany,* Vol. 33 (1946), pp. 83–90.

Zeuner, F. E., "The Neolithic-Bronze Age Gap on the Tell of Jericho," *Palestine Exploration Quarterly,* May–October, 1954, pp. 64–68.

———, "Loess and Paleolithic Chronology," *Proceedings of the Prehistoric Society,* Vol. 21 (1955a), pp. 51–64.

———, "Notes on the Bronze Age Tombs of Jericho, I," *Palestine Exploration Quarterly,* October, 1955b, pp. 118–128.

———, *Dating the Past; An Introduction to Geochronology,* 4th ed. London: Methuen, 1958.

———, *The Pleistocene Period.* London: Hutchinson, 1959.

———, "Advances in Chronological Research," *Viking Fund Publications in Anthropology,* No. 28 (1960), pp. 325–350.

———, *A History of Domesticated Animals.* London: Hutchinson, 1963.

INDEX

A

Aboo-Habba, excavations at, 18
Aboriginal intertribal trade, 189
Aborigines, 121, 212
  Australian, 5, 180, 195–196
Absolute dating, 29, 65, 66, 153–154,
  170, 176–177
Abu Simbel, 20
Academic discipline, archeology as, 13
Accumulation, rate of, dating by 181–
  183
Adaura cave, 46
Adena culture group, 200
Aerial photography, 47, 89–90, 114
Aggradation of rivers, 162–163
Agricultural fields, 34
Agriculture, 187, 188, 194, 197, 199,
  233, 246
Akerblad, J. D., 17
Albright, W. F., 26, 178, 245
Alexander VI, 15
Ameilhon, H. P., 17
American Indians
  Blackfoot, 209
  culture of, changes in, 31
  economic exchange among, 189, 202
  Hopewell, 36, 202
  Hopi, 226
  Iroquois, 218–219, 226
  Maidu, 64
  mound-building, 36, 228
  Navajo, 189, 229
  origin of, studies on, 230–231
  Plains, 198, 209, 233
  population studies on, 221
  prehistory of, ending of, 4
  pueblo-dwelling, 207
  social organization of, 209, 226,
    227
  social and religious systems of, 101

specialization practiced by, 204, 233
trade routes established by, 189, 202
American prehistory (see American
  Indians; United States, archeological data on)
Analysis, technical (see Technical
  analyses)
Anatolia, 25, 38, 206
Anasazi culture, 203
Angel Mounds, Indiana, 89
Animal bones, 35, 42, 44
  cultural significance of, 189
  dating and, 152–153, 155–157, 170–
    172
  identification of as to species, 189–
    190
  preservation of, 81, 116, 190
  technical analysis of, 134–138, 152–
    153, 155–157, 189–192, 218–
    219
  uses of, determination of, 218–219
Animal teeth, analysis of, 135
Animal transport, 209
Animals
  butchering of, 35, 136–137, 188,
    190–192
  extinction of, 170–171
  hunting of, 136–137, 188, 190–193,
    195–199, 232
  preservation of, 72–73
Antevs, Ernst, 161
Anthropology, 6, 8, 29–31, 72, 195
Antiquities protection laws, 11, 80
Arbitrary levels, 53, 55, 58–59, 110
*Archaeology and Prehistoric Annals
  of Scotland,* 4
"Archeological salvage," 22
Archeologists
  academic training of, 10
  amateur, 10
  difficulties encountered by, 10–11

293

Archeologists *(continued)*
kinds of, 12–32
salvage, 32
Archeology, 3–32
as academic discipline, 13
anepigraphic, 26
beginning and development of, 13–14
classical, 24–26
collecting as center of, 13
culture and, 8–9, 66–67
ecological method in, application of, 9, 192
history and, 4–6, 8
kinds of, 12–32
looting and, 14–23, 36, 77, 80, 96
meaning of, 3
natural science and, 9–10
Paleolithic, 30
and philology, combining of, 25
romance of, 13
salvage, 10, 31–32, 99
treasure hunting and, 14–23
underwater, 22–23
Architecture, 25, 34, 81, 116
changes in, 247
Area exposure, 57–58
Arkell, W. J., 163
Arrowheads, 6, 12, 49, 180
Artifacts, 8
assemblages of, 8–9, 21, 49, 66, 97, 110, 123–124, 177–178
chronological arrangement of, 237–239
attributes of, 123–126, 128, 130
cluster analysis of, 123–124
dating of *(see* Dating)
descriptions of, 124–129
pictorial, 124–125, *126*
statistical, 125–126, 128
symbolic, 128–129
verbal, 124
destruction of, 77–80, 124
examples of, 8
imitation of, 63–64
natural or man-made, question of 217–219
preservation of
in laboratory, 18, 81, 114–117, 190
natural, 69–77

reports on, 124–129, 236–237
technical analysis of *(see* Technical analyses)
type, 96, 97
types of, 119–124
convenient, 121–122
cultural, 123–124
designed, 122
discovered, 122
functional, 120–121
use of, determination of, 210–219
context and, 214
dissection, use of in, 216
by ethnographic analogy, 211–214
reproduction, experiments on, 214–216
Arundel, Earl of, 15–16
Ashmolean Museum, 15–16
Ashur-bani-pal, Palace of, 18
Assemblages, 8–9, 21, 49, 66, 97, 110, 123–124, 177–178
chronological arrangement of, 237–239
Assyrian sculpture, mammalian forms on, 196
Assyriology, crowning blow to, 19
Astronomical dating, 175–176
Aswan dam, 31
Atkinson, R. J. C., 101
Aurignacian culture, 177, 178
Australian aborigines, 5, 180, 195–196
Australian ceremonial exchange, 189
Australian populations, study on, 221
Australopithecines, 218
Aztec shrines, 42, 44
destruction of, 79
Aztecs, 29
economic exchange among, 203

B

Babbage, Charles, 172
Bagdad, British Consulate in, establishment of, 16
Bailey, James, 17
Bannerstones, 214
Bannister, B., 173
Barbarism, 28, 227, 240, 242, 245

Barter, 201, 203–204
Basket Maker culture, 181–182
Basketry, 73, 81, 132–133, 213, 216
Bâton de comandement, 214
Battle-axe culture, 27
Beach deposits, dating of, 161–162
Beads, preservation of, *76*
Beaker Culture, 66
Beaker-folk, 27
Beersheba, underground houses in, 206
Belshazzar, 14
Belt Cave, 190
Belzoni, Giovanni Battista, 14, 20, 22, 80, 158
Berlin Museum, 6
Beta-activity dating, 152–153
Billitonites, 66
Biological evolution, 30–31, 239
Bird, J. B., 193–194
Birds
    migratory, 137–138, 223
    ritual importance of, 213–214
Blocks, stratigraphic, 58
    isolation of, 59
Blood groups, bone analysis to determine, 157
Boats, 209
Bog butter, chemical analysis of, 138
Bogs
    bodies found in, 70, 193
    pollen analysis in, 168, 169
Bones (*see* Animal bones; Human bones)
Borremose bog body, 193
Botany, 9, 134
Botta, Paul Emile, 18
Boussard, André Joseph, 16–17
B.P. dating, 150
Braidwood, R. J., 57, 87, 104, 243–245
Breton Passage Graves, 122
British Egyptology, 20
British Museum, 16–19, 140
British prehistory, 4, 132
Bronze Age, 23, 29, 35, 50, 70, 73, 136, 194
Bulldozers, use of, 106
Burial sites, 36–37
Burkitt, M. C., 122
Butchering, 35, 136–137, 188, 190–192

C

Caesar, Gaius Julius, 15, 28
Calendars, 29, 65, 176–177
Carter, Howard, 20
Caves, 21, 40, 42, 47, 53, 95–96
    painted, 37–38, 53, 70, 196, 215, 231
    pollen analysis in, 169–170
    preservation in, 74–76
    soils in, climate determined by, 133
    stratigraphic layers in, 50, 53
    test digging in, 99
Celts, 27, 28, 194
Cemeteries, 36–37
    looting of, 14–16, 19–20, 36, 77, 96
Center of Documentary Analysis for Archaeology, 129
Ceramics (*see* Pottery)
Ceremonial sites, 35–36
Champollion, Jean François, 17
Charles I, 31
Cheese residues, analysis of, 138
Chemical analysis (*see* Technical analyses)
Cheops, pyramid of, 64
Chichen Itza, 69
Childe, V. G., 8–9, 40, 180, 212, 216, 227, 244–246
China
    culture in, continuity of, 213
    excavations in, negotiations over, 11
    Shang dynasty, 80–81, 228
    tomb robberies in, 14–15
Cholula, pyramid of, 111
Christian calendar, 65, 176
Christy, Henry, 21
Chronology (*see* Dating)
Churches, 42, 44
Cienega Site, Arizona, 109
    See also Surveying
Clark, Grahame, 5, 10, 106, 137, 180, 187, 194, 207, 210, 236
Clark, J. G. D., 60, 120, 213
Clarksville site, tooth wear in, analysis of, 197
Classic Maya, collapse of, 248
Classic Maya site of Palenque, 36
Classical archeology, 24–26

Clay tablets, 4, 16, 21
  preservation of, 18
Cliff dwellings, 22, 34
Climate, 187–188
  dating and, 170–172
  information sources on
    animal bones, 137, 170–172, 191
    cave soils, 133
    plant remains, 137
  preservation, dependence of on,
    69–77
Climatic succession, 163
Clisby, K., 170
Cluster analysis, 123–124
Codices, 29
Coe, Michael, 249
Coffins, glazed, 19
Coins, 13, 16, 25, 203, 204
Collagen fiber shrinkage, 157
Collecting, 13
Columbus, Christopher, 28
Communism, 246
Conifers, use of in dating, 173
Context, 6, 9, 10, 49–67, 214
Control pits, 108, 110
Control walls, stratigraphic, 57
Convenient types, 121–122
Coombs Site, Nevada, plan of, 105
  See also Excavation
Copenhagen, National Museum in,
  26
Cordage, 75
Cordova Cave, 58, 74, 75
Cortes, Hernando, 28, 79
Courses Toward Urban Life, 244
Creel, H. G., 11, 15, 80
Cross-dating, 66, 173, 180–181
Cultural development, 31, 199, 235,
  241–243
Cultural evolution, 29–30, 199, 239–
  241, 243
Cultural levels, 55, 110
Cultural types, 123–124
Culture(s)
  and archeology, 8–9, 66–67
  changes in, 246–249
  classification of, 241–242
    Paleolithic, 21–22
  identification of, 229–231
  nonmaterial, 8
  and space, 66–67

Culture history, 86, 234–249
Cuneiform texts, 13, 16, 18, 25
Currency, 203
Cushing, F. H., 179
Cutler, Reverend Manasseh, 172
Cylinder seals, 16, 202

D

Danger Cave, 183
Daniel, G. E., 122, 227
Darien, tomb robbery in, 15
Darwin, Charles, 29–30
Dark Ages, 28
Dating, 9–10, 64–66, 145–184
  absolute, 29, 65, 66, 153–154, 170,
    176–177
  accuracy in, differing degrees of,
    65
  archeological-cultural, 184
  archeological-geological, 184
  astronomical, 175–176
  beta-activity, 152–153
  bones and, 152–153, 155–157, 170–
    172
  B.P., 150
  calendars and, 29, 65, 175–176
  by chemical analysis, 155–157
  climate, influence of on, 170–172
  cross-, 66, 173, 180–181
  gaps in, 50
  geochronological methods, 151, 160–
    166
  geographical location and, 183
  K-A, 151–152
  magnetic, 153–155, 154
  natural low-level radioactivity, 152–
    153
  obsidian-hydration, 158–159
  patina formation, use of in, 157–
    158
  of Pleistocene, 161–167, 171, 175–
    176
  by pollen analysis, 167–170, 169
  potassium-argon, 34, 66, 151–152,
    205
  of pottery, 25, 152–155, 178–179
  radiocarbon, 145–151, 157, 161, 165,
    168, 176, 178, 182–184
  by rate of accumulation, 181–183
  by rate of sedimentation, 165, 176

Dating *(continued)*
  relative, 65–66, 157, 162, 170–172
  sequence, 177–180, 202
  of similar occurrences, 65–66
  statistical methods, application of
    in, 128
  stratigraphy, use of in, 53, 63–64,
    67, *62*
  surveying and, 95–97
  thermoluminescence, 152
  tree-ring, 160, 172–174, 177, 184,
    174
  zoological, 196
Dating the Past, 176
Davis, J. T., 189, 195
Dawkins, W. B., 27
Dead Sea scrolls, 12, 157
Death Valley, 166
Deetz, J., 61
Defensible villages, 34
De Geer, Baron Gerard, 160
Degradation of rivers, 162–163
Deh Luran Valley, Iran, *94, 95*
  See also Surveying
de Menou, Jacques François, 17
Demography, 220–225
Dendrochronology, 160, 172–174, 177,
  184
Denmark
  Iron Age, diet in, 193
  stratigraphic succession in, 26
de Perthes, Jacques Boucher Crêve-
  coeur, 30, 37, 140
Deposition, geological, 165
de Sacy, Silvestre, 17
Desert Culture, 66, 242
Designations, site, 99–100
Destruction of artifacts, 77–80, 124
Dethlefsen, E., 61
Diet, 135–138, 171–172, 189–197, 223–
  224
Diffusion, stimulus, 238–239
Dilettanti, 15
Direct historical approach, 213, 229,
  242–243
Disintegration, 40, 68, 115, 116
Dorpfeld, Wilhelm, 24
Douglass, A. E., 172
Drumkelin house, 72
"Drumsticks," 214
Dubois, Eugene, 47

Dump areas, 36, 42, 44, 53, 60, 98–99,
  181–183, 191, 207
Dunes, 48
  dating and, 133, 162
Dynastic Period Egyptian tombs, 213,
  214

E

E. primigenius, 171
Earth mounds, 38–46
Ecology, 9, 192, 226
Economy, 187–209
  diet, 135–138, 171–172, 189–197,
    223–224
  exchange, standards of, 203–204
  shelter, 204–208
  technology, 30, 197–201, 243, 246–
    249
  trade, 188–189, 200–203, 233
  transportation and travel, 209
Eggan, F., 226
Egypt
  collecting of antiquities in, 16–17
  Eighteenth Dynasty, 60, 191
  Eleventh Dynasty, 60
  First Dynasty, 138, 200, 202
  Predynastic, 179
  Second Dynasty, 138, 193
  tomb robberies in, 14
Egyptian hieroglyphs, 24
Egyptian monuments, inscriptions on,
  38
Egyptian pyramids, 20, 36, 64
Egyptian royal tombs, 200–202, 213,
  214
Elephas antiquus, 170–171
Elgin marbles, 9, 17
Emery, W. B., 10–11, 14, 213
Engels, Friedrich, 246
English Egyptology, 20
English prehistory, 4, 132
Enrichment, isotopic, 149
Environment, 9, 48, 187–188
  animals, preference of for, 172,
    191, 192
  changes in, effects of, 239
  effect of
    on food, 189–197, 223–224
    on preservation, 69–77
Epigraphy, 25, 81

Eskimos
  artifacts of, 212–213
  Greenland, 196
  infanticide among, 222
  Point Barrow, 63
    disappearance of, 233
Ethnographic analogy, 211–214
Ethnography, 34, 228
Ethnology, 30, 63, 200, 220, 240–242
Euphrates valley, 16, 44
Evans, John, 30
Evolution, 29–31, 64
  biological, 30–31, 239
  cultural, 29–30, 199, 239–241, 243
Excavation, 101–111
  bulldozers, use of in, 106
  control pits, 108, 110
  hazards in, 10–11
  horizontal stripping, 108, 110, *109*
  of large areas, 104–111, *105, 107*
  object of, 102–103
  permits for, negotiations over, 11
  recovery and, 80–81
  reports on, 81–82, 111–114, 236–237
  staff of, selection of, 117–118
  test pits, 57–58, 103–104
  tools used in, 106, 108
  trenches, 57–59, 103–104, 108
  tunneling operations, 110–111
Exchange, standards of, 203–204
Extinction of animals, 170–171

F

Fabric analysis, 132
Faience beads, 132
Fakes, problem of, 64–65, 140–141, 152
Falconer, H., 30
Farming, 187, 188, 194, 197, 199, 233, 246
Feces, human, technical analysis of, 138
  diet determined by, 138, 194–195
Fewkes, J. W., 179
Fifth Radiocarbon Dating Conference, 150
Fiorelli, Giuseppe, 24
Fire, first use of, 204–205
Fiske, M., 172

Flint artifacts, 13, 21, 37, 46, 47, 96, 112, 116, 158, 165
Flint-chopping, studies, on, 212
Flotation, 193
Flower, W. H., 30
Food, 135–138, 171–172, 189–197, 223–224
Food taboos, 192, 224
Ford, J. A., 50
Foreman, F., 170
Forgeries, 140–141
Fowler, M. L., 182
Functional types, 120–121

G

Gar Arjenah, Iran, deposit at, *56*
Garbage dumps, 36, 42, 44, 53, 60, 98–99, 181–183, 191, 207
Garrod, Dorothy, 6
Geiger counter, 149
Geiger-Muller counter, 149
Geochronology, 151, 160–166
  varve analysis, 160–161
Geographical location, dating and, 183
Geological deposition, 165
Geology, 6, 9, 29, 48, 133, 193
  Pleistocene, 163–166
Gerzean period tombs, 202
Gifford, E. W., 42, 60
Glaciation, 67, 77, 160–165, 168–170, 175, 205
Glazed coffins, 19
Glottochronology, 229
Goodman-Thompson-Martinez correlation, 176
Graffiti, 38
Grauballe Man, 193
Graves (*see* Royal tombs)
Green, F. E., 170
Griffin, J. B., 50
Grimes Graves, 35
Gypsum Cave culture, 181–182

H

Habitation sites, 33–34, 38, 40, 42, 44, 50
Hafsten, U., 170
Hamitic herders, 199

Harappan civilization, 26, 183
Hauser, Otto, 21
Hawkes, C., 26
Helicigona banatica, 164
Herculaneum, 15, 73
Herodotus, 26–28
Hieroglyphs, Egyptian, 24
Hissarlik, 24
Histograms, 128
History
  and archeology, 4–6, 8
  beginning of, 4
  culture, 86, 234–249
  divisions of, 3–5
  and prehistory, dividing line be-
    tween, 4
Hitler, Adolf, 245–246
Hittite civilization, 25, 26
Hoaxes, 64–65, 140-141
Hodgson, J., 5–6
Hohokam culture, 203
Holmes, W. H., 69, 179
Horizons, 53, 59, 60, 63, 162, 164
Horizontal stripping, 108, 110
Houses, 8, 38, 40, 205–207, *39, 41*
Howard, Thomas, 15–16
Howe, B., 87, 104, 117
Human bodies, preservation of, 20,
  72, 73, 196
Human bones, 30, 66, 151, 152
  population data obtained from,
    221–222
  preservation of, 81, 116, 190
  technical analysis of, 152–153, 155–
    157
Human feces, technical analysis of,
  138
  diet determined by, 138, 194–195
Human sacrifice, 222
Human teeth, analysis of, 197
Humboldt Cave, 75
Hunting, 136–137, 188, 190–193, 195–
  199, 232
Huntington, Ellsworth, 245
Hutchinson, Lord, 17
Hydration dating, 158–159

I

Iban ceremonials, 216–217
Iconoclasm, 79–80

Iliad, 29
Incas, 29
Indo-European languages, 230
Indus valley civilization, 25
Industries, 8, 123
Infanticide, 222
Intaglio figures, 38
Intertribal trade, aboriginal, 189
Iron Age, 193, 194
Isotopic enrichment, 149
Italian Renaissance, 15

J

Jamestown, Virginia, 4
Jennings, J. D., 121–122, 162
Jericho, 50, 57, 59, 73
Jewell, P. A., 136
Judd, N. M., 60, 194, 196, 210
Julien, Fort, 17

K

K-A dating, 151–152
Kehoe, T. F., 213
Kennedy, George, 152
Kenyon, Kathleen, 57–58
Khafaje
  looting at, 19–20
  Oval Temple at, 206
Kill sites, 35, 44, 137
Kroeber, A. L., 179, 195, 238
"Kula-ring," Trobriand, 189
Kunji cave, Iran, *52*

L

Labor, division of, 232
Lafitau, Père, 211
La Madeleine, excavation at, 21
Lamar pottery, 59
Laming-Emperaire, A., 87
Languages, study of, 25
Lartet, Eduard, 21, 215–216
Laugerie Haute, excavation at, 21
Layard, Austen Henry, 17–18, 79, 80,
  110
Layers, stratigraphic (*see* Stratigraphic
  layers)
Leakey, L. S. B., 34, 151, 217–218

Le Moustier, excavation at, 21
Les Eyzies, excavation at, 21
Levels, stratigraphic (see Stratigraphic levels)
Lexiocastatistics, 229
Libby, W. F., 146–149
Linear A script, 25
Linear B script, 25, 29
Linguistic data, identification of cultures by, 229–231
"Living floors," 35
Lloyd, S., 19–20, 40, 57, 106
Loess regions, 163–164
Loftus, W. K., 19
Looting, 14–23, 36, 77, 80, 96
Lovelock Cave, 74, 75
Lowe, Van Riet, 181
Lower Paleolithic, 21–22, 72
Luxor, obelisk of, 6, 9, 7
Lyell, Sir Charles, 23, 73, 77

M

Macalister, R. A. S., 211
Macaws, ritual importance of, 213
Magdalenian culture, 21, 177, 178
Magnetic dating, 153–155
Magnetometry, 90–91, 99
Mammoth Cave, 47
Man, evolution of, 29–31, 64
    biological, 30–31, 239
    cultural, 29–30, 199, 239–241, 243
Man Makes Himself, 244
Mapping, 81, 87, 90, 93, 95, 111–113
Marbles, 15–16
    Elgin, 9, 17
Marsh Arabs, 44
Marx, Karl, 246
Mason, Charley, 22
Matteson, M. R., 136
Maya, archeological data on
    calendar, 29, 65, 176–177
    paintings, 70
    Palenque, site of, 36
    stelae, 63, 132, 176, 177
    temples, 69
Medicine men, 200, 228, 231
Megalithic monuments, 36

Meso-America, archeological data on
    ceremonial centers, 35–36
    looting, 22
    mound building, 42
    pyramids, 36, 110–111
    surveying, 86
    trade routes, 202–203
Mesopotamia, archeological data on
    clay tablets, 4
    cuneiform inscriptions, 25
    cylinder seals, 16, 202
    excavations, 17–19, 108
    fauna, 196
    glazed coffins, 19
    mineral and plant resources, 188
    mud houses, 206
    wheeled vehicles, 209
Metal artifacts, technical analysis of, 132
Metrical stratigraphy, 55
Mexican Indians, 64
Midwestern Taxonomic Method, 241–242
Migration Period, 28
Migratory birds, 137–138, 223
Milankovitch, M., 175–176
Mimbres pottery, 196
Mindel glaciation, 169–170, 205
Minoan civilization, 24–26
Minos, Palace of, 77
Modoc Rock Shelter, 182
Mohenjo-daro, test pits in, 103
Mohenjo-daro script, 25
Monagrillo shell mound, 98
Mongolon culture, 203
Montelius, G., 27
Moraines, 163–164
Morgan, L. H., 240, 245, 246
Morro Rock, 37–38
Moslem shrines, 63
Mosques, 63–64
Mounds
    earth, 38–46, 43
    shell, 42, 98, 110
Mousterian culture, 21, 177, 183, 198
Mud houses, 205–206
Mummification, 20, 73, 196
Munsell Soil Color Charts, 131
Mycenaean economic and political structure, 29
Mycenaean shaft tombs, 24, 227

N

Nabonidus, 14, 15
Nachikufan III, 53
Natural low-level radioactivity dating, 152–153
Natural science and archeology, 9–10
Neanderthal burials, 36
Neanderthal groups, diet of, 192
Neanderthal skulls, 30
Nefertiti, bust of, 6
Nelson, N. C., 60
Neolithic Age, 35, 50, 72, 217
New World prehistory, 15, 28–29, 243–244
Niah Cave, 218
Nile valley, 16, 199
Nimes, Roman amphitheatre in, 44
Nimrud, excavation at, 17–18
Nineveh, 18, 78, 79, 110
Nordenskiöld, Baron Gustav, 22
Nordic race, excavations to prove superiority of, 86, 245–246
Nubia, 10–11
    royal tombs in, 200, 213, 214

O

Oakley, K. P., 140
Obelisks, 6, 9, 20
Obsidian blades, 63, 188
    trade in, 202
Obsidian-hydration dating, 158–159
Occupation sites, 33–34, 38, 40, 42, 44, 50
Odyssey, 211
Old World prehistory, 28, 31, 240–243
Olduvai Gorge, 34, 47, 151, 204–205
On the Origin of Species, 30
Oseberg Viking ship, 15, 115
Osteodontokeratic culture, 218
Oxford University, History of Art at, 154

P

Painted caves, 37–38, 53, 70, 196, 215, 231
Palenque, Classic Maya site of, 36
Paleoanthropology, 8

Paleobotany, 48, 193
Paleo-Indian implements, 139
Paleolithic archeology, 30
Paleolithic culture, 21–22, 33, 77
    Lower, 21–22, 72
    Upper, 21–22, 53, 72, 196, 201, 214, 231
Paleolithic sociology, 229
Paleontology, 6, 21, 120, 170–172, 193
Paleoserology, 157
Paleozoology, 48
Palisaded villages, 34
Palynology, 6, 167–170
Panama, tomb robberies in, 15
Papyrus scrolls, 21, 73
Pathological idiot, 30
Patination, 157–158
Paudorf soil formation, 164
Pedological analysis, 133–134
Peking Man, 169, 205
Permits, excavation, negotiations over, 11
Peru
    avalanche in, 77
    Early Nazca period, 216
    tomb robberies in, 15, 22
Peruvian quipus, 29
Peruvian rulers, 29
Petrie, Sir Flinders, 121, 178–179, 181
Petroglyphs, 37–38, 196, 231
Petrographic analysis, 131–132
Petrological analysis, 35
Philae obelisk, 20
Phillips, P. J., 31, 50, 244
Philology, 25, 31
Photography, 93, 113–114
    aerial, 47, 89–90, 114
    artifacts and, 124–125
Pictographs, 37–38, 196
Pictorial descriptions, 124–125
Piggott, S., 28, 29
Piltdown hoax, 64–65, 140–141
Piltdown skull, 156
Pinus aristata, 173
Pinus ponderosa, 173
Pithecanthropus erectus, 47
Pithecanthropus fossil human remains, 66
Pits
    control, 108, 110
    test, 57–58, 103–104

Plant remains
  reports on, 237
  technical analysis of, 137–138, 195
Plants, use of in diet, 193–194
Playa Miller, 74, 75
Pleistocene, 21, 30, 72, 77
  dating of, 161–167, 171, 175–176
  Middle, 66
Pleistocene Period, The, 176
Plotting, 111–113
Pollen analysis, 6, 167–170
Pompeii, 15, 24, 38, 73, 77
Population studies, 220–225
Post-Columbian period, 4
Potassium-argon dating, 34, 66, 151–152, 205
Potsherds, 58–59, 81, 98, 112, 116
  dating and, 178
  petrographic analysis of, 131
Pottery, 8, 13, 46, 58, 96–98
  dating of, 25, 152–155, 178–179
  fish-forms portrayed on, 196
  intrusive, 203
  Lamar, 59
  Mimbres, 196
  plumbate, 203
  Swift Creek, 59
  technical analysis of, 130–131
  trade, 203
  trade in, 202–203
Pottery-making, studies on, 212, 215
Powell, J. W., 79
Prehistoric archeology (*see* Archeology)
Prehistory
  American (*see* American Indians; United States, archeological data on)
  British, 4, 132
  change, pervasiveness of throughout, 238–239
  and history, dividing line between, 4
  meaning of, 3
  models of, 238–249
  New World, 15, 28–29, 243–244
  Old World, 38, 31, 240–243
  primary, 5
  as subfield of anthropology, 6
Preservation of artifacts
  in laboratory, 18, 81, 114–117, 190

  natural, 68–77
Prestwich, J., 30
Primary prehistory, 5
Private collecting, 13
Prodromus, 26
Proportional flow counter, 152
Protohistory, 5, 26–29
Protoliterate period, 202
Ptolemy V, 17
Punta Pichalo, 74, 75
Pyddoke, E., 50, 61
Pyramids, 38, 177, 231, 247, 248
  Egyptian, 20, 36, 64
  Meso-American, 36, 110–111

Q

Quarry sites, 35
Quipus, 29

R

Rachid, Fort, 17
Radioactivity, 152
Radiocarbon, 150
Radiocarbon dating, 145–151, 157, 161, 165, 168, 176, 178, 182–184
Rameses II, 20
Rampart Cave, 170
Random-sampling technique, 97–99
Rassam, Hormuzd, 11, 18
Rawlinson, Henry Creswick, 16
Records (*see* Reports)
Refuse deposits, 36, 42, 44, 53, 60, 98–99, 181–183, 191
Regional sequences, 237–239
Regional studies, 86
Relative dating, 65–66, 157, 162, 170–172
  See also Dating
Religion, 228, 231–232
Religious structures, 42, 44, 228
  destruction of, 79–80
Reports
  on artifacts, 124–129, 236–237
  excavation, 81–82, 111–114, 236–237
  forms, *88, 89*
Research Laboratory for Archaeology, 154
Residues, technical analysis of, 138–139

Resistivity surveying, 91, 93, 99
Reversed stratigraphy, 60–61
Rich, Claudius, 16, 78
Ring ditch at Stanton Harcourt, Oxon, *92*
    See also Surveying
River Basin survey program, 99
Rivers, aggradation and degradation of, 162–163
Rock shelters, 50, 55, 96, 182
Roman amphitheatre in Nimes, 44
Roman arena in Arles, *45*
Roman roads, 34, 46
Rome, collecting of art treasures in, 15
Rosetta Stone, 16–17
Rowe, J. H., 29, 64, 115
Royal tombs
    Egyptian, 200–202, 213, 214
    looting of, 14–16, 19–20, 36, 77, 96
    Mycenaean shaft, 24, 227
    Nubian, 200, 213, 214
    technological objects found in, 200, 202
    Tutankhamen's, 20, 227
    of Ur, 36, 38, 80, 227
Russians, social organization of, 227

S

Sacrifice, human, 222
"Salvage, archeological," 22
Salvage archeology, 10, 31–32, 99
Samoan Material Culture, 211
Sand dunes, 48
    dating and, 133, 162
Sandford, K. S., 163
Sardanapalus, Palace of, 19
Savagery, 227, 240, 242
Schliemann, Heinrich, 24–26, 47, 80, 86
Screen-wall technique, 149
Scripts, 24–25, 29
Scrolls, Papyrus, 21, 73
Scythians, 26–28, 72, 233
    marriage customs of, 225
Sears, W. H., 101
Seasonal occupation of sites, 191, 221
Sedimentation, rate of, dating by, 165, 176
Seneca graves, 63

Sequence dating, 177–180, 202
Sequoia gigantea, 173
Seriation graphs, 98
Settlements, 207–208
Sexual division of labor, 232
"Shaft-straighteners," 214
Shaft tombs, Mycenaean, 24, 227
Shamans, 200, 228, 231
Shang tombs, looting of, 15
Shell beads, stringing of, 75
Shell mounds, 42, 98, 110
Shelter, 204–208
Sheppey, Isle of, fossil fruits from, 191
Sherds, 59, 96–98, 112, 116
    chemical tests for, 131
Shore lines, 162–163
Shrines, 42, 44, 63, 231
    destruction of, 79
Similar development, law of, 240
Sites, 33–48
    burial, 36–37
    ceremonial, 35–36
    classification of, 33
    defensible, 34
    designations for, 99–100
    finding of, 46–48
        See also Surveying
    habitation, 33–34, 38, 40, 42, 44, 50
    kill, 35, 44, 137
    mounds
        earth, 38–46
        shell, 42, 98, 110
    petroglyphic, 37–38
    pictographic, 37–38
    quarry, 35
    reports on, 81–82, 111–114, 236–237
    seasonal occupation of, 191, 221
    surface scatters, 37
    technical analysis of, 139–140
    trading centers, 34
    unstratified, 53, 55
Sixtus IV, 15
Smiley, T. L., 173
Smithsonian Institution, 99
Smuggling, 22
Social correlates, 216–217
Social Evolution, 245
Social organization, 209, 225–229, 243
    changes in, 247–248
Societies, decline and fall of, 248

Society, 8, 220–233, 243
cultures, identification of, 229–231
demographic data on, 220–225
labor, division of, 232
religion, 228, 231–232
specialization, 232–233
and technology, causal relation between, 246
Soil
Paudorf formation, 164
pH determinations, 61, 89, 134, 169
Pleistocene, 163–164
technical analysis of, 133–134, 139–140
Solutrean 4 layer, 135
Sondages, 103
Soundings, 103–104
Space and culture, 66–67
Spanish conquest, 29, 42, 78, 176
Spanish conquistadors, 15
Spanish missions, 4
Spaulding, A. C., 124
Specialization, 192, 199, 204, 232–233
Spinden correlation, 176
Staff, excavation, selection of, 117–118
Statistical descriptions, 125–126, 128
Stelae, 63, 132, 176, 177
Steno, Nicolaus, 26
Steno's Law, 26
Step-trench, 103–104
Steward, J. H., 166
Stimulus diffusion, 238–239
Stone Age, Middle, 218
Stone artifacts, 21, 96–97
dating of, 165–166
technical analysis of, 35, 132
Stonehenge, 35
Strabo, 15, 28
Stratification, 26
deriving stratigraphy from, 60–64
Stratigraphic blocks, 58
isolation of, 59
Stratigraphic control walls, 57
Stratigraphic layers, 50–53, 104, 51, 52
actual, 58
at Ali Kosh, Iran, 54
natural, 53, 55, 57, 58
photographing of, 113

Stratigraphic levels, 53, 104
arbitrary, 53, 55, 58–59, 110
cultural, 55, 110
natural, 55
numbering of, 112
photographing of, 113
time-based, 110
Stratigraphic succession, principle of, 26
Stratigraphy, 49–64, 103, 104, 106, 108, 158
dating and, 53, 63–64, 67
metrical, 55
principle of, 49–50
reversed, 60–61
Stripping, horizontal, 108, 110
Study of History, 245
Sultantepe mound, 38
Superposition, principle of, 26
Surface scatters, 37
Surveying, 85–100
for age and cultural contents, 95–97
magnetic, 90–91, 99, 92
mapping, 81, 87, 90, 93, 95, 111–113, 94, 95
photography, use of in
aerial, 47, 89–90
underground, 93
probe, use of in, 93
random-sampling technique, 97–99
regional studies, 86
resistivity, 91, 93, 99
sites
contents of, judging of, 90–99
finding of, 87–90
special problems in, 86–87
test digging, 99
Swift Creek pottery, 59
Swiss lakes, draining of, 23
Symbolic descriptions, 128–129

T

Taboos, food, 192, 224
Tacitus, 28
Tattooing, 72, 228, 71
Taxonomy, 241–243
Technical analyses, 130–141
of bones, 134–138, 152–153, 155–157, 189–192, 218–219

Technical analyses *(continued)*
  fabric, 132
  of human feces, 138, 194–195
  of metal and stone, 35, 132
  pedological, 133–134
  petrographic, 131–132
  of plant remains, 137–138, 195
  pollen, 6, 167–170
  of pottery, 130–131
  of residues, 138–139
  of sites, 139–140
  of soil, 133–134, 139–140
  of teeth, 135, 152, 156, 197
  of textiles, 132–133
  varve, 160–161
Technology, 30, 197–201, 243
  advances in, 199, 247–249
  and society, causal relation between, 246
Tectonic action, 162
Teeth, technical analyses of, 135, 152, 156, 197
Tektites, 66
Tells, 38, 40, 44
Temple of the Inscriptions, 36
Temples, 231
  destruction of, 79
Tents, 206–207
Teotihuacan, pyramid of, 110–111
Terraces, 34
  dating of, 162–163
Test digging, 99
Test pits, 57–58, 103–104
Textiles, 73, 81
  dissection of, 216
  technical analysis of, 132–133
Thermoluminescence dating, 152
Thermo-remnant magnetism, 153, 155
Thompson, J. Eric, 36
Thomsen, Christian Jurgensen, 26, 27, 199, 240
"Thong-stroppers," 214
Three-Age system, 26, 199, 240
Tiahuanaco, 78–79, *107*
Tigris valley, 16, 44
Time-based levels, 110
Tollifero site, tooth wear in, analysis of, 197
Tollund Man, 70, 193
Tombs *(see Royal tombs)*

Tournal, 4
Toynbee, Arnold, 245
Trade, 188–189, 200–203, 233
Trading centers, 34
Transportation, 209
Trash areas, 36, 42, 44, 53, 60, 98–99, 181–183, 191, 207
Travel, 209
Treasure hunting, 14–23
Tree-ring dating, 160, 172–174, 177, 184
Trenches, 57–59, 103–104, 108
Trobriand "Kula-ring," 189
Troy, 24, 47
Tularosa Cave, 58, 74, 75
Tunneling operations, 110–111
Tutankhamen, tomb of, 20, 227
"Twitches," 214

U

Underwater archeology, 22–23
United States, archeological data on
  Adena culture group, 200
  bannerstones, 214
  caves, 47, 58, 74, 170
    painted, 37
    pollen analysis in, 169–170
    preservation in, 74–76
  Clarksville site, tooth-wear studies in, 197
  cliff dwellings, 22, 34
  cultures, identification of, 229–231
  glaciation, 161
  Jamestown, early settlements in, 4
  Morro Rock, 37–38
  petroglyphs and pictographs, 37, 196, 231
  Pliocene deposits, 218
  pottery
    Lamar, 59
    Mimbres, 196
    Swift Creek, 59
  refuse heaps, 60, 191
  Seneca graves, 63
  sites
    burial, 36, 231
    defensible villages, 34
    kill, 35, 44, 137
    mounds, 36, 40, 42
    quarry, 35

United States, archeological data on
   (continued)
   Spanish missions, 4
   Tollifero site, tooth-wear studies in,
      197
   trade routes, 34, 189, 202
   tree-ring dating, 173, 177
   Williamsburg, early settlements in,
      4
   See also American Indians
Upper Paleolithic, 21–22, 53, 72, 196,
   201, 214, 231
Ur, royal tombs of, 36, 38, 80, 227
   looting of, 15
Uruk, Jemdet Nasr period, 202
U.S.S.R., social organization in, 227

V

Varve analysis, 160–161
Vehicles, wheeled, 209
Venus figures, 231
Verbal descriptions, 124
Vesuvius, 15, 73
Viking ship, Oseberg, 15, 115
Villages, defensible, 34
Visigoths, 44
von Post, Lennar, 167

W

Warka, 19
Watson, V., 136
Weaving, technical analysis of, 132–
   133
Weiss, L., 132

Wessex culture, 38, 132
Wetherill, Richard, 22
Wheeled vehicles, 209
Wheeler, M., 13, 50, 55, 57, 59, 102–
   104, 106, 108, 117, 118, 182–183
Whetstones, ceremonial blessing of,
   216–217
Willey, G. R., 31, 58–59, 90, 212, 243–
   245
Windeby Bog-body No. 1, head of, 71
Williamsburg, Virginia, 4
Wilson, Daniel, 4
Wiltshire barrows, 136
Winlock, H. S., 60, 79
Wood, disintegration of, 40, 81
   preservation of, 72, 73
Wooley, Sir Leonard, 38, 53, 80, 114
Worsaae, J. J. A., 26
Writing, earliest form of, 4
Wylie, J. C., 40, 69

X

X-ray crystallographic method, 156

Y

Young, Arthur, 17

Z

Zinjanthropus, 205
Zoological dating, 196
Zoology, 9, 134, 190
Zuni, ritual importance of macaw
   among, 213